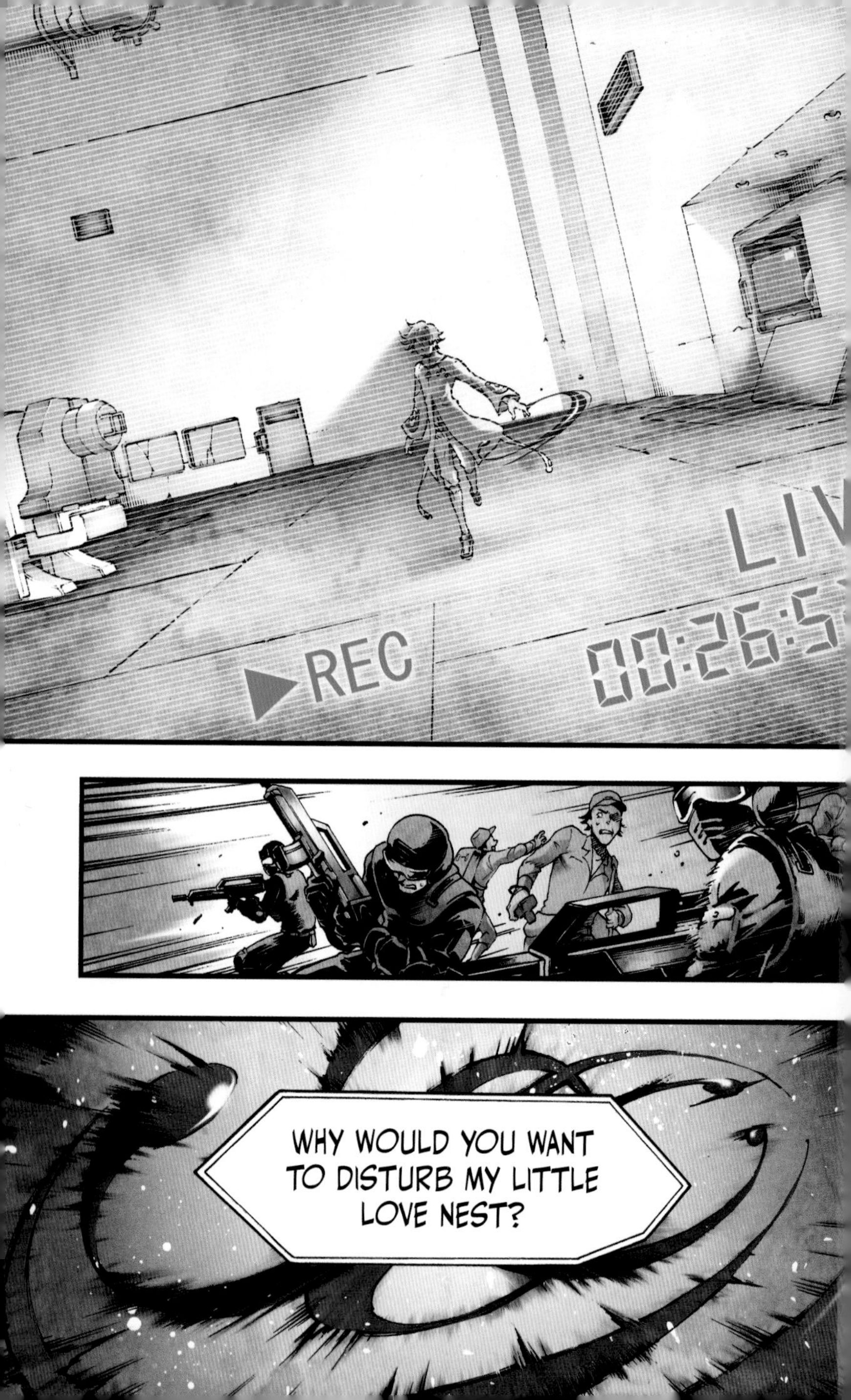
LIV
▶REC
00:26:5
WHY WOULD YOU WANT TO DISTURB MY LITTLE LOVE NEST?

DEADMAN WONDERLAND

STORY & ART BY JINSEI KATAOKA, KAZUMA KONDOU

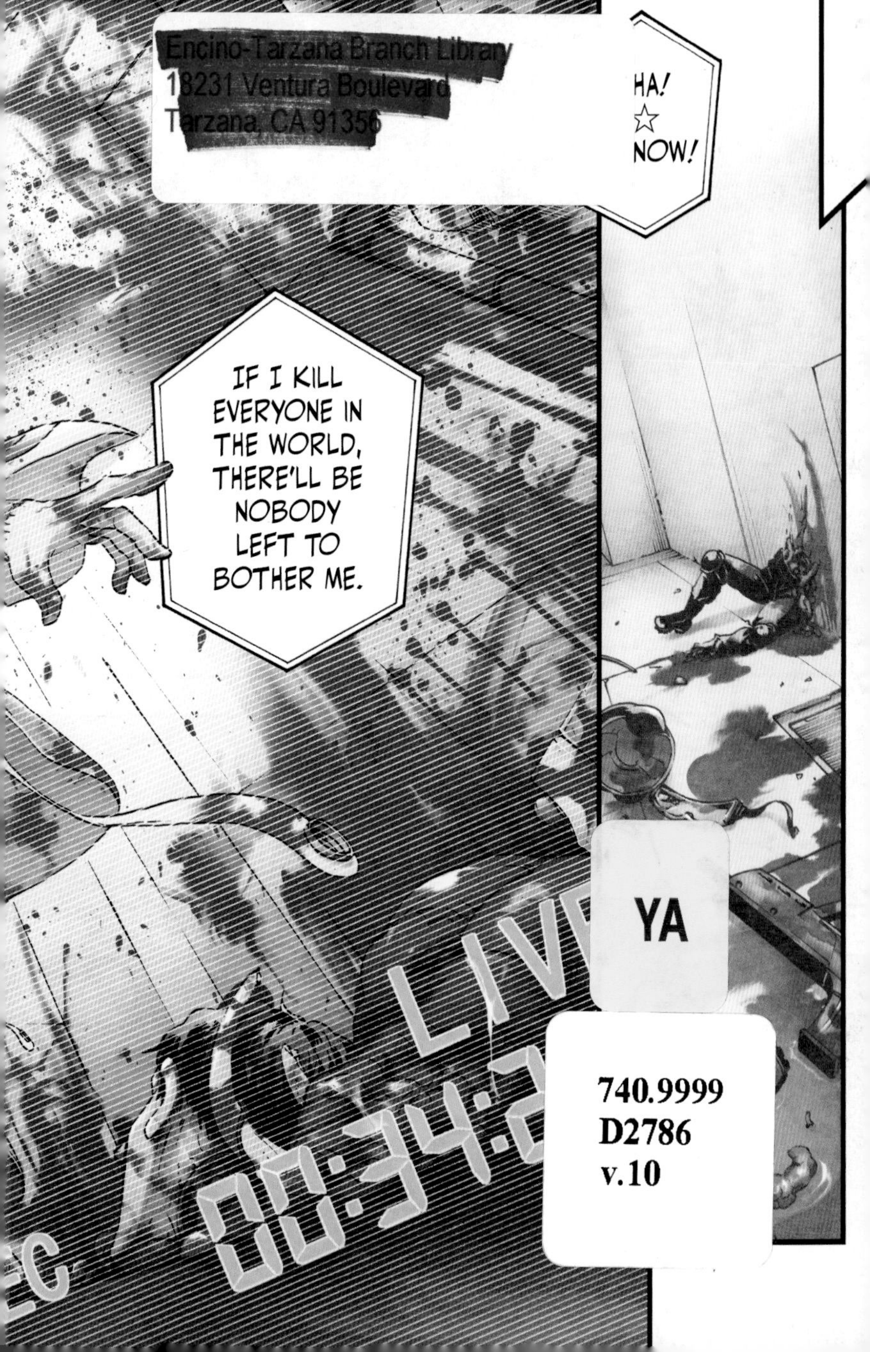
HA!
NOW!
IF I KILL EVERYONE IN THE WORLD, THERE'LL BE NOBODY LEFT TO BOTHER ME.

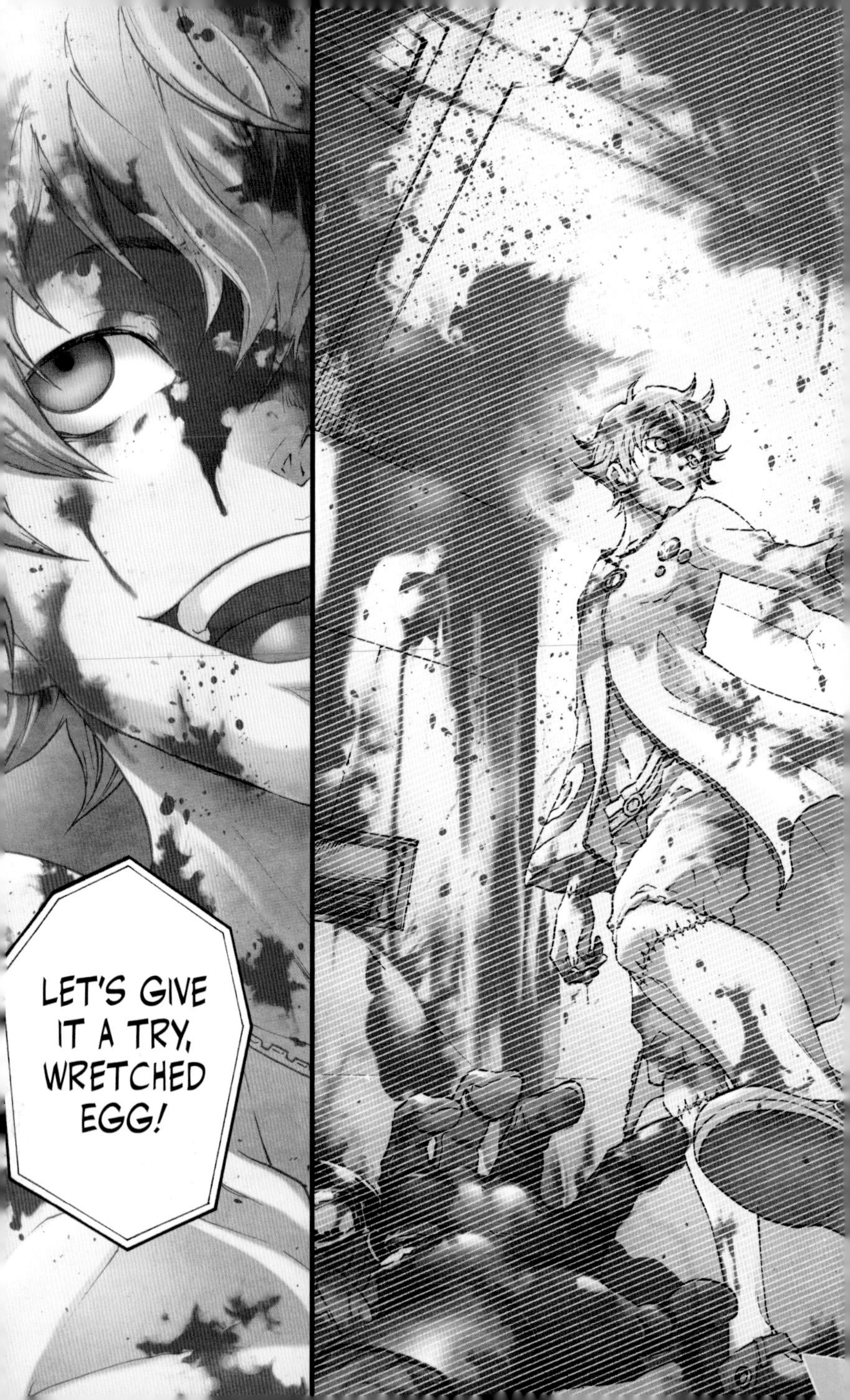
LET'S GIVE IT A TRY, WRETCHED EGG!

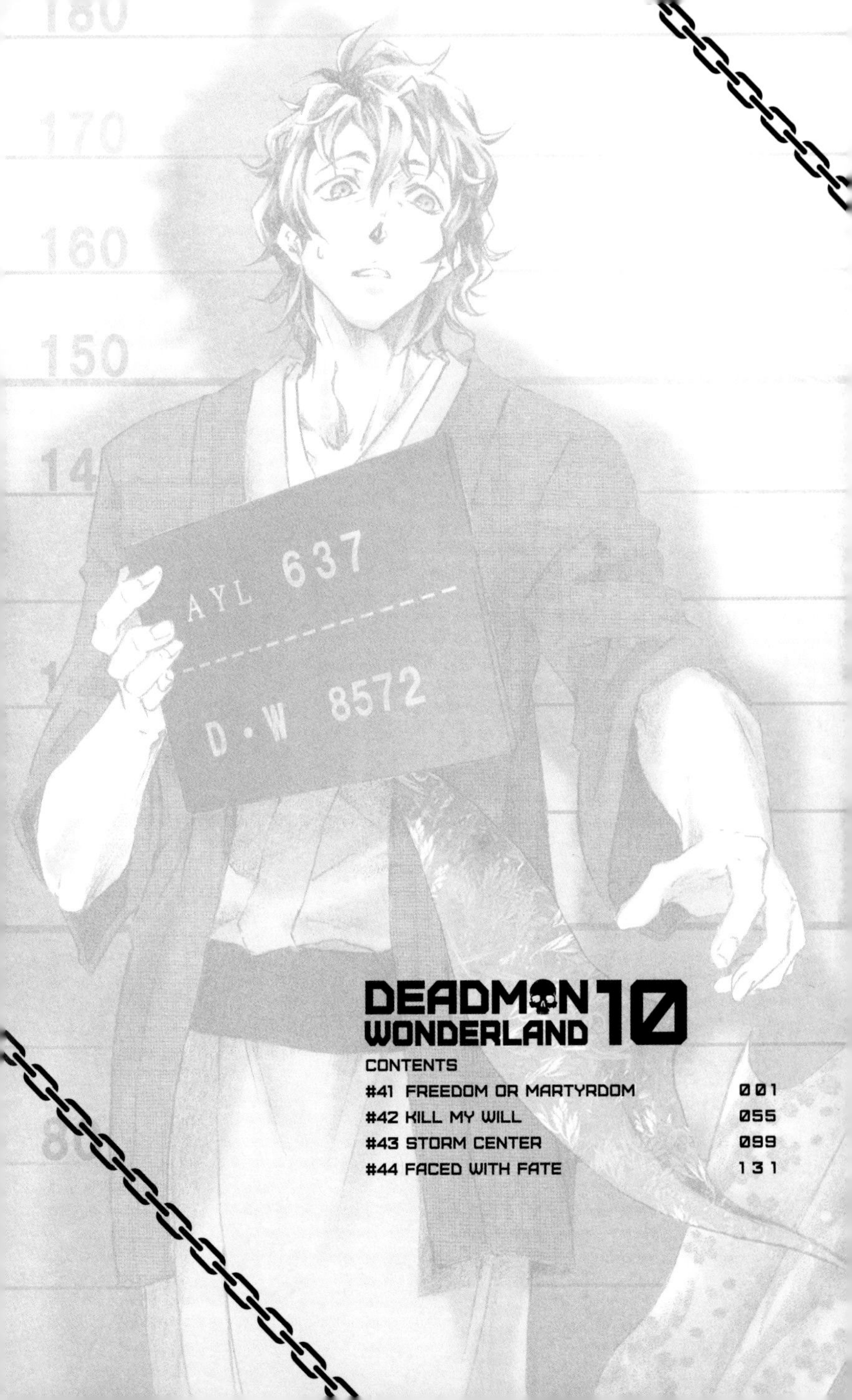
170
160
150
AYL 637
D・W 8572

DEADMAN WONDERLAND 10

CONTENTS

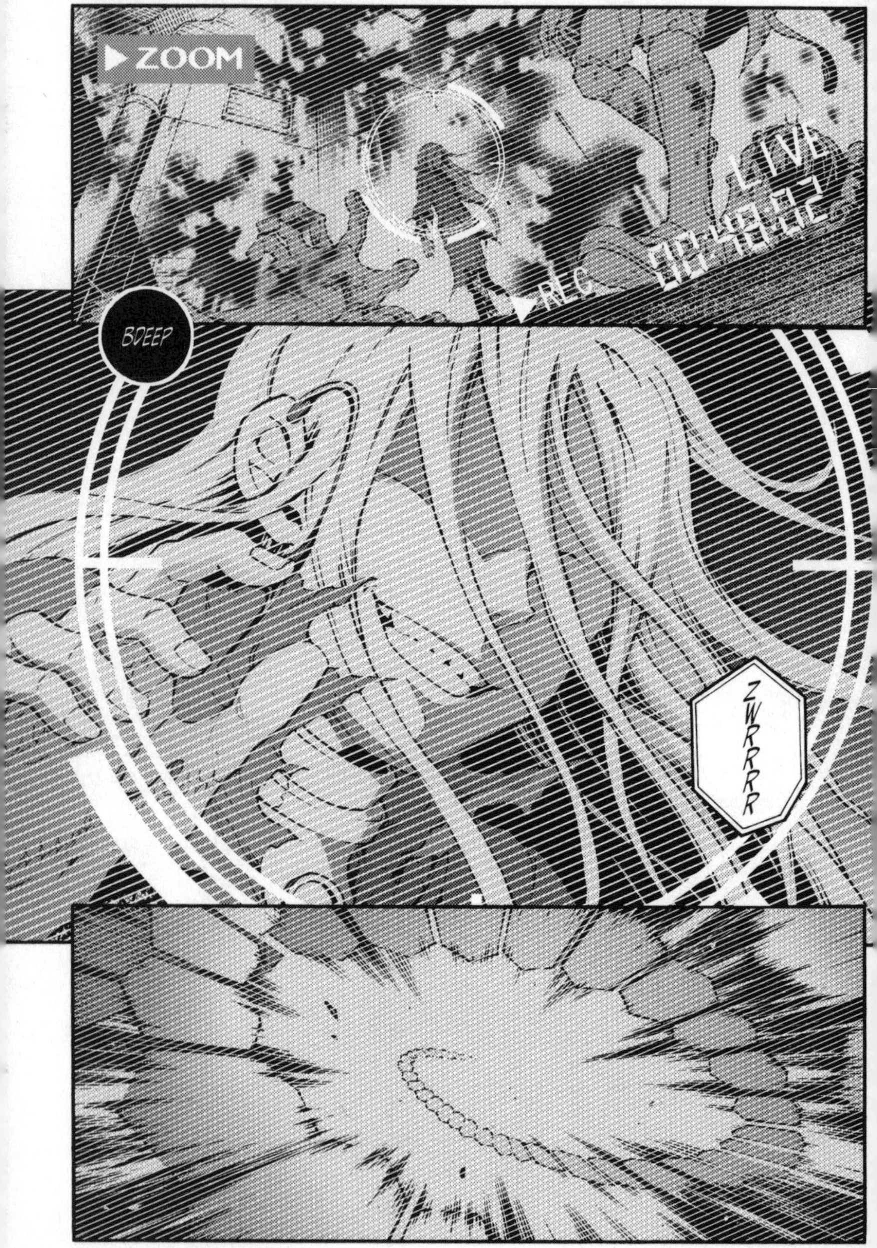
▶ZOOM
LIVE
▶REC
BDEEP
ZWRRRRR

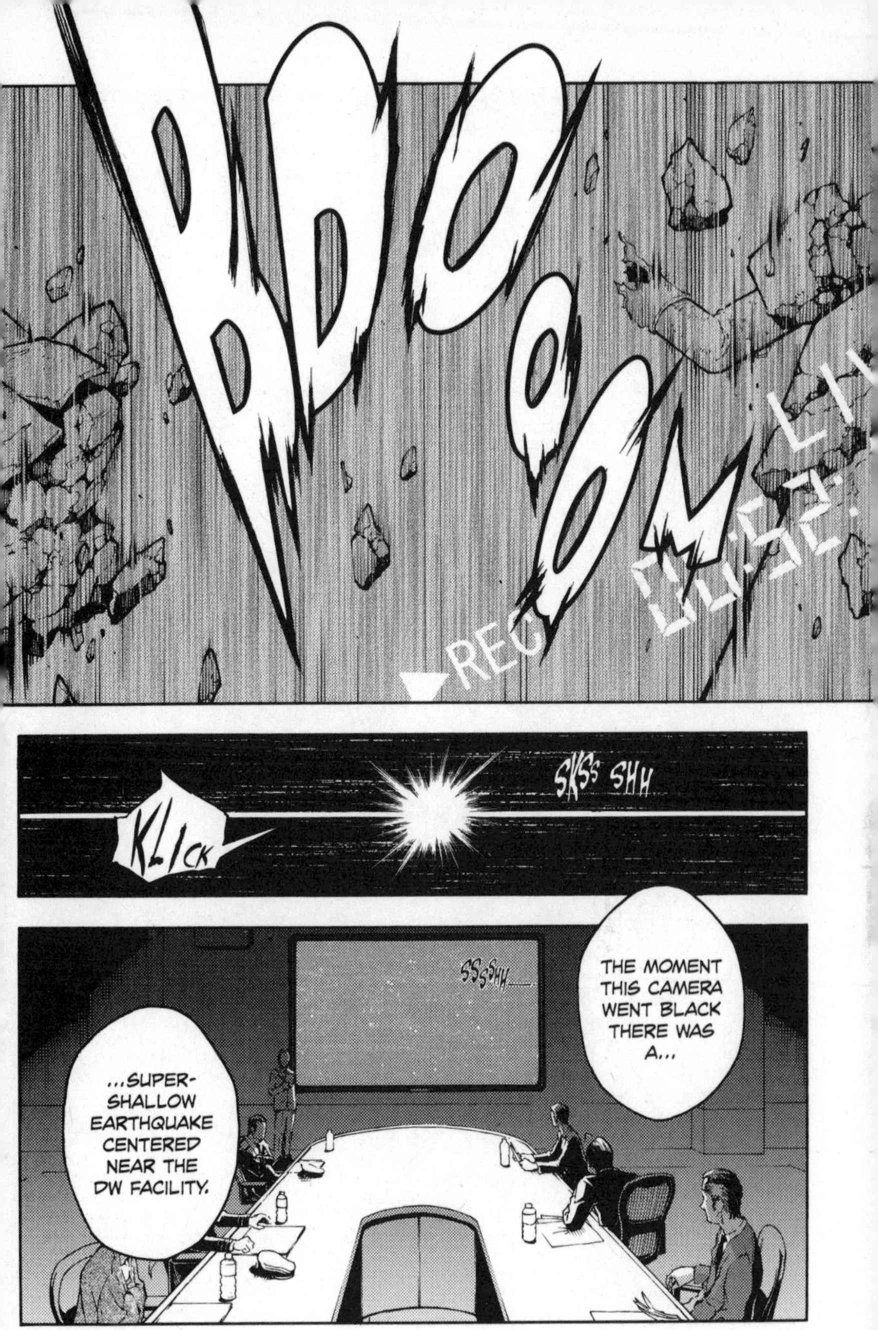
BADOOOOM
REC
SKSS SHH
KLICK
THE MOMENT THIS CAMERA WENT BLACK THERE WAS A...
SSSSHH...
...SUPER-SHALLOW EARTHQUAKE CENTERED NEAR THE DW FACILITY.

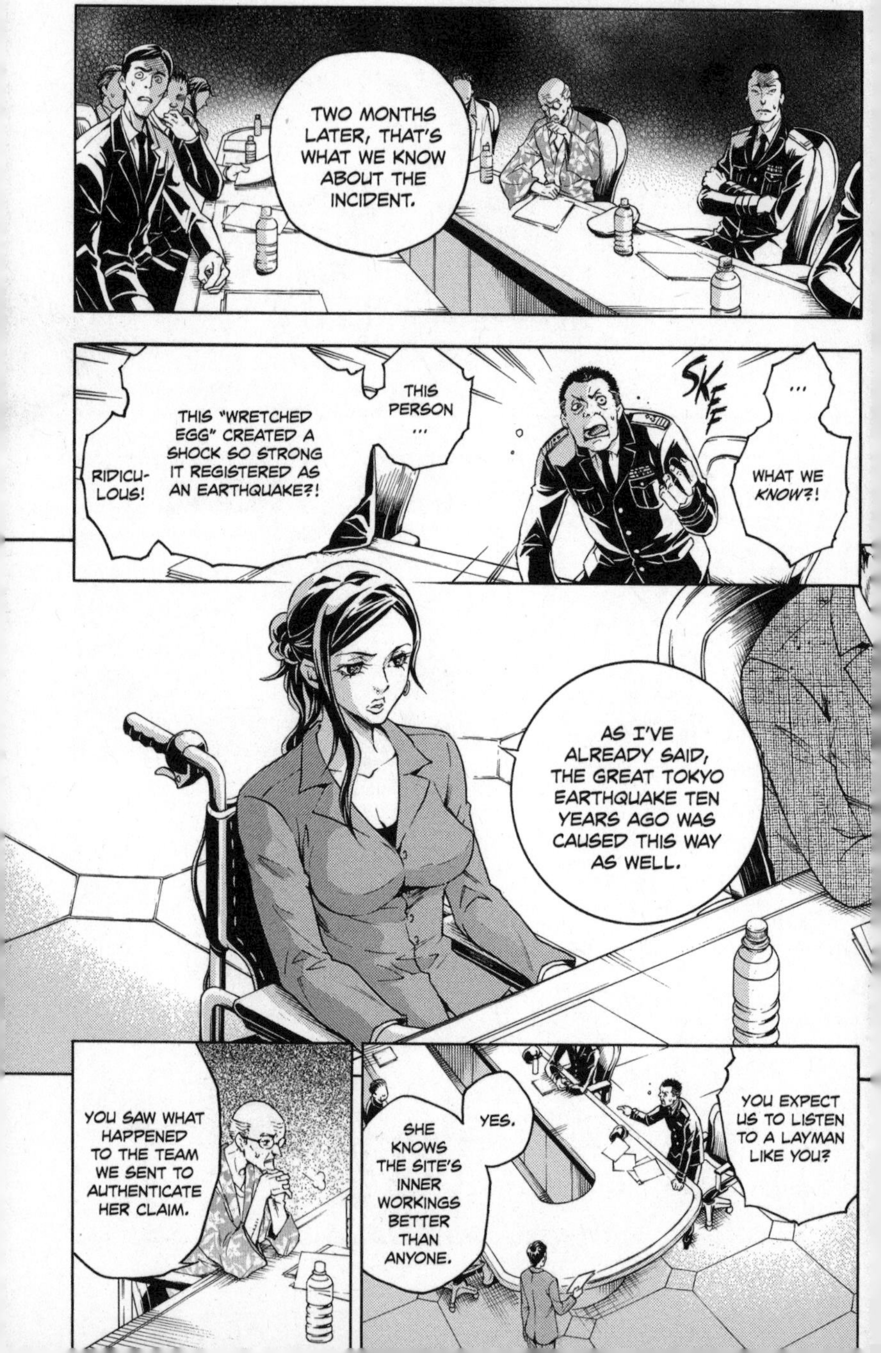
TWO MONTHS LATER, THAT'S WHAT WE KNOW ABOUT THE INCIDENT.
SKEE
...
WHAT WE *KNOW*?!
THIS PERSON ...
THIS "WRETCHED EGG" CREATED A SHOCK SO STRONG IT REGISTERED AS AN EARTHQUAKE?!
RIDICU-LOUS!
AS I'VE ALREADY SAID, THE GREAT TOKYO EARTHQUAKE TEN YEARS AGO WAS CAUSED THIS WAY AS WELL.
YOU EXPECT US TO LISTEN TO A LAYMAN LIKE YOU?
YES.
SHE KNOWS THE SITE'S INNER WORKINGS BETTER THAN ANYONE.
YOU SAW WHAT HAPPENED TO THE TEAM WE SENT TO AUTHENTICATE HER CLAIM.

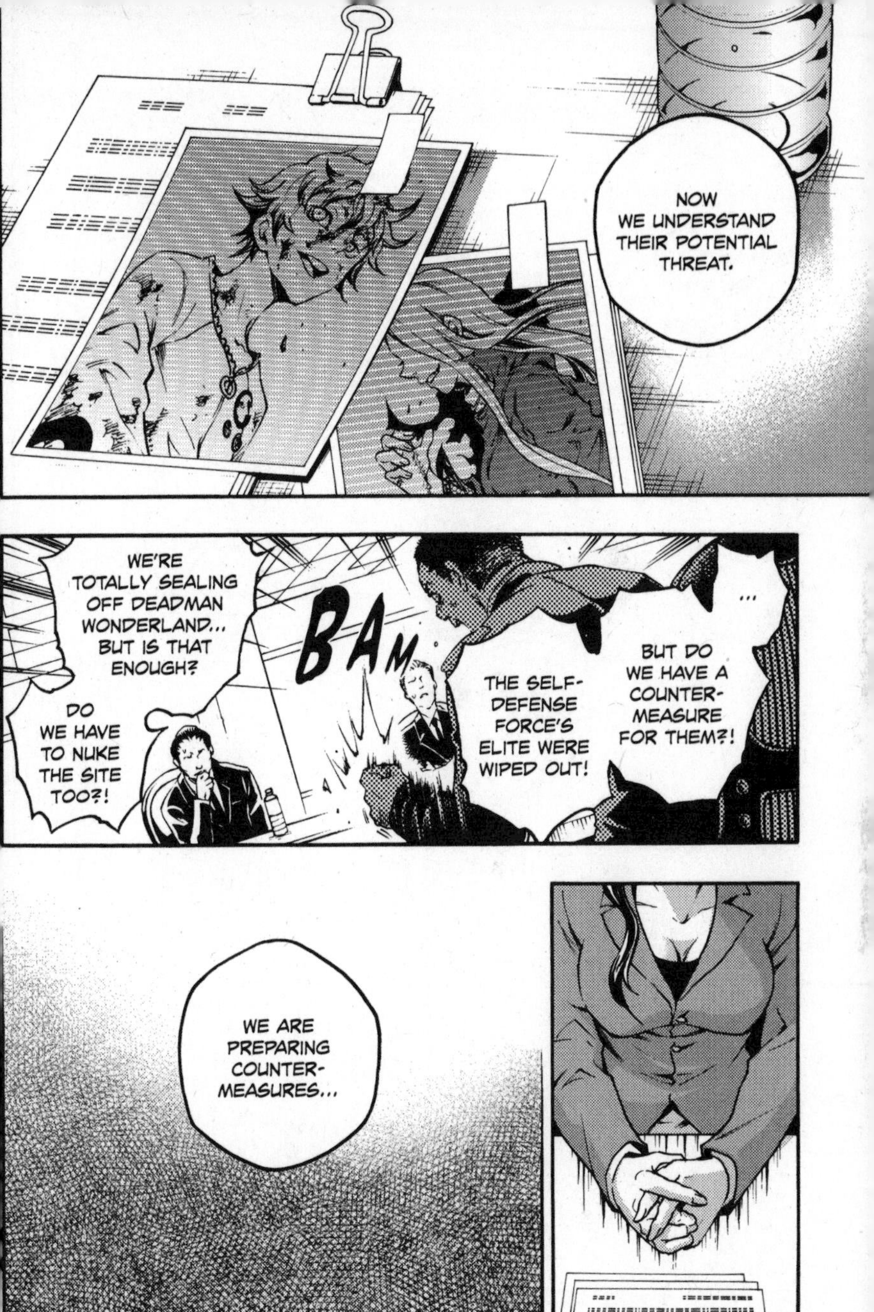
NOW WE UNDERSTAND THEIR POTENTIAL THREAT.
...
BUT DO WE HAVE A COUNTER-MEASURE FOR THEM?!
THE SELF-DEFENSE FORCE'S ELITE WERE WIPED OUT!
BAM
WE'RE TOTALLY SEALING OFF DEADMAN WONDERLAND... BUT IS THAT ENOUGH?
DO WE HAVE TO NUKE THE SITE TOO?!
WE ARE PREPARING COUNTER-MEASURES...

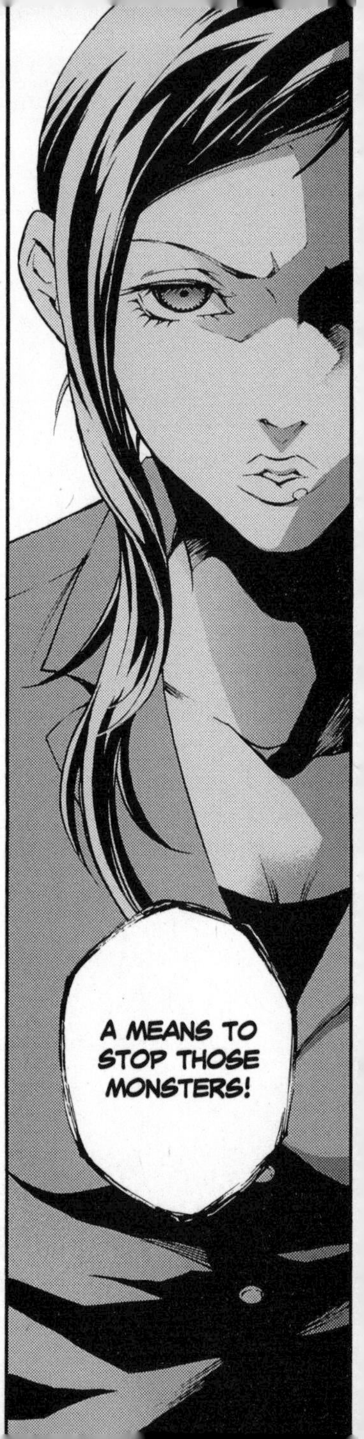
A MEANS TO STOP THOSE MONSTERS!

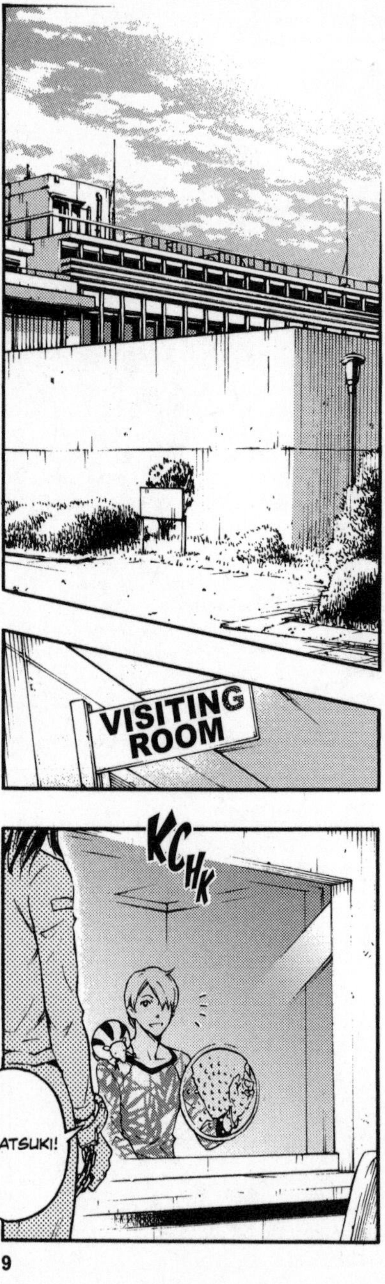
VISITING ROOM
KCHK
MINATSUKI!

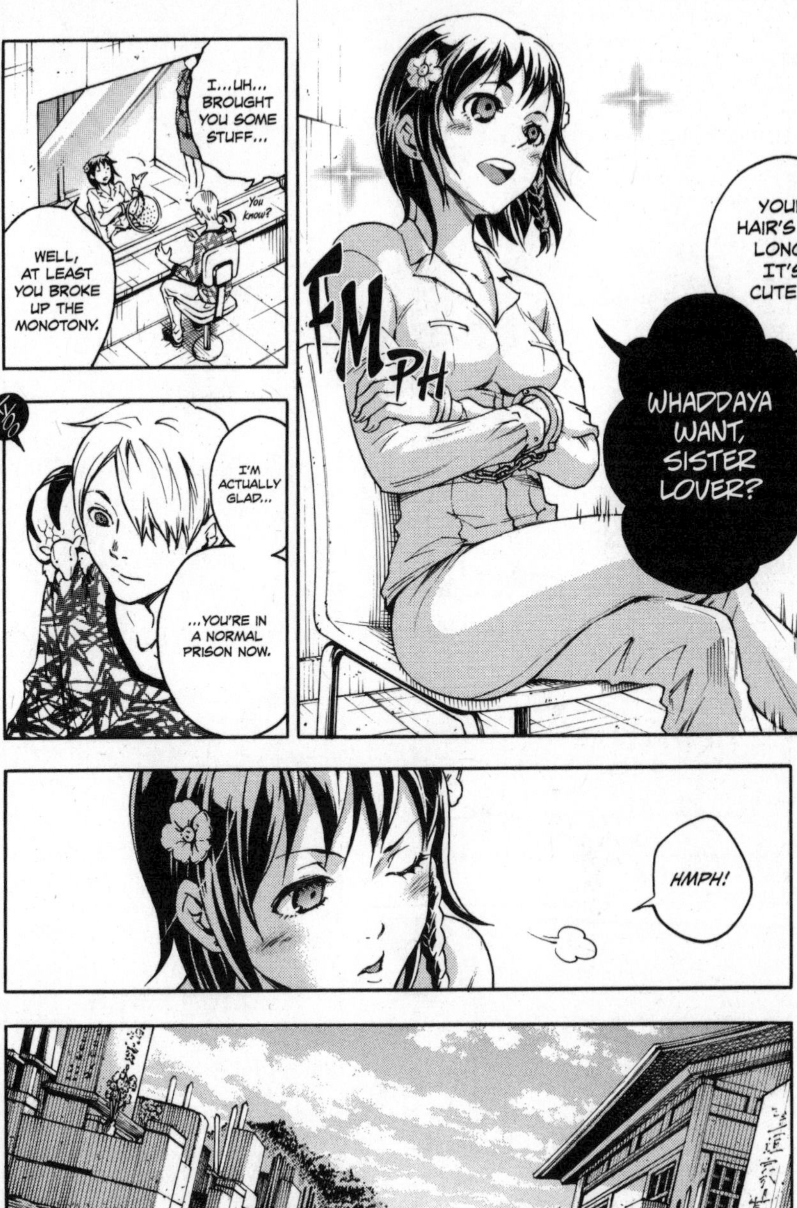
YOUR HAIR'S SO LONG. IT'S CUTE...
FMPH
WHADDAYA WANT, SISTER LOVER?
I...UH... BROUGHT YOU SOME STUFF...
You know?
WELL, AT LEAST YOU BROKE UP THE MONOTONY.
KYOO
I'M ACTUALLY GLAD...
...YOU'RE IN A NORMAL PRISON NOW.
HMPH!

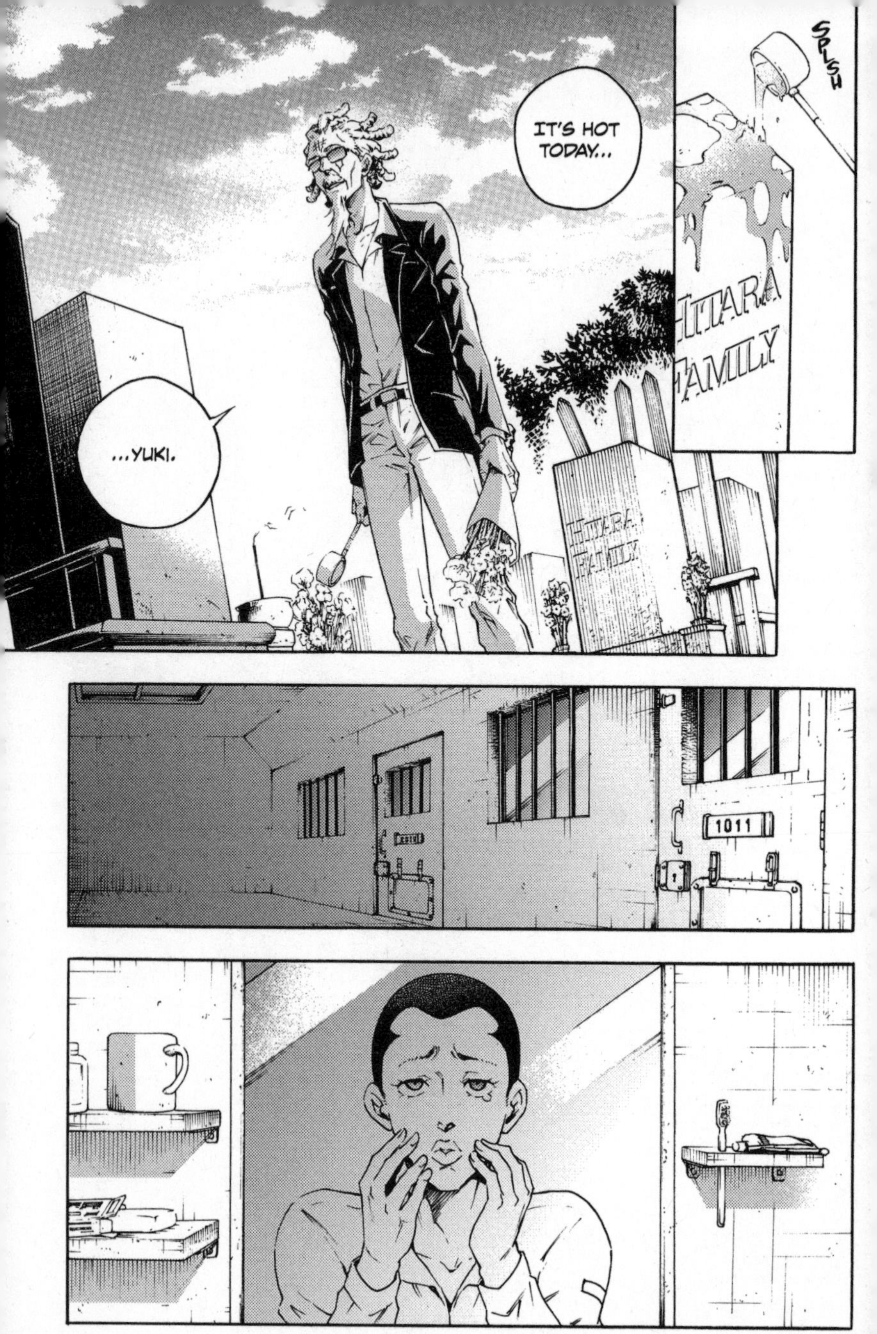
SPLSH
IT'S HOT TODAY...
...YUKI.
1011

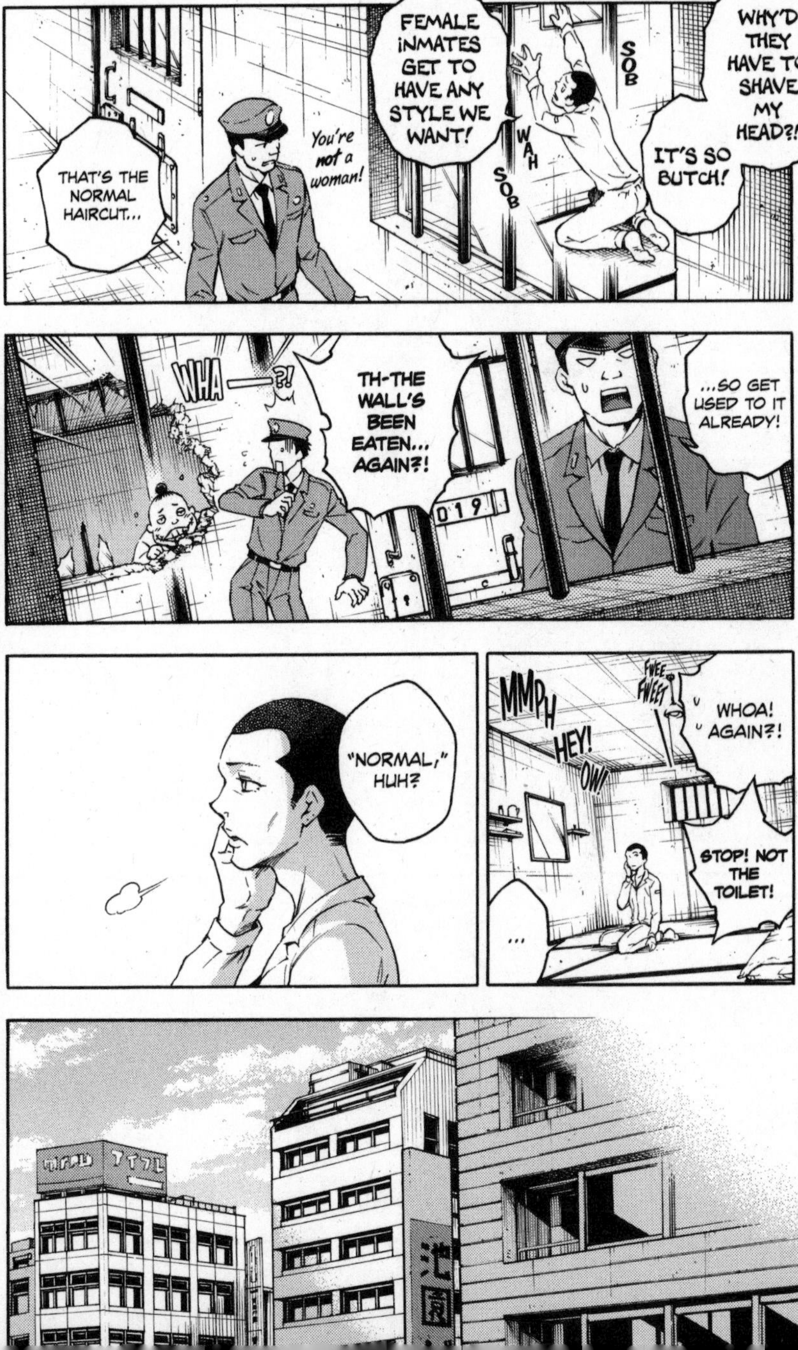
WHY'D THEY HAVE TO SHAVE MY HEAD?!
IT'S SO BUTCH!
SOB
WAH
SOB
FEMALE INMATES GET TO HAVE ANY STYLE WE WANT!
You're not a woman!
THAT'S THE NORMAL HAIRCUT...
...SO GET USED TO IT ALREADY!
019
TH-THE WALL'S BEEN EATEN... AGAIN?!
WHA—?!
WHOA! AGAIN?!
FWEE FWEET
MMPH
HEY!
OW!
STOP! NOT THE TOILET!
...
"NORMAL," HUH?

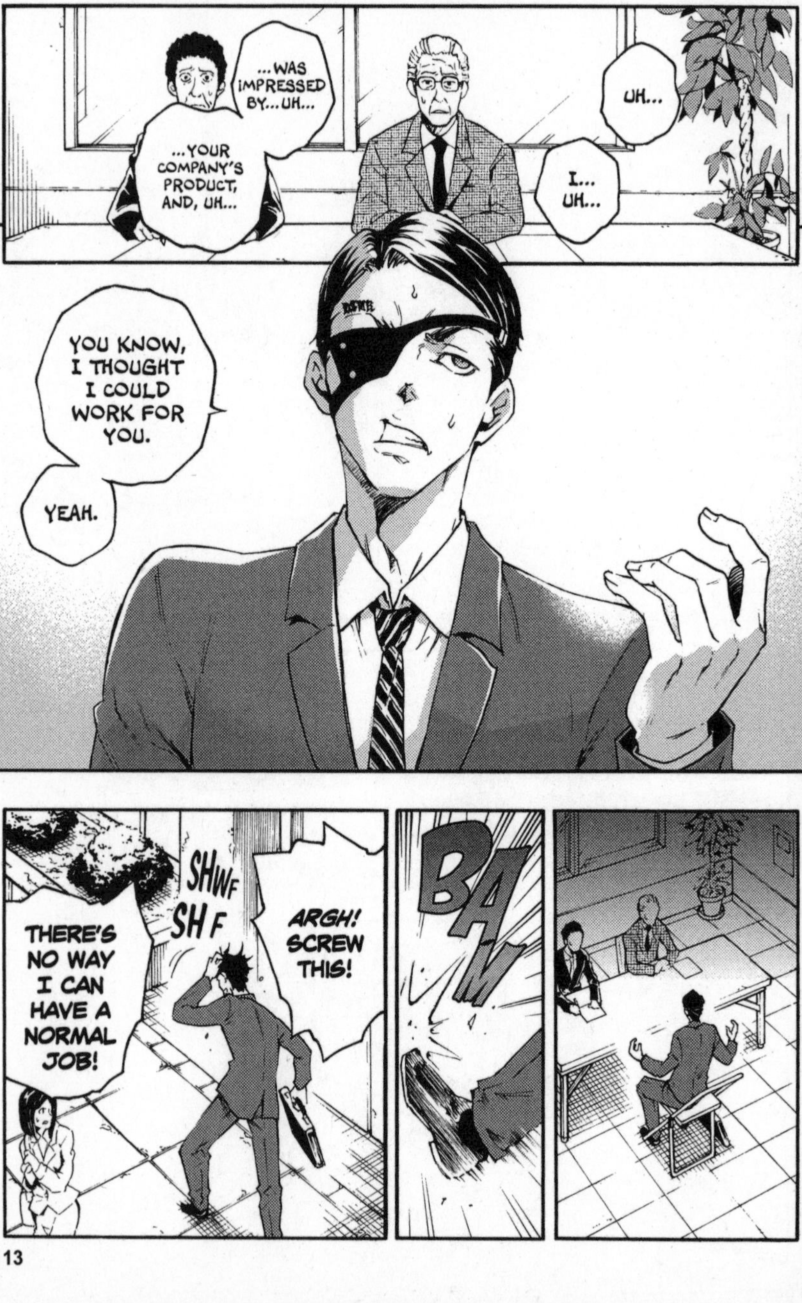
UH...
I... UH...
...WAS IMPRESSED BY...UH...
...YOUR COMPANY'S PRODUCT, AND, UH...
YOU KNOW, I THOUGHT I COULD WORK FOR YOU.
YEAH.
BAM
ARGH! SCREW THIS!
SHWF
SHF
THERE'S NO WAY I CAN HAVE A NORMAL JOB!

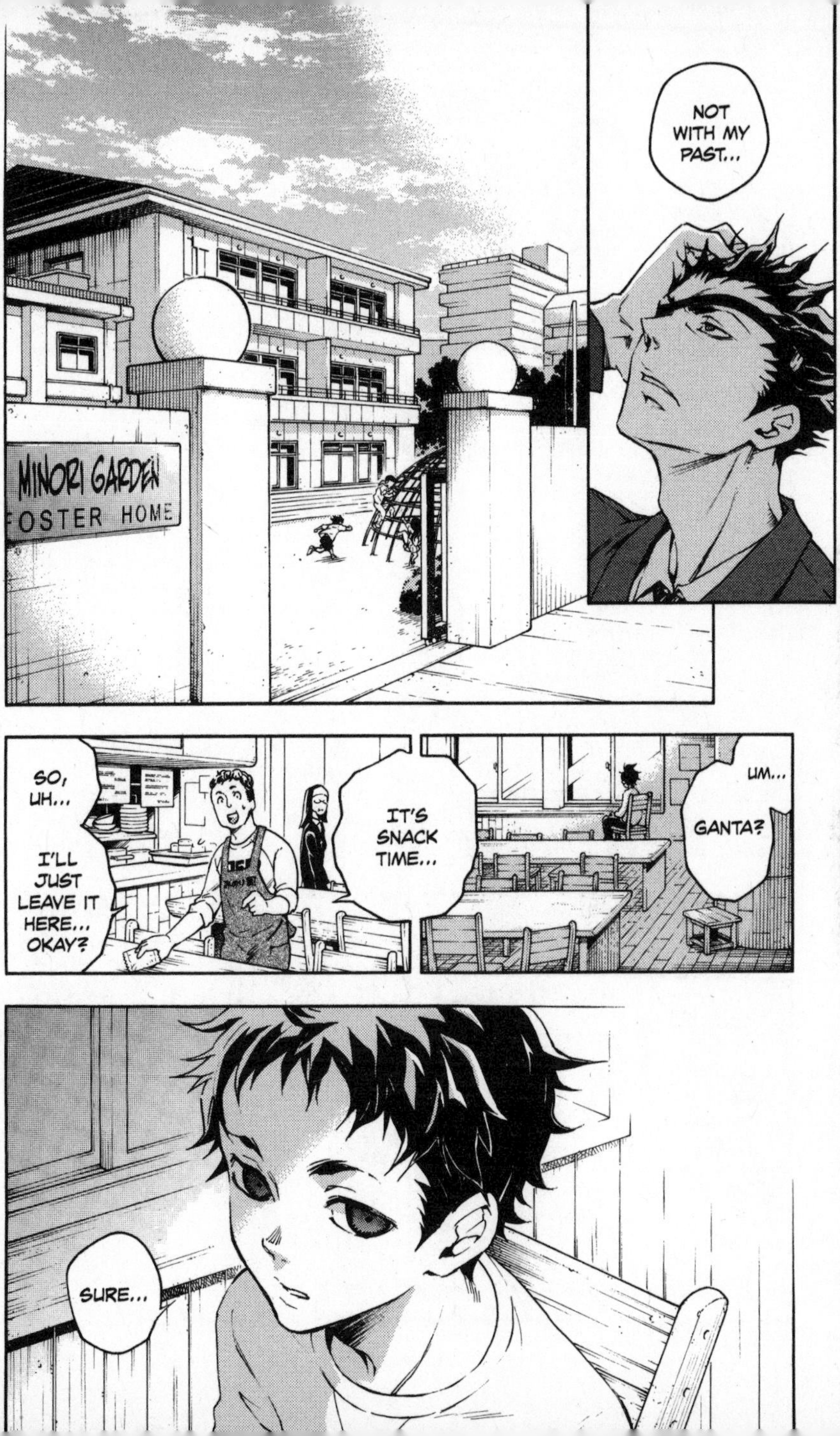
NOT WITH MY PAST...
MINORI GARDEN
FOSTER HOME
UM...
GANTA?
SO, UH...
IT'S SNACK TIME...
I'LL JUST LEAVE IT HERE... OKAY?
SURE...

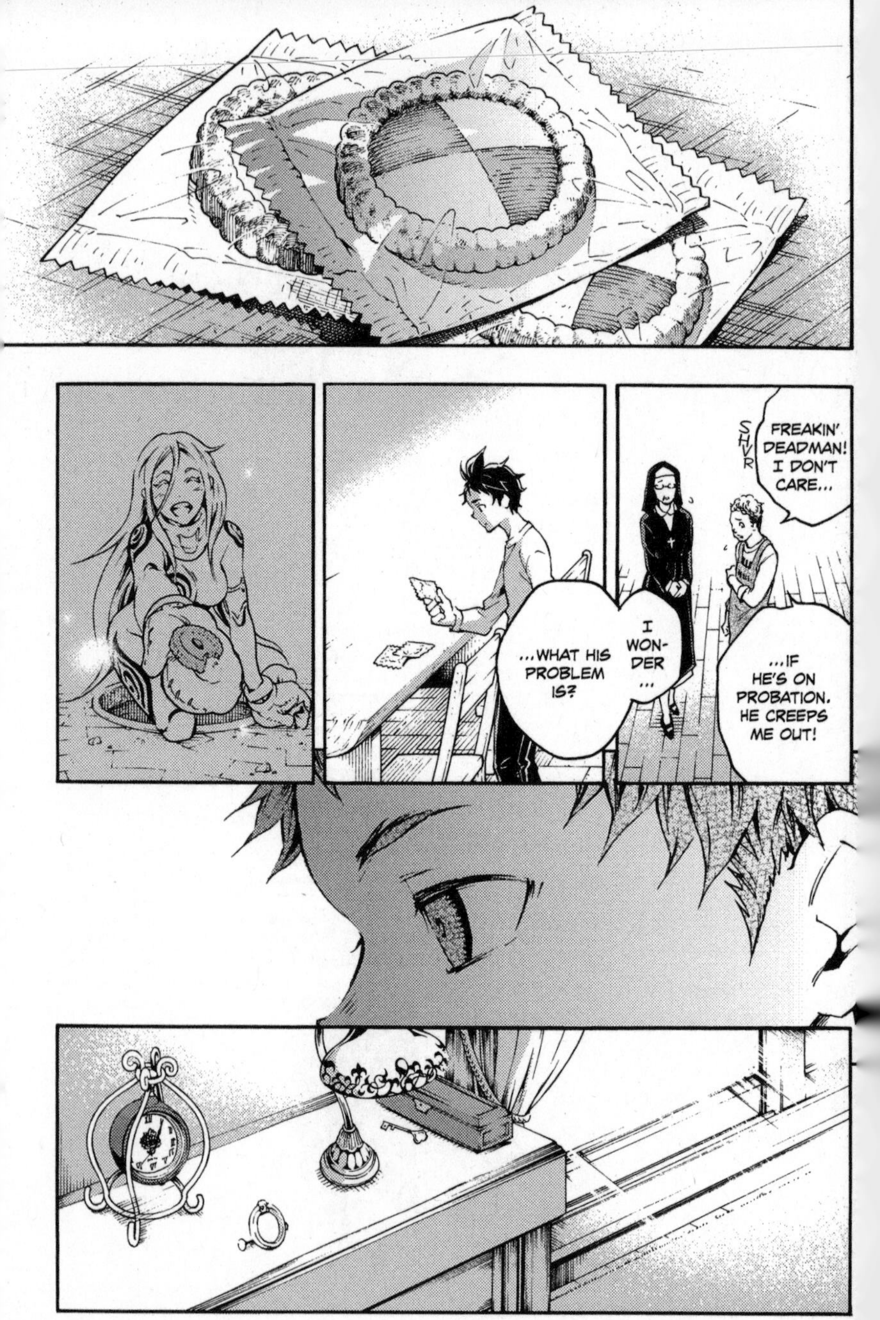
SHVR
FREAKIN' DEADMAN! I DON'T CARE...
...IF HE'S ON PROBATION. HE CREEPS ME OUT!
I WONDER...
...WHAT HIS PROBLEM IS?

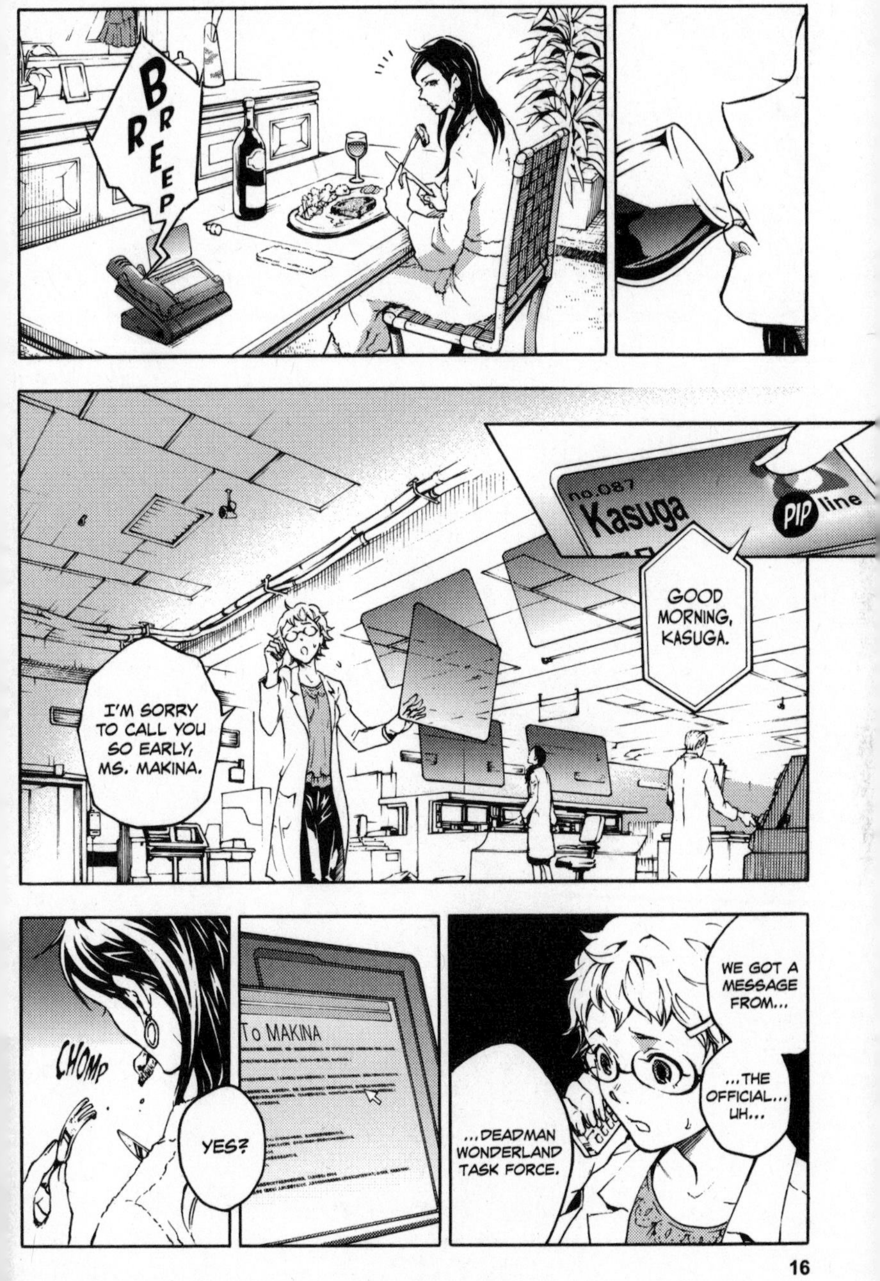
BRREEP
no.087
Kasuga
PIP line
GOOD MORNING, KASUGA.
I'M SORRY TO CALL YOU SO EARLY, MS. MAKINA.
WE GOT A MESSAGE FROM...
...THE OFFICIAL... UH...
...DEADMAN WONDERLAND TASK FORCE.
To MAKINA
YES?
CHOMP

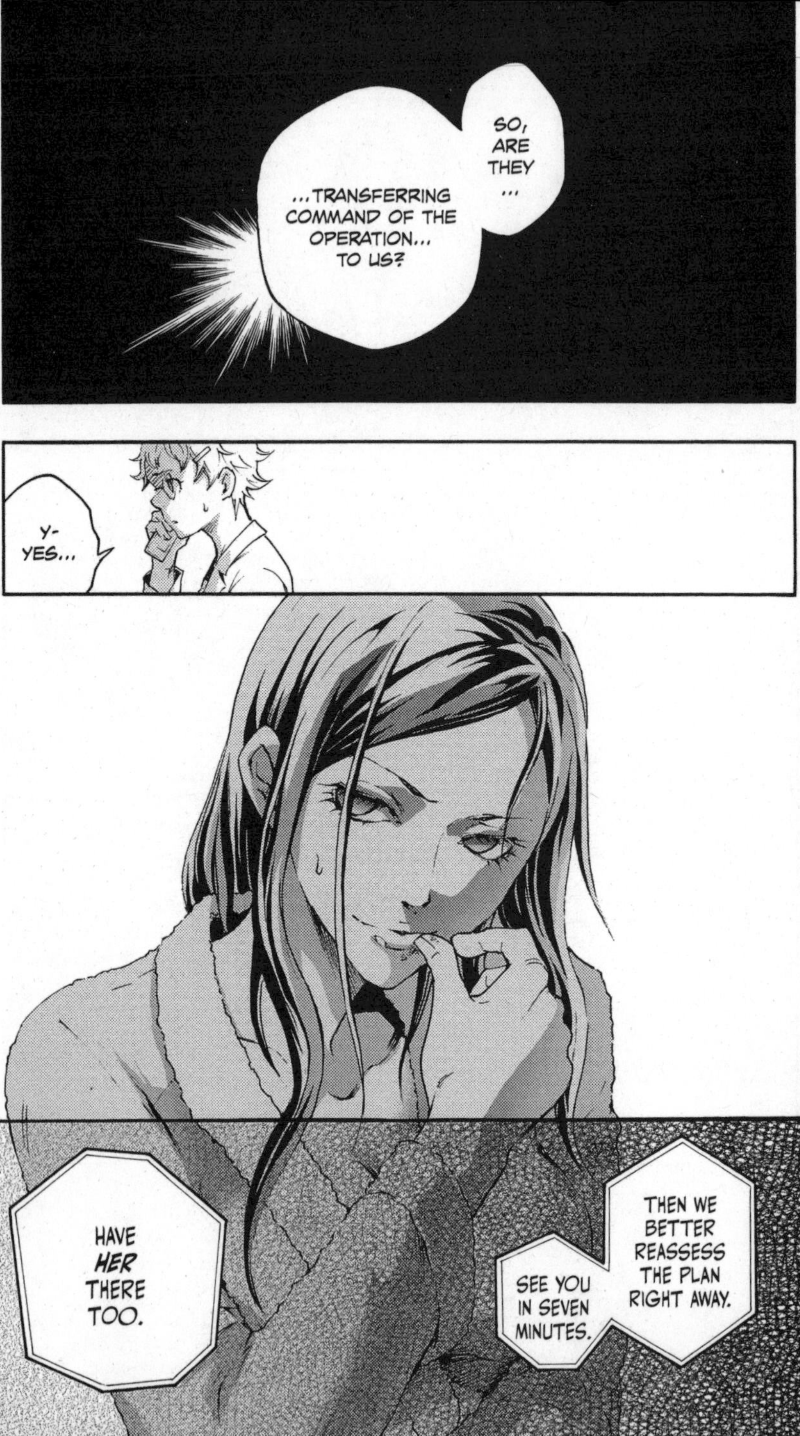
SO, ARE THEY ...
...TRANSFERRING COMMAND OF THE OPERATION... TO US?
Y-YES...
THEN WE BETTER REASSESS THE PLAN RIGHT AWAY.
SEE YOU IN SEVEN MINUTES.
HAVE ***HER*** THERE TOO.

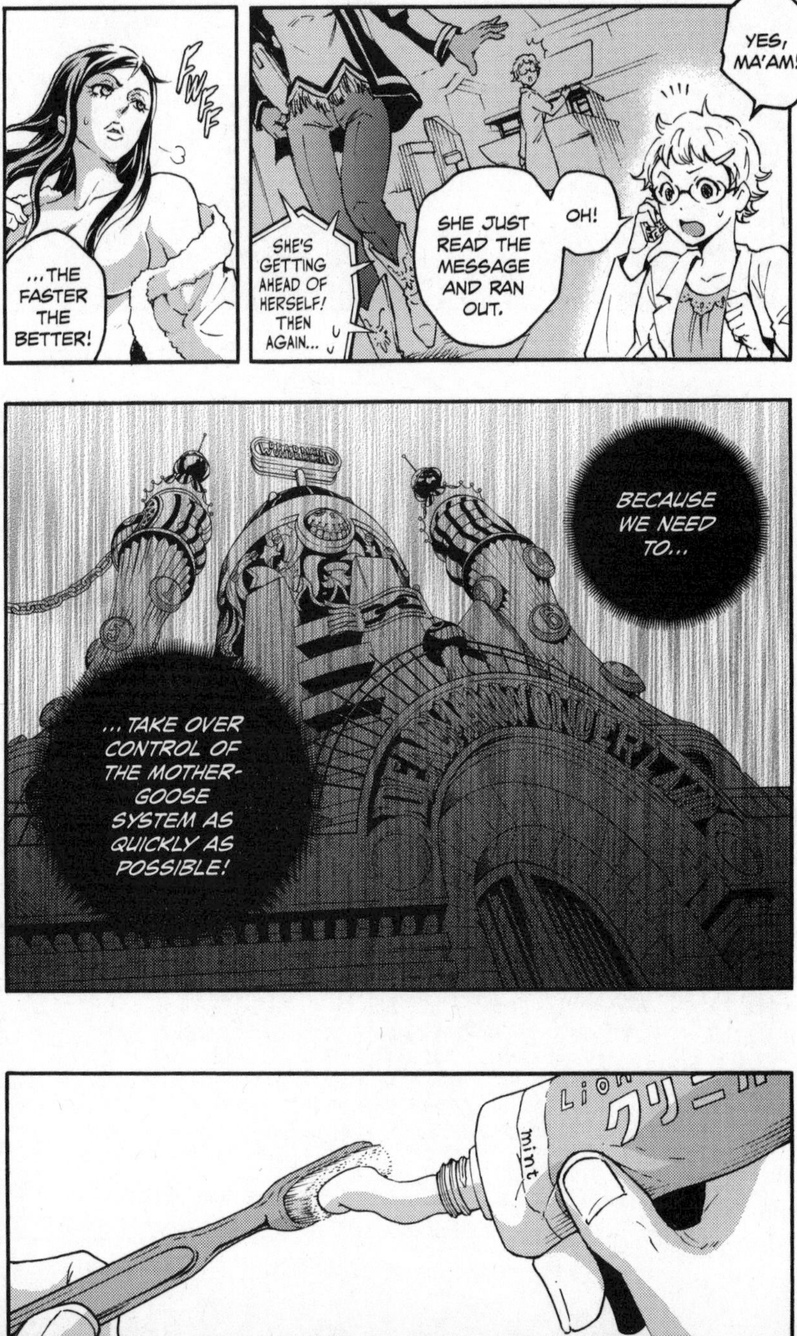
YES, MA'AM!
OH!
SHE JUST READ THE MESSAGE AND RAN OUT.
SHE'S GETTING AHEAD OF HERSELF! THEN AGAIN...
FWFF
...THE FASTER THE BETTER!
BECAUSE WE NEED TO...
...TAKE OVER CONTROL OF THE MOTHER-GOOSE SYSTEM AS QUICKLY AS POSSIBLE!
mint

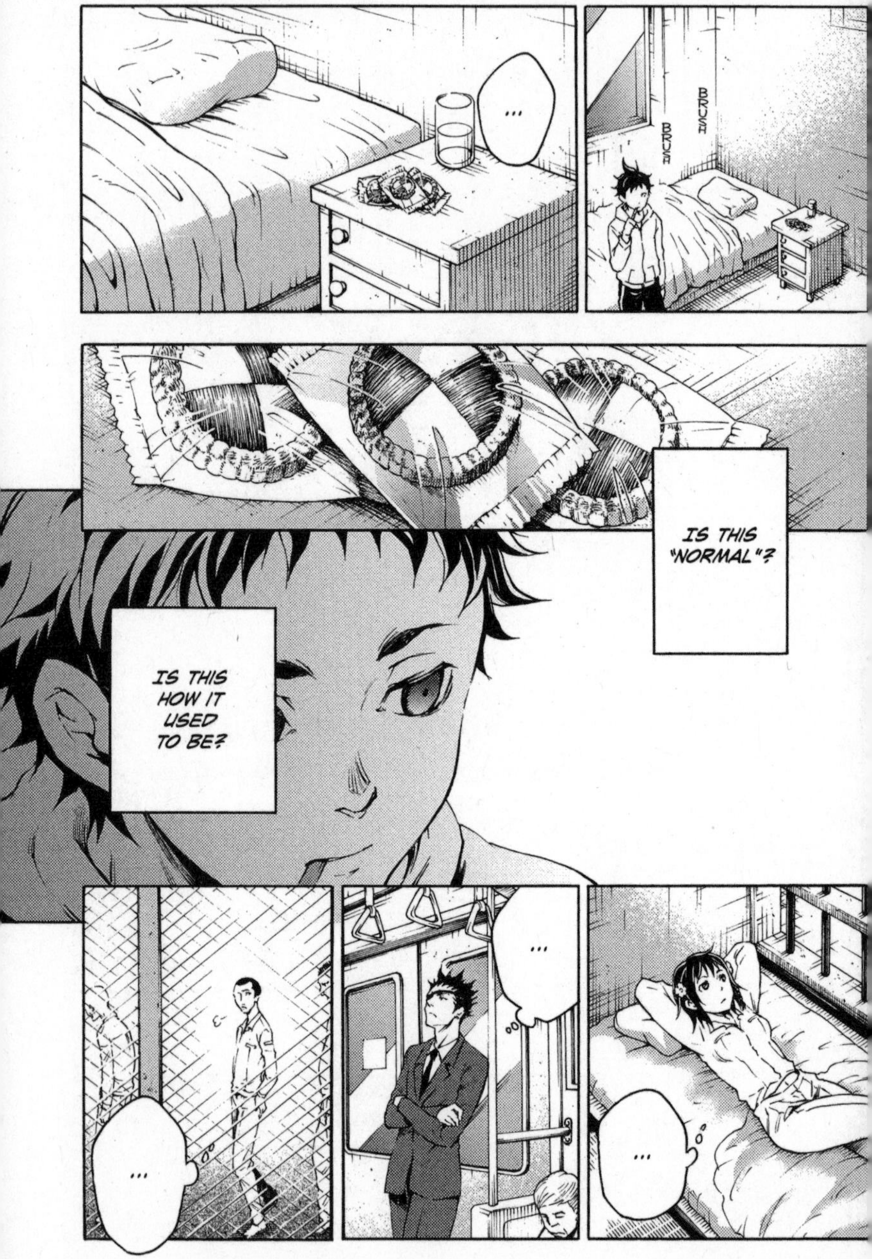
BRUSH
BRUSH
...
IS THIS "NORMAL"?
IS THIS HOW IT USED TO BE?
...
...
...

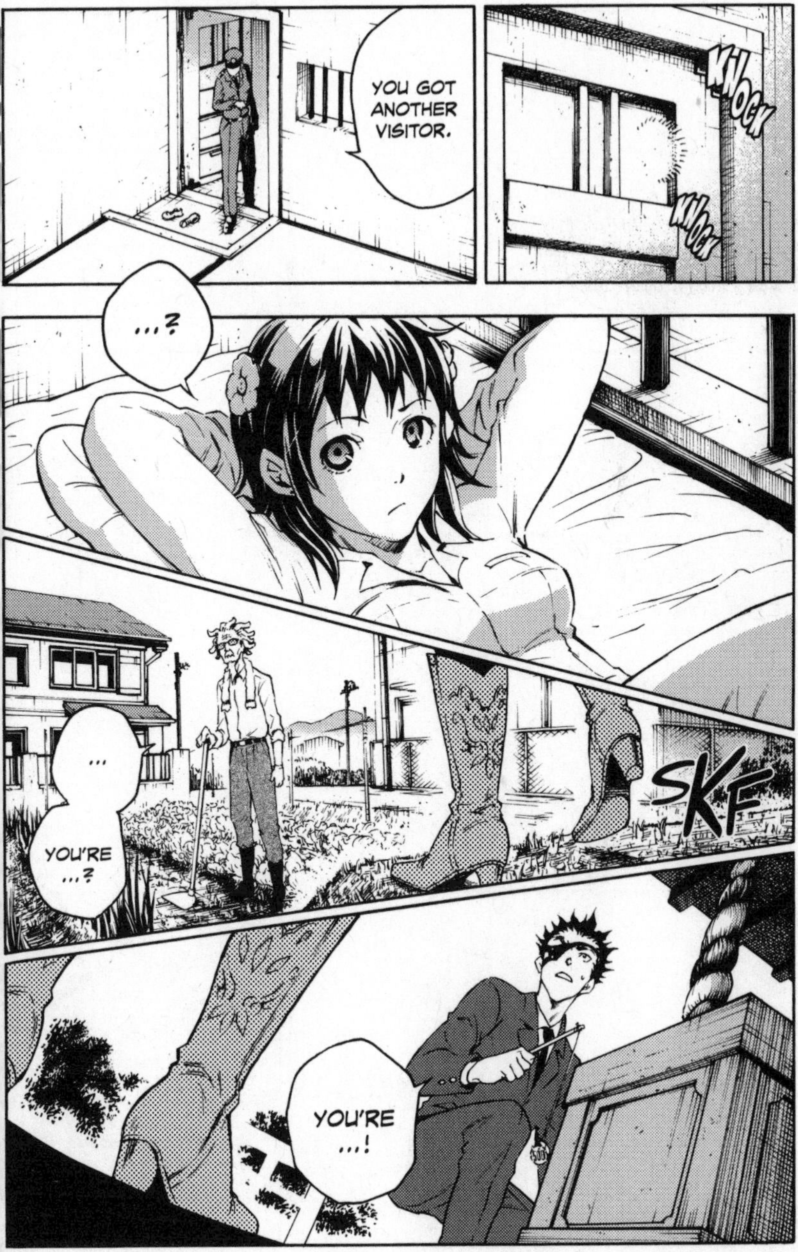
KNOCK
KNOCK
YOU GOT ANOTHER VISITOR.
...?
...
YOU'RE ...?
SKF
YOU'RE ...!

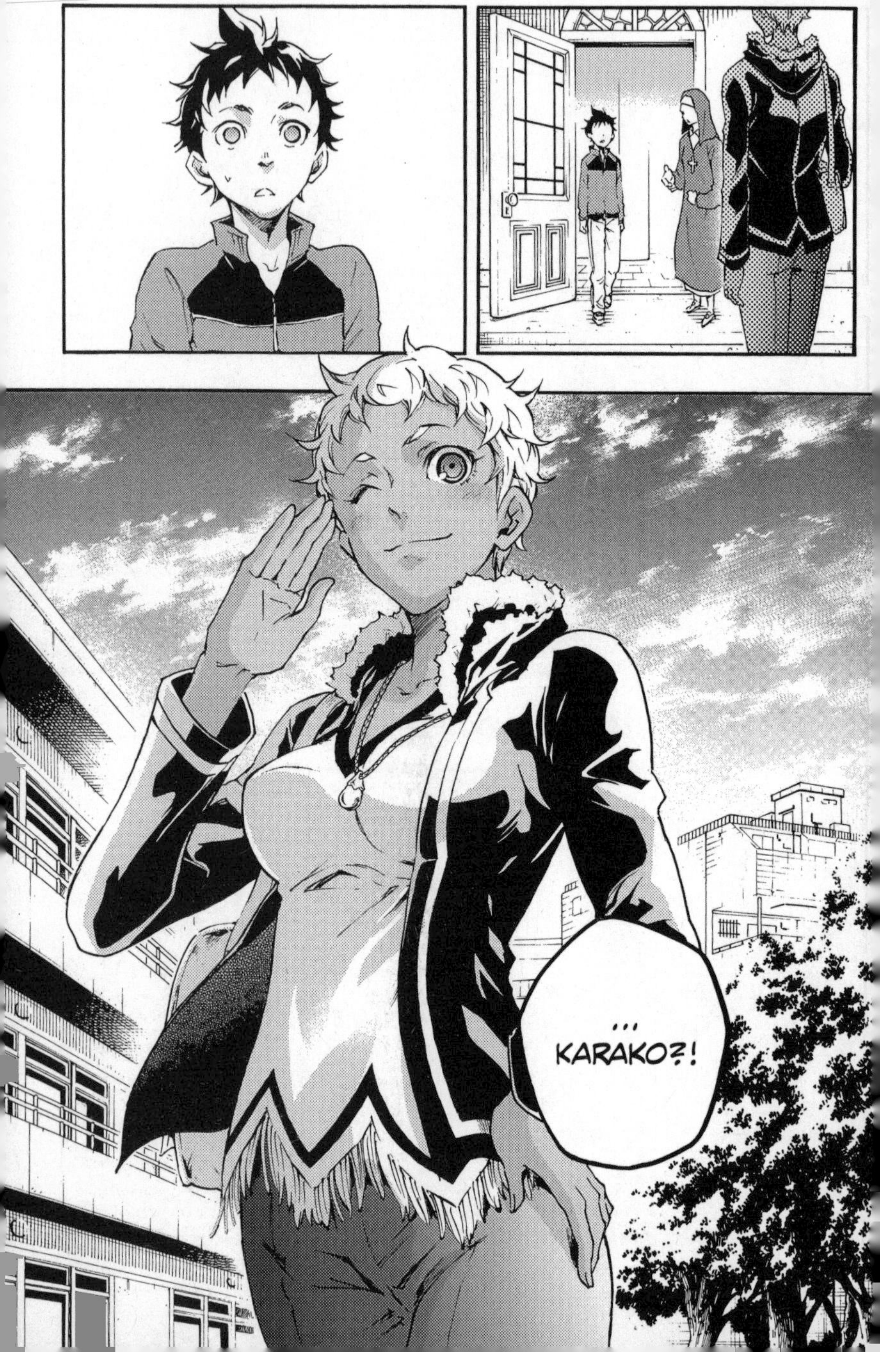
... KARAKO?!

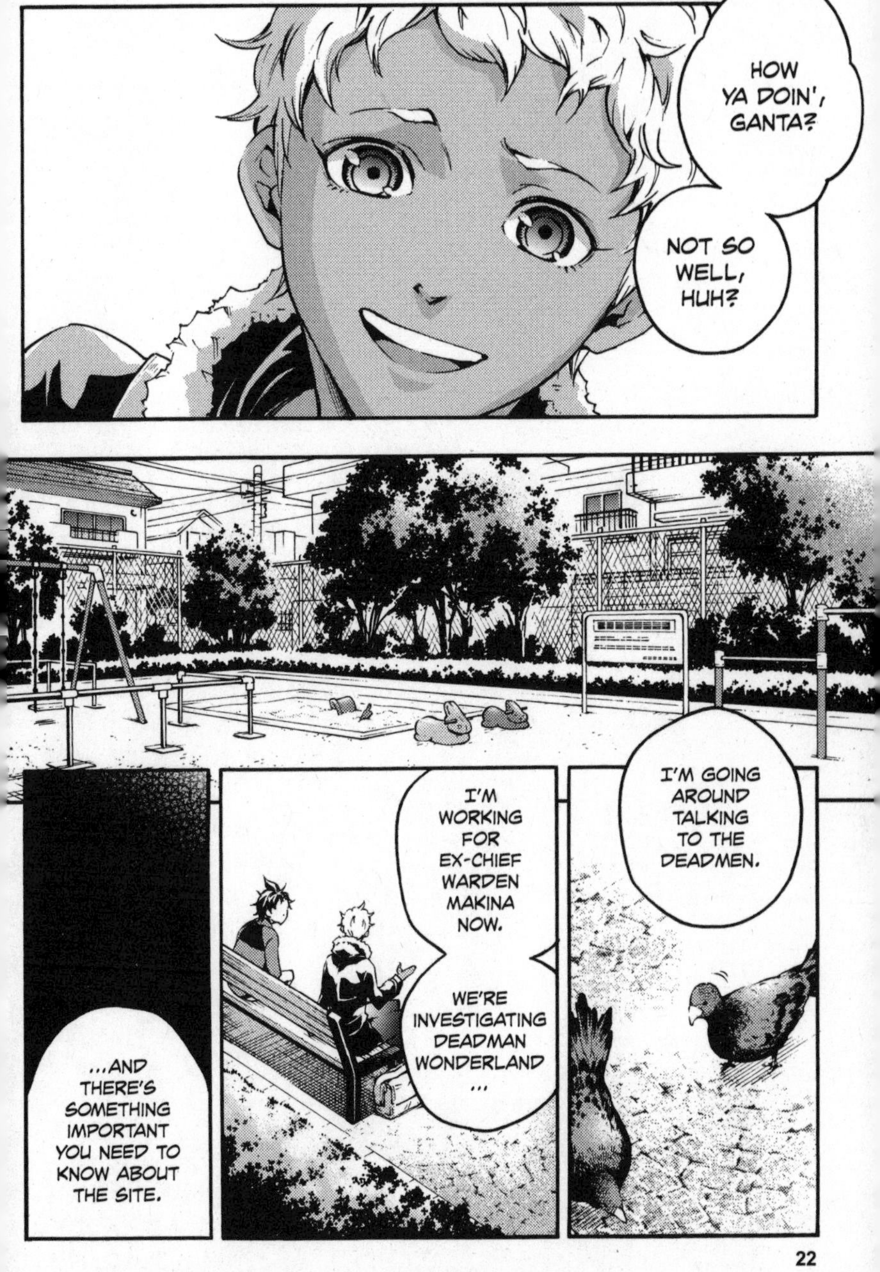
HOW YA DOIN', GANTA?
NOT SO WELL, HUH?
I'M GOING AROUND TALKING TO THE DEADMEN.
I'M WORKING FOR EX-CHIEF WARDEN MAKINA NOW.
WE'RE INVESTIGATING DEADMAN WONDERLAND ...
...AND THERE'S SOMETHING IMPORTANT YOU NEED TO KNOW ABOUT THE SITE.

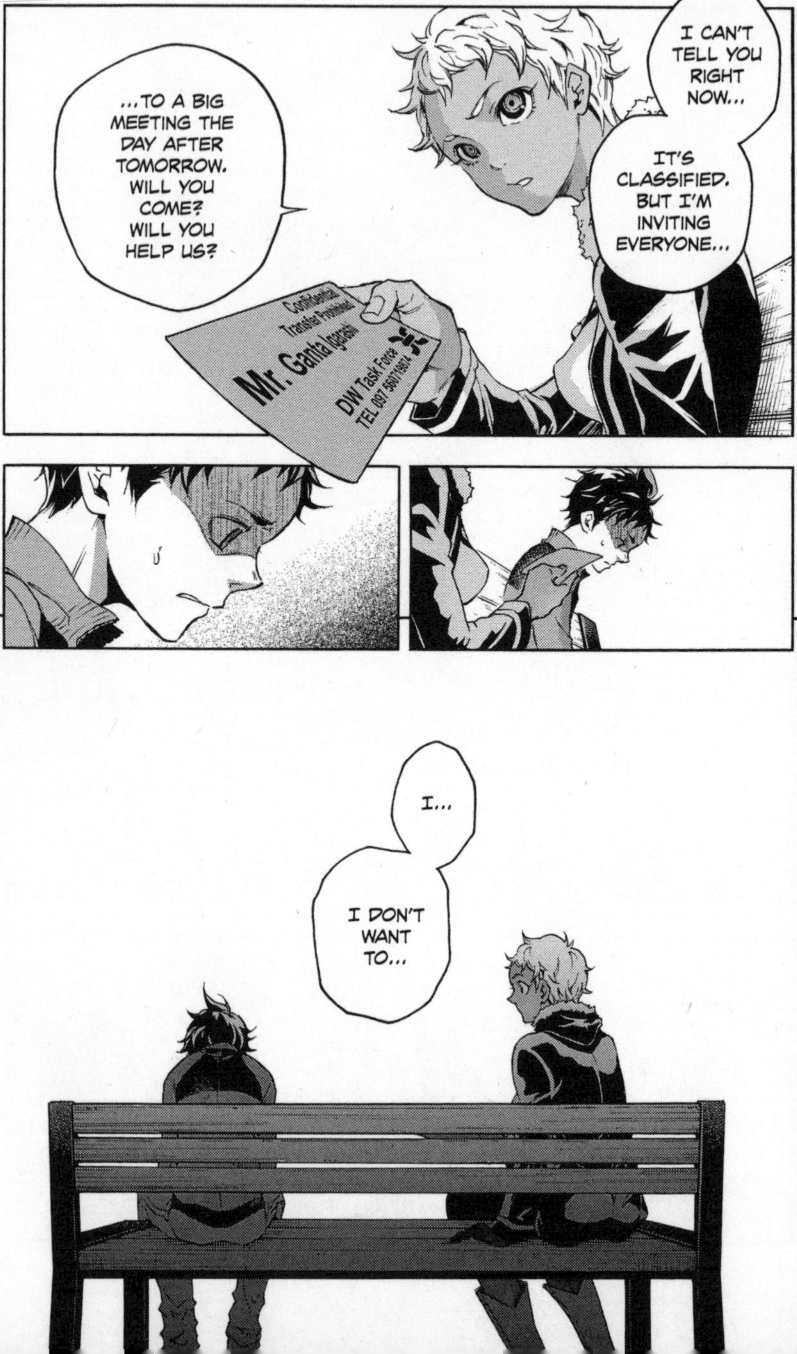
I CAN'T TELL YOU RIGHT NOW...
IT'S CLASSIFIED. BUT I'M INVITING EVERYONE...
...TO A BIG MEETING THE DAY AFTER TOMORROW. WILL YOU COME? WILL YOU HELP US?
Confidential
Transfer Prohibited
Mr. Ganta Igarashi
DW Task Force
I...
I DON'T WANT TO...

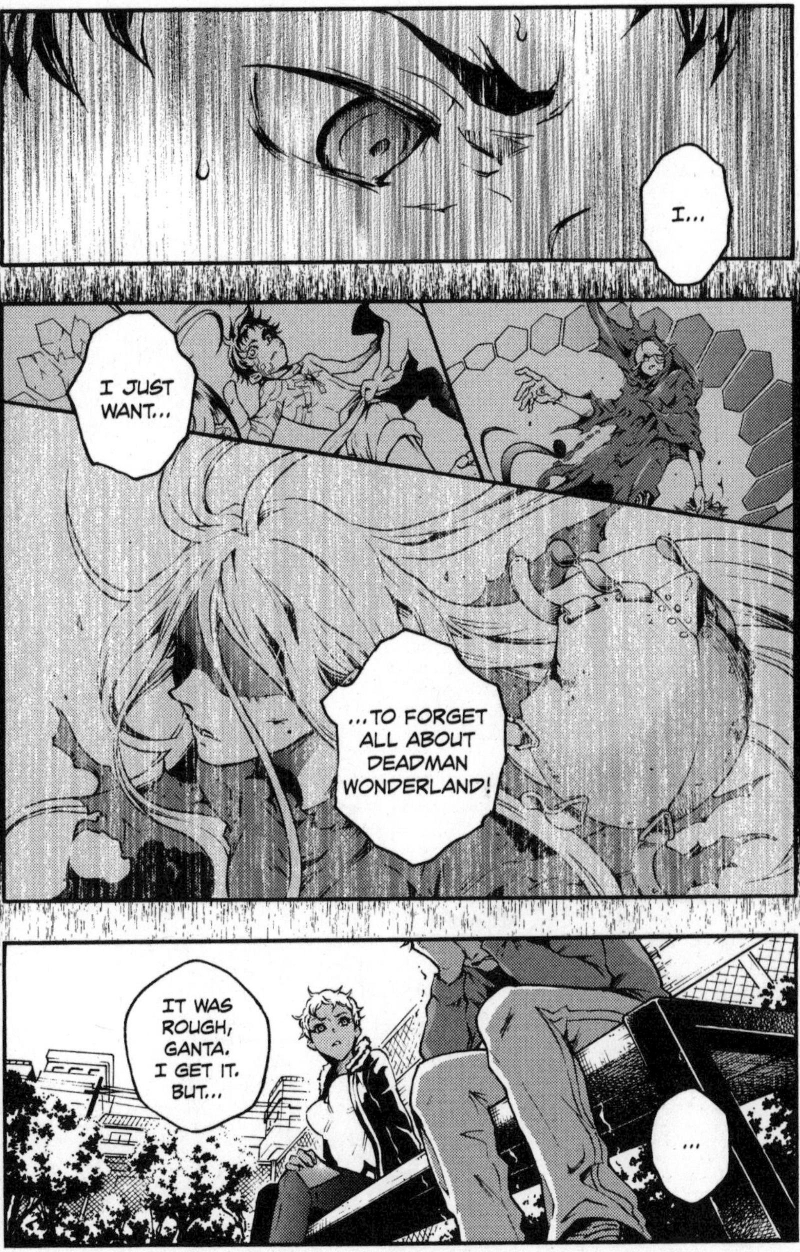
I...
I JUST WANT...
...TO FORGET ALL ABOUT DEADMAN WONDERLAND!
...
IT WAS ROUGH, GANTA. I GET IT. BUT...

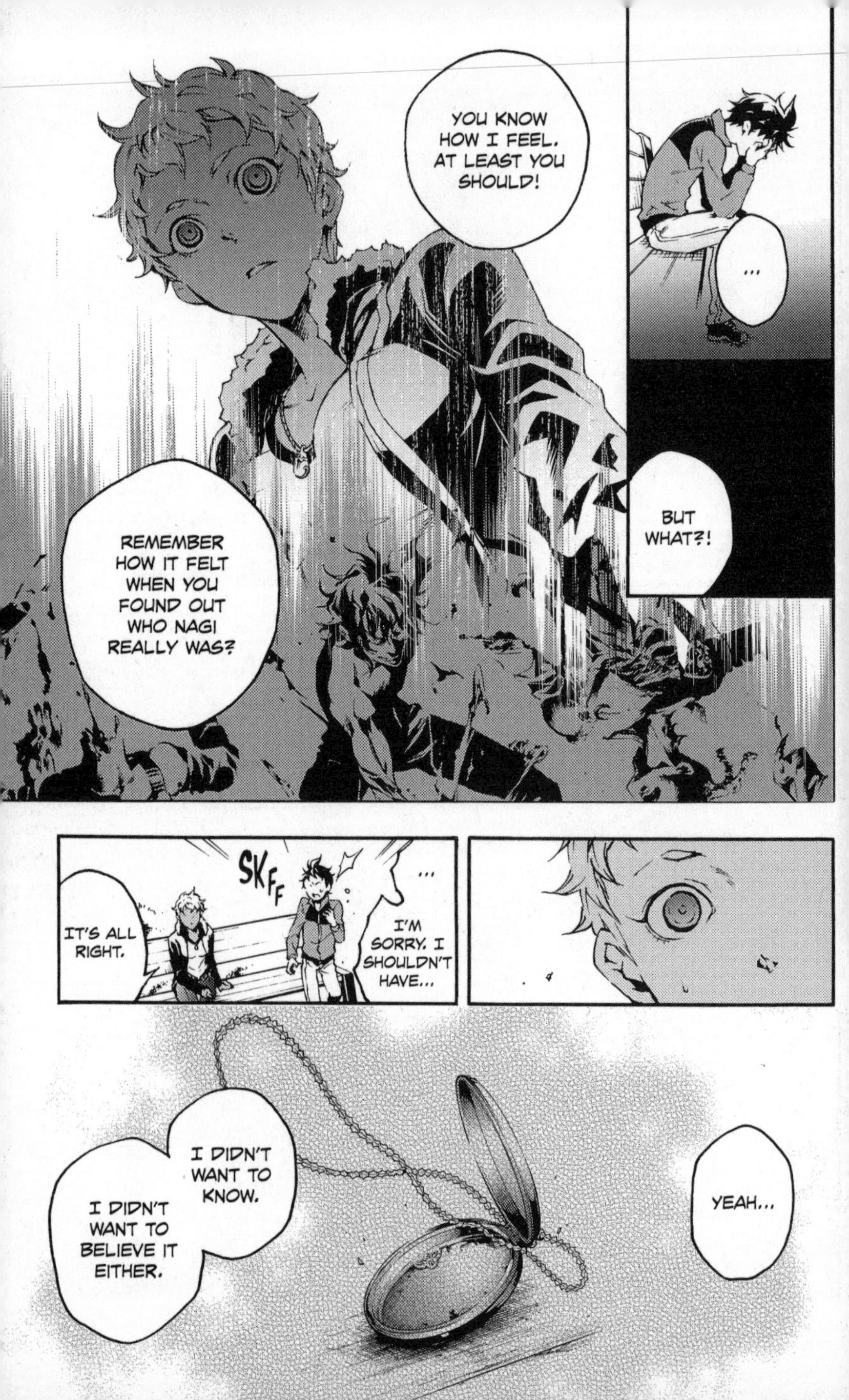
...
BUT WHAT?!
YOU KNOW HOW I FEEL. AT LEAST YOU SHOULD!
REMEMBER HOW IT FELT WHEN YOU FOUND OUT WHO NAGI REALLY WAS?
...
SKFF
I'M SORRY. I SHOULDN'T HAVE...
IT'S ALL RIGHT.
YEAH...
I DIDN'T WANT TO KNOW.
I DIDN'T WANT TO BELIEVE IT EITHER.

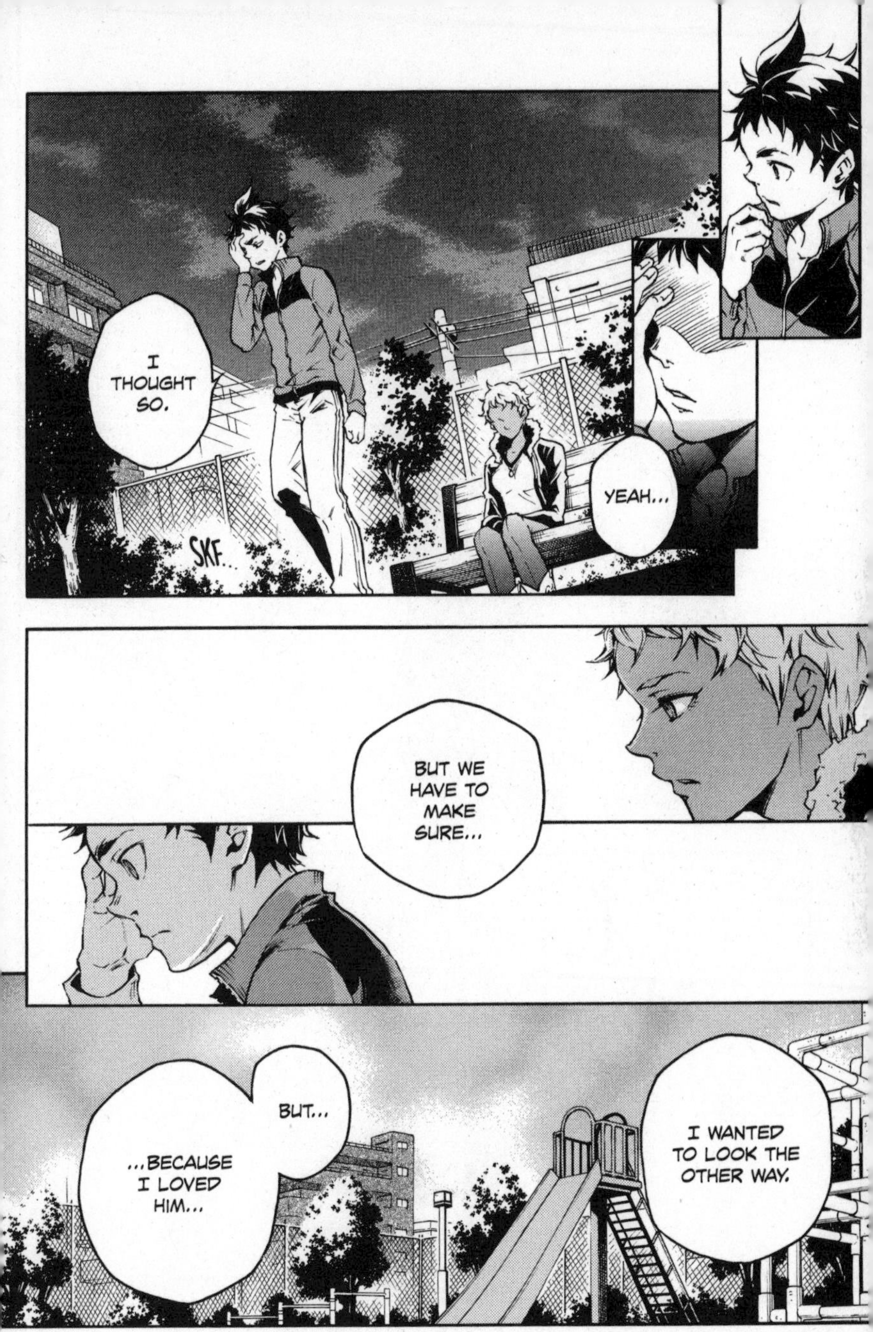
YEAH...
I THOUGHT SO.
SKF...
BUT WE HAVE TO MAKE SURE...
I WANTED TO LOOK THE OTHER WAY.
BUT...
...BECAUSE I LOVED HIM...

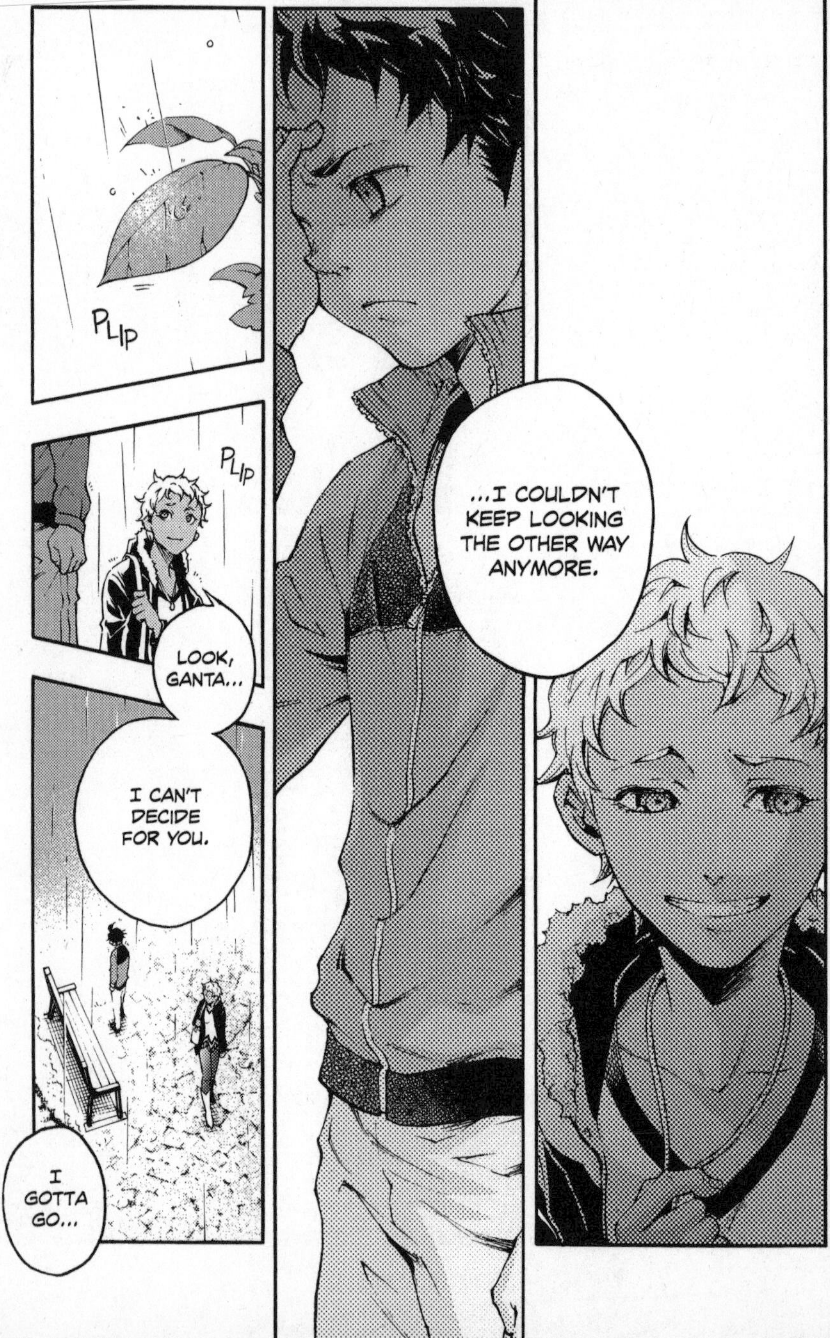
...I COULDN'T KEEP LOOKING THE OTHER WAY ANYMORE.
PLIP
PLIP
LOOK, GANTA...
I CAN'T DECIDE FOR YOU.
I GOTTA GO...

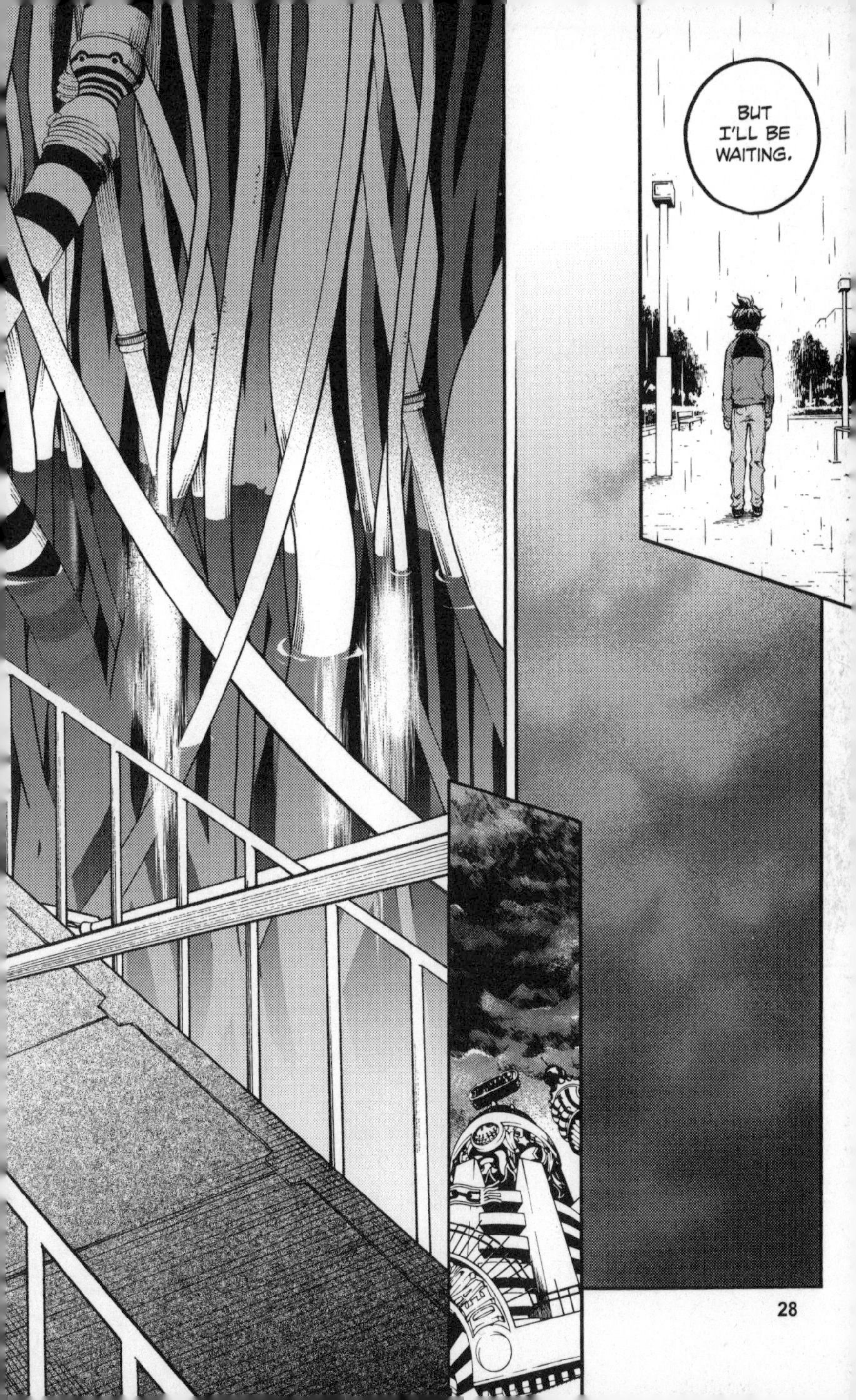
BUT I'LL BE WAITING.

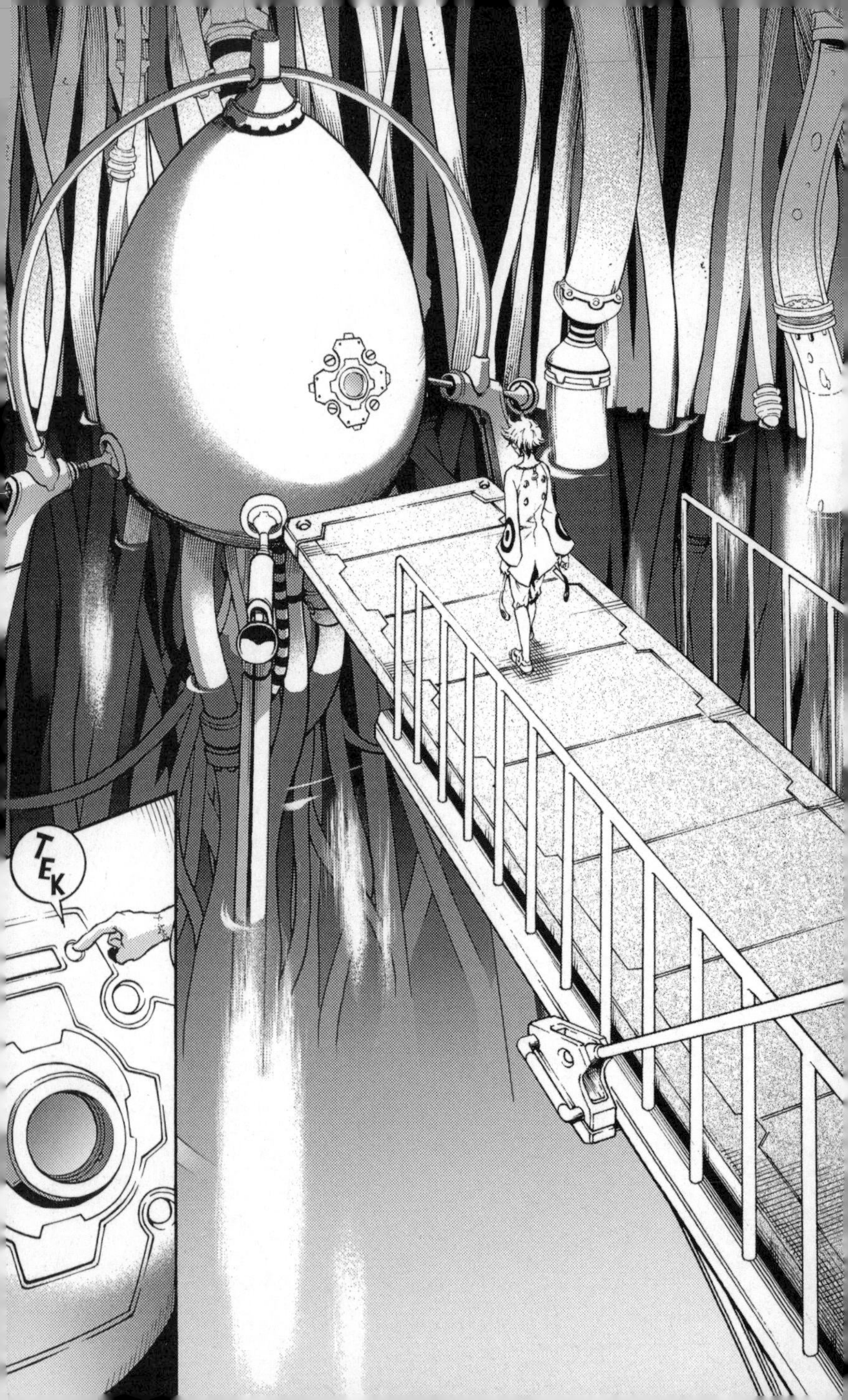
TEK

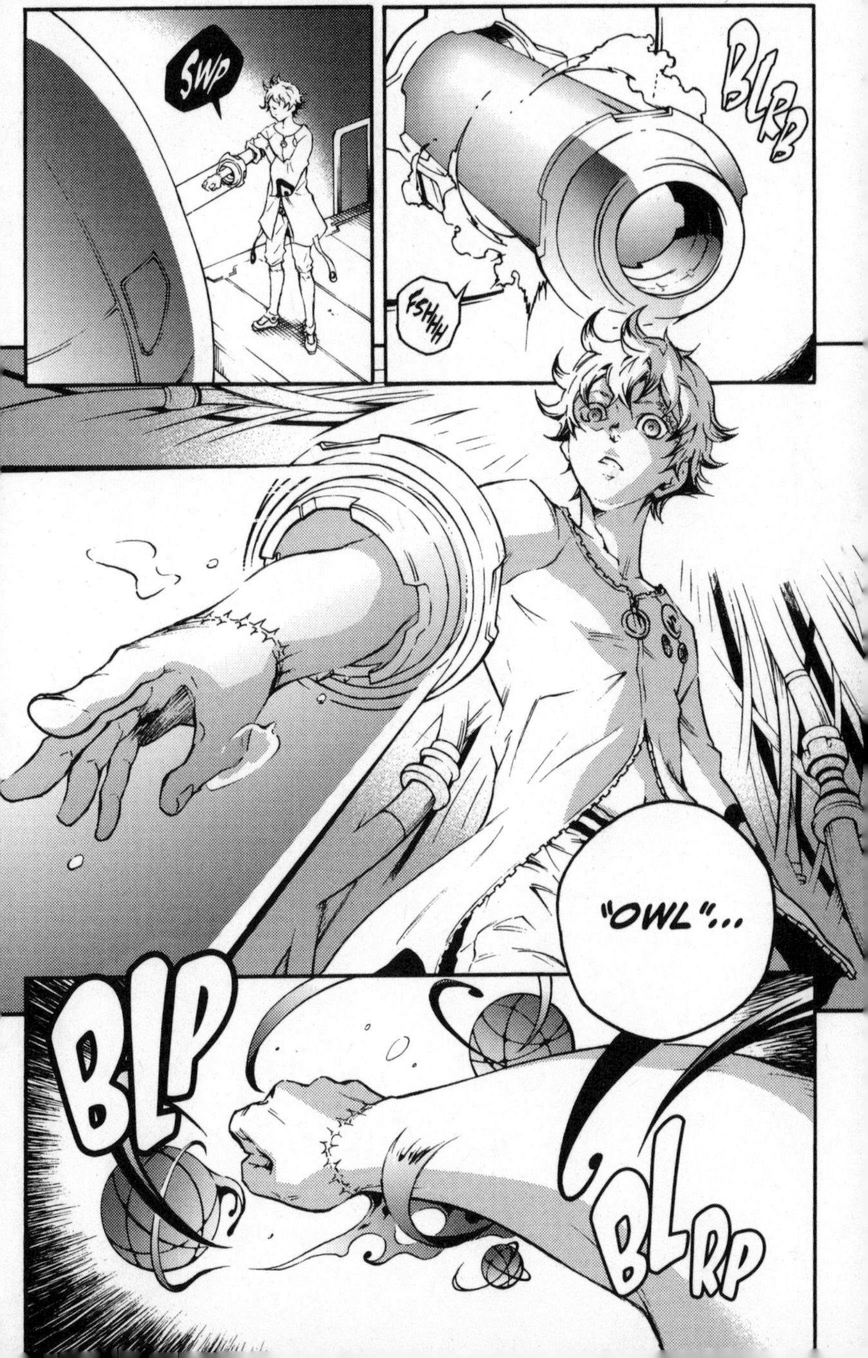
BLRB
FSHHH
SWP
"OWL"...
BLRP
BLP

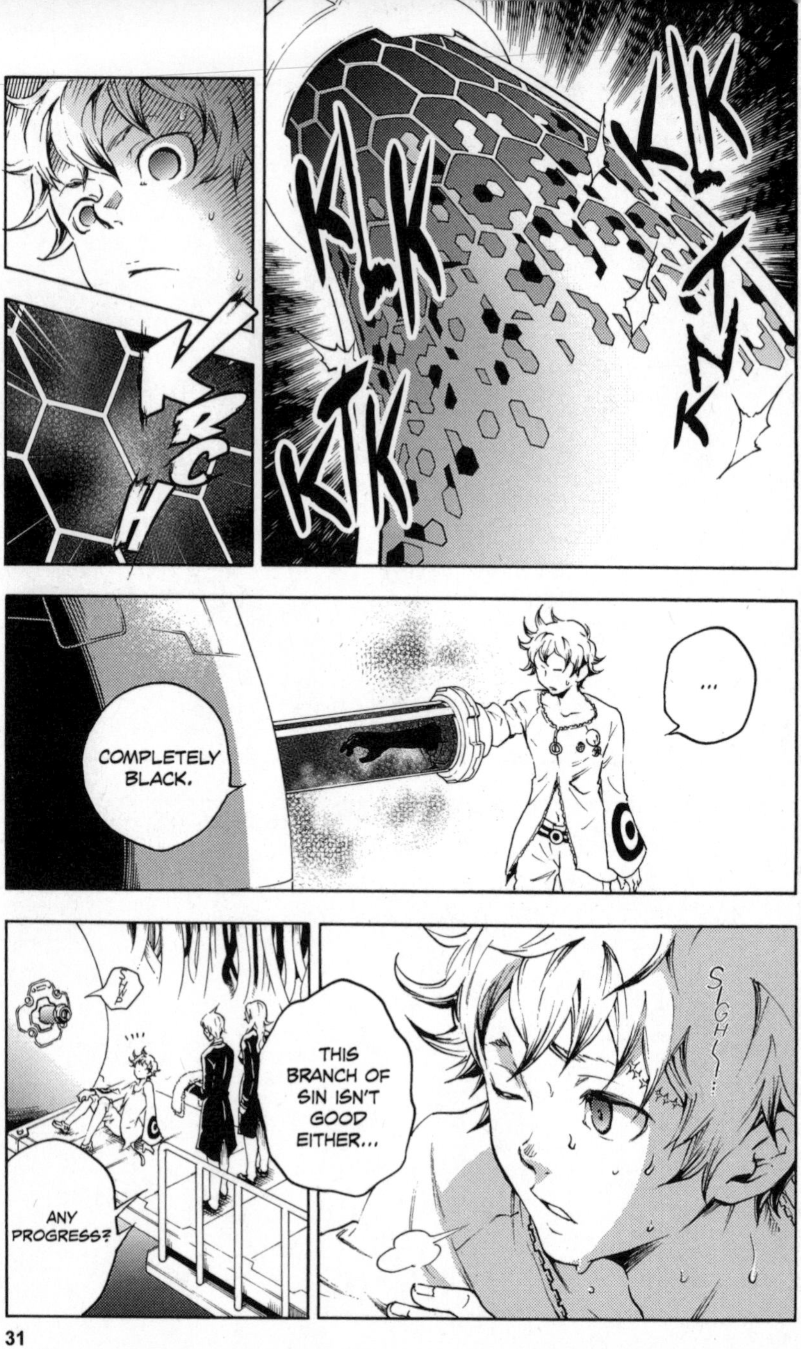

KLIK
TINK
KLIK
KTIK
KRCH
...
COMPLETELY BLACK.
SIGH...
THIS BRANCH OF SIN ISN'T GOOD EITHER...
SHWP
!!!
ANY PROGRESS?

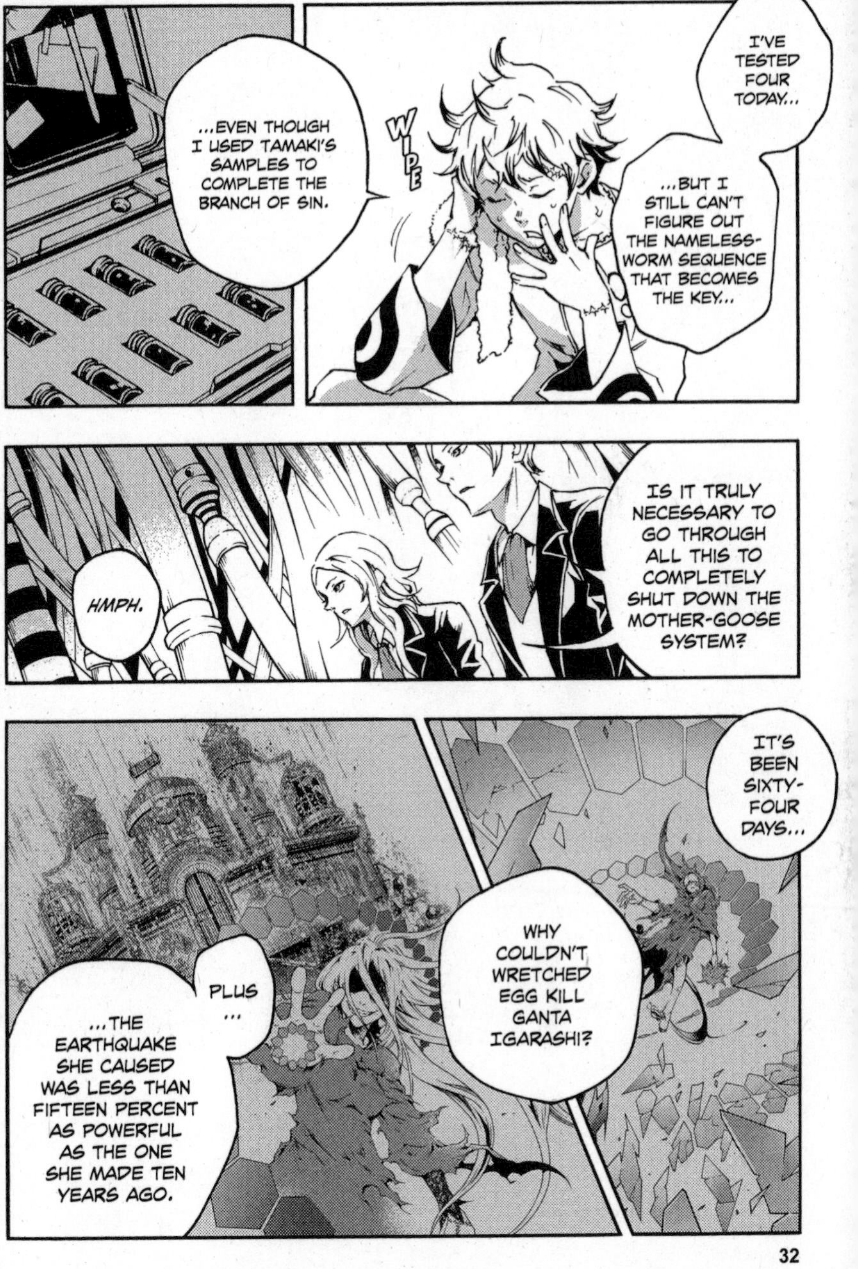
I'VE TESTED FOUR TODAY...
WIPE
...BUT I STILL CAN'T FIGURE OUT THE NAMELESS-WORM SEQUENCE THAT BECOMES THE KEY...
...EVEN THOUGH I USED TAMAKI'S SAMPLES TO COMPLETE THE BRANCH OF SIN.
IS IT TRULY NECESSARY TO GO THROUGH ALL THIS TO COMPLETELY SHUT DOWN THE MOTHER-GOOSE SYSTEM?
HMPH.
IT'S BEEN SIXTY-FOUR DAYS...
WHY COULDN'T WRETCHED EGG KILL GANTA IGARASHI?
PLUS...
...THE EARTHQUAKE SHE CAUSED WAS LESS THAN FIFTEEN PERCENT AS POWERFUL AS THE ONE SHE MADE TEN YEARS AGO.

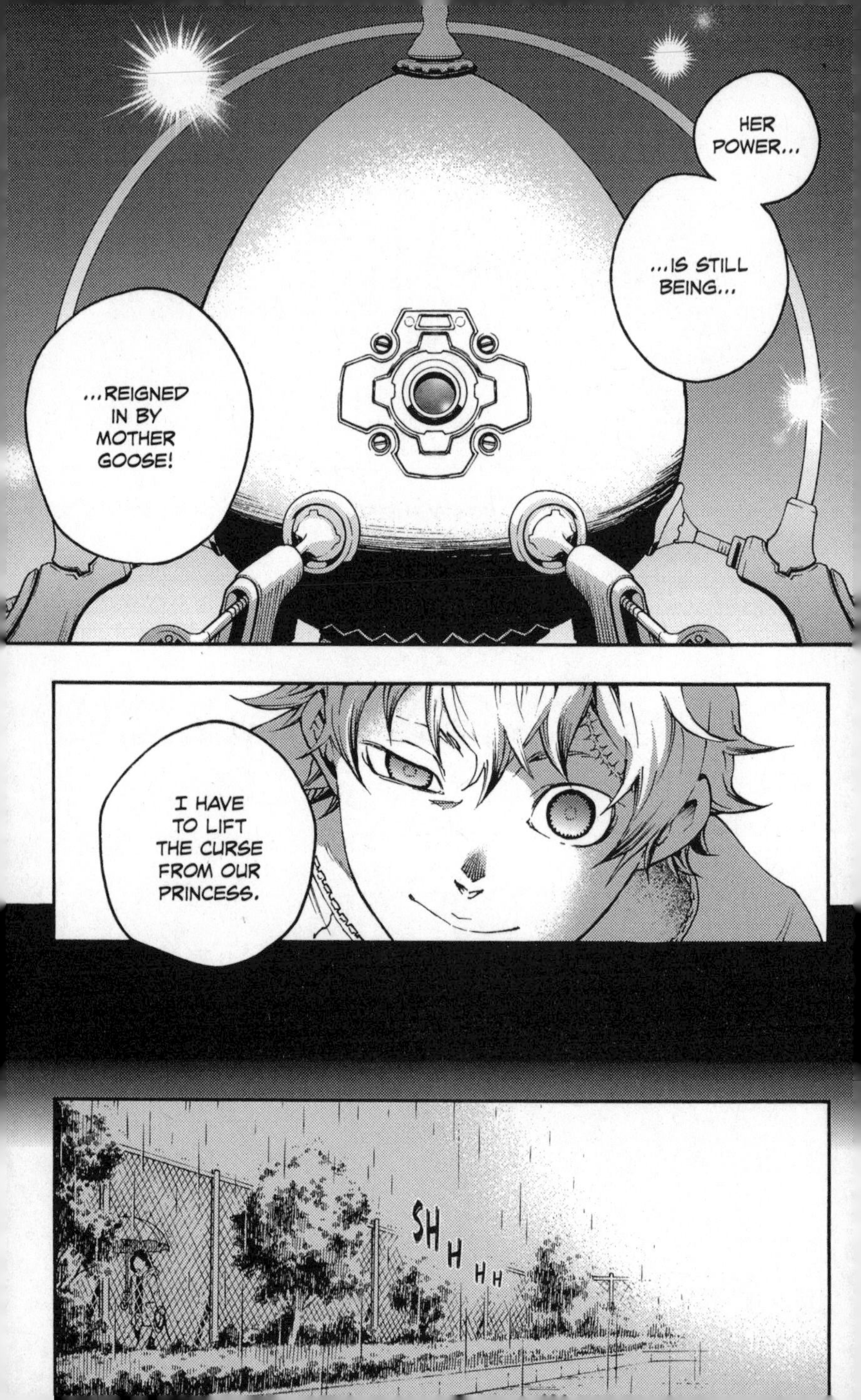
HER POWER...
...IS STILL BEING...
...REIGNED IN BY MOTHER GOOSE!
I HAVE TO LIFT THE CURSE FROM OUR PRINCESS.
SHHHH

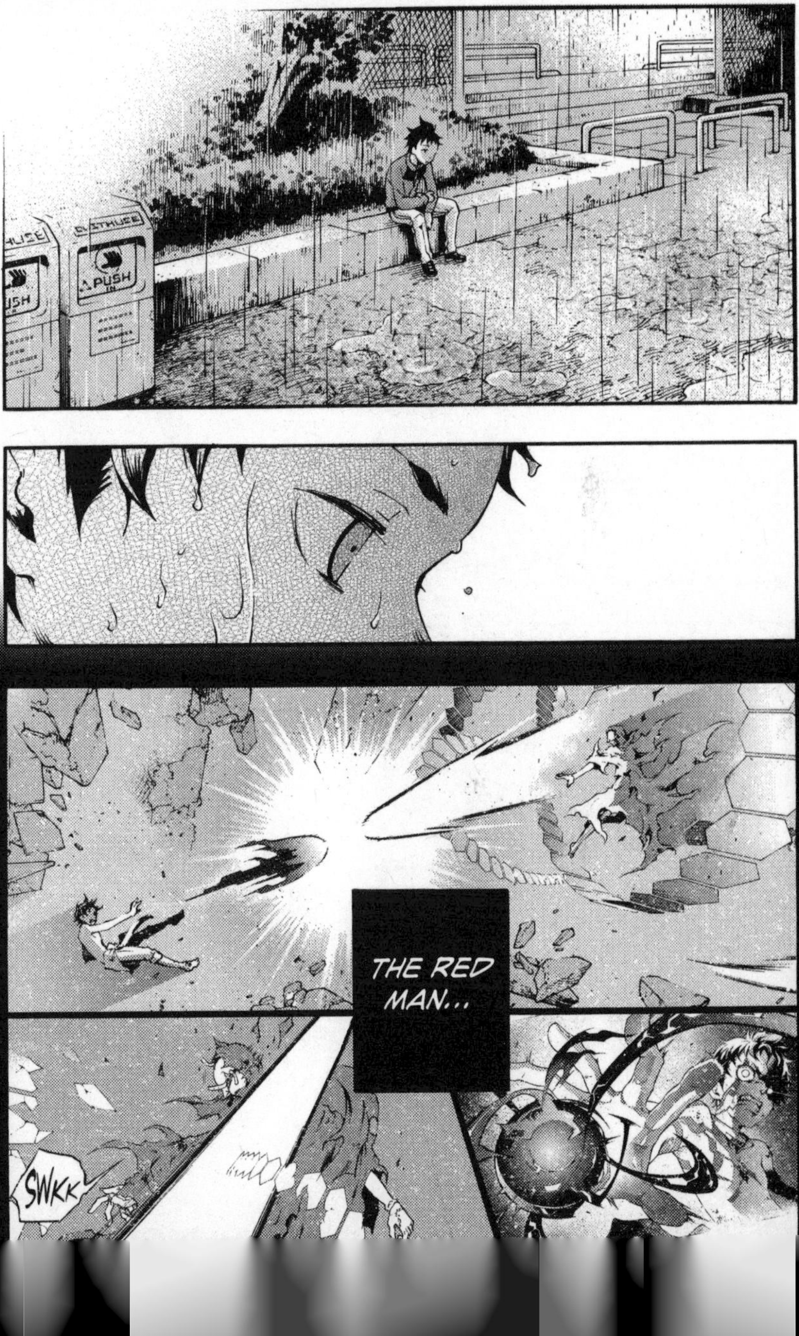
PUSH
PUSH
THE RED MAN...
SWKK

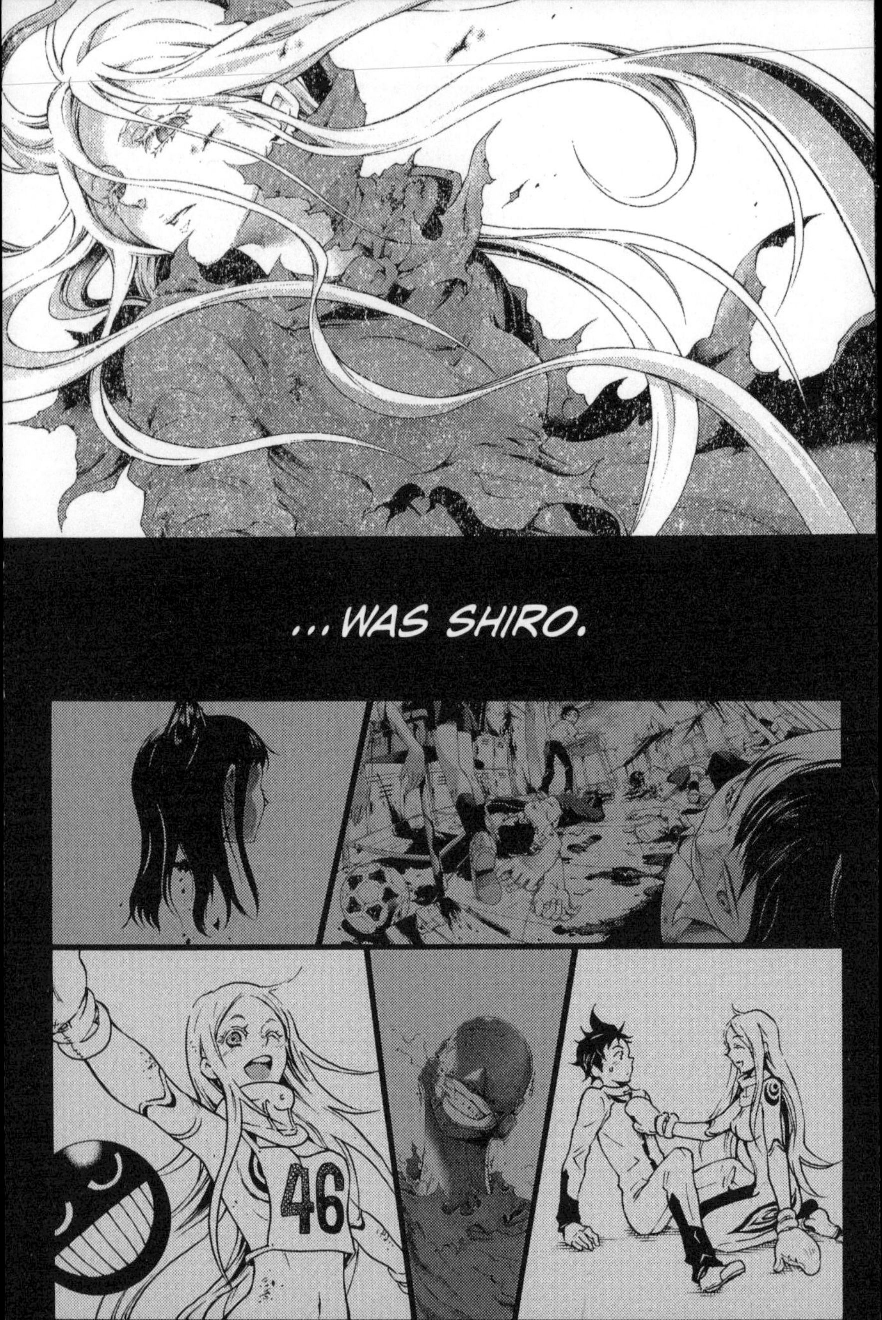
...WAS SHIRO.
46

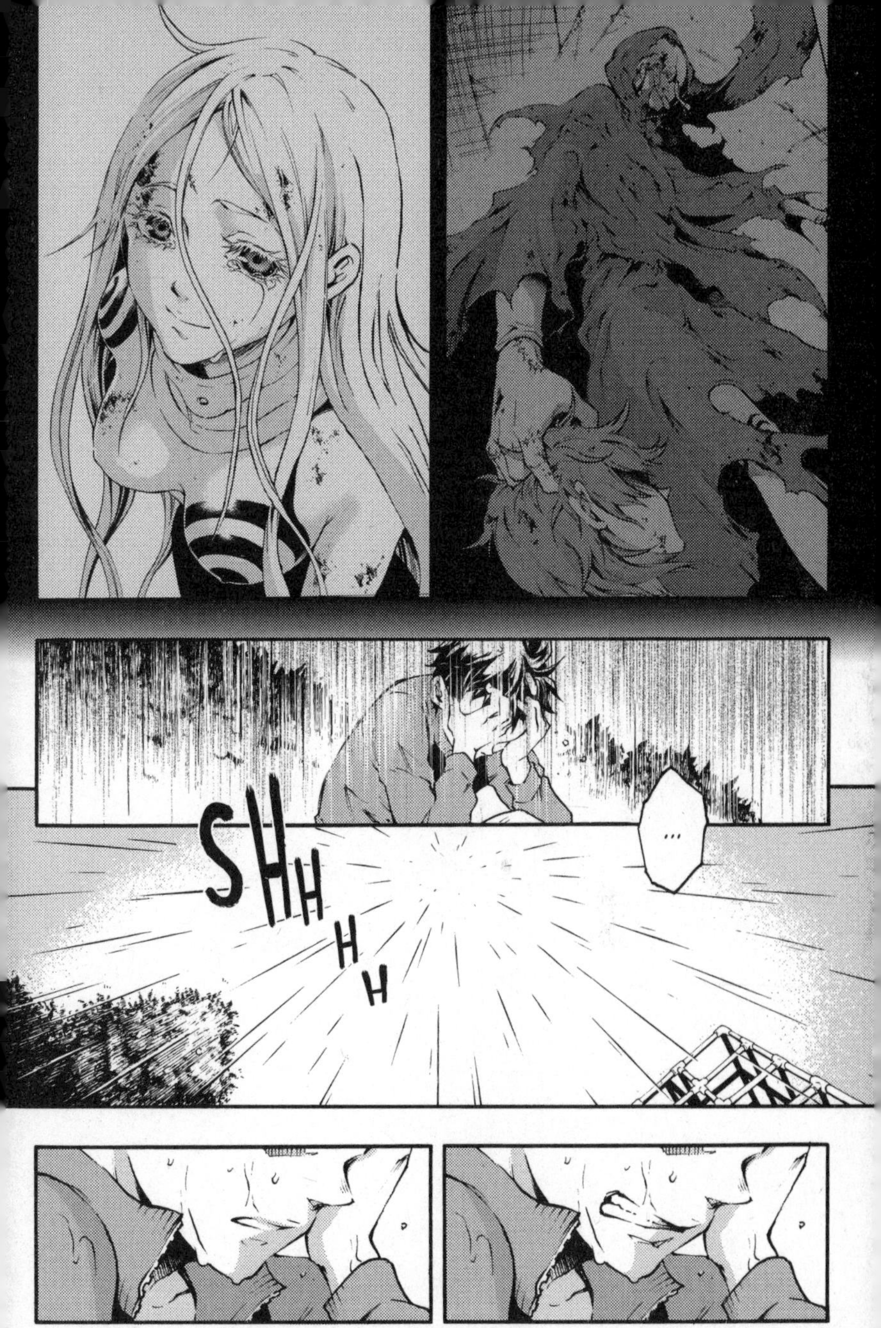
...
SHHHH

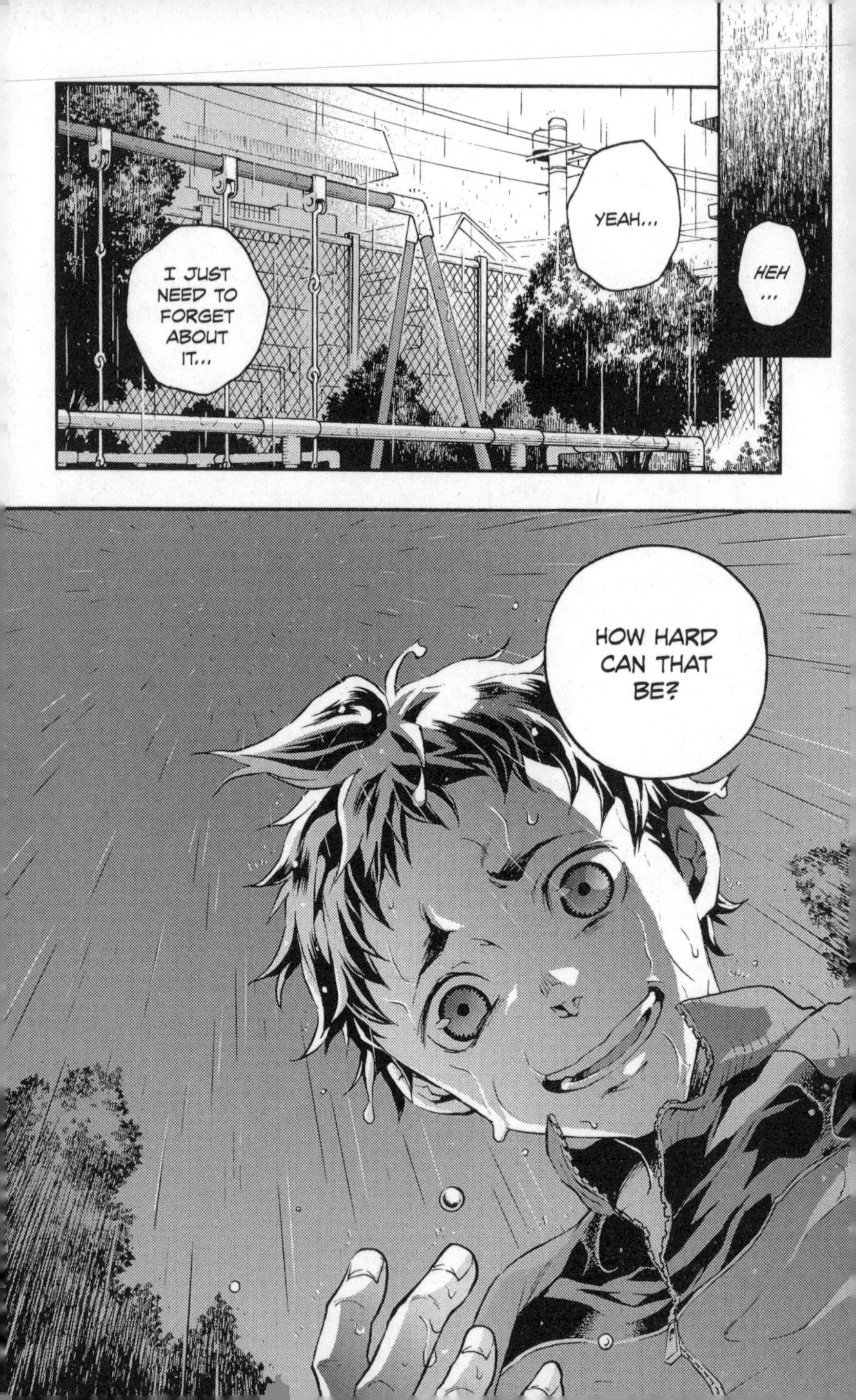
HEH ...
YEAH...
I JUST NEED TO FORGET ABOUT IT...
HOW HARD CAN THAT BE?

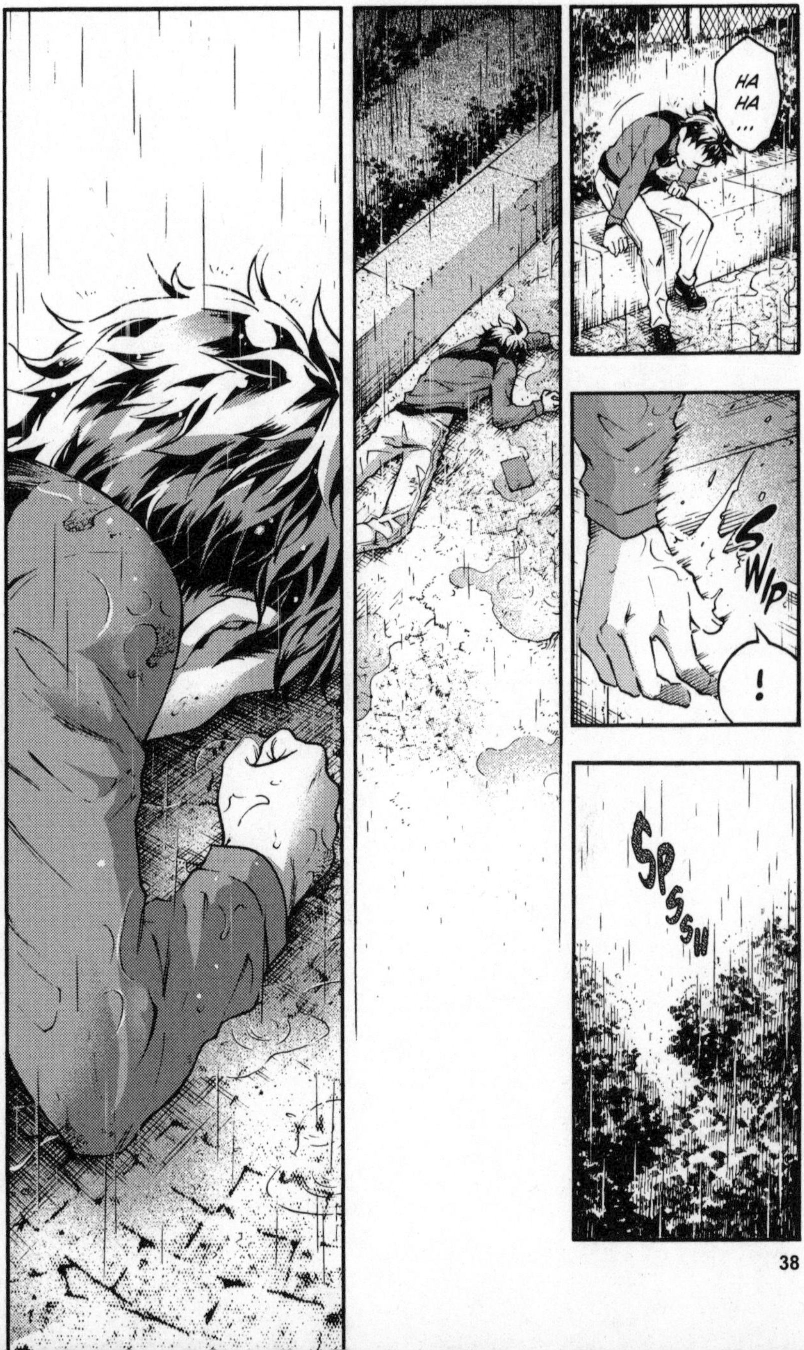
HA HA ...
SWIP
!
SPSSSH

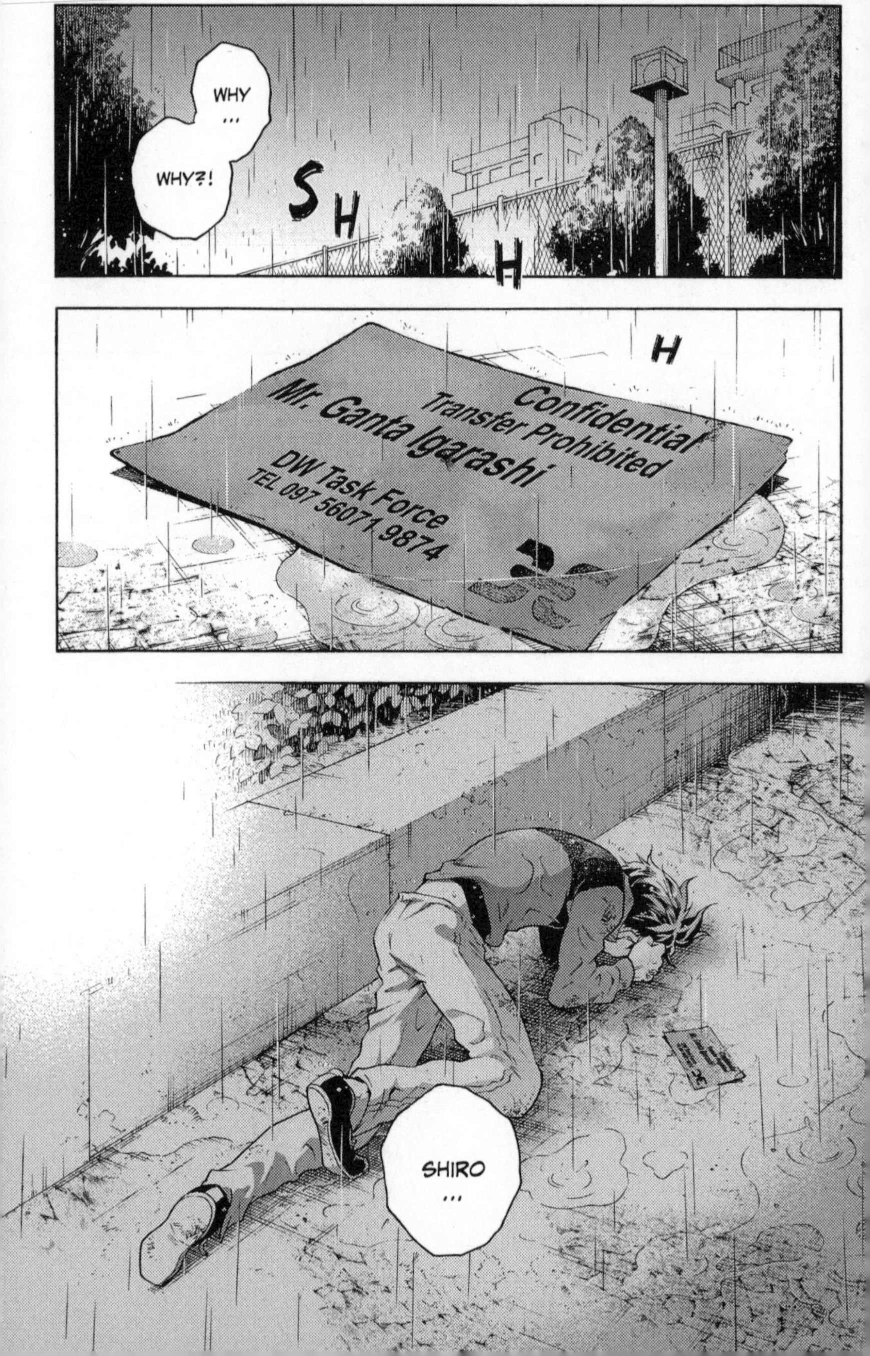
WHY ...
WHY?!
SH
H
H
Confidential
Transfer Prohibited
Mr. Ganta Igarashi
DW Task Force
TEL 097 56071 9874
SHIRO ...

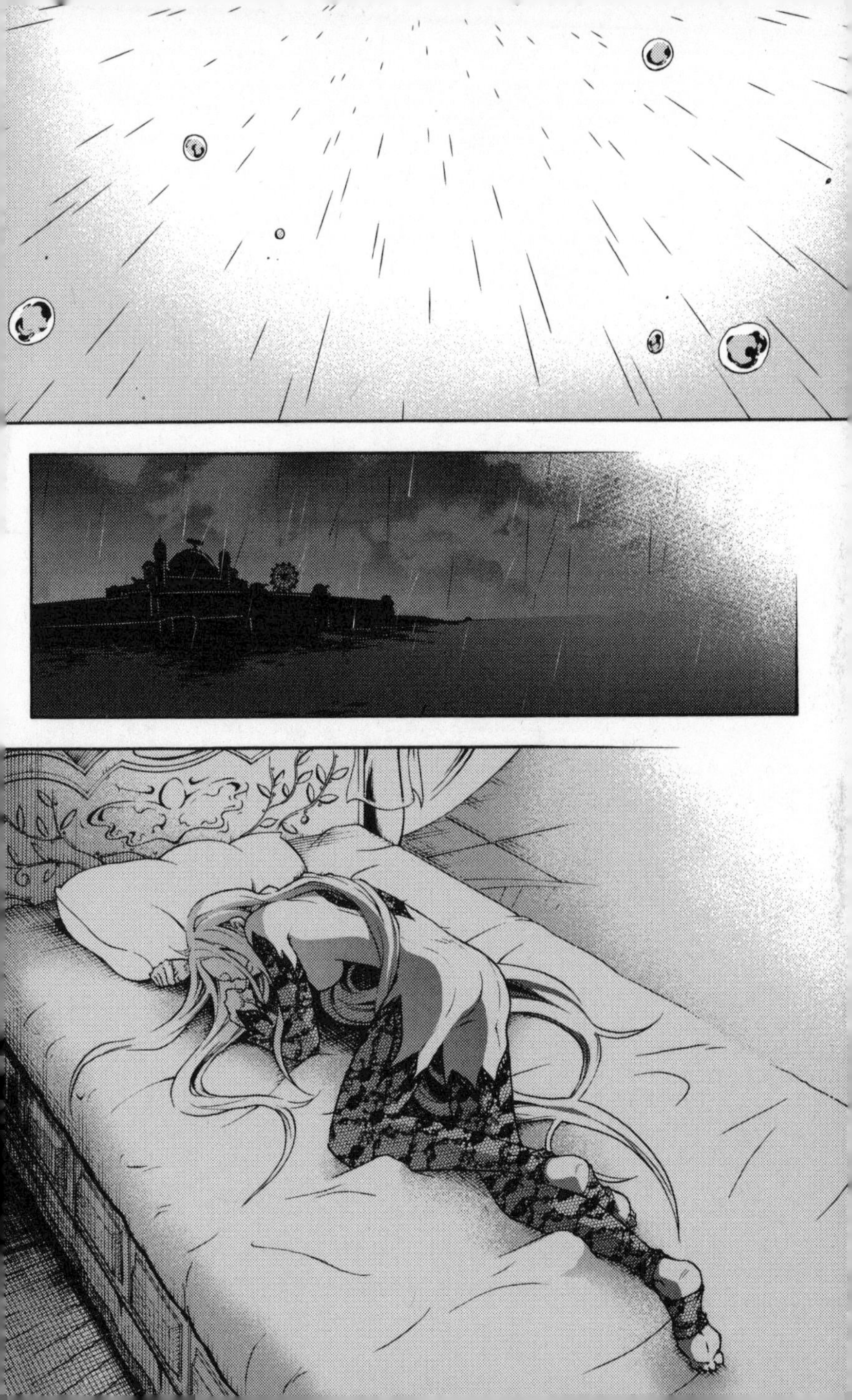

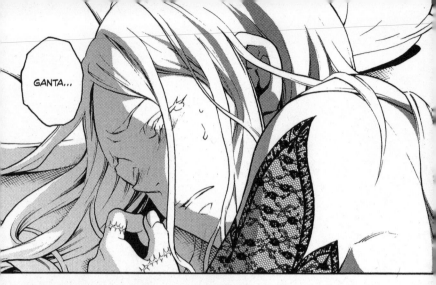

GANTA...

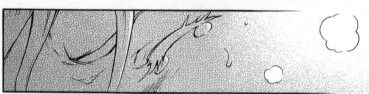

...

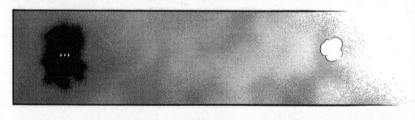

STOP...

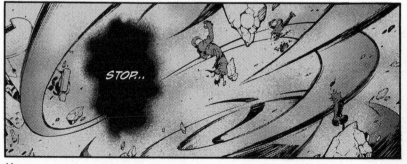

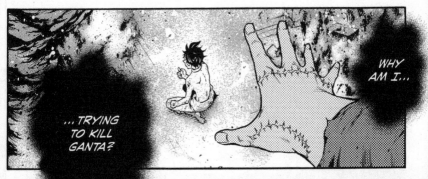

...TRYING TO KILL GANTA?

WHY AM I...

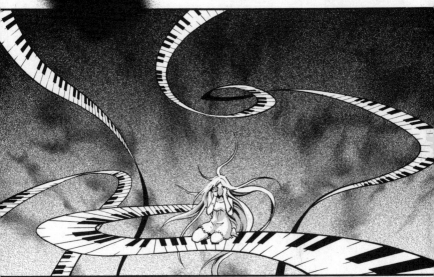

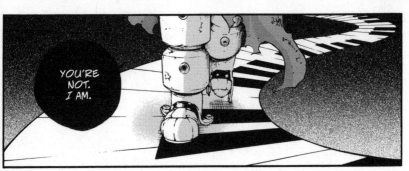

YOU'RE NOT. I AM.

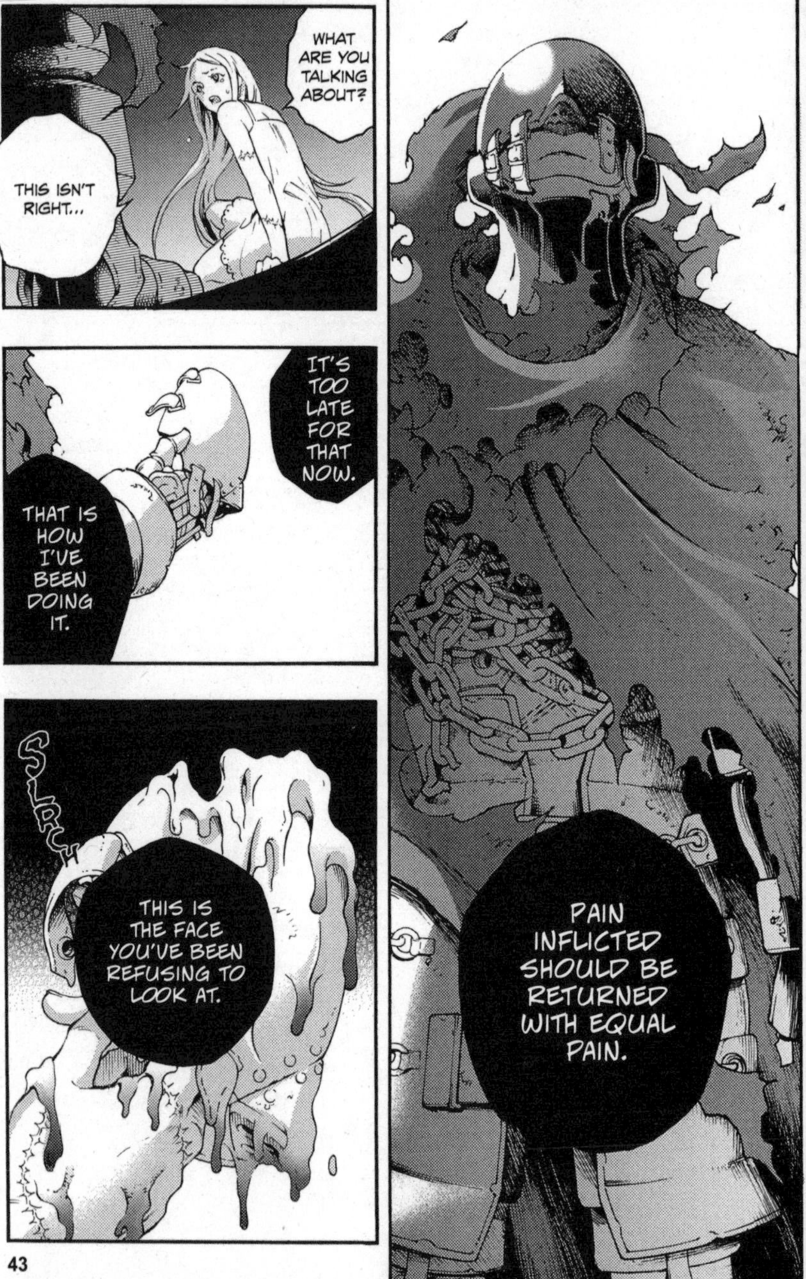
PAIN INFLICTED SHOULD BE RETURNED WITH EQUAL PAIN.
WHAT ARE YOU TALKING ABOUT?
THIS ISN'T RIGHT...
IT'S TOO LATE FOR THAT NOW.
THAT IS HOW I'VE BEEN DOING IT.
SLRCH
THIS IS THE FACE YOU'VE BEEN REFUSING TO LOOK AT.

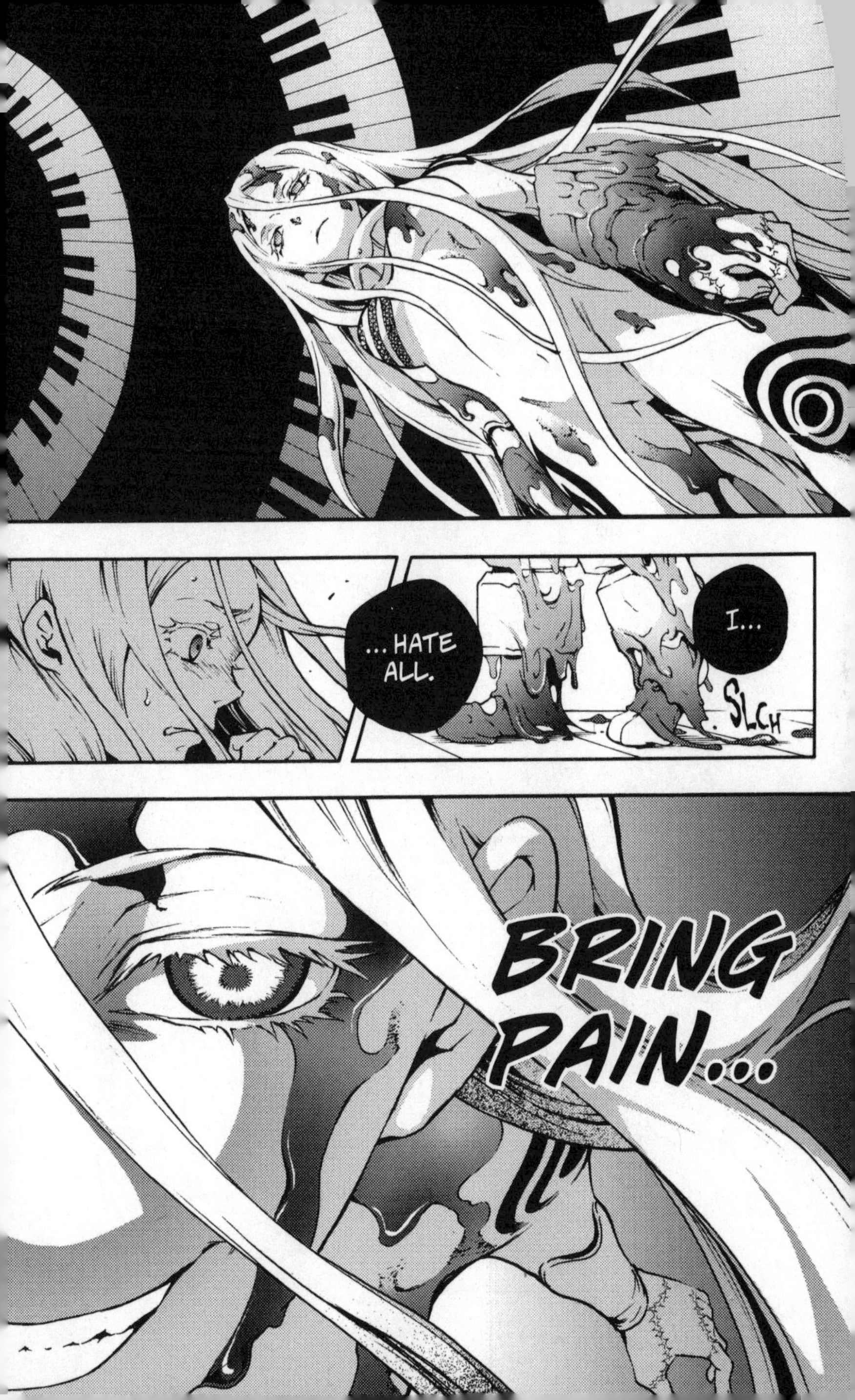
I...
... HATE ALL.
SLCH
BRING PAIN...

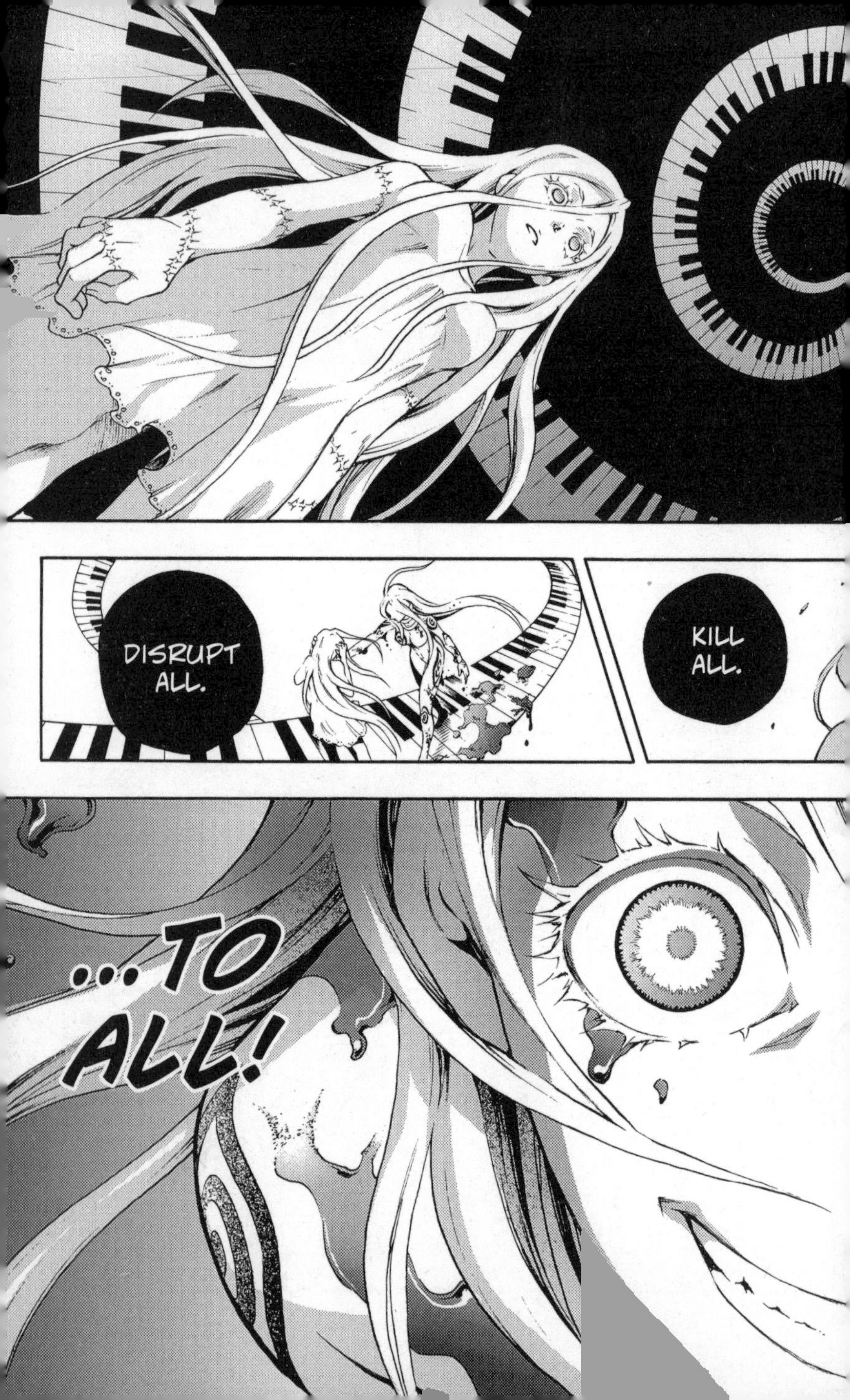
KILL ALL.
DISRUPT ALL.
...TO ALL!

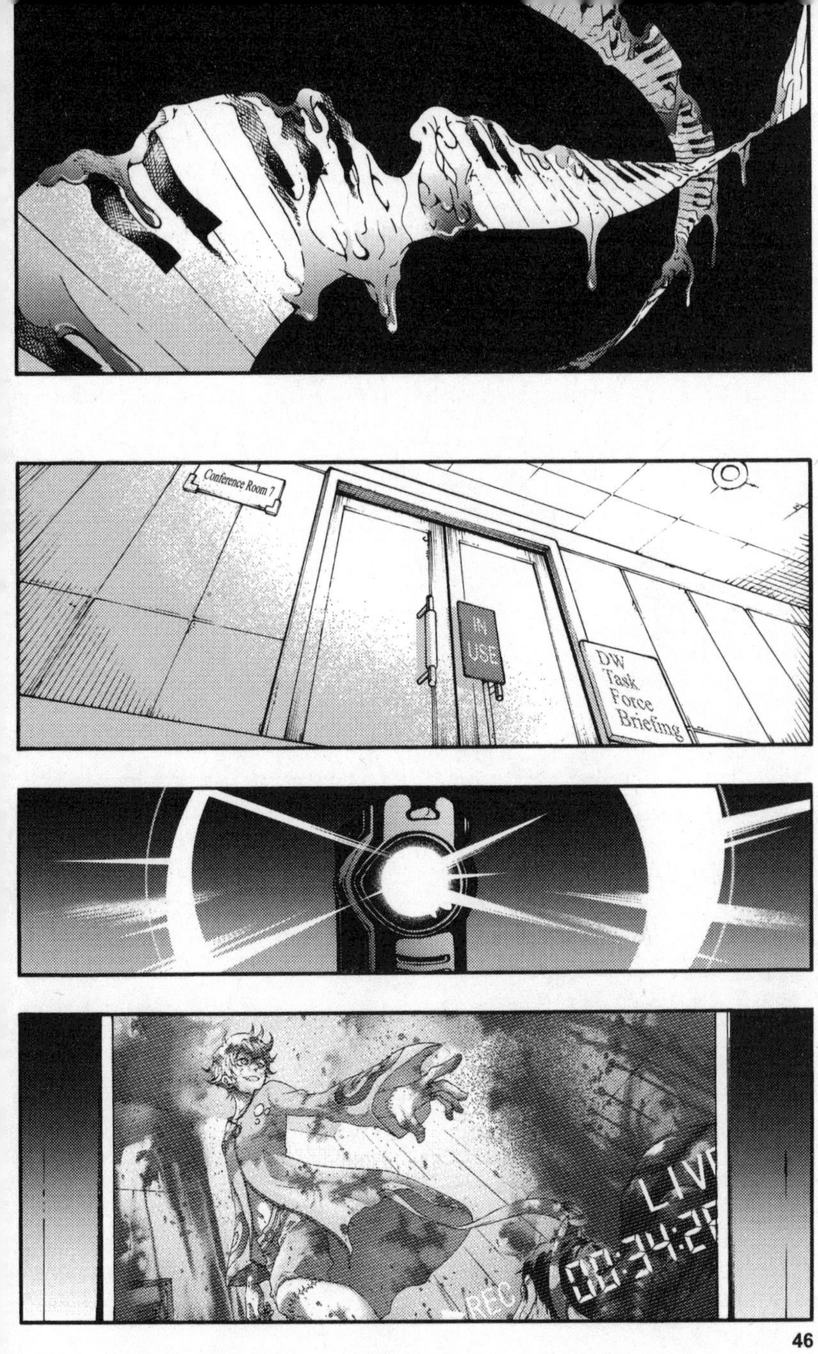
Conference Room 7
IN USE
DW Task Force Briefing
REC

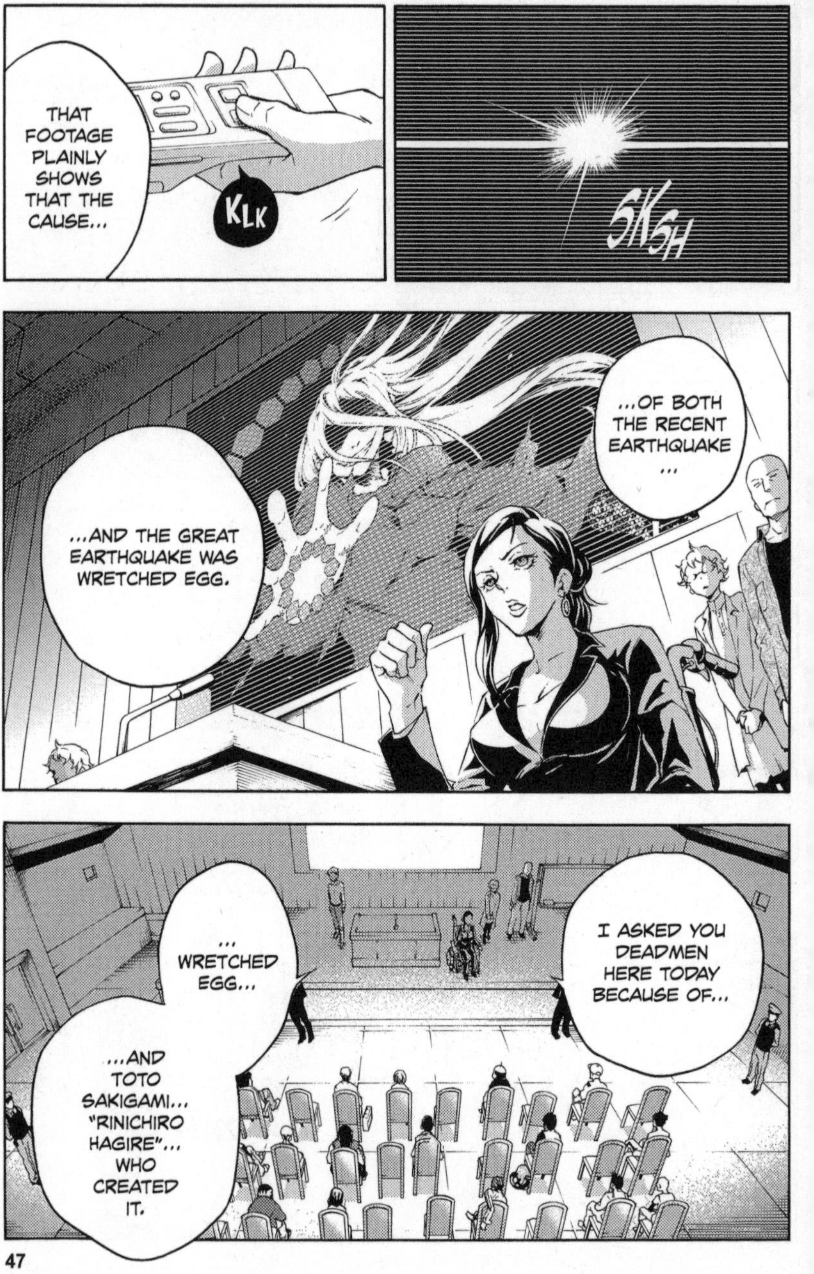
SKSH
THAT FOOTAGE PLAINLY SHOWS THAT THE CAUSE...
KLK
...OF BOTH THE RECENT EARTHQUAKE ...
...AND THE GREAT EARTHQUAKE WAS WRETCHED EGG.
I ASKED YOU DEADMEN HERE TODAY BECAUSE OF...
... WRETCHED EGG...
...AND TOTO SAKIGAMI... "RINICHIRO HAGIRE"... WHO CREATED IT.

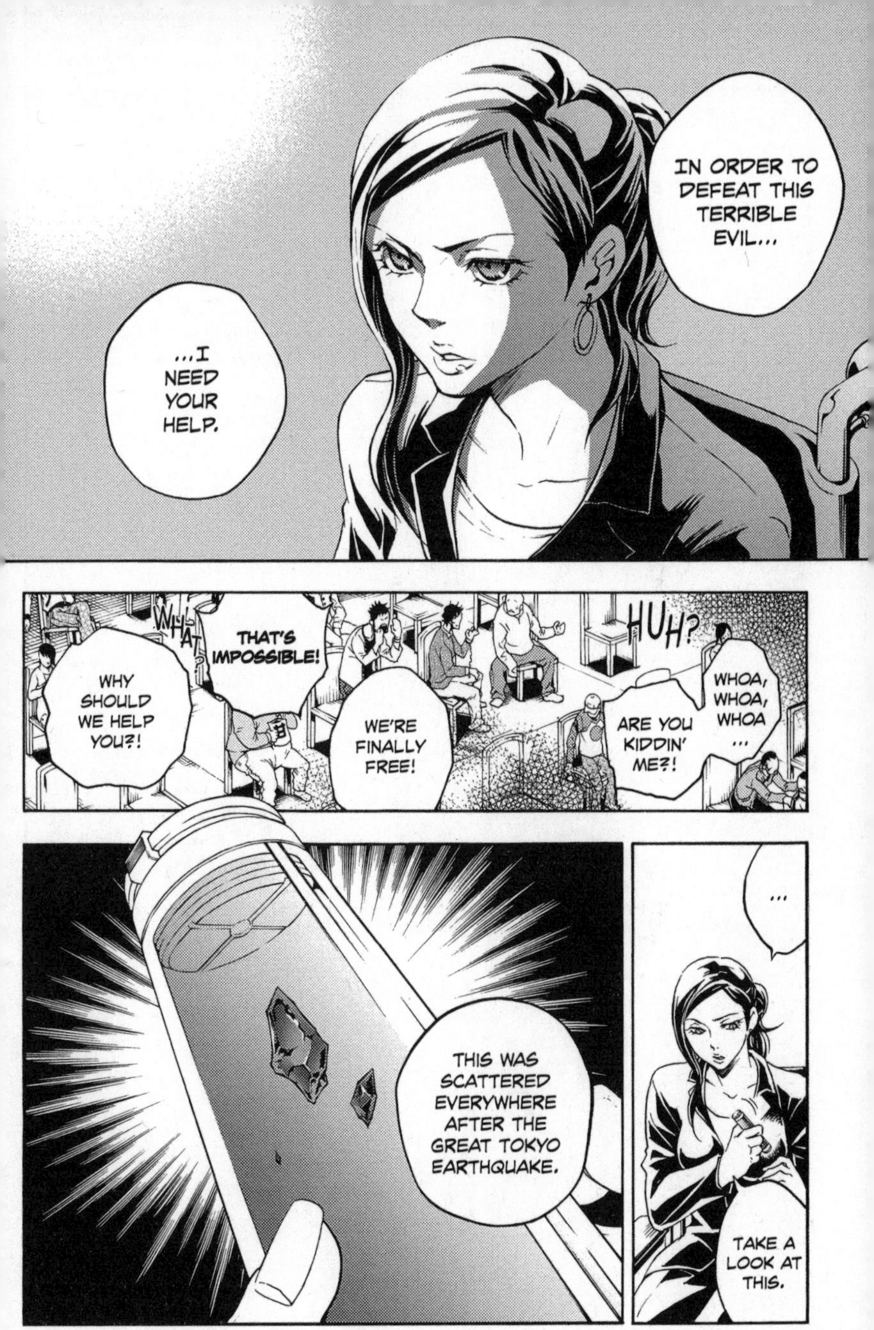
IN ORDER TO DEFEAT THIS TERRIBLE EVIL...
...I NEED YOUR HELP.
WHOA, WHOA, WHOA ...
HUH?
ARE YOU KIDDIN' ME?!
WE'RE FINALLY FREE!
THAT'S IMPOSSIBLE!
WHAT?
WHY SHOULD WE HELP YOU?!
...
TAKE A LOOK AT THIS.
THIS WAS SCATTERED EVERYWHERE AFTER THE GREAT TOKYO EARTHQUAKE.

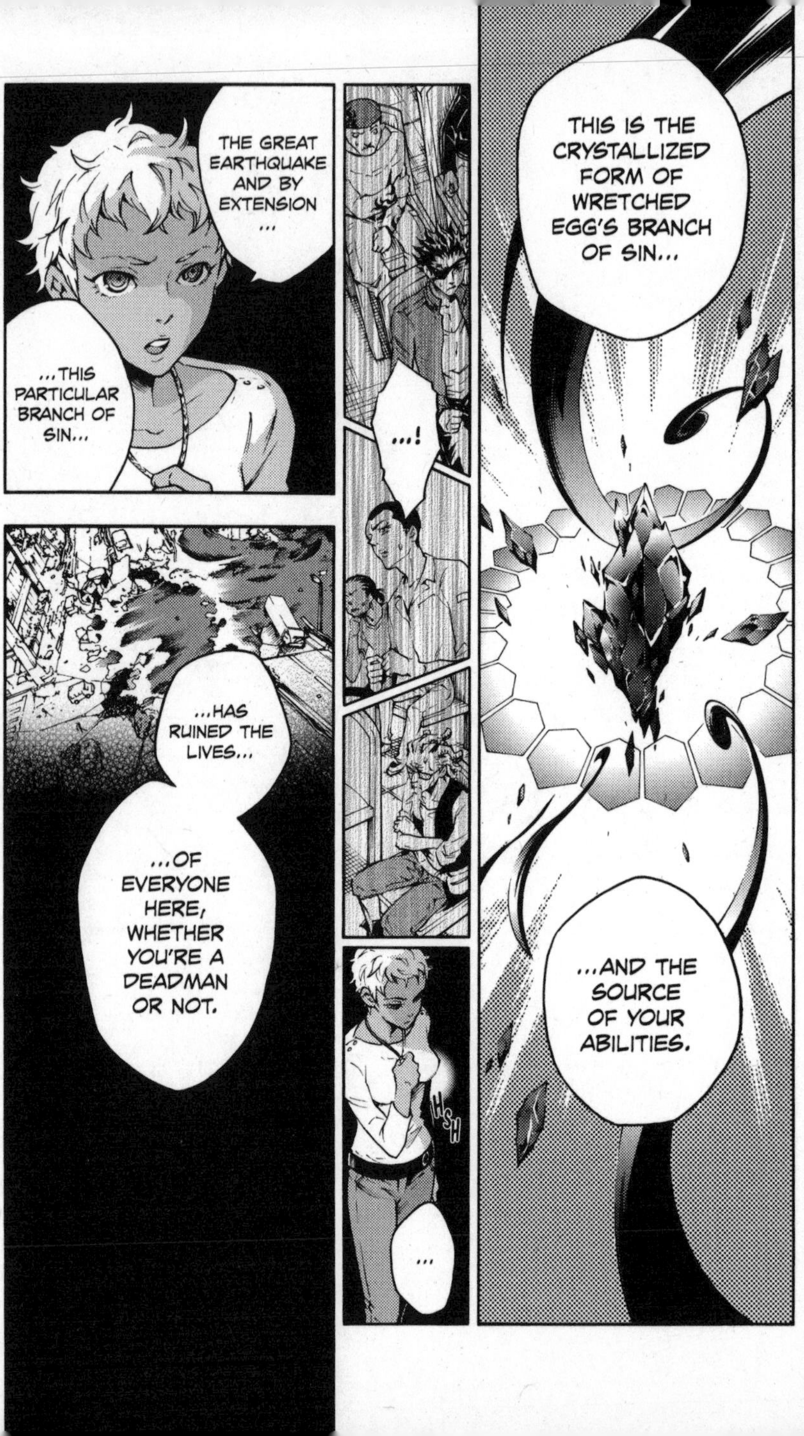
THIS IS THE CRYSTALLIZED FORM OF WRETCHED EGG'S BRANCH OF SIN...
...AND THE SOURCE OF YOUR ABILITIES.
...!
HSH
...
THE GREAT EARTHQUAKE AND BY EXTENSION ...
...THIS PARTICULAR BRANCH OF SIN...
...HAS RUINED THE LIVES...
...OF EVERYONE HERE, WHETHER YOU'RE A DEADMAN OR NOT.

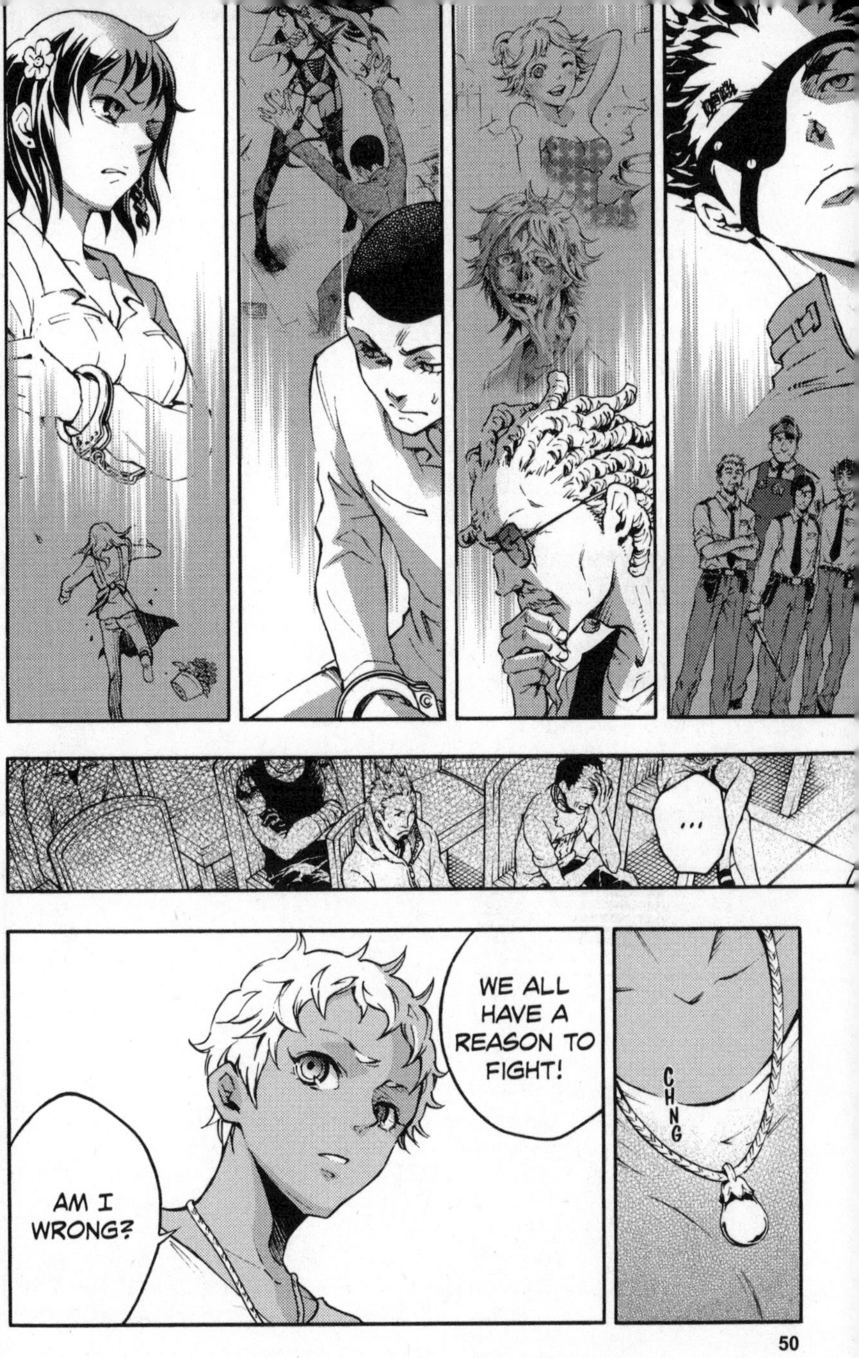
...
CHNG
WE ALL HAVE A REASON TO FIGHT!
AM I WRONG?

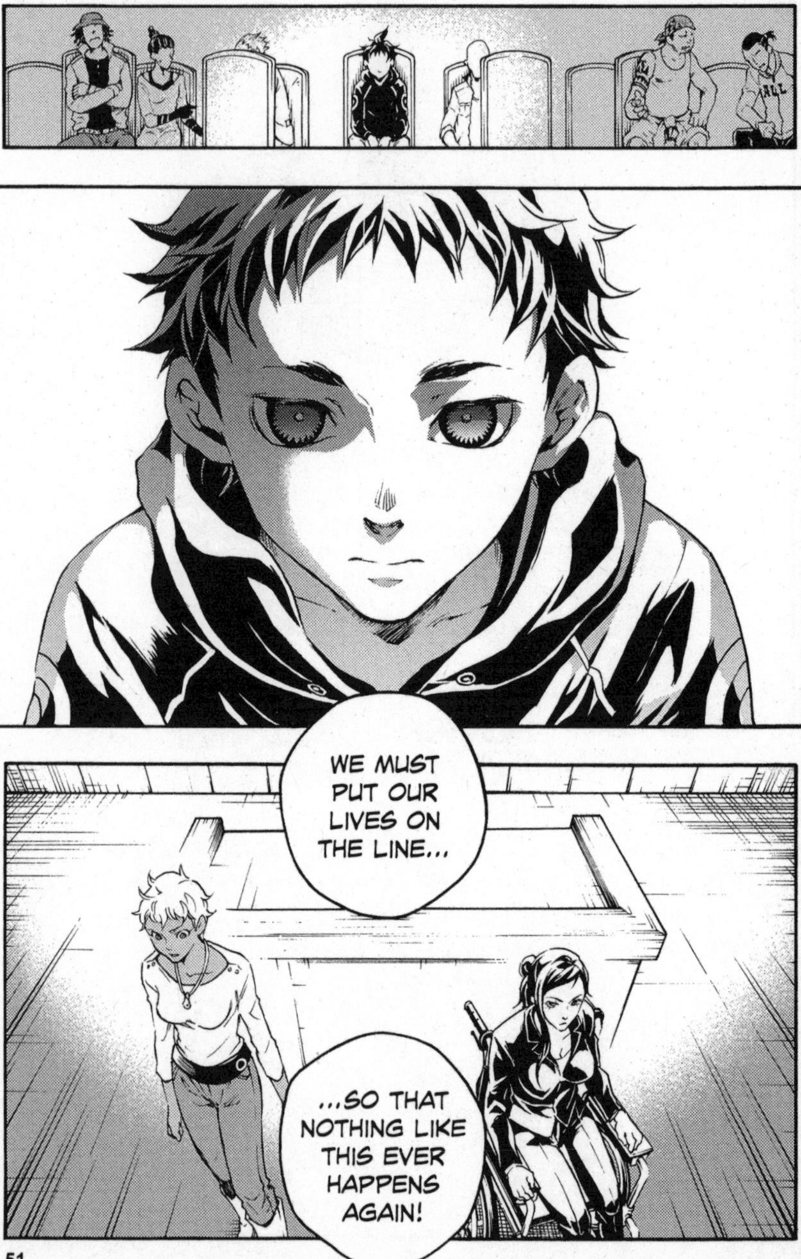
WE MUST PUT OUR LIVES ON THE LINE...
...SO THAT NOTHING LIKE THIS EVER HAPPENS AGAIN!

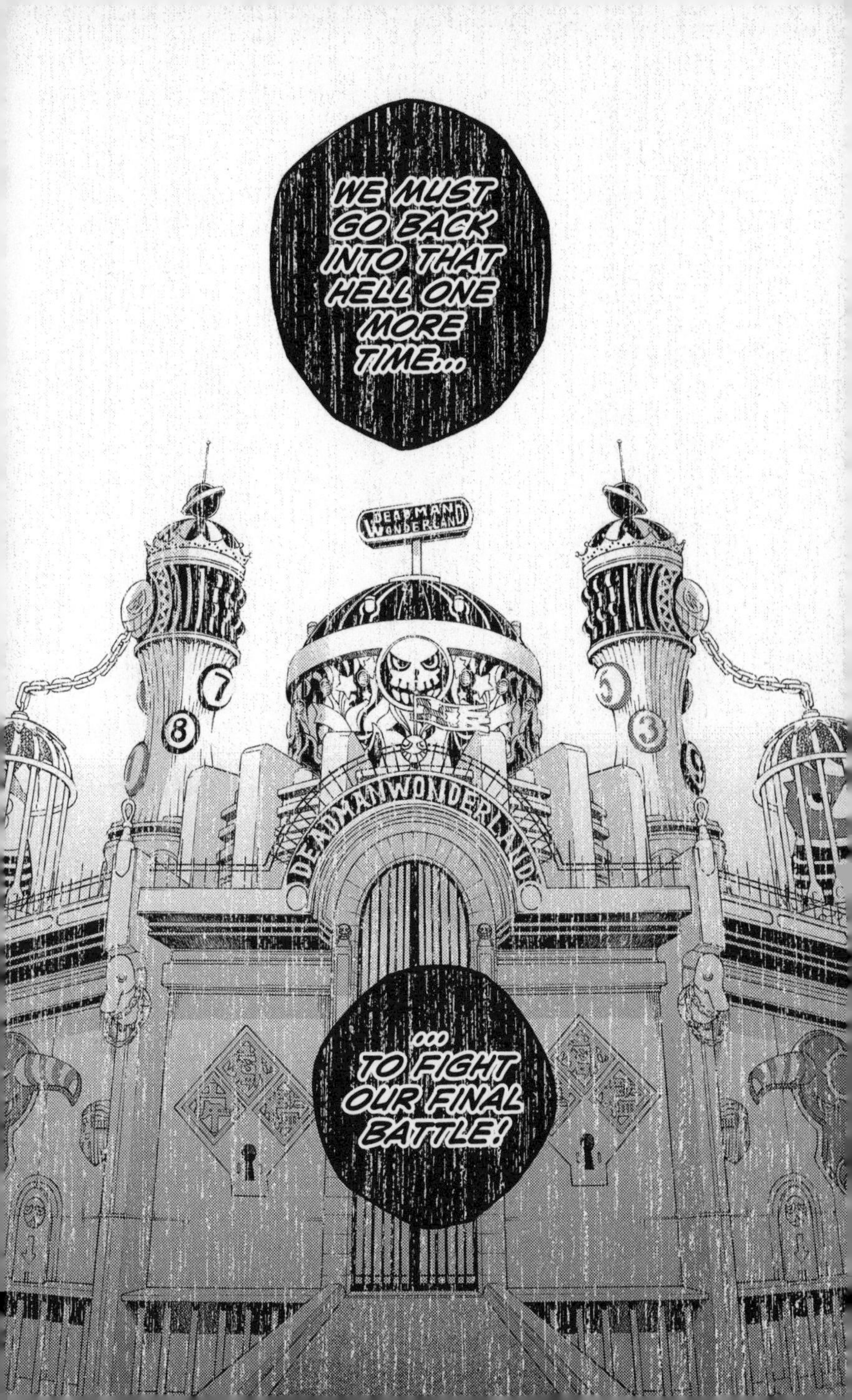
WE MUST GO BACK INTO THAT HELL ONE MORE TIME...
DEADMAN WONDERLAND
DEADMAN WONDERLAND
...TO FIGHT OUR FINAL BATTLE!

DEADMAN
WONDER
LAND

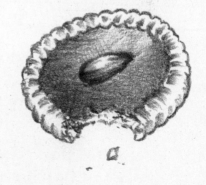

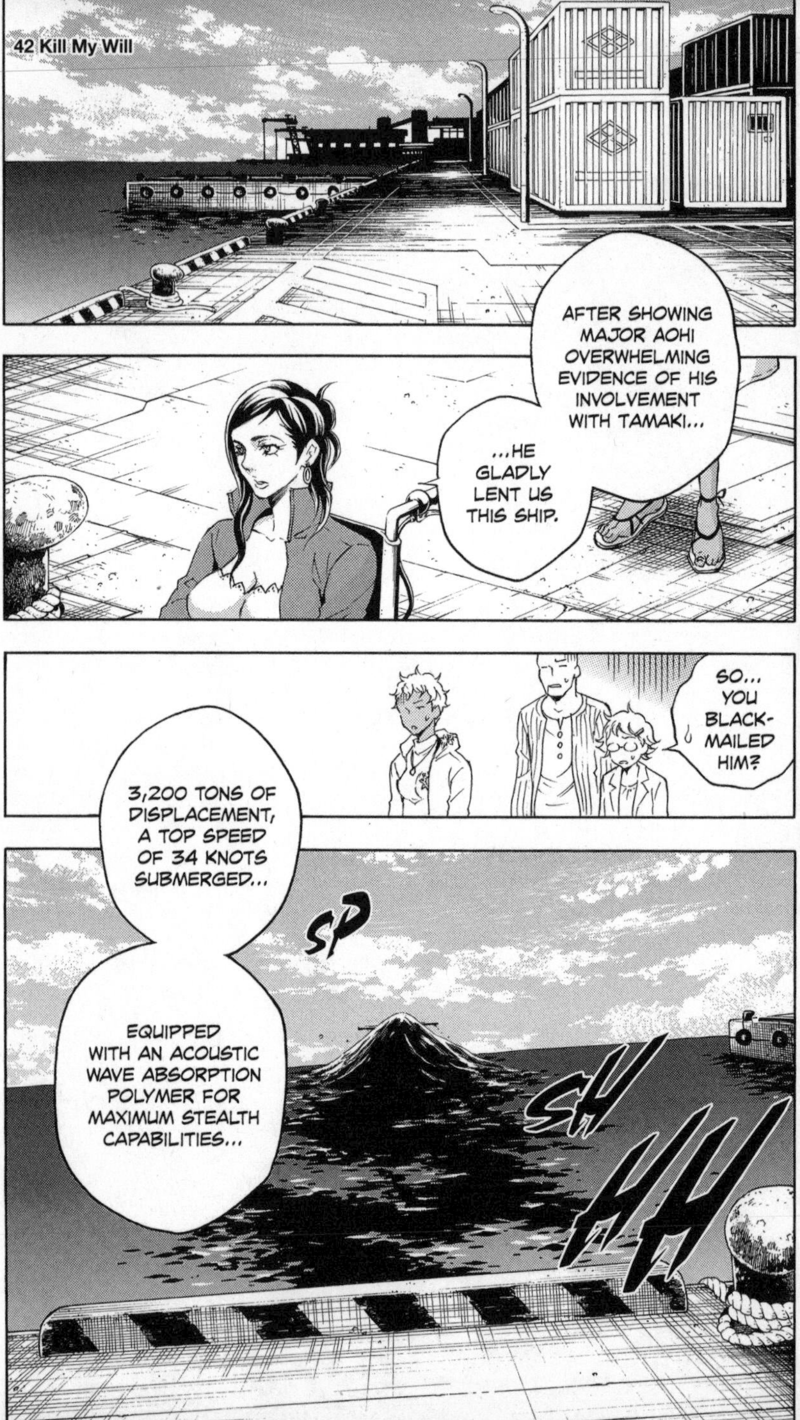
AFTER SHOWING MAJOR AOHI OVERWHELMING EVIDENCE OF HIS INVOLVEMENT WITH TAMAKI...
...HE GLADLY LENT US THIS SHIP.
SO... YOU BLACK-MAILED HIM?
3,200 TONS OF DISPLACEMENT, A TOP SPEED OF 34 KNOTS SUBMERGED...
SP
EQUIPPED WITH AN ACOUSTIC WAVE ABSORPTION POLYMER FOR MAXIMUM STEALTH CAPABILITIES...
SHHH

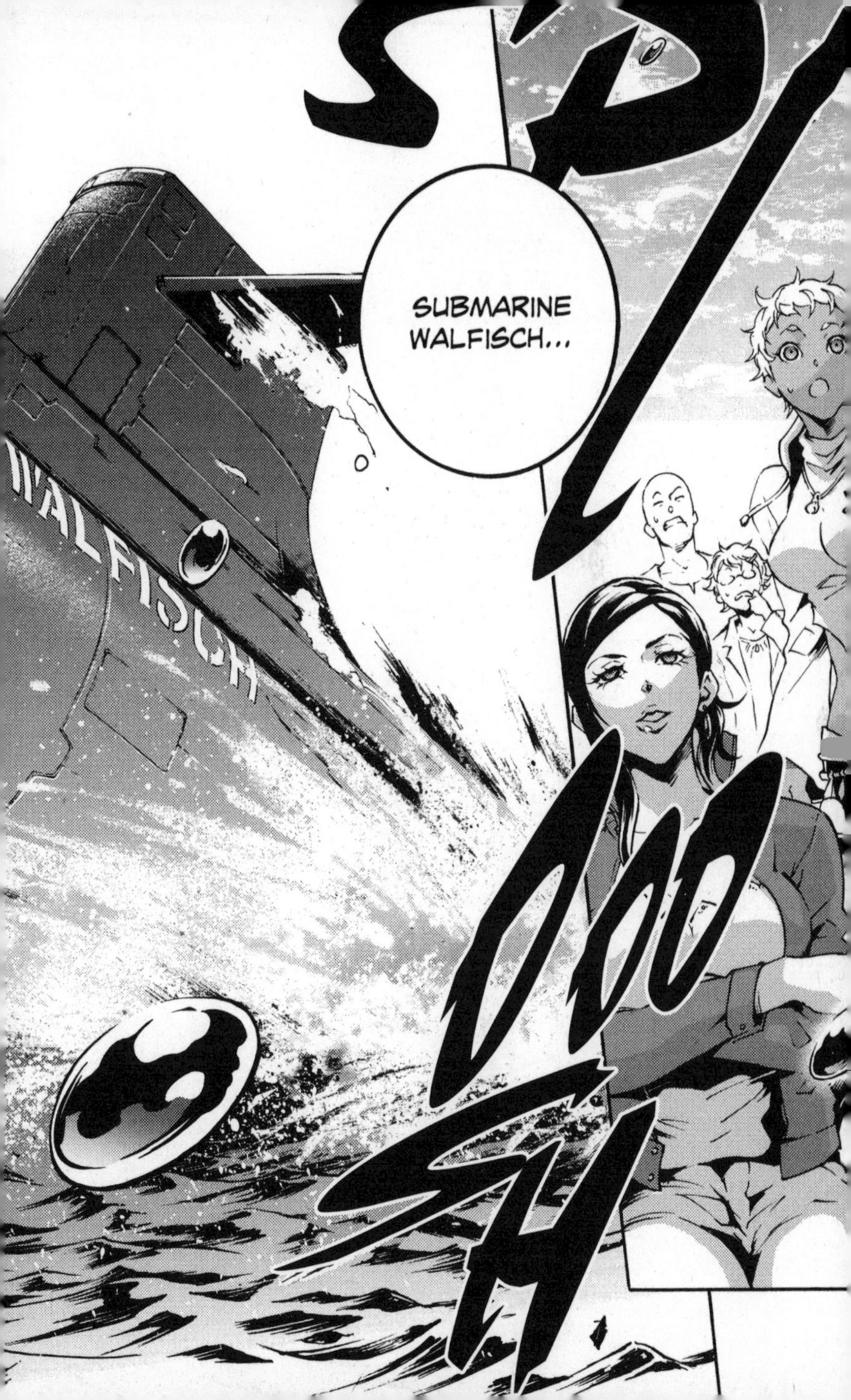
SPLSH
SUBMARINE WALFISCH...
WALFISCH
SWOOSH

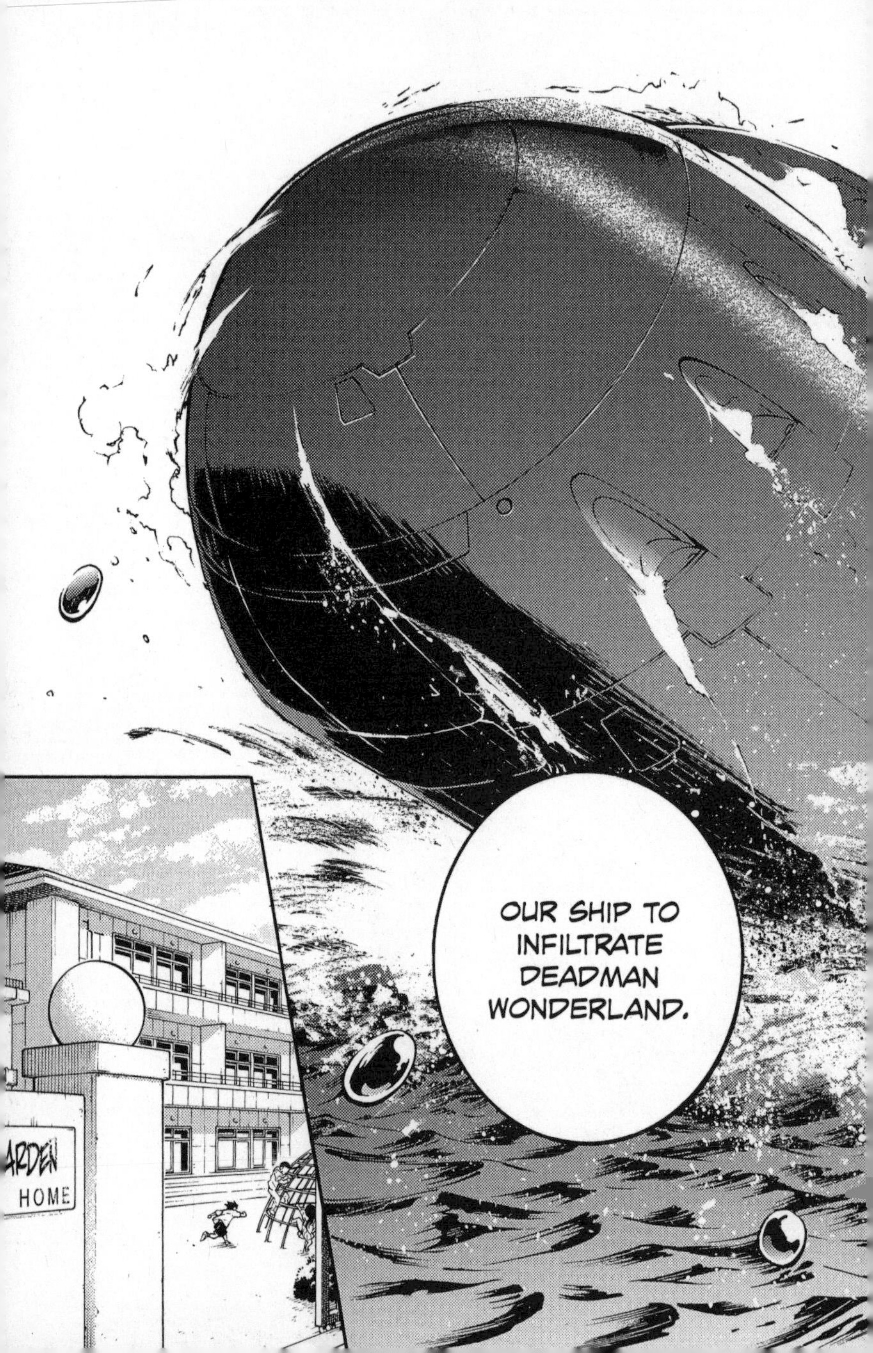
OUR SHIP TO INFILTRATE DEADMAN WONDERLAND.
ARDEN
HOME

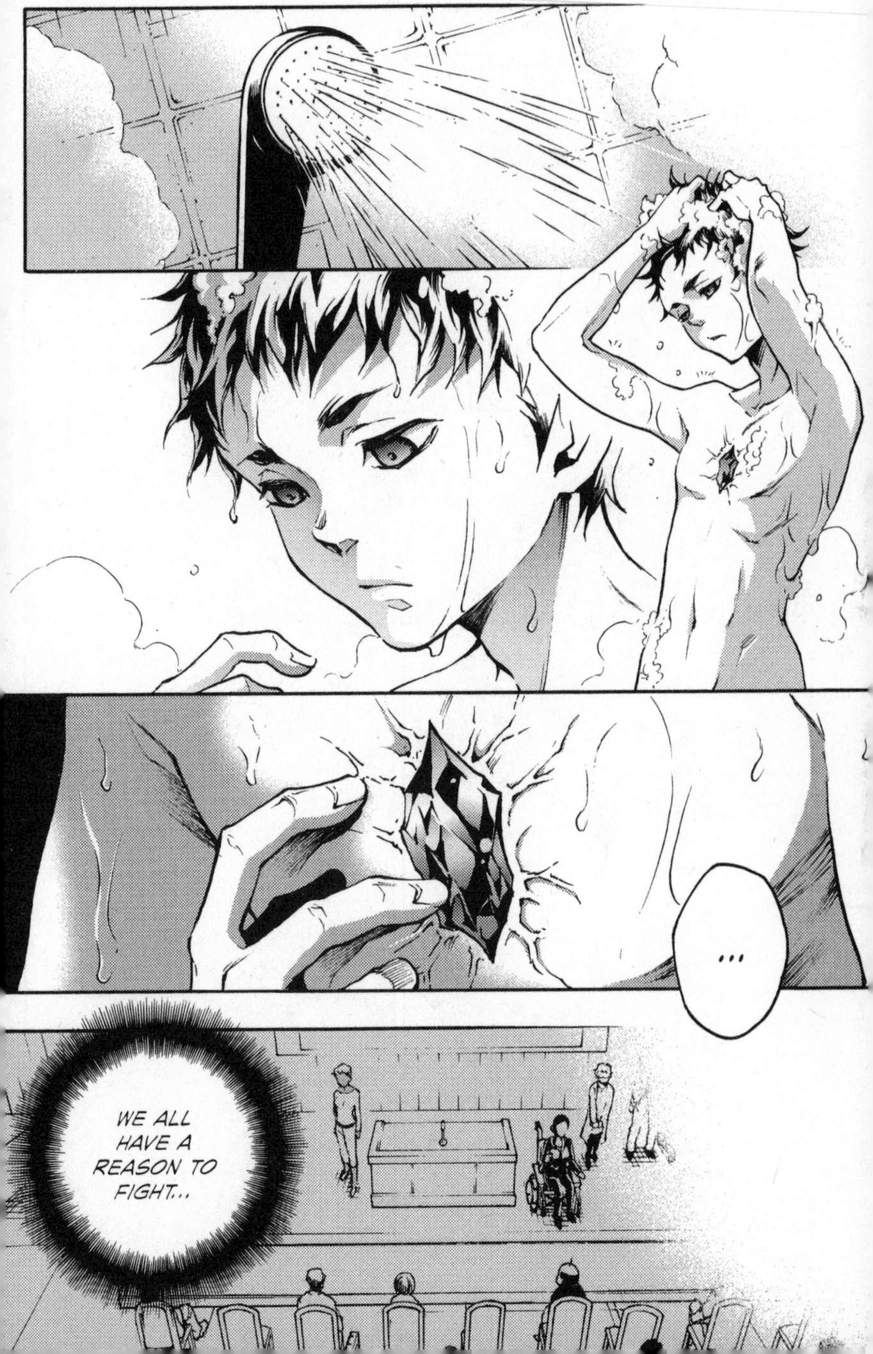
...
WE ALL HAVE A REASON TO FIGHT...

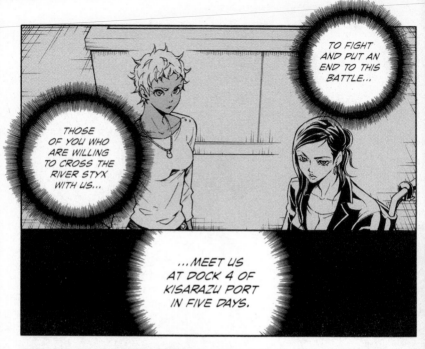

TO FIGHT AND PUT AN END TO THIS BATTLE...

THOSE OF YOU WHO ARE WILLING TO CROSS THE RIVER STYX WITH US...

...MEET US AT DOCK 4 OF KISARAZU PORT IN FIVE DAYS.

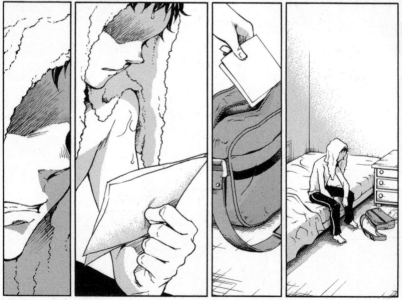

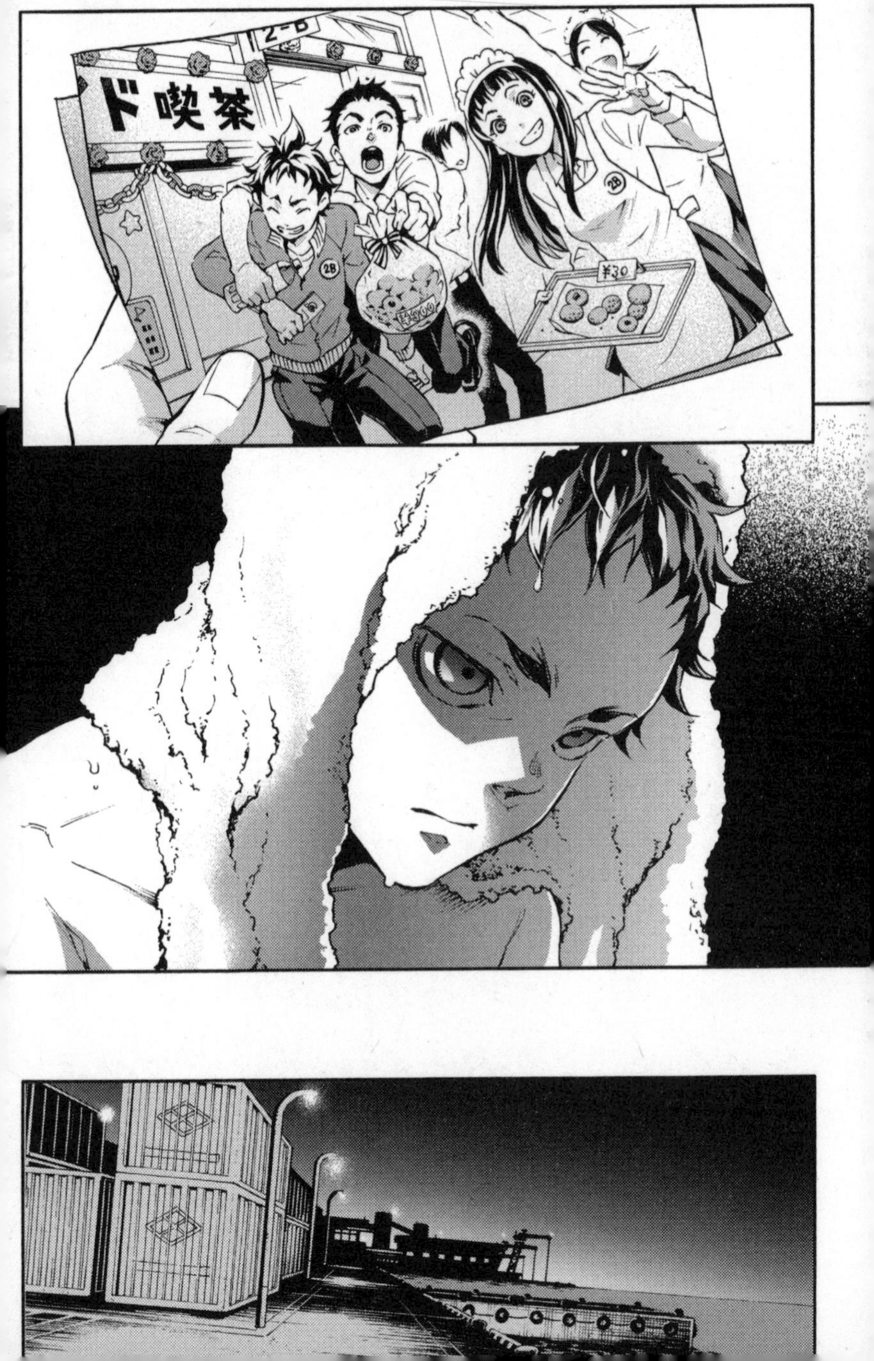
2-B
ド喫茶
2B
2B
¥30

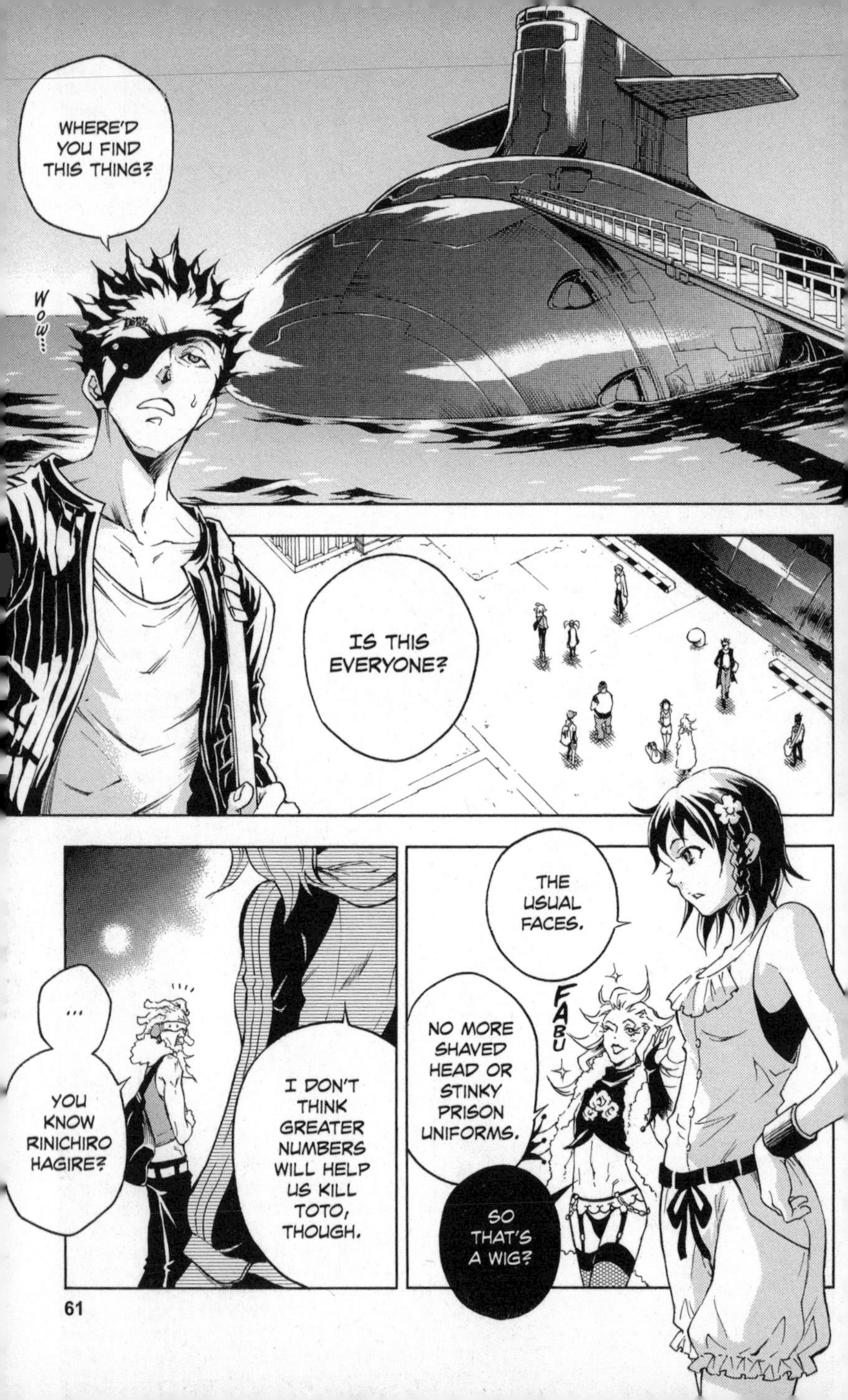
WHERE'D YOU FIND THIS THING?
WOW...
IS THIS EVERYONE?
THE USUAL FACES.
FABU
NO MORE SHAVED HEAD OR STINKY PRISON UNIFORMS.
SO THAT'S A WIG?
I DON'T THINK GREATER NUMBERS WILL HELP US KILL TOTO, THOUGH.
...
YOU KNOW RINICHIRO HAGIRE?

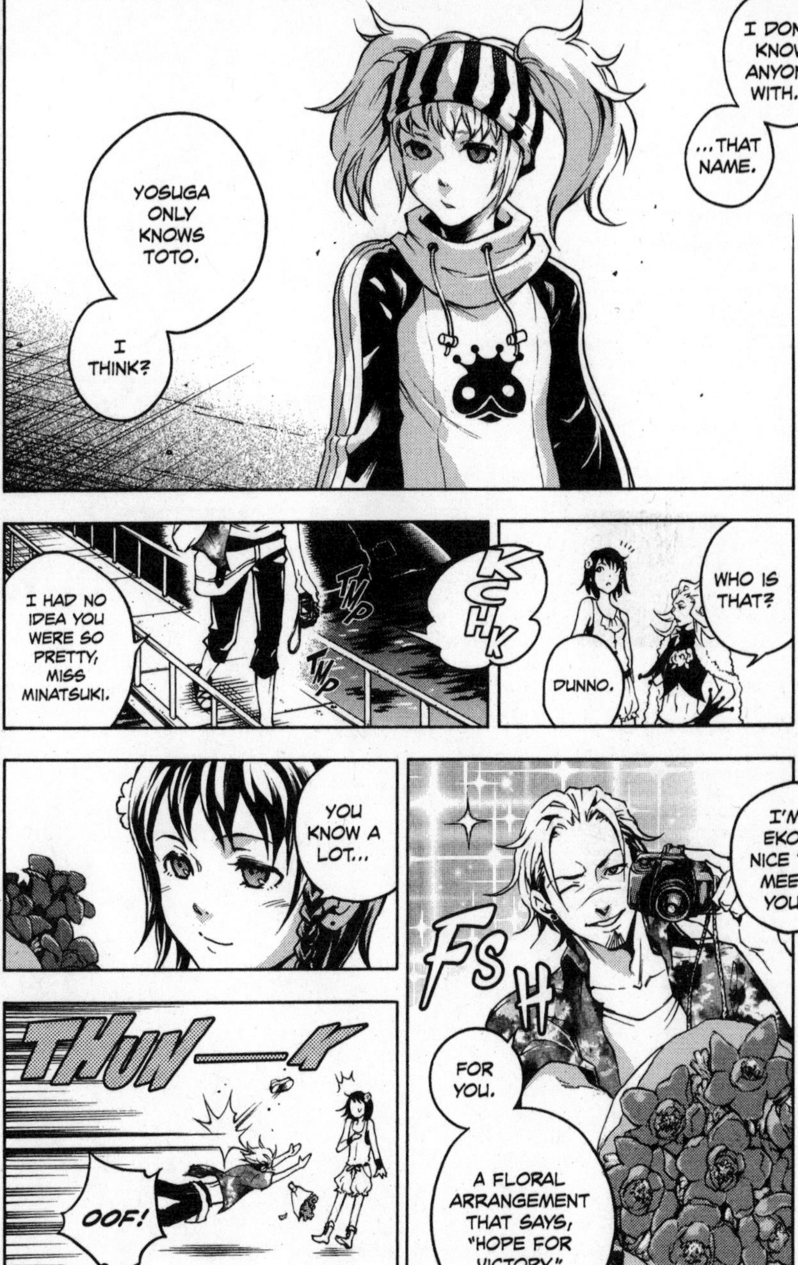
I DON'T KNOW ANYONE WITH...
...THAT NAME.
YOSUGA ONLY KNOWS TOTO.
I THINK?
WHO IS THAT?
DUNNO.
KCHK
TMP
TMP
I HAD NO IDEA YOU WERE SO PRETTY, MISS MINATSUKI.
I'M EKO. NICE TO MEET YOU.
FSH
FOR YOU.
A FLORAL ARRANGEMENT THAT SAYS, "HOPE FOR VICTORY."
YOU KNOW A LOT...
THUN—!
OOF!

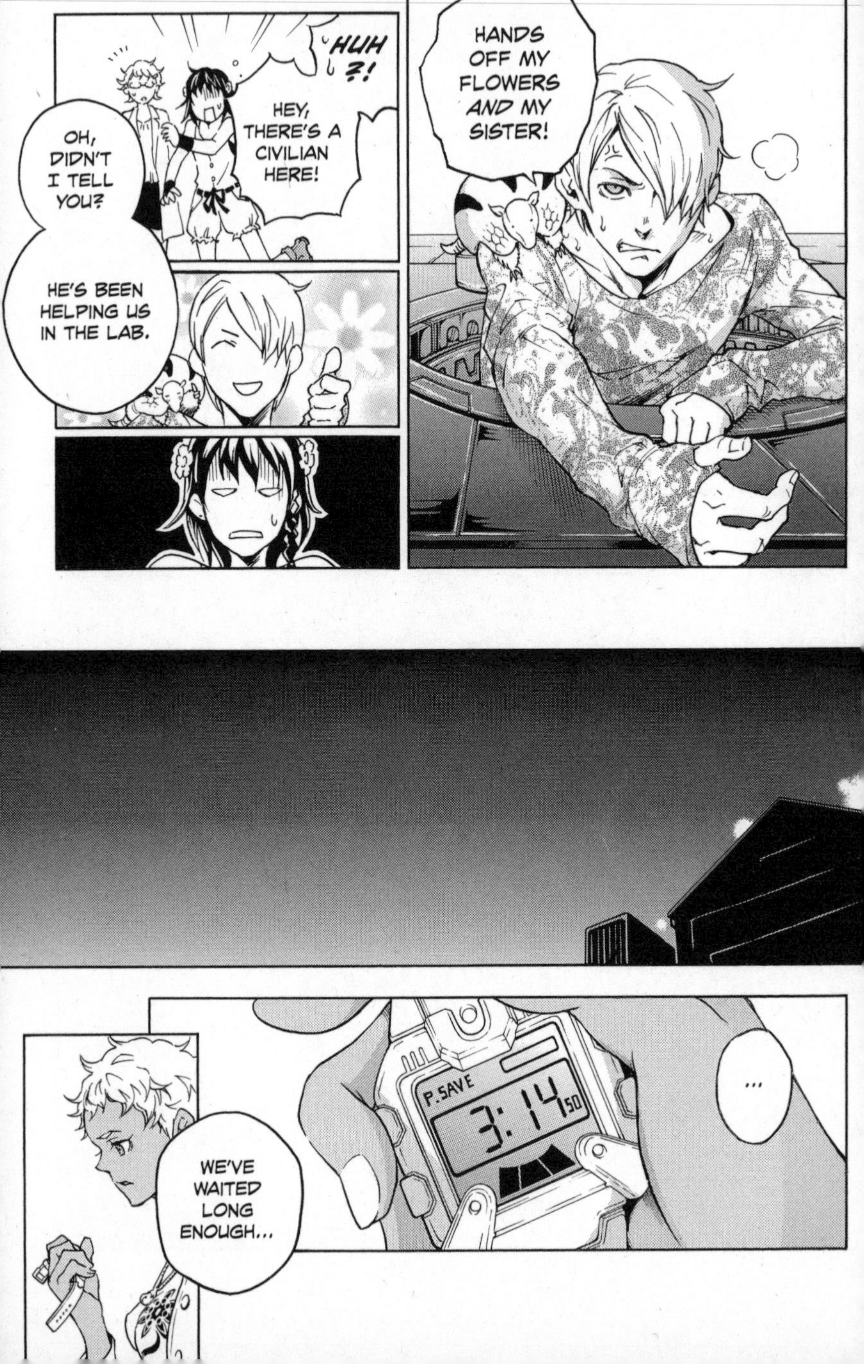
HANDS OFF MY FLOWERS AND MY SISTER!
HUH?!
HEY, THERE'S A CIVILIAN HERE!
OH, DIDN'T I TELL YOU?
HE'S BEEN HELPING US IN THE LAB.
...
P.SAVE
3:14 50
WE'VE WAITED LONG ENOUGH...

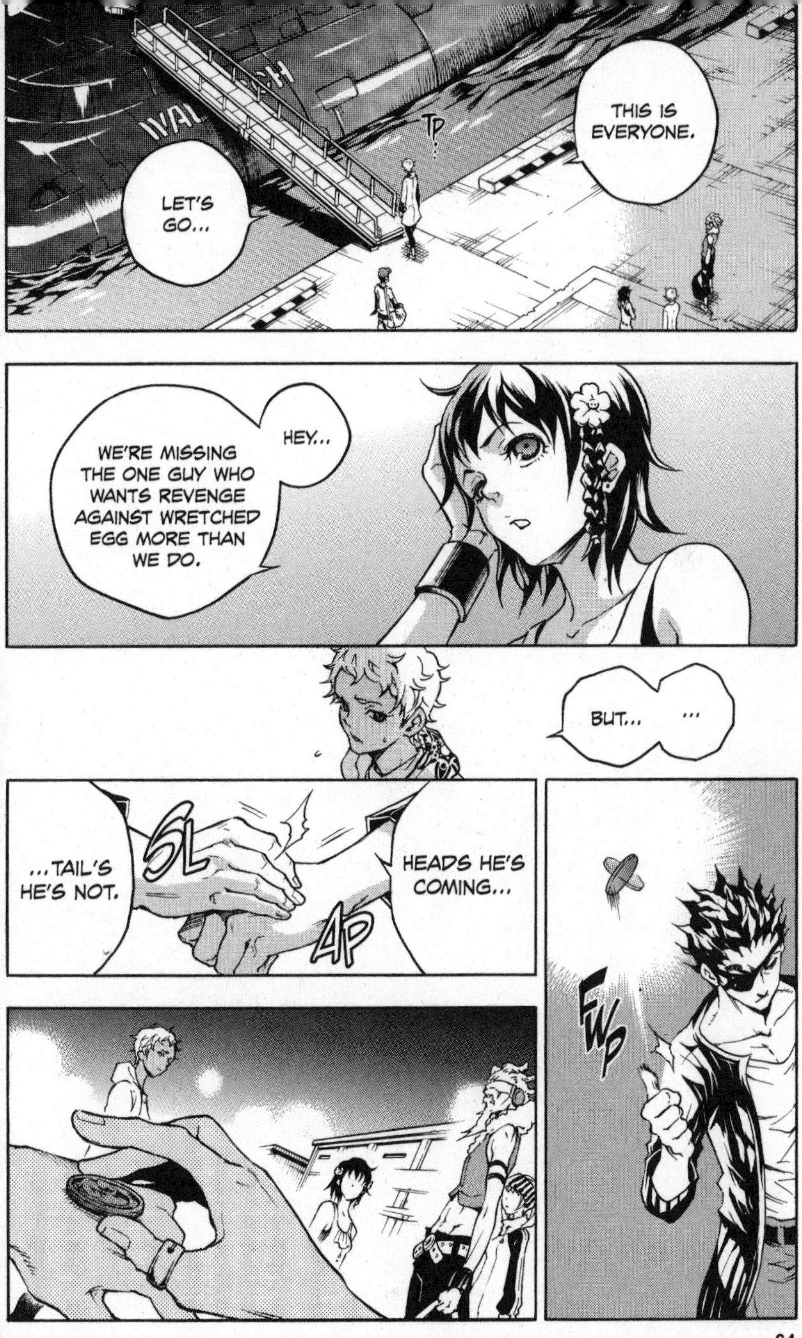
THIS IS EVERYONE.
TP...
LET'S GO...
HEY...
WE'RE MISSING THE ONE GUY WHO WANTS REVENGE AGAINST WRETCHED EGG MORE THAN WE DO.
BUT... ...
FWP
HEADS HE'S COMING...
SL
...TAIL'S HE'S NOT.
AP

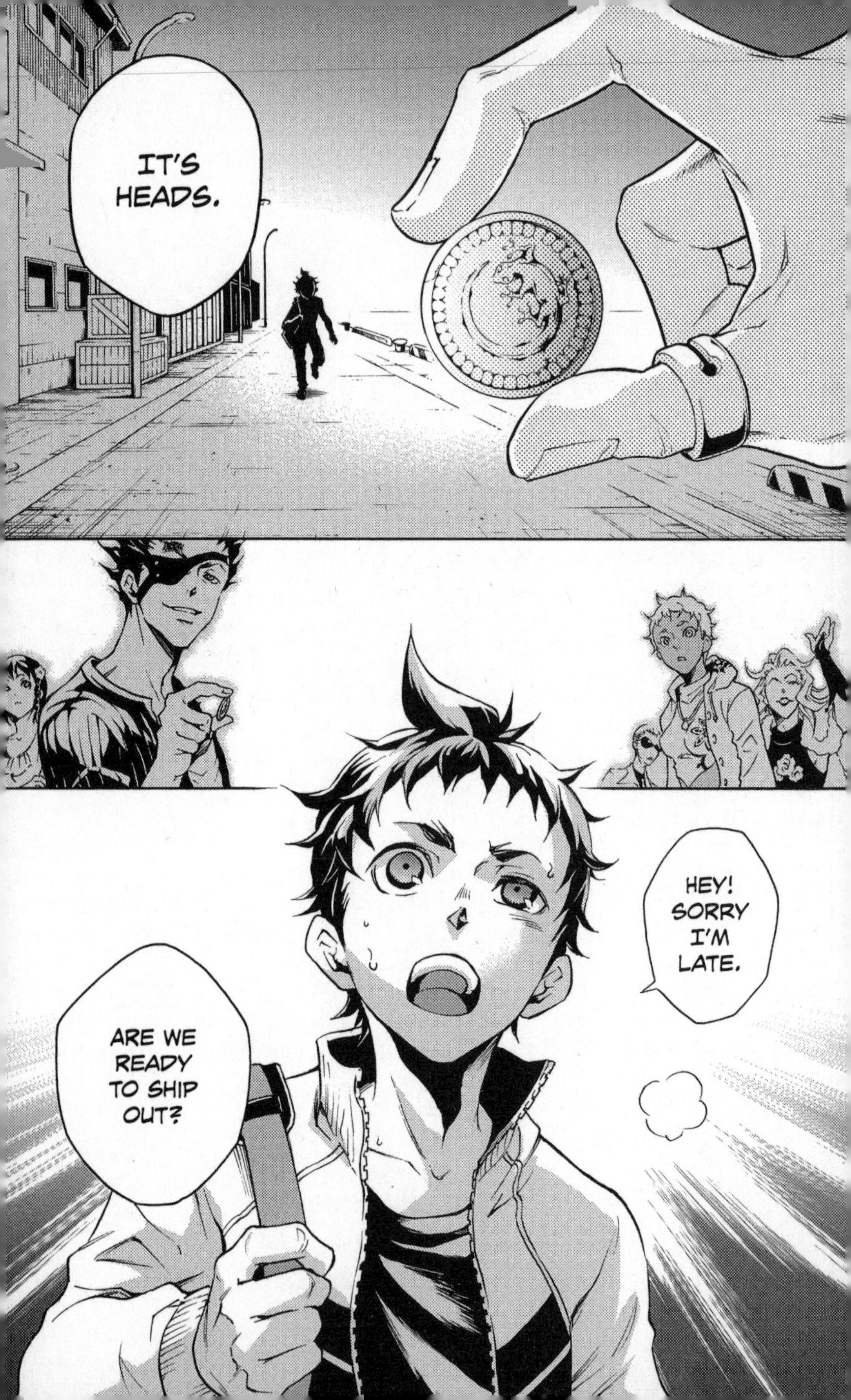
IT'S HEADS.
HEY! SORRY I'M LATE.
ARE WE READY TO SHIP OUT?

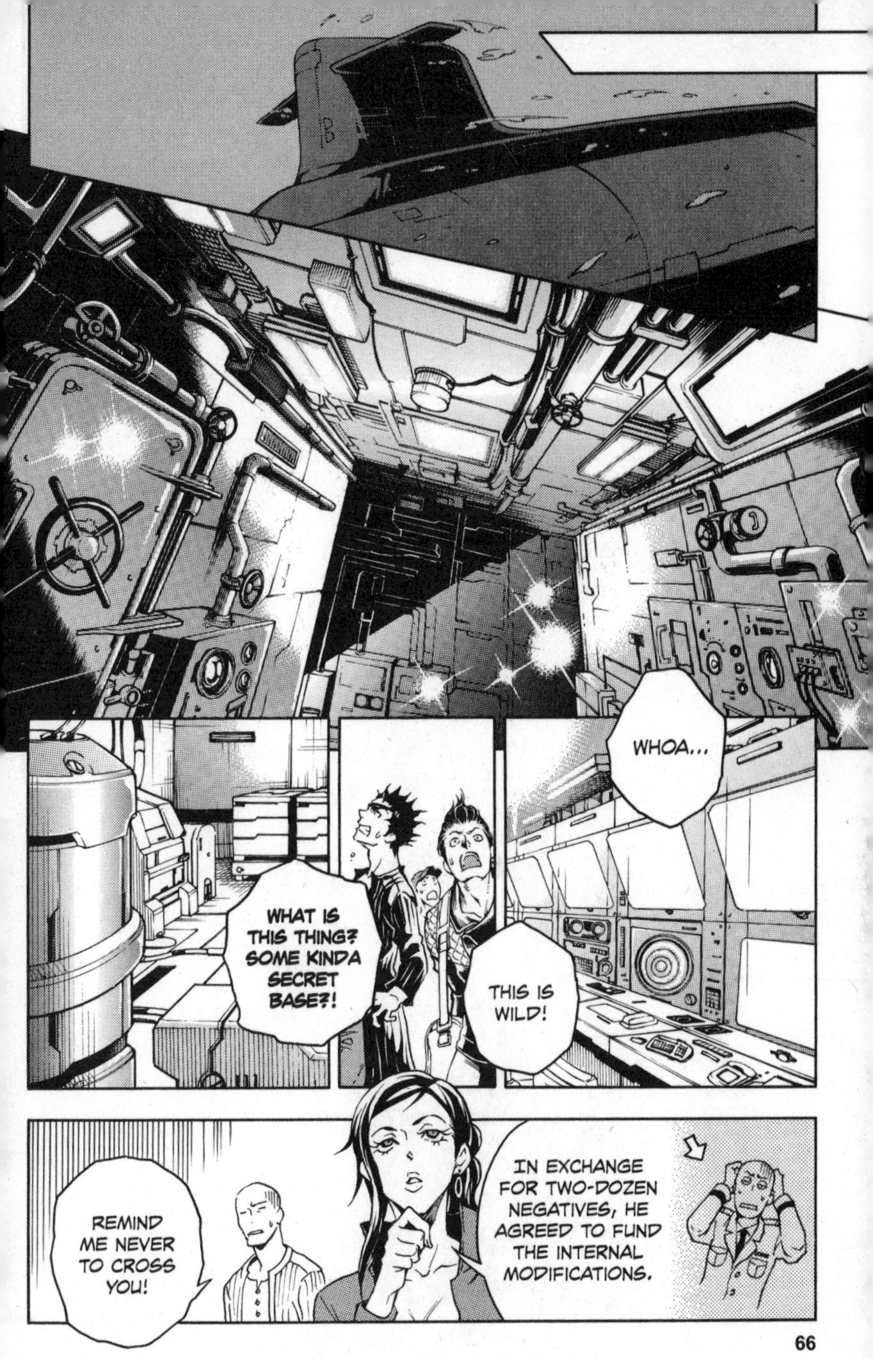
WHOA...
WHAT IS THIS THING? SOME KINDA SECRET BASE?!
THIS IS WILD!
IN EXCHANGE FOR TWO-DOZEN NEGATIVES, HE AGREED TO FUND THE INTERNAL MODIFICATIONS.
REMIND ME NEVER TO CROSS YOU!

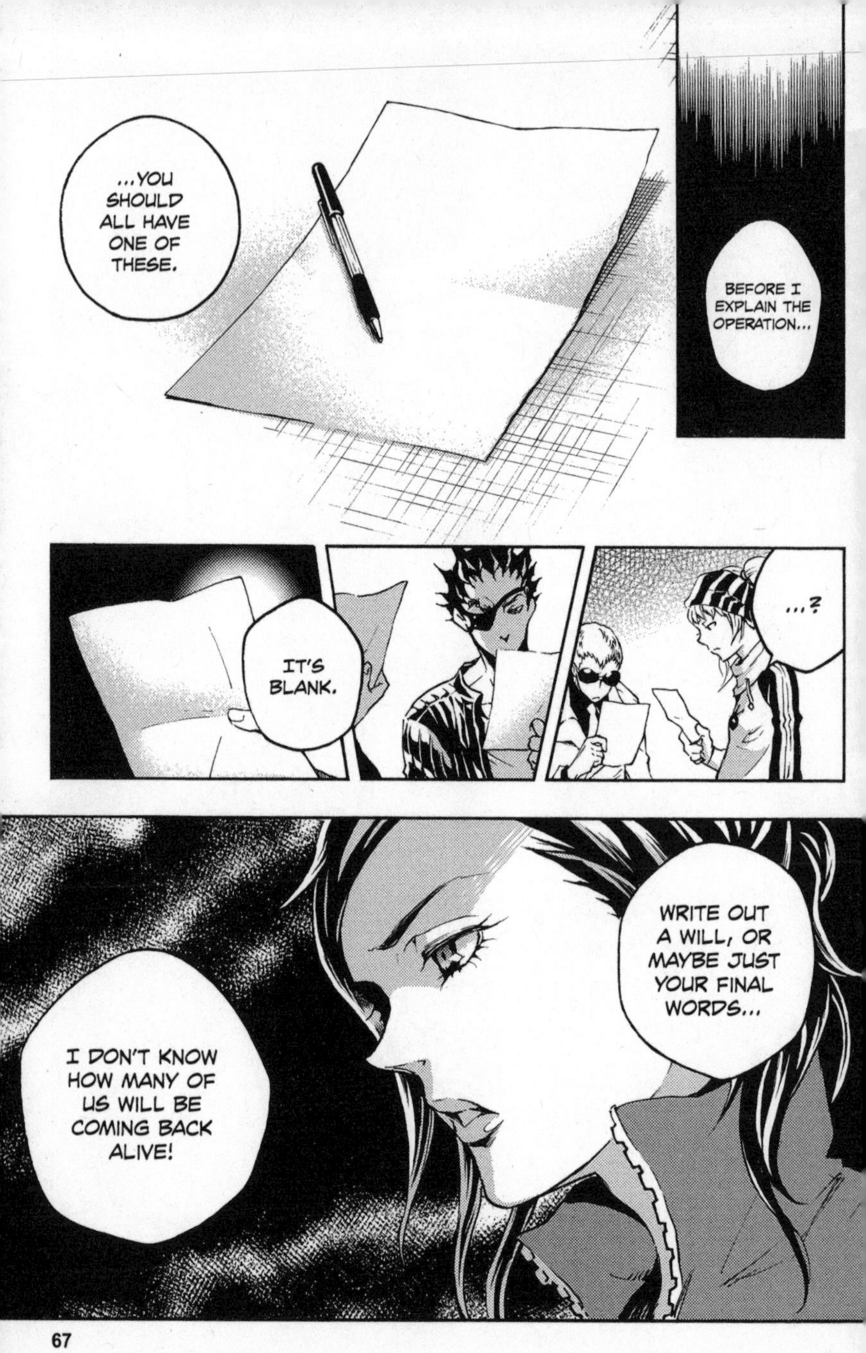
BEFORE I EXPLAIN THE OPERATION...
...YOU SHOULD ALL HAVE ONE OF THESE.
...?
IT'S BLANK.
WRITE OUT A WILL, OR MAYBE JUST YOUR FINAL WORDS...
I DON'T KNOW HOW MANY OF US WILL BE COMING BACK ALIVE!

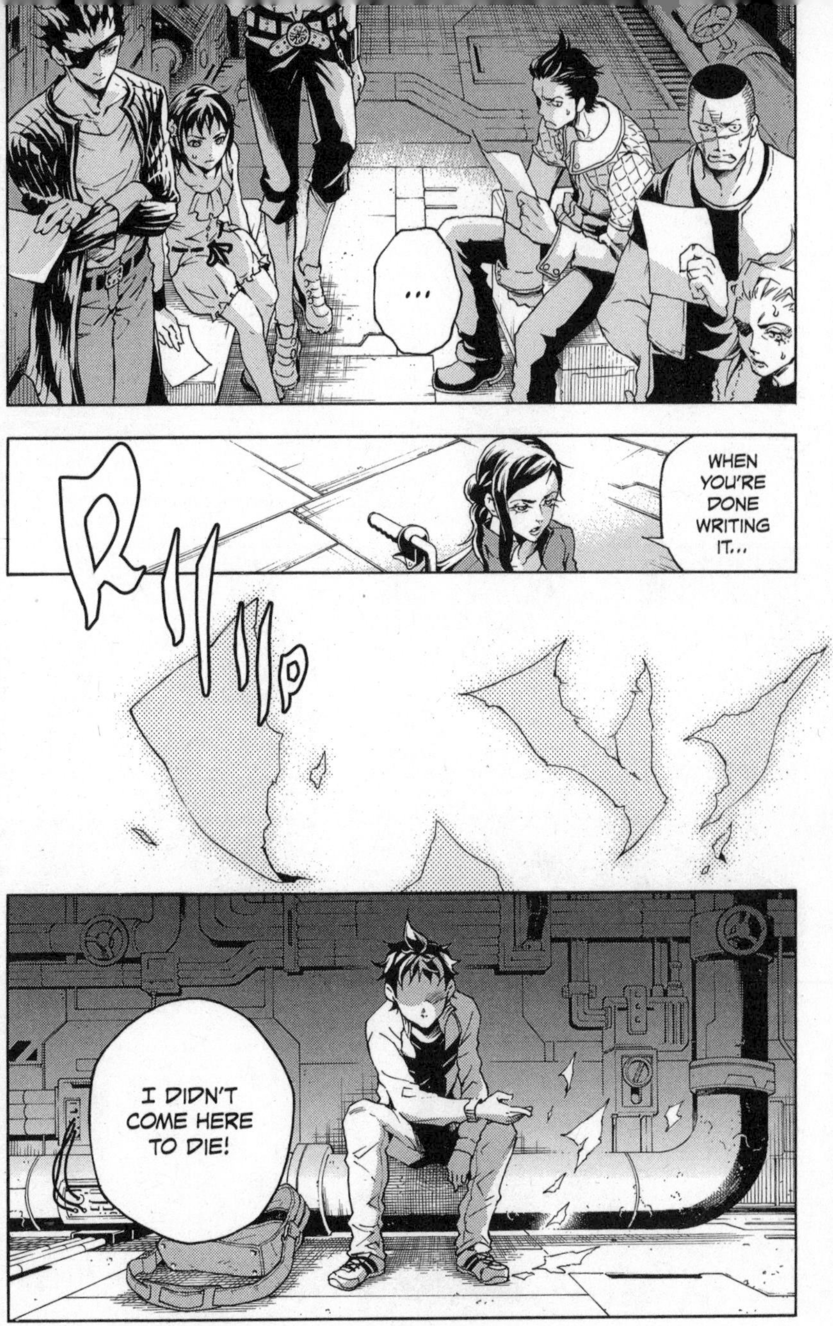
...
WHEN YOU'RE DONE WRITING IT...
RIIIIP
I DIDN'T COME HERE TO DIE!

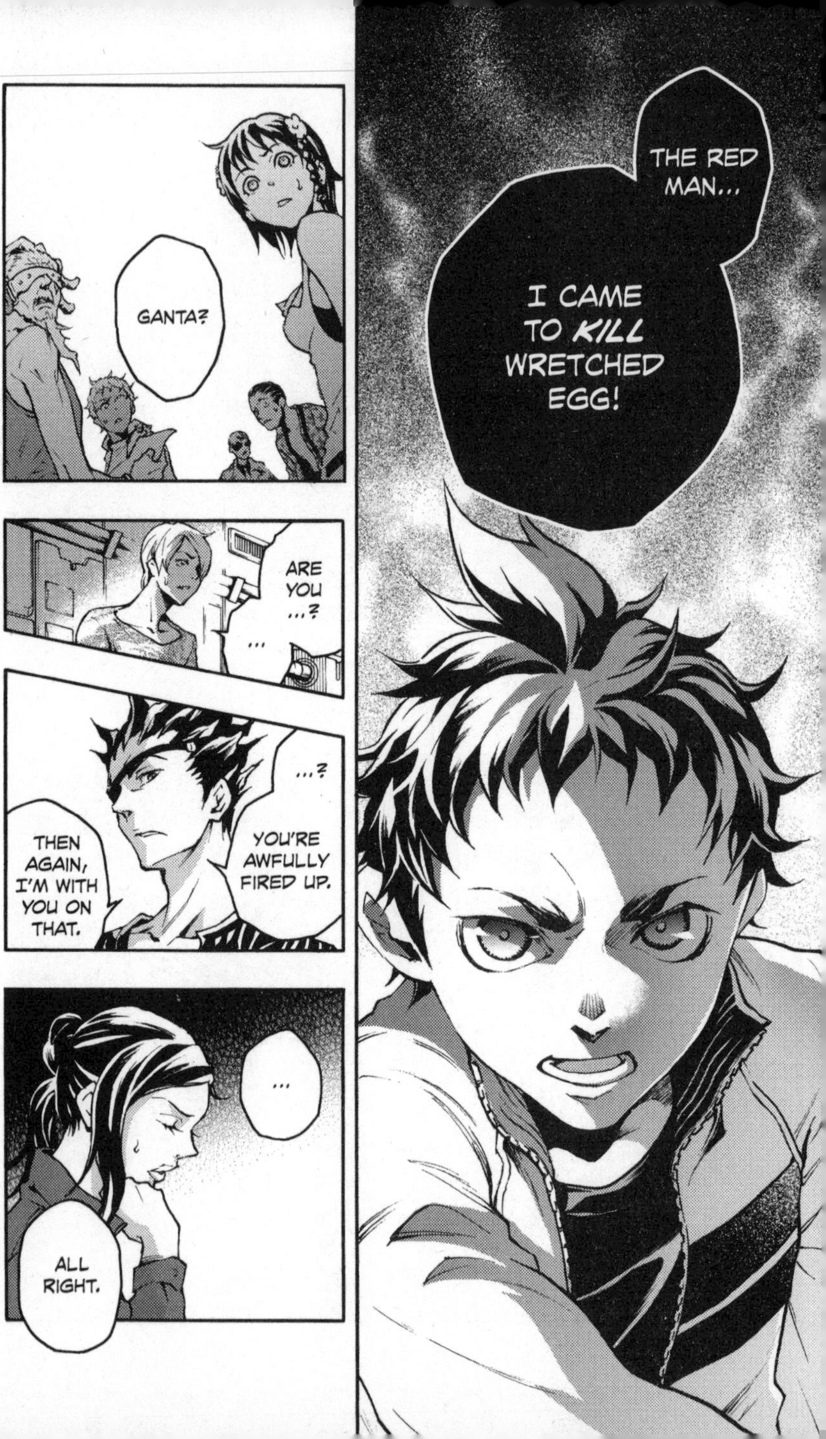
THE RED MAN...
I CAME TO KILL WRETCHED EGG!
GANTA?
ARE YOU ...?
...
...?
YOU'RE AWFULLY FIRED UP.
THEN AGAIN, I'M WITH YOU ON THAT.
...
ALL RIGHT.

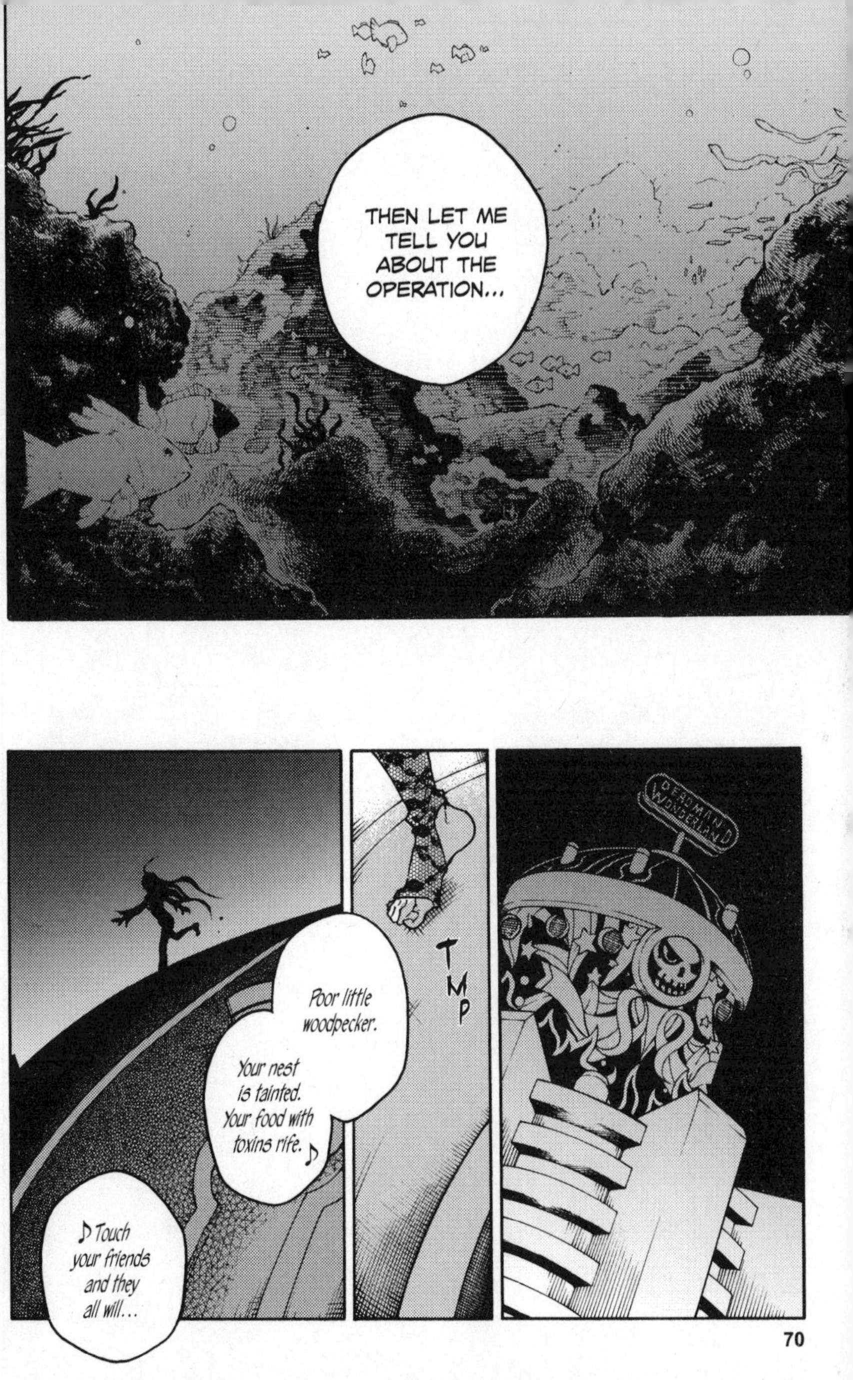
THEN LET ME TELL YOU ABOUT THE OPERATION...
DEADMAN WONDERLAND
TMP
Poor little woodpecker.
Your nest is tainted. Your food with toxins rife. ♪
♪ Touch your friends and they all will...

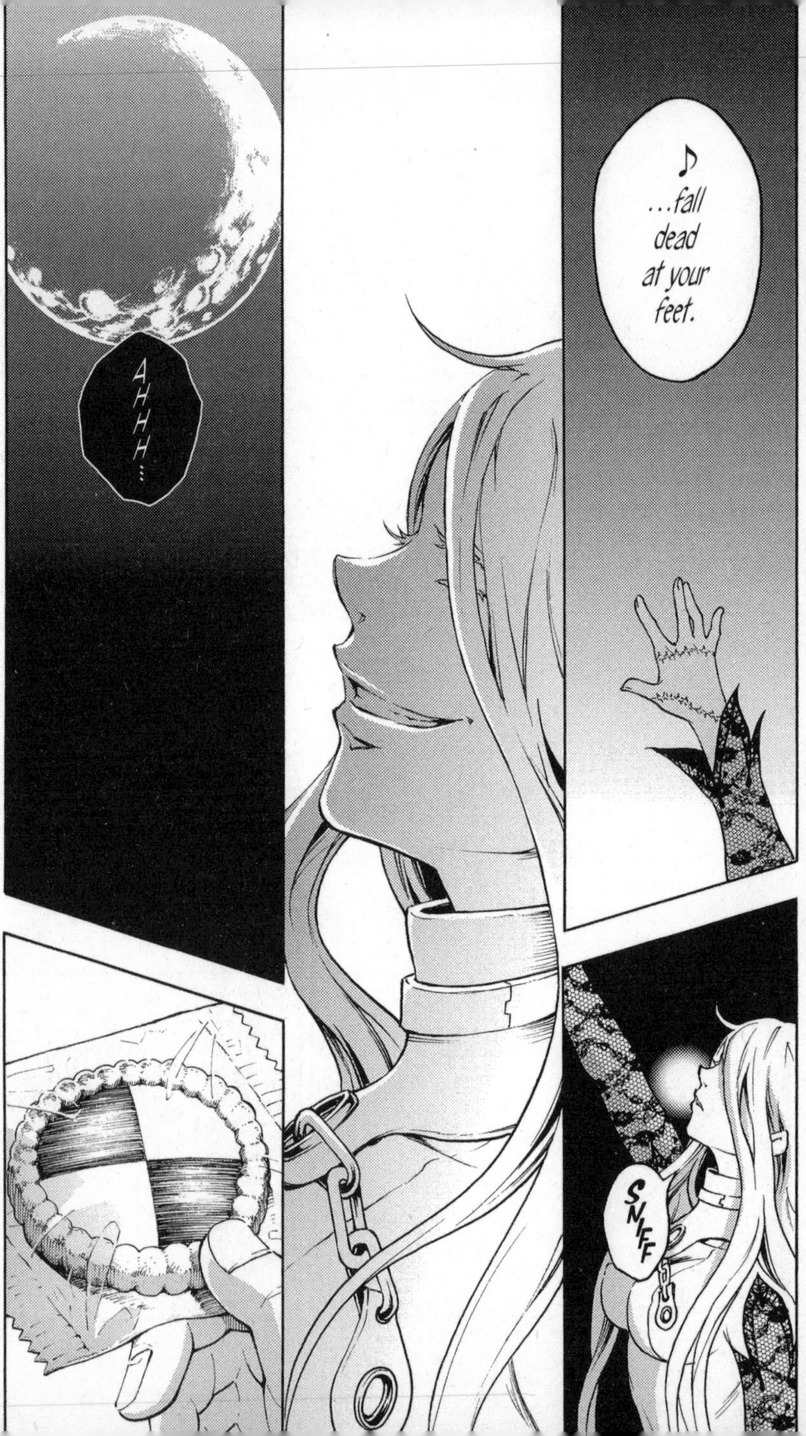
♪ …fall dead at your feet.
AHHH…
SNIFF

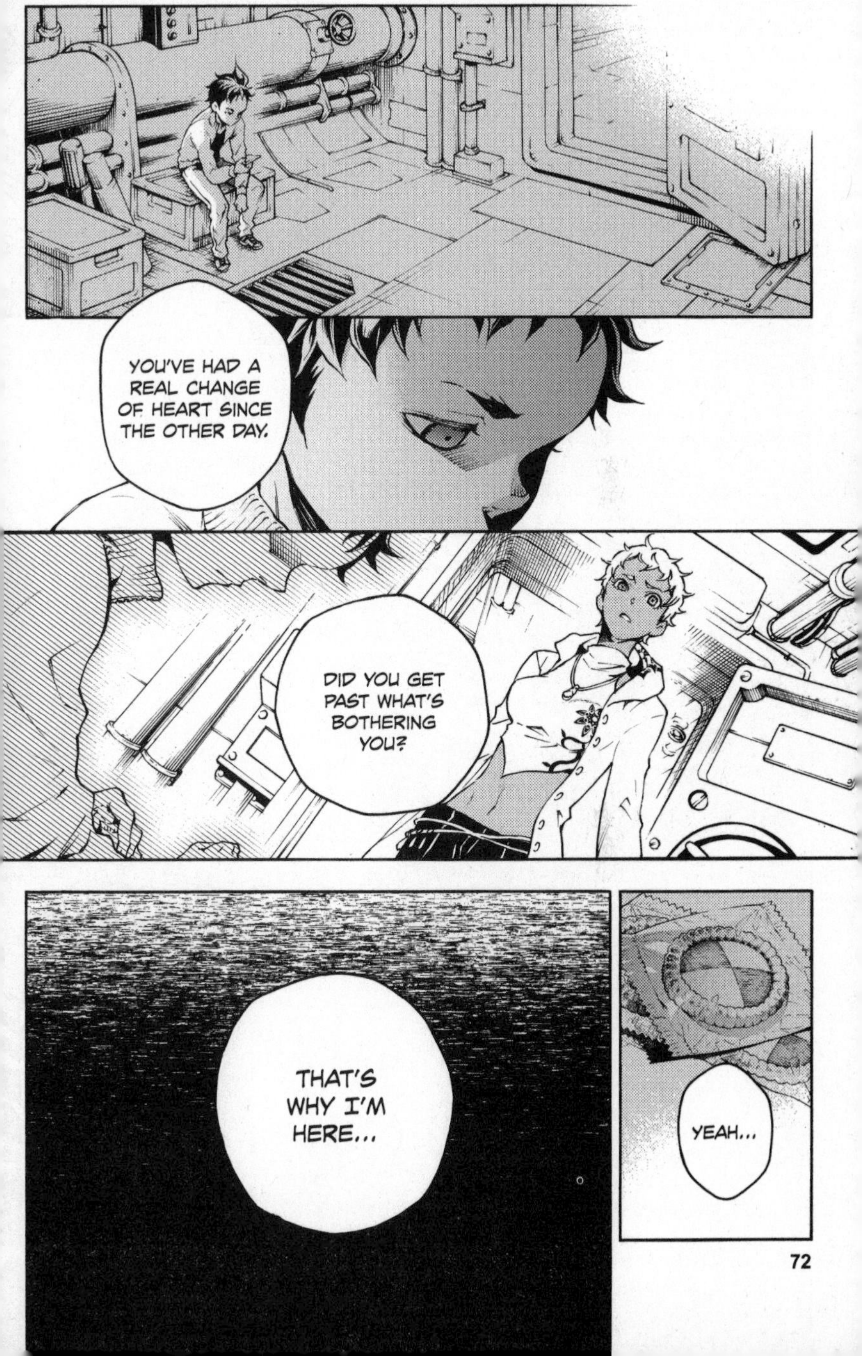
YOU'VE HAD A REAL CHANGE OF HEART SINCE THE OTHER DAY.
DID YOU GET PAST WHAT'S BOTHERING YOU?
YEAH...
THAT'S WHY I'M HERE...

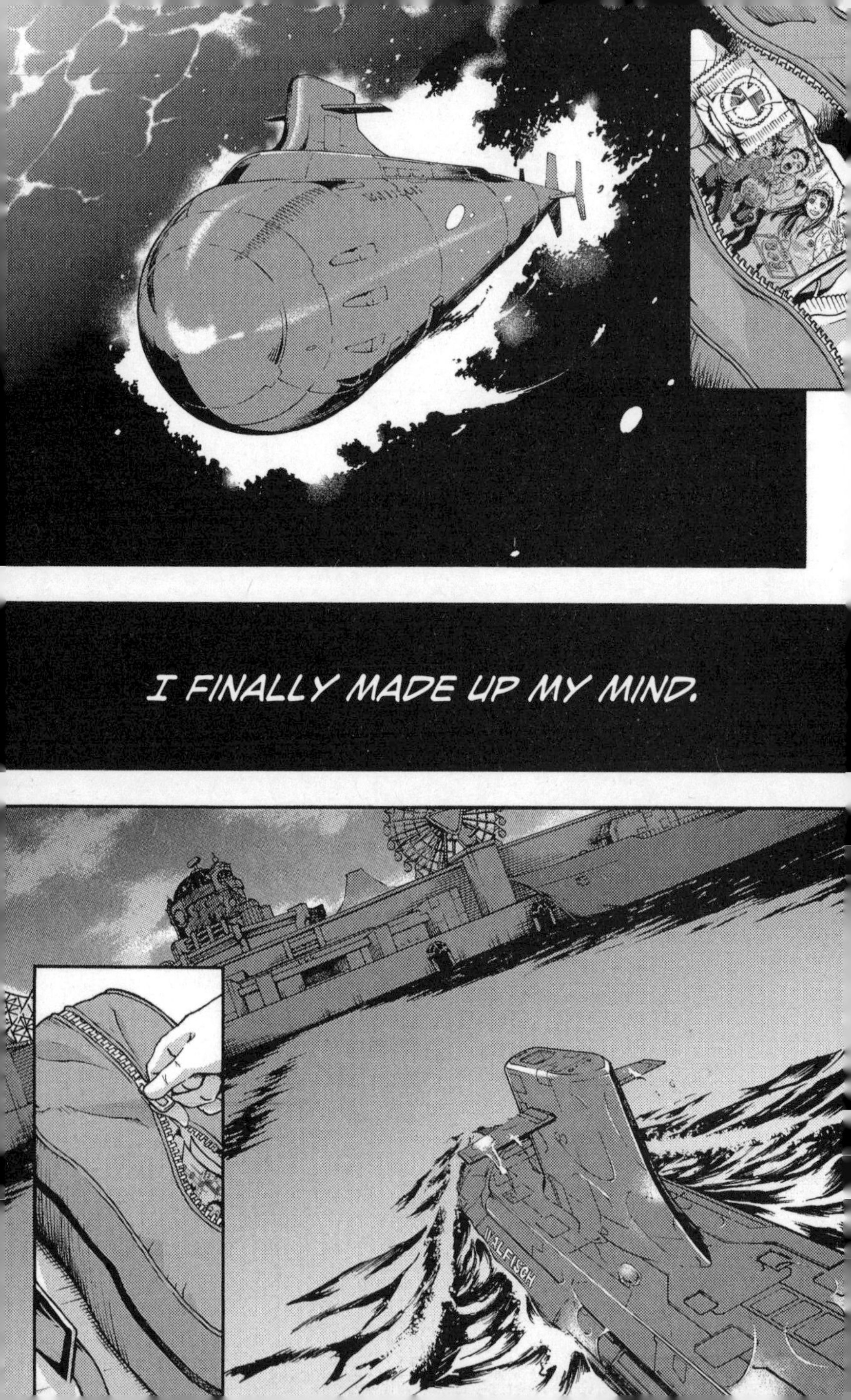
I FINALLY MADE UP MY MIND.
WALFISCH

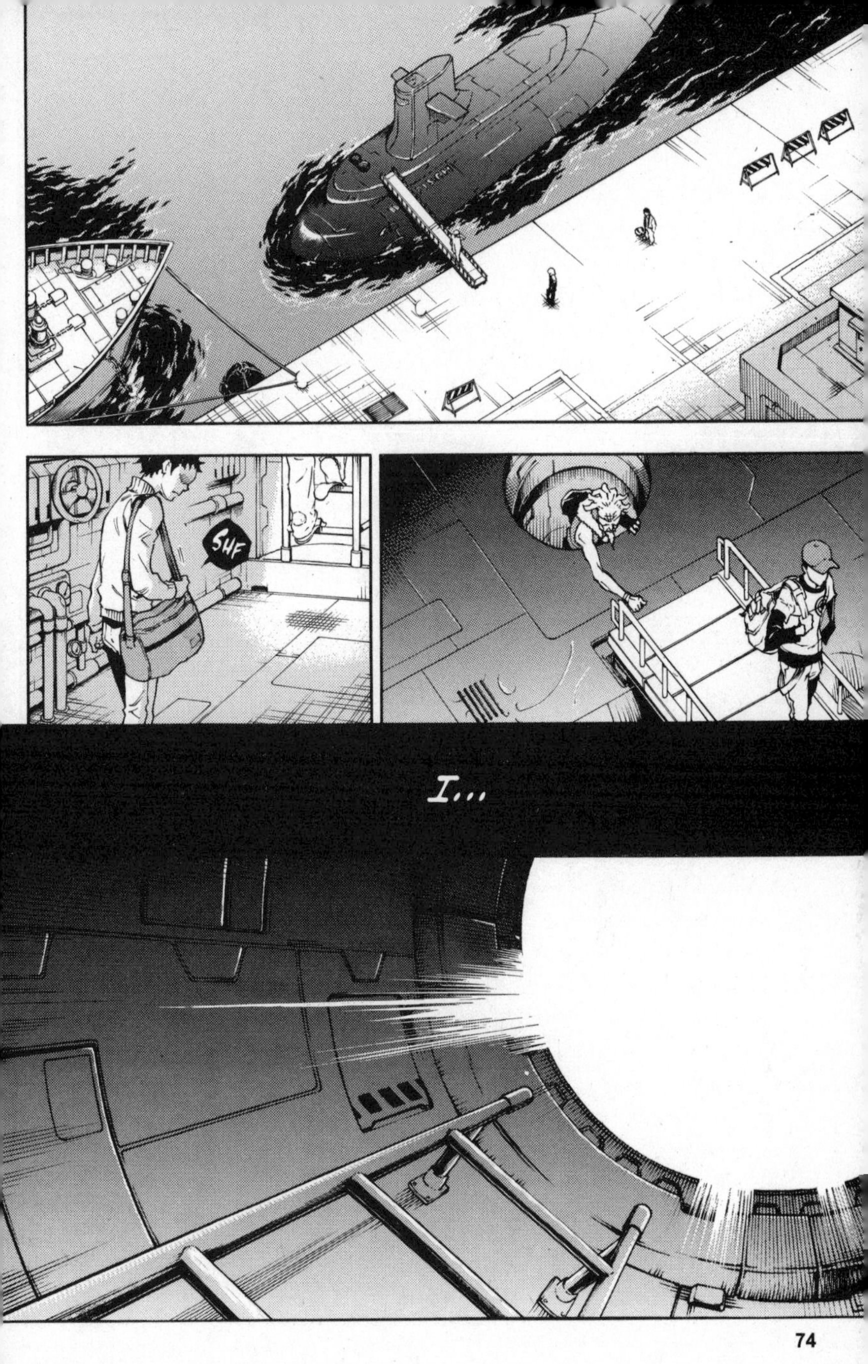
SHF
I...

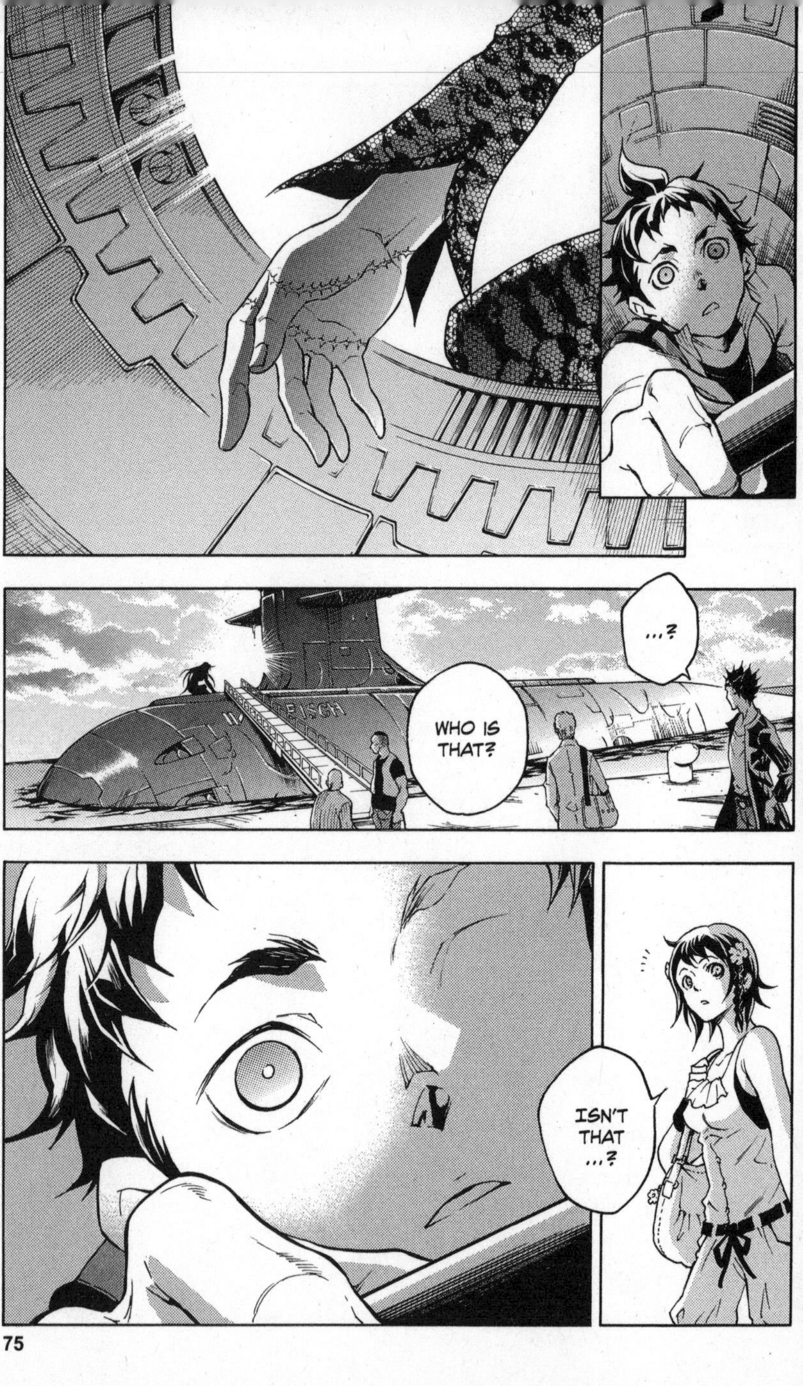
...?
WHO IS THAT?
ISN'T THAT ...?

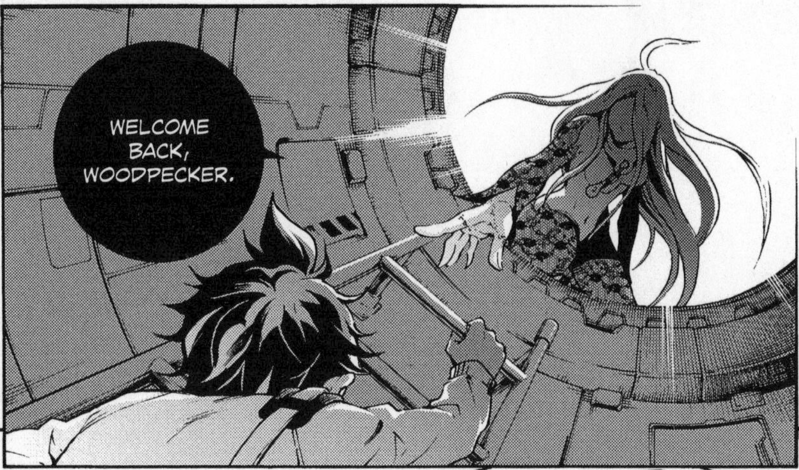
WELCOME BACK, WOODPECKER.

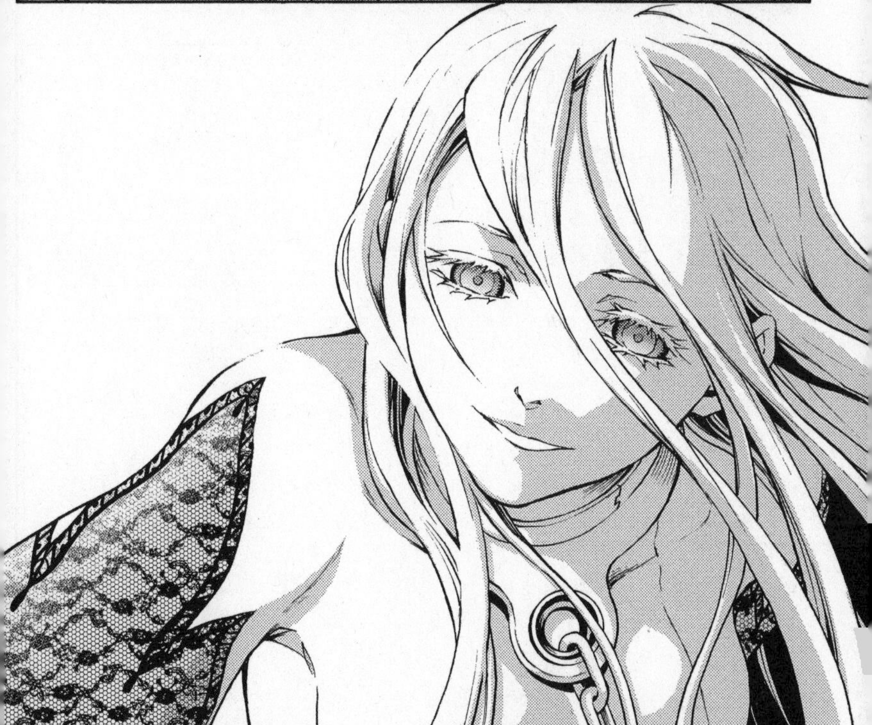

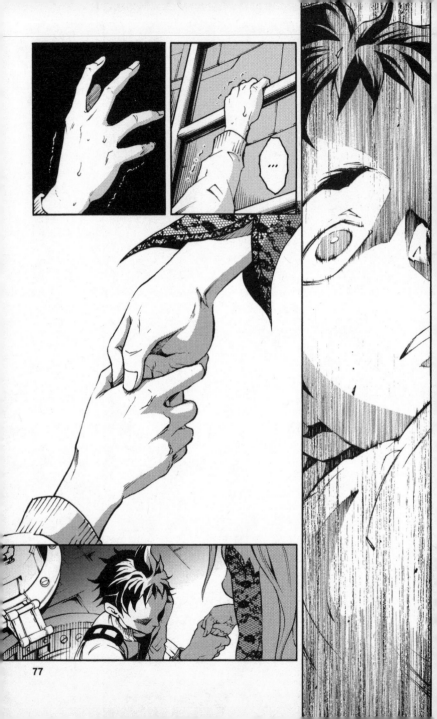

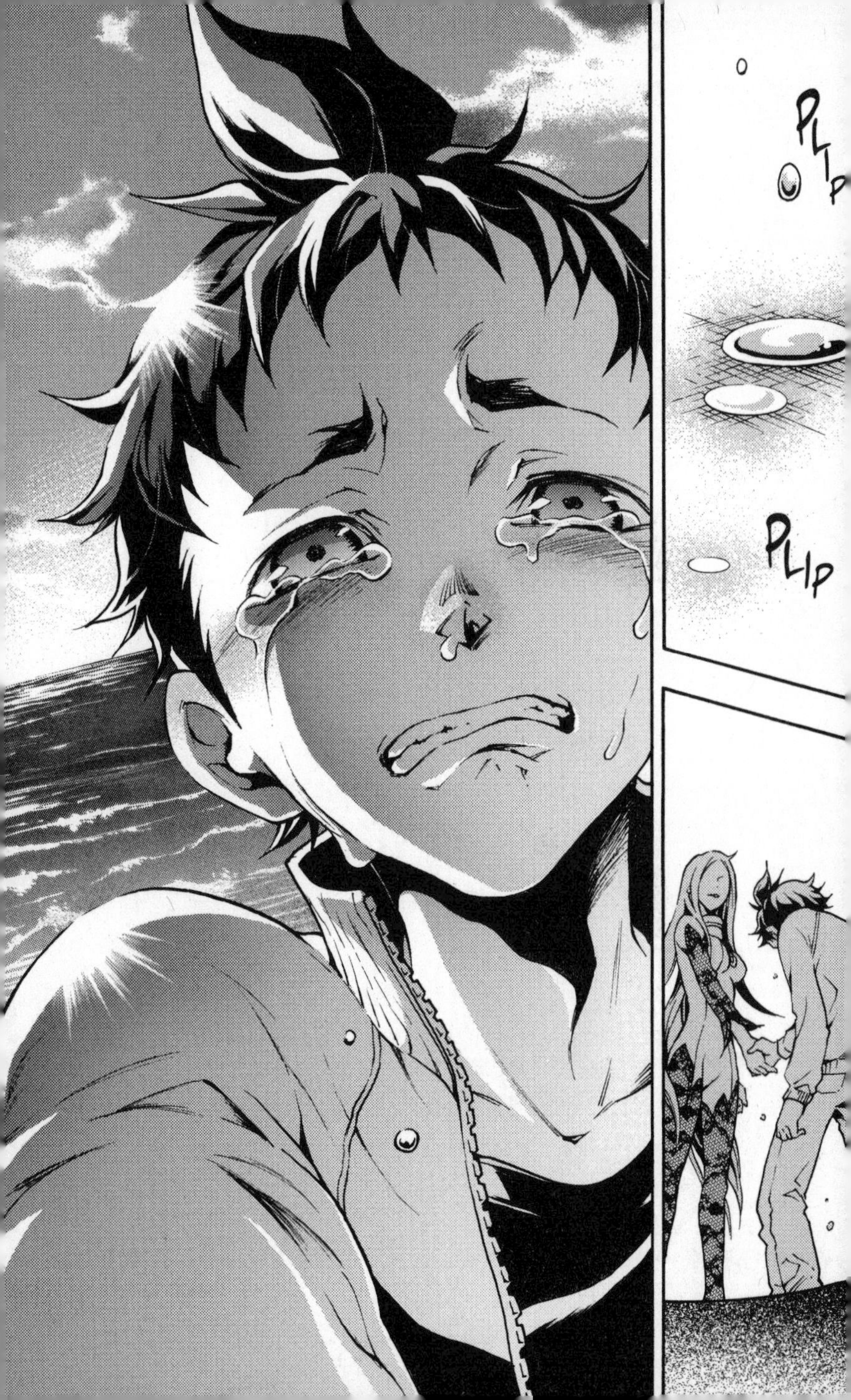
PLIP
PLIP

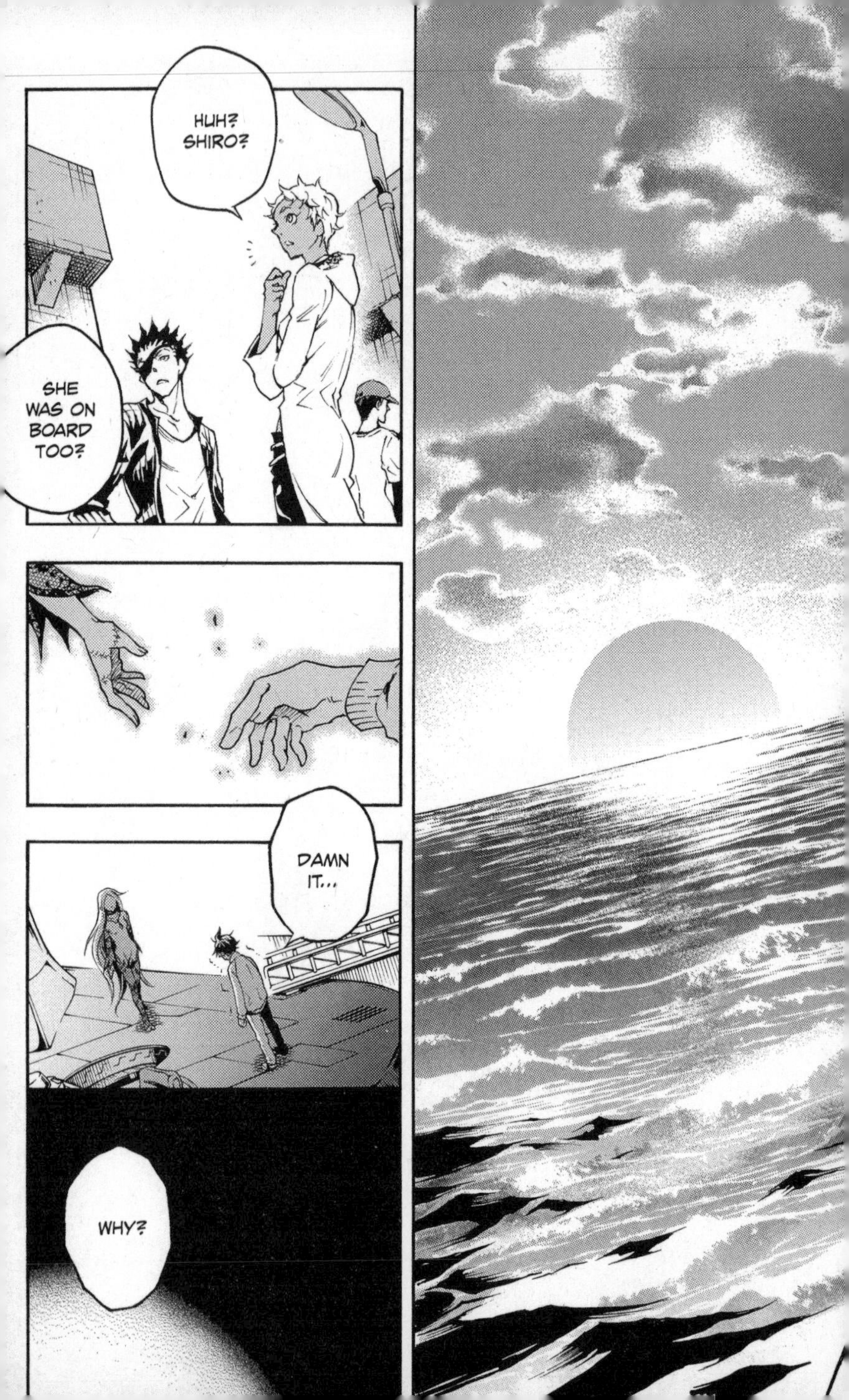
HUH? SHIRO?
SHE WAS ON BOARD TOO?
DAMN IT...
WHY?

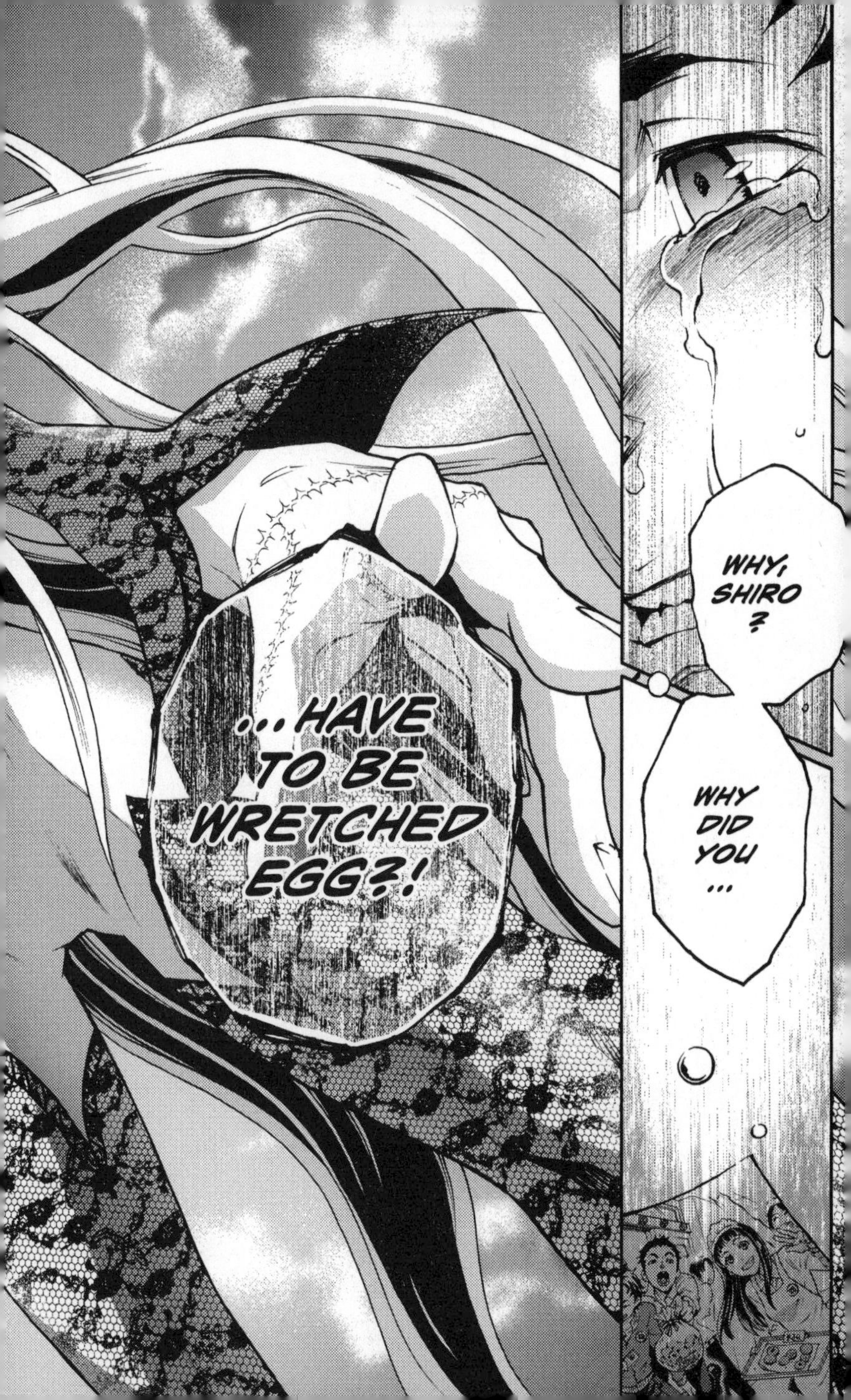
WHY, SHIRO?
WHY DID YOU...
...HAVE TO BE WRETCHED EGG?!

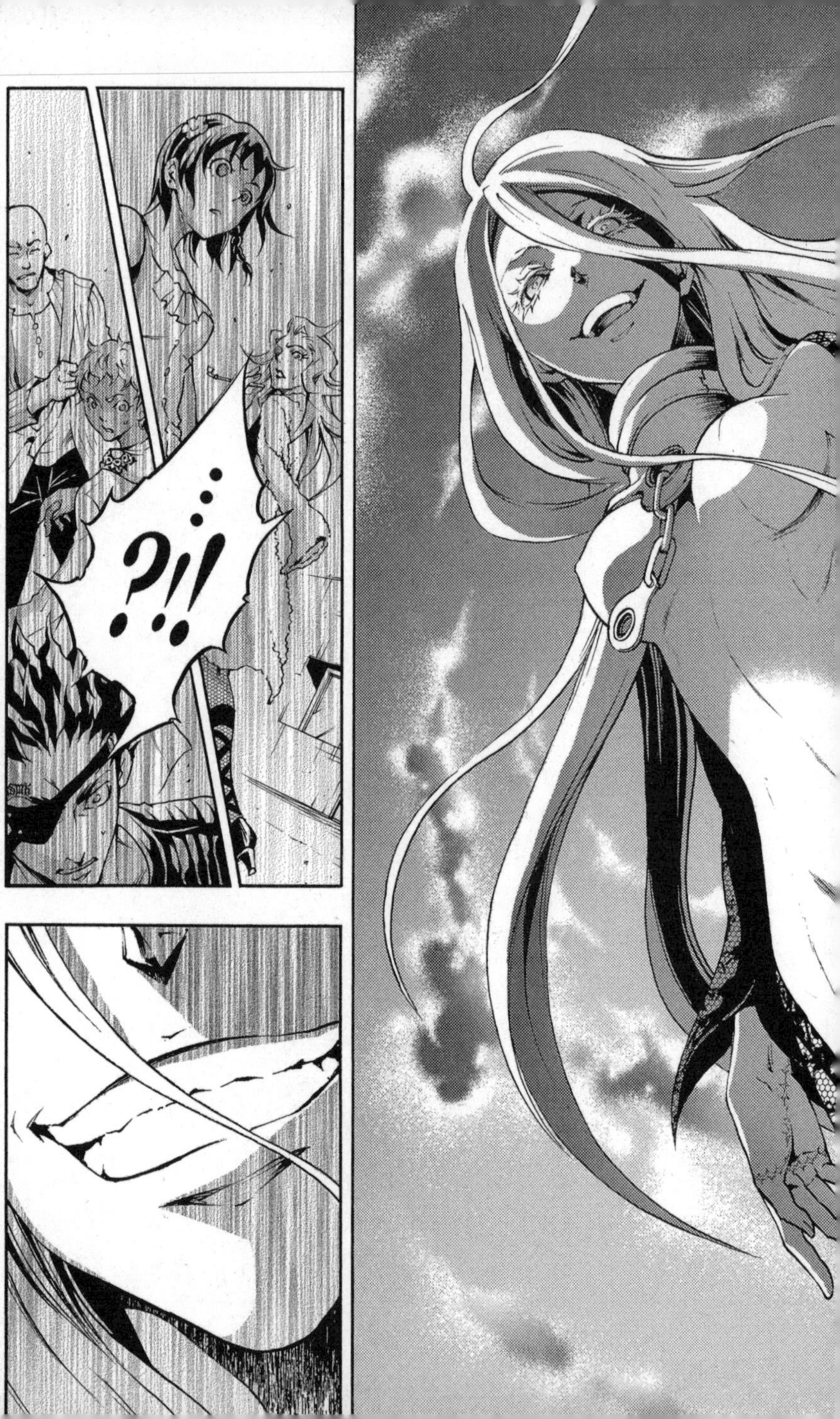
...?!!

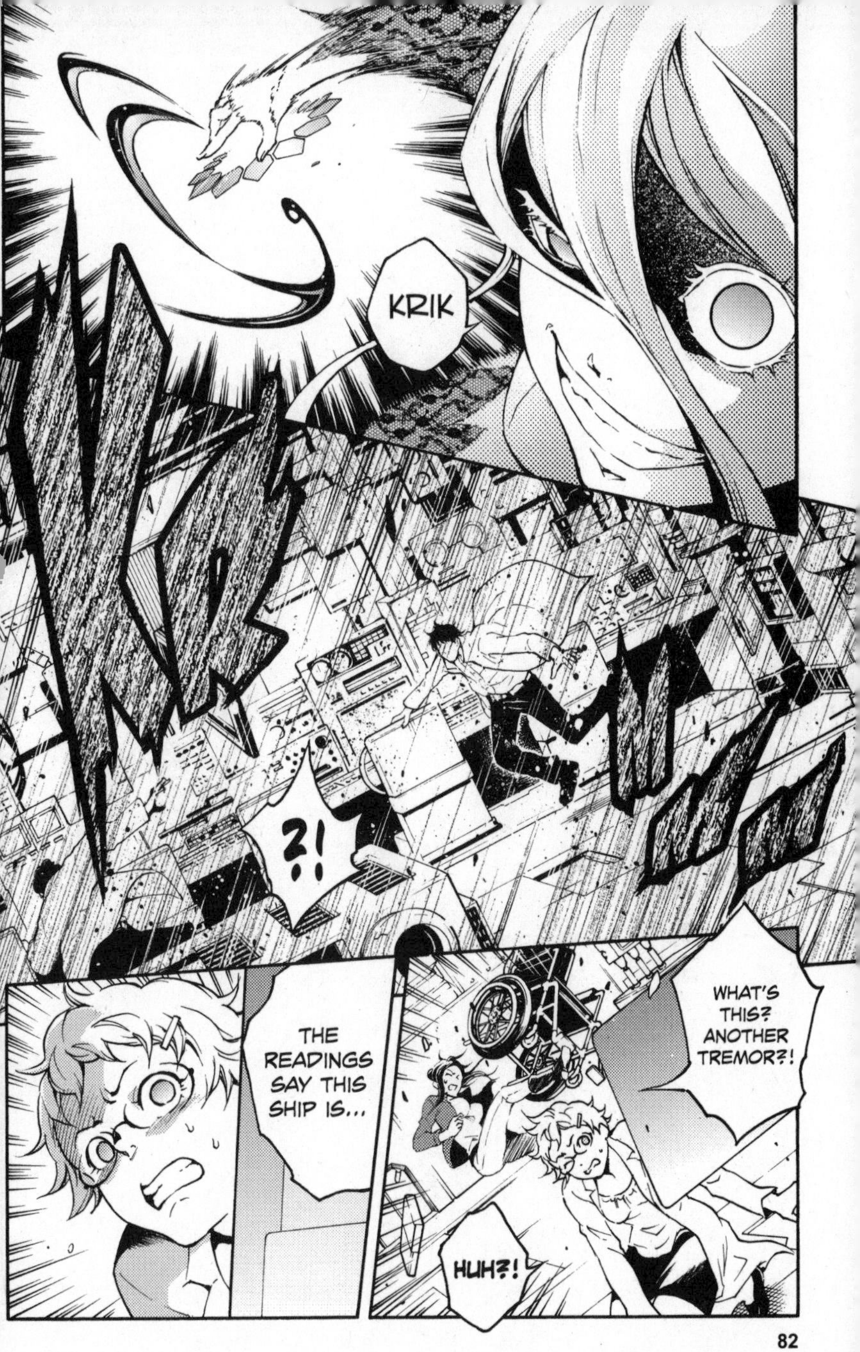
KRIK
?!
WHAT'S THIS? ANOTHER TREMOR?!
HUH?!
THE READINGS SAY THIS SHIP IS...

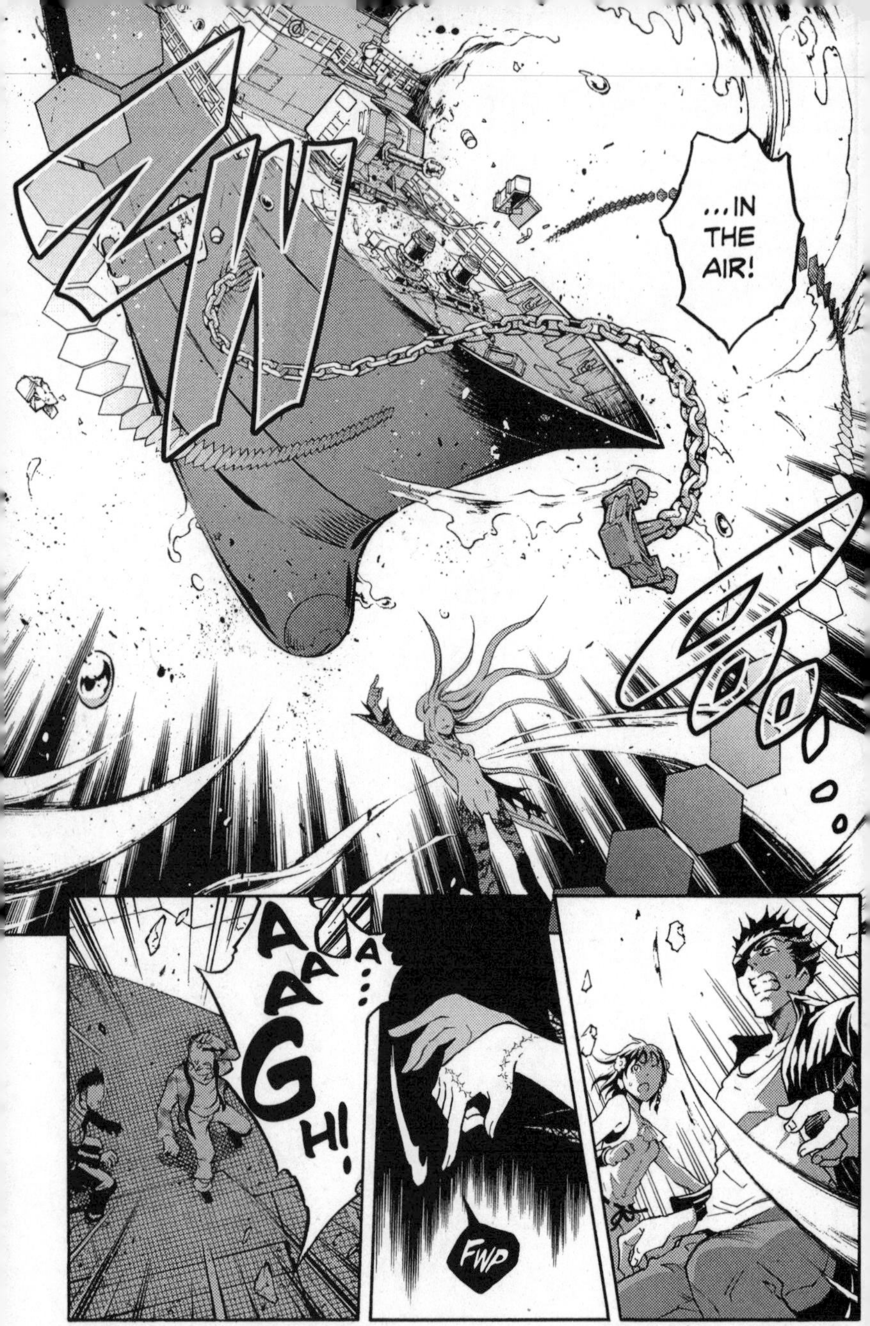
...IN THE AIR!
FWP
AAAAGH!...

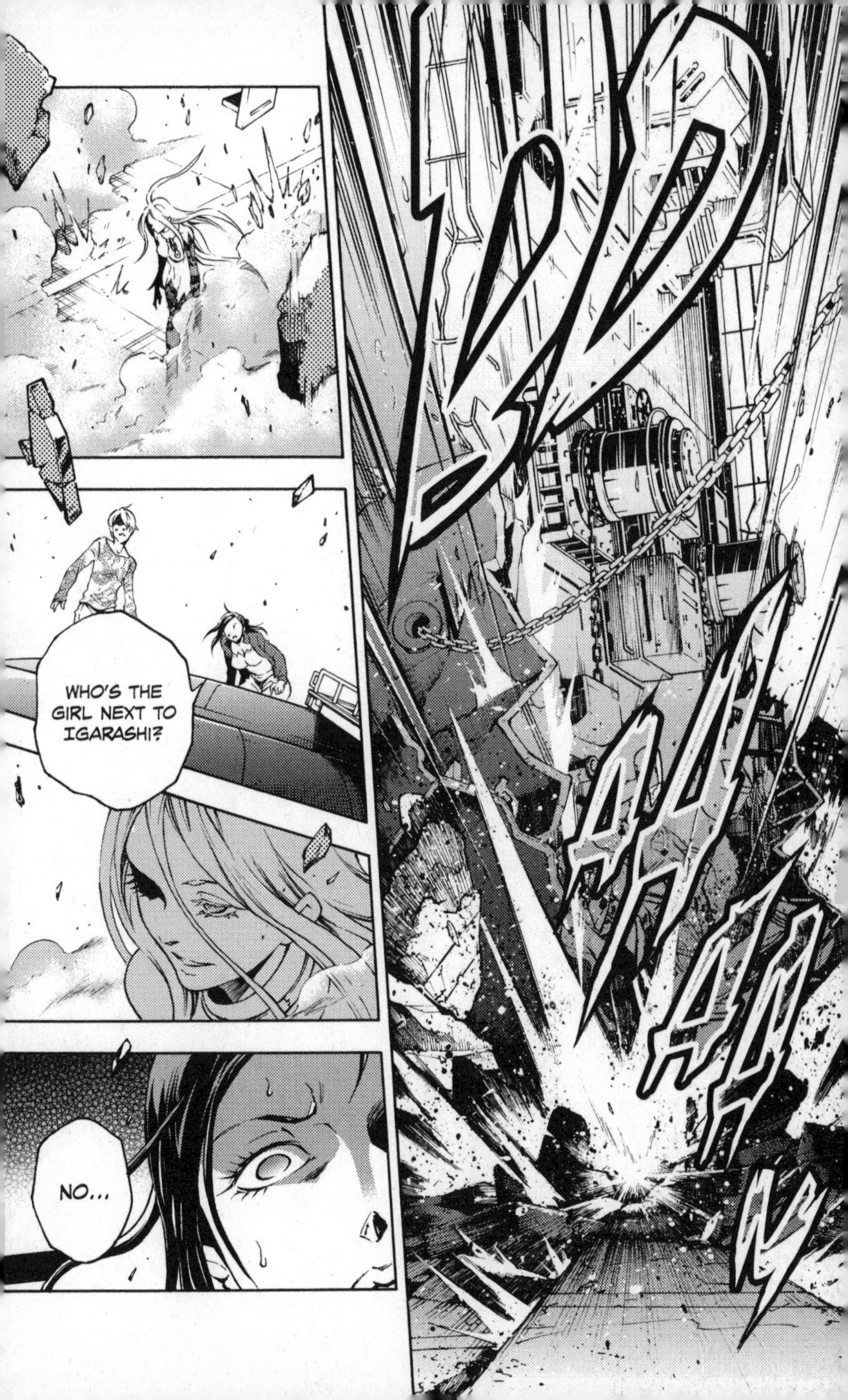
WHO'S THE GIRL NEXT TO IGARASHI?
NO...

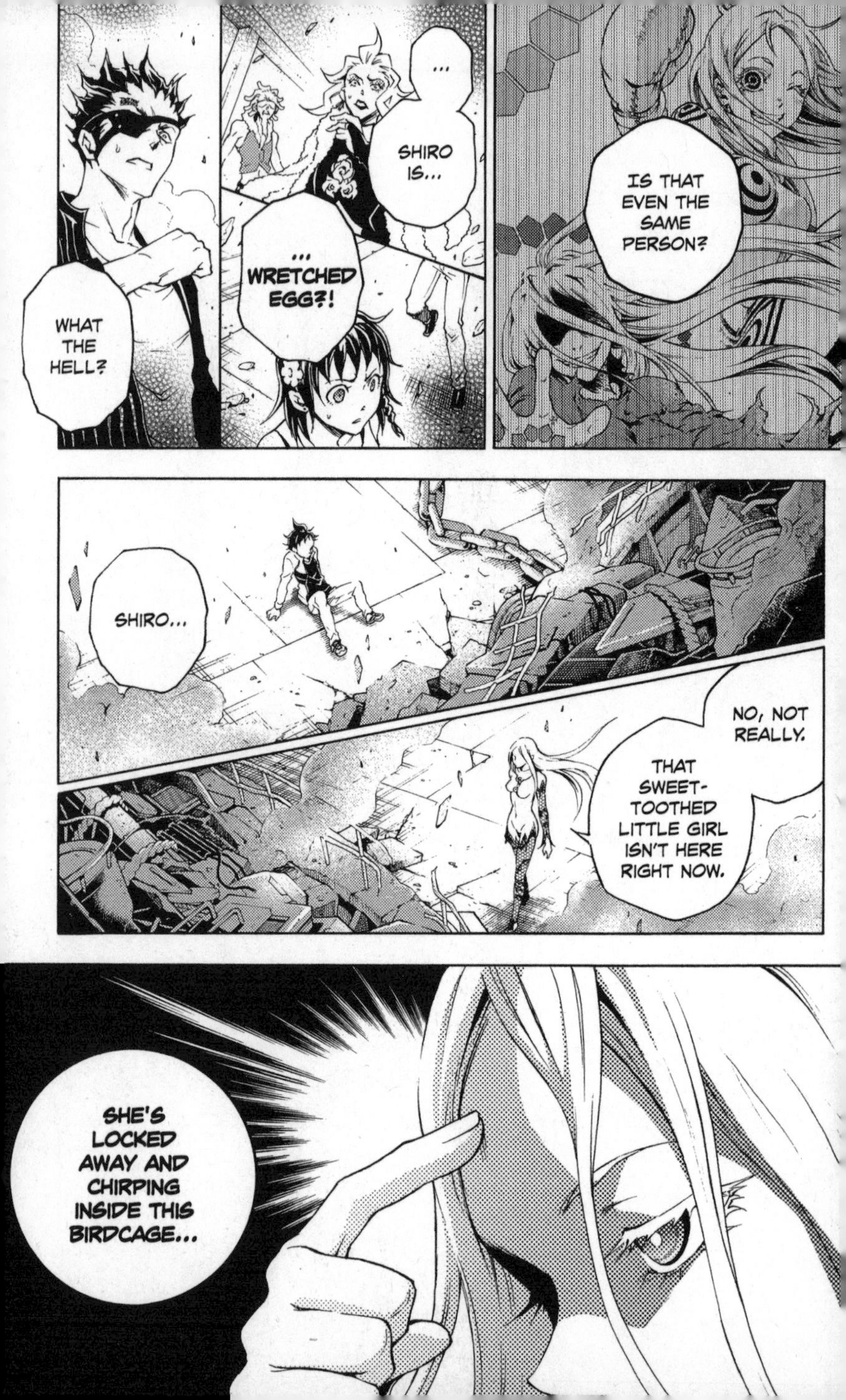
IS THAT EVEN THE SAME PERSON?
...
SHIRO IS...
...WRETCHED EGG?!
WHAT THE HELL?
SHIRO...
NO, NOT REALLY.
THAT SWEET-TOOTHED LITTLE GIRL ISN'T HERE RIGHT NOW.
SHE'S LOCKED AWAY AND CHIRPING INSIDE THIS BIRDCAGE...

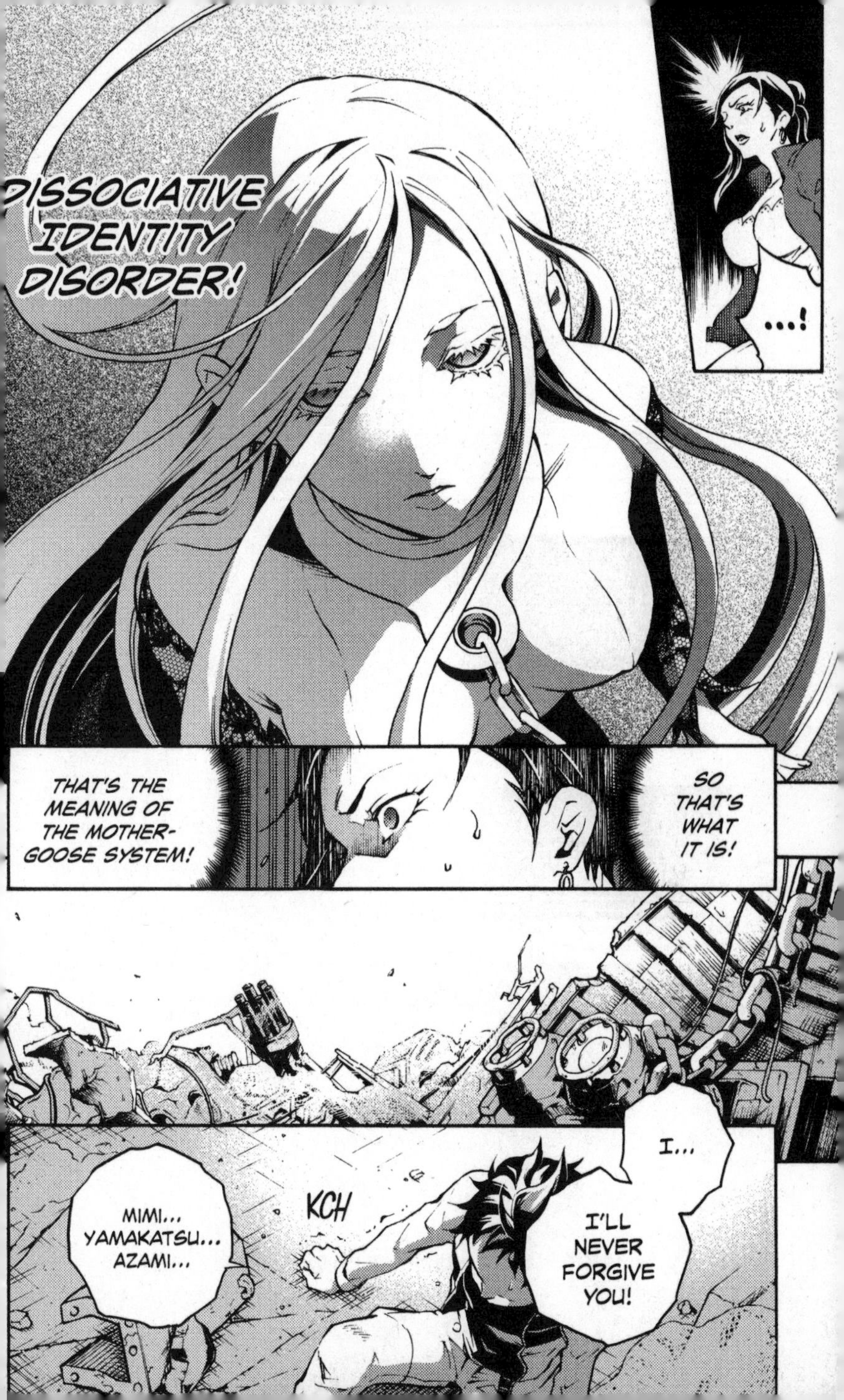
...!
DISSOCIATIVE IDENTITY DISORDER!
SO THAT'S WHAT IT IS!
THAT'S THE MEANING OF THE MOTHER-GOOSE SYSTEM!
I...
I'LL NEVER FORGIVE YOU!
KCH
MIMI... YAMAKATSU... AZAMI...

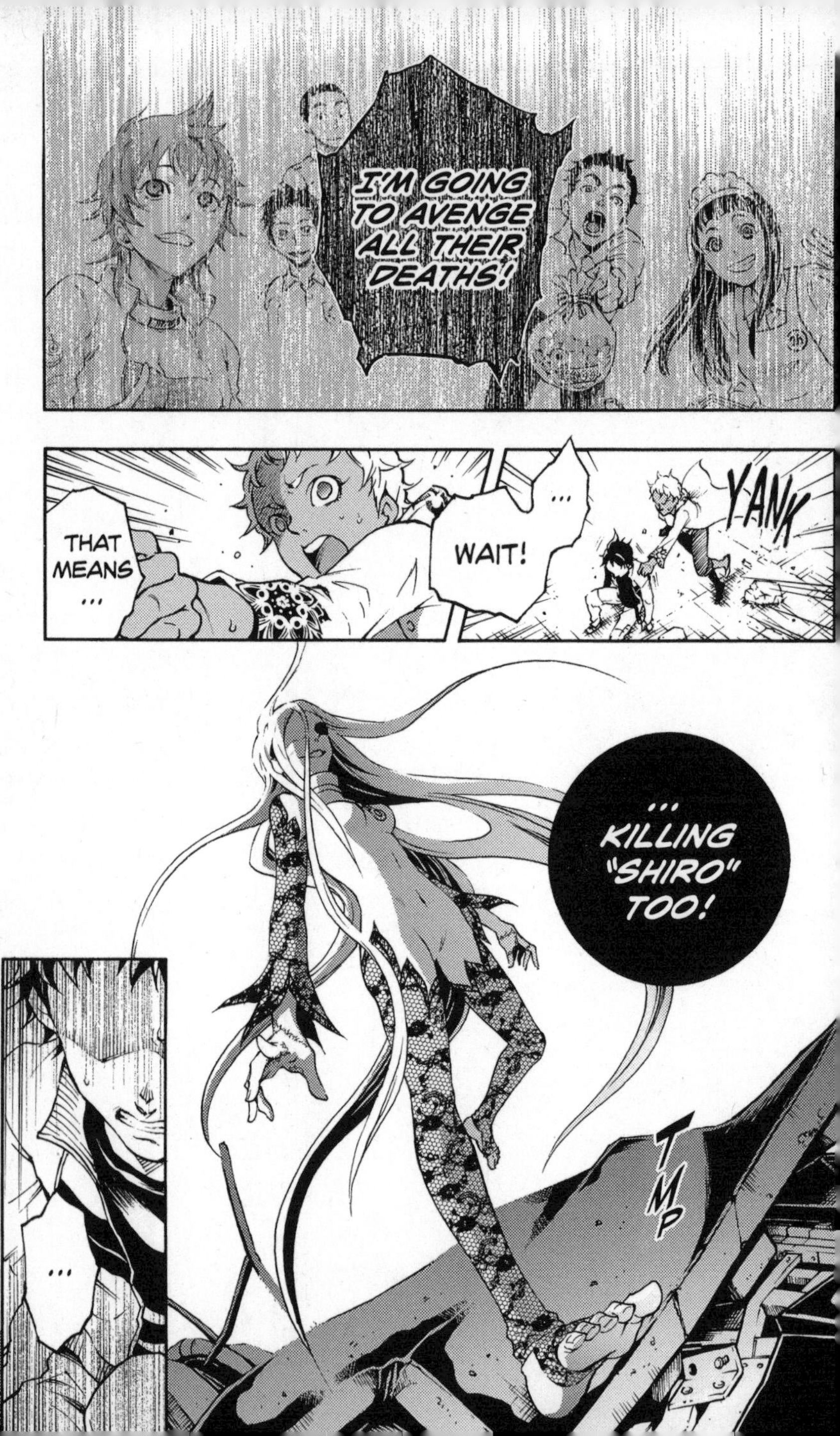
I'M GOING TO AVENGE ALL THEIR DEATHS!
...
WAIT!
YANK
THAT MEANS ...
... KILLING "SHIRO" TOO!
TMP
...

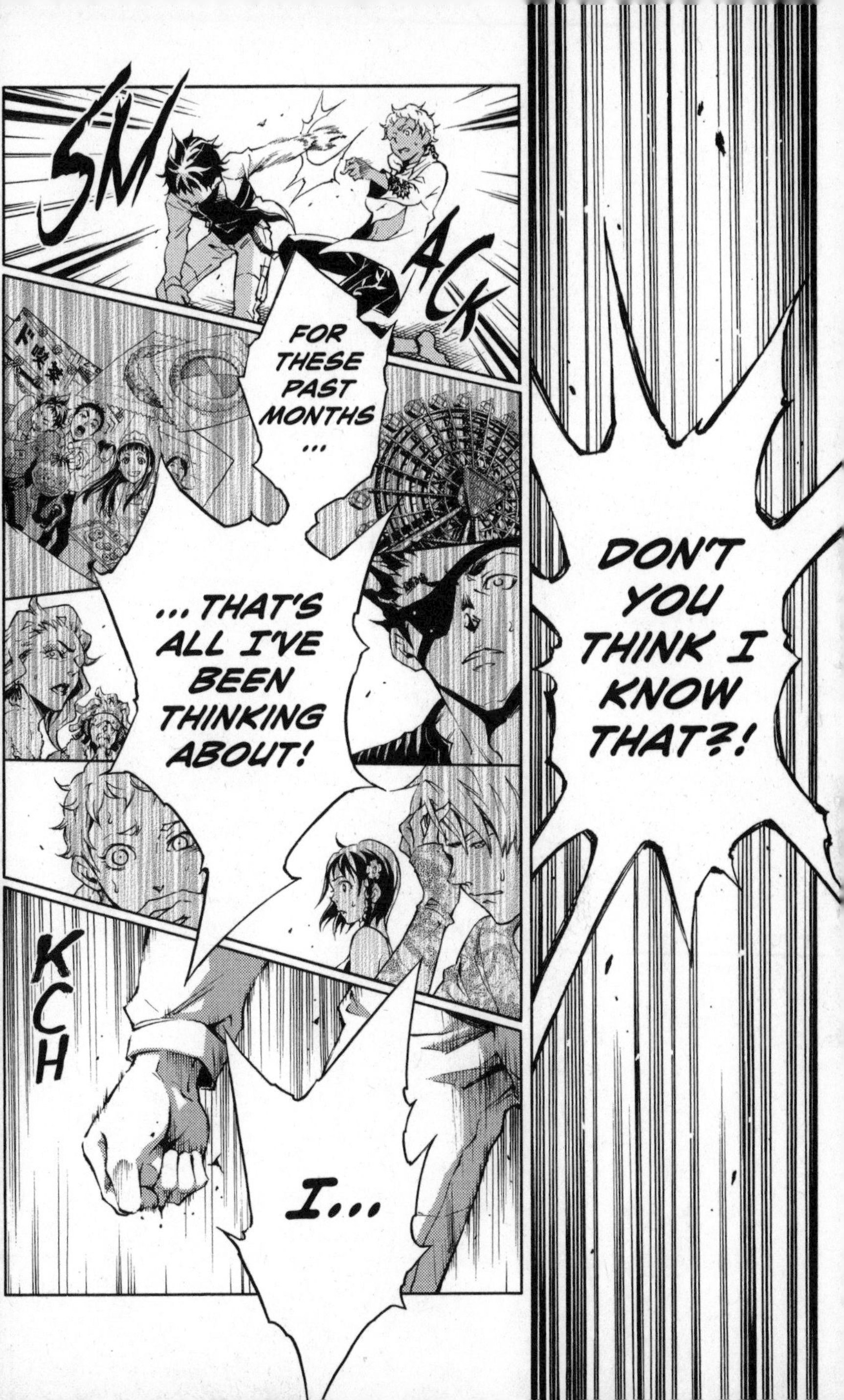
DON'T YOU THINK I KNOW THAT?!
SMACK
FOR THESE PAST MONTHS...
...THAT'S ALL I'VE BEEN THINKING ABOUT!
KCH
I...

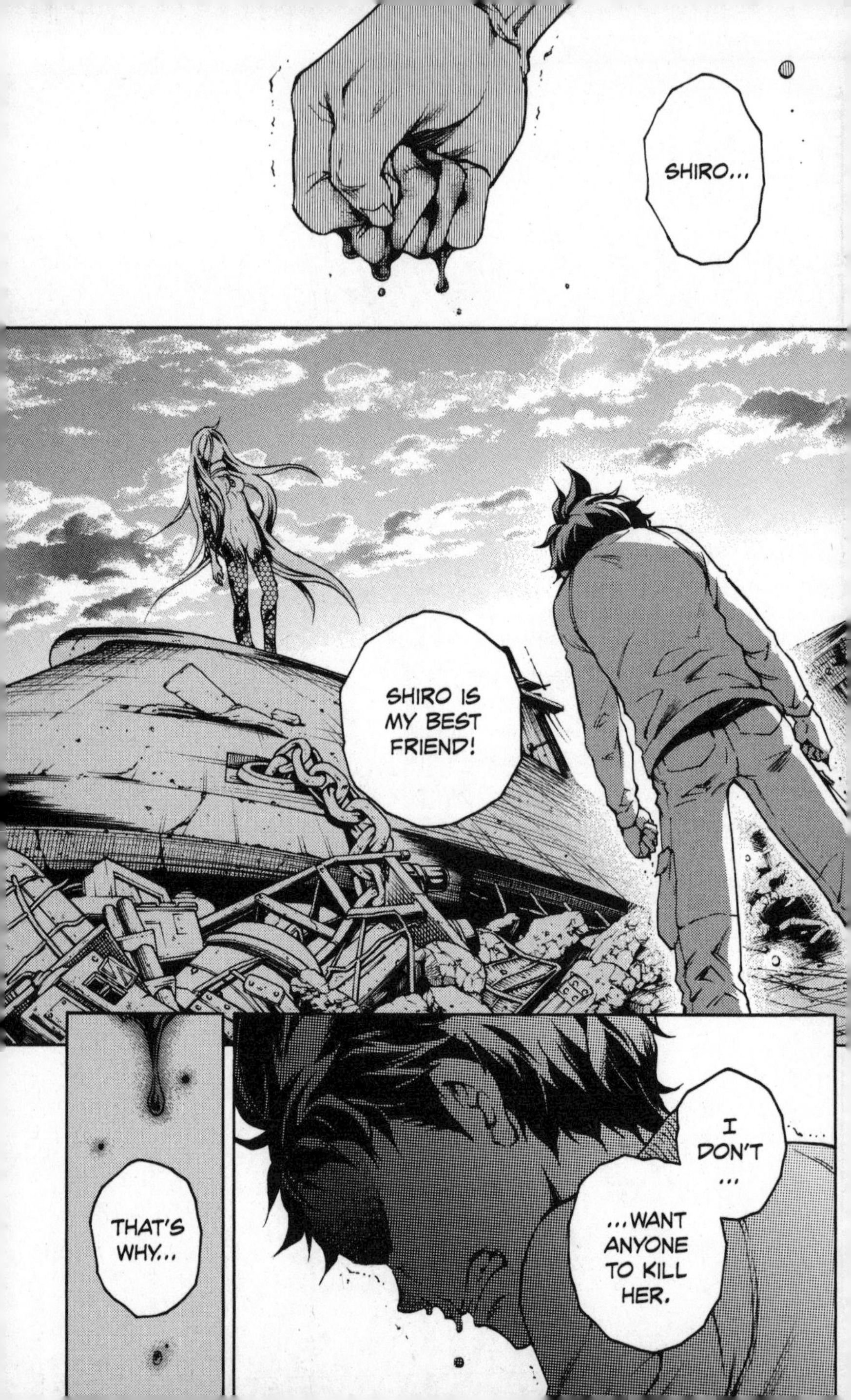
SHIRO...
SHIRO IS MY BEST FRIEND!
I DON'T ...
...WANT ANYONE TO KILL HER.
THAT'S WHY...

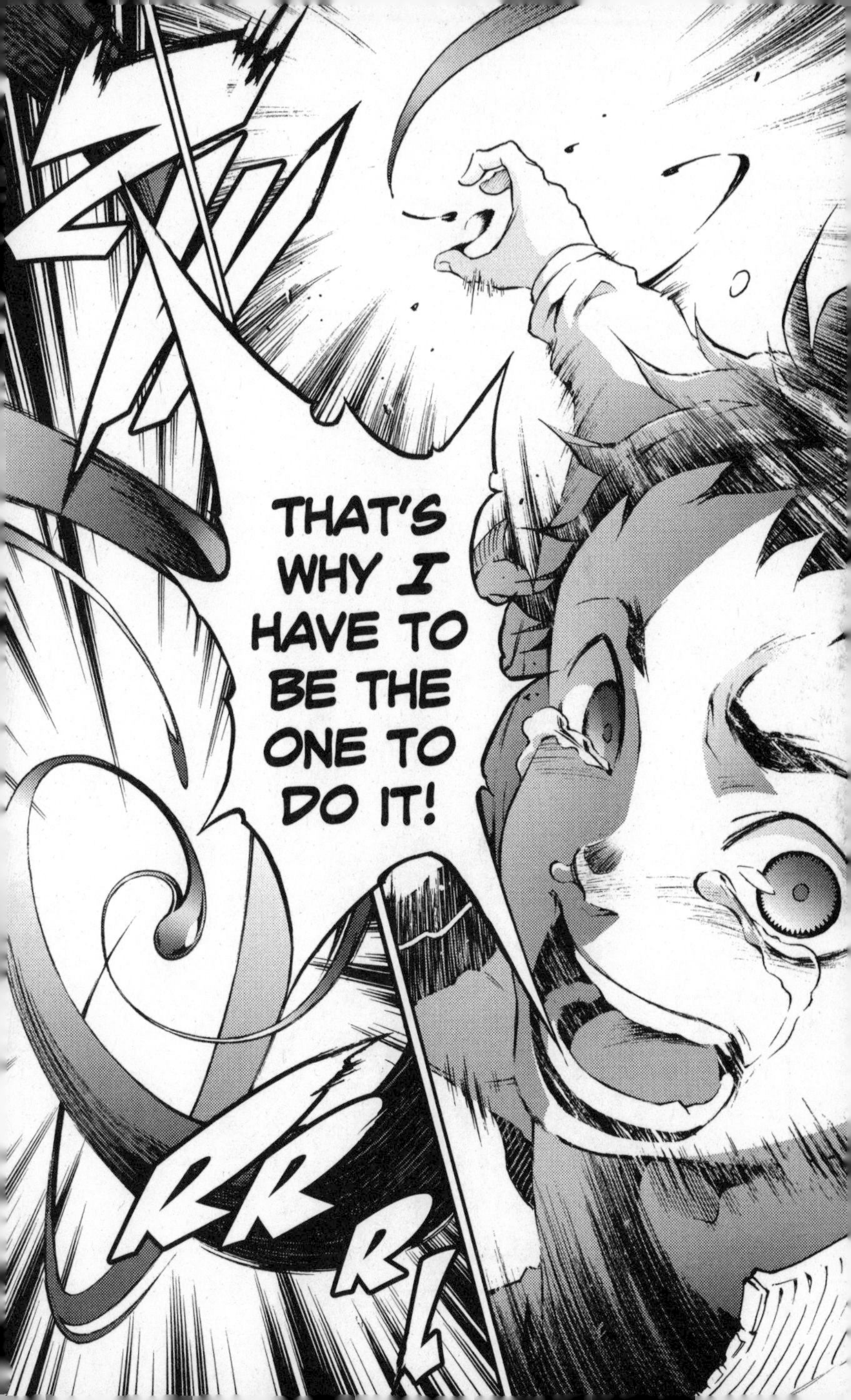
THAT'S WHY I HAVE TO BE THE ONE TO DO IT!
KRRK!

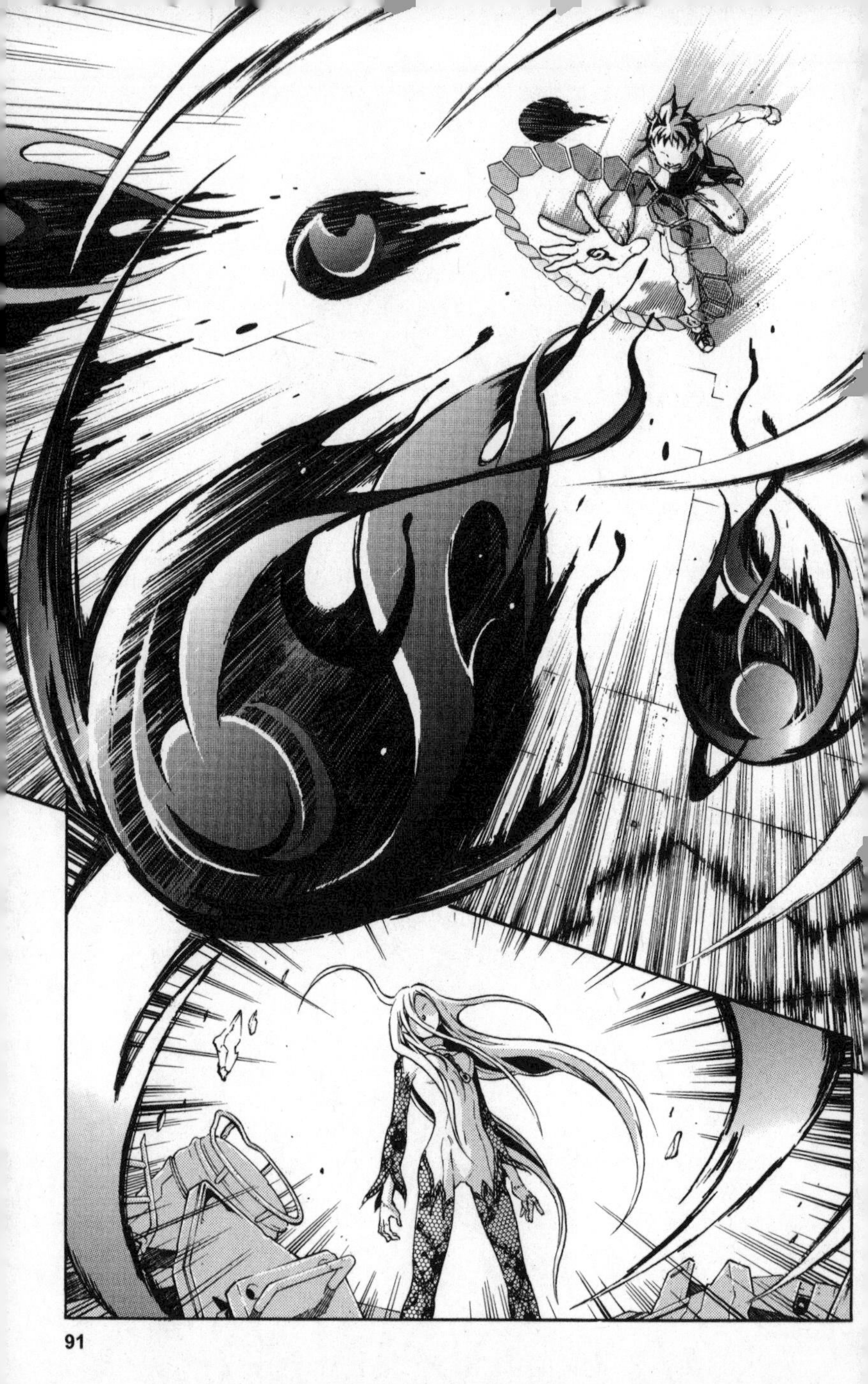

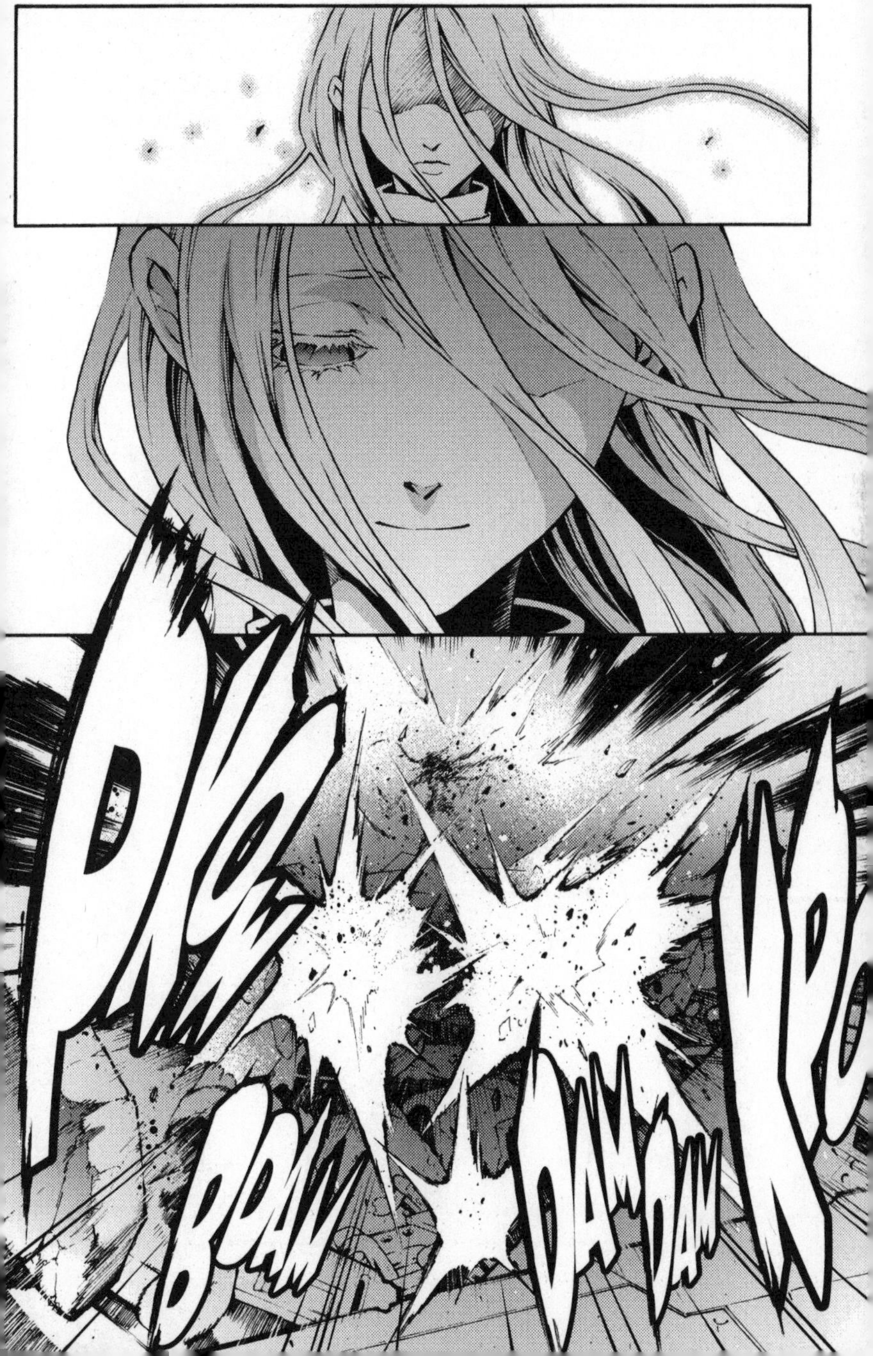
DAM
DAM
BDAM

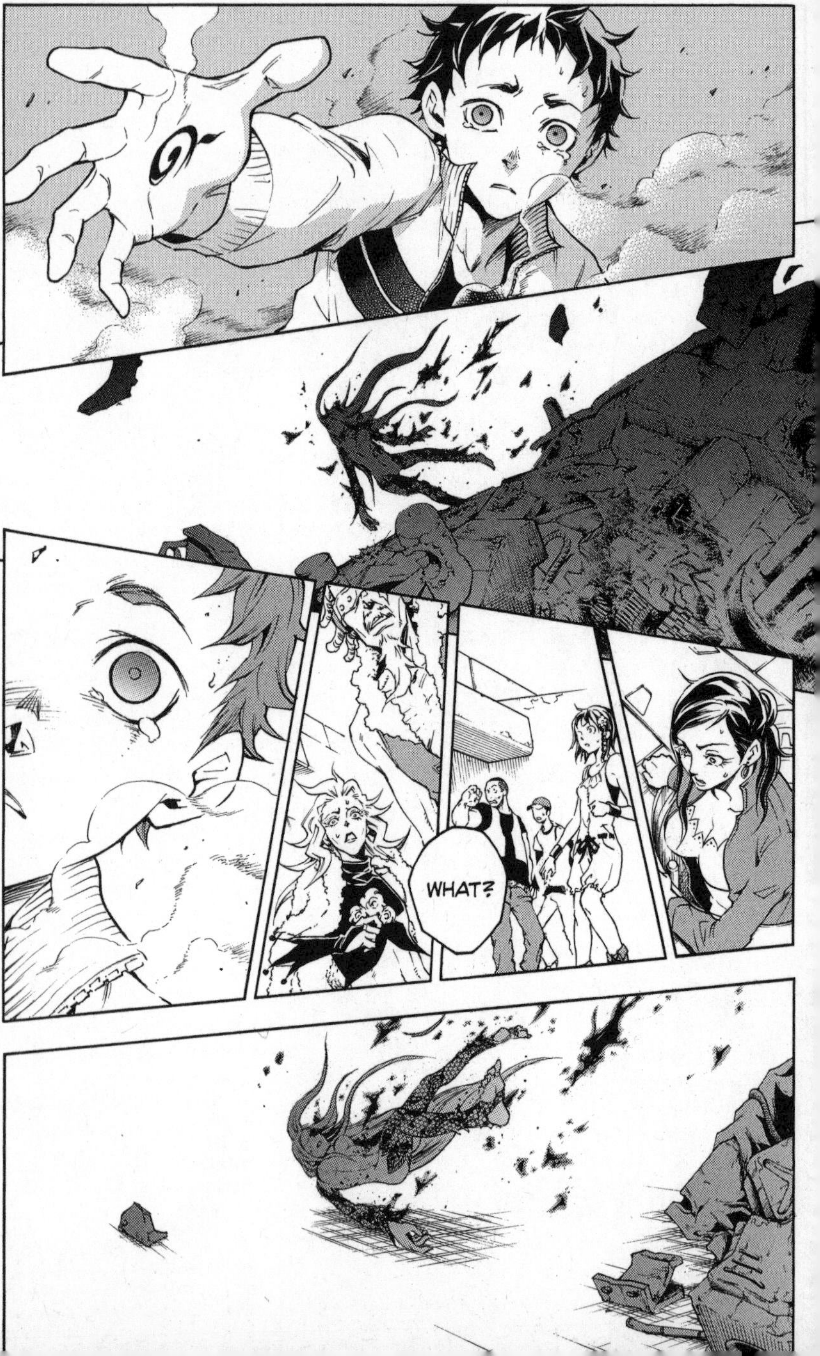
WHAT?

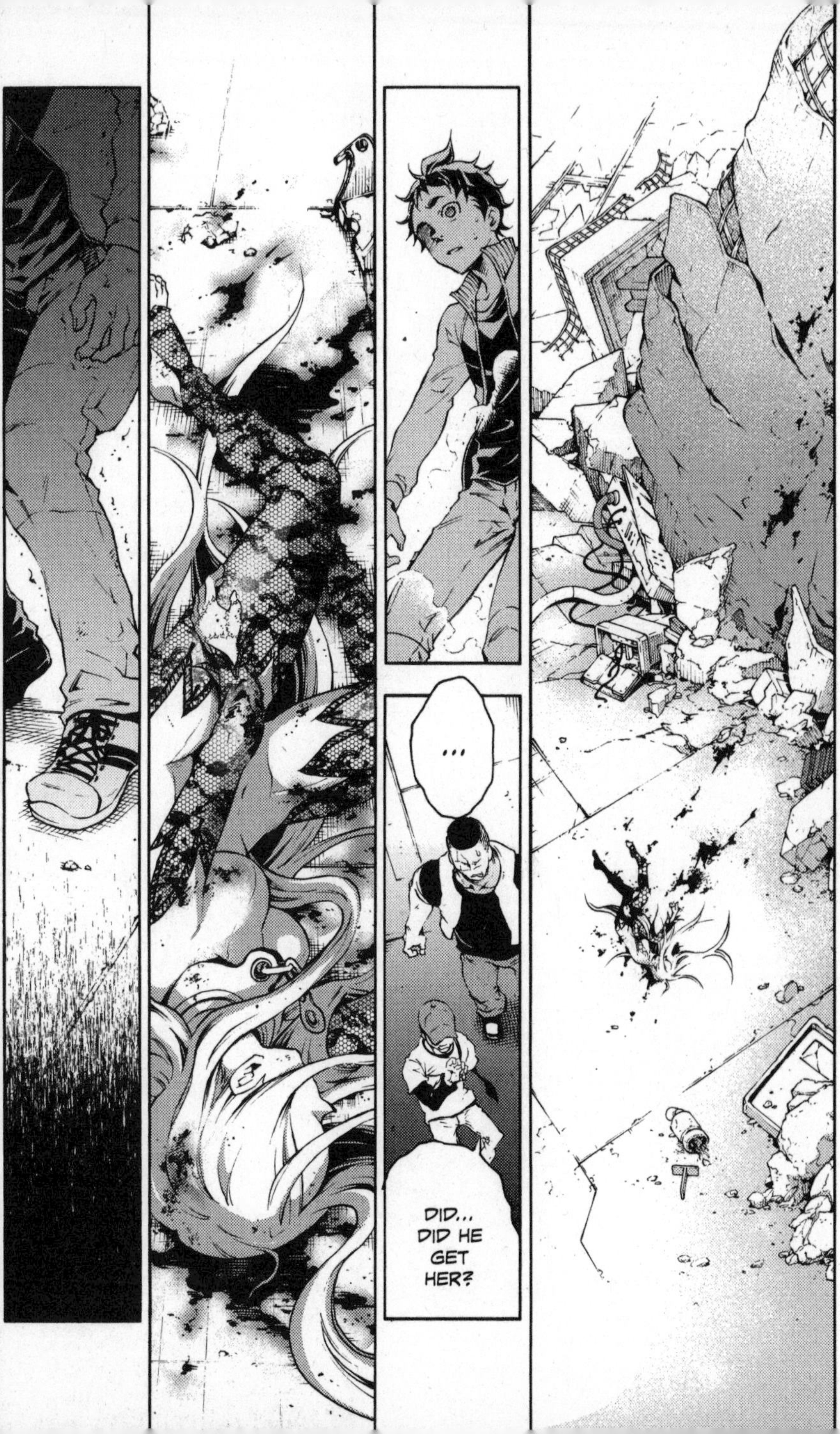
...
DID... DID HE GET HER?

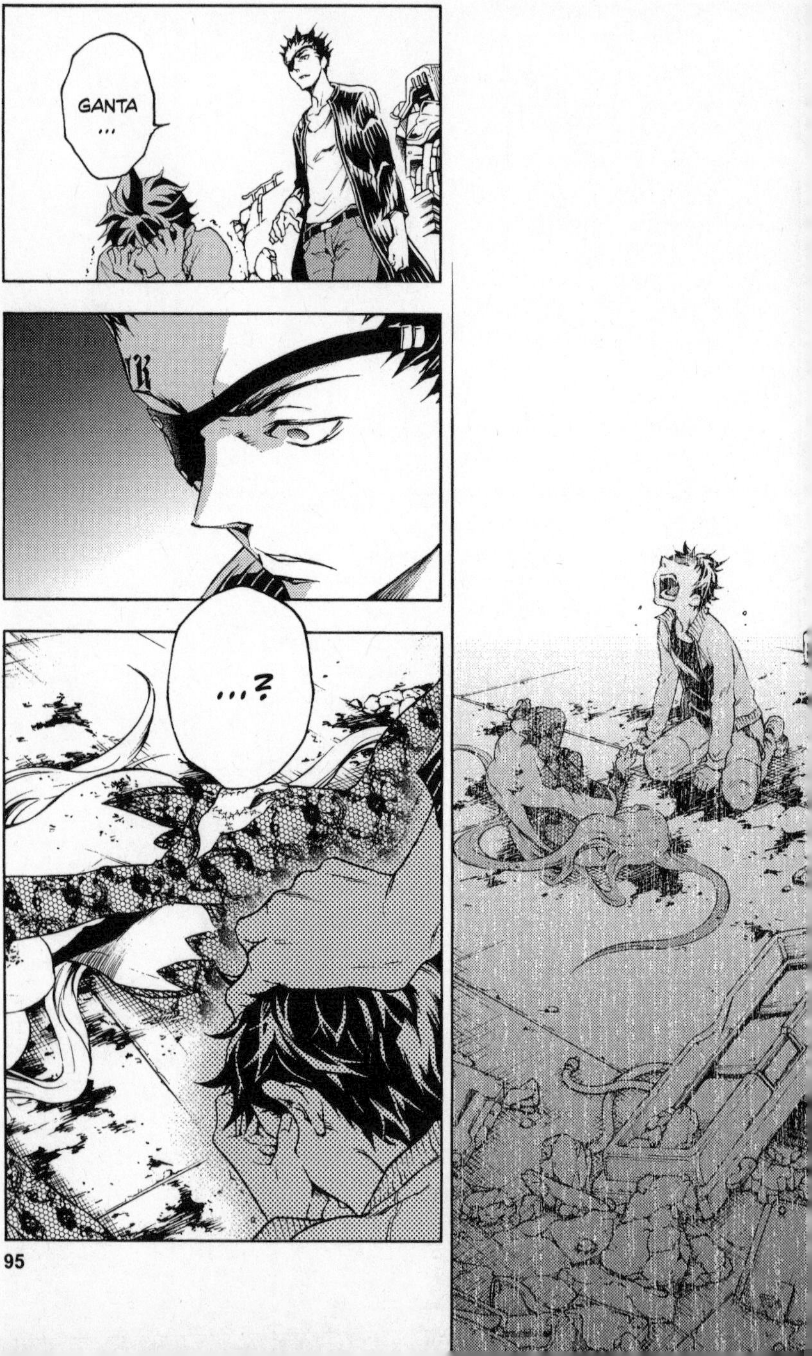
GANTA ...
...?

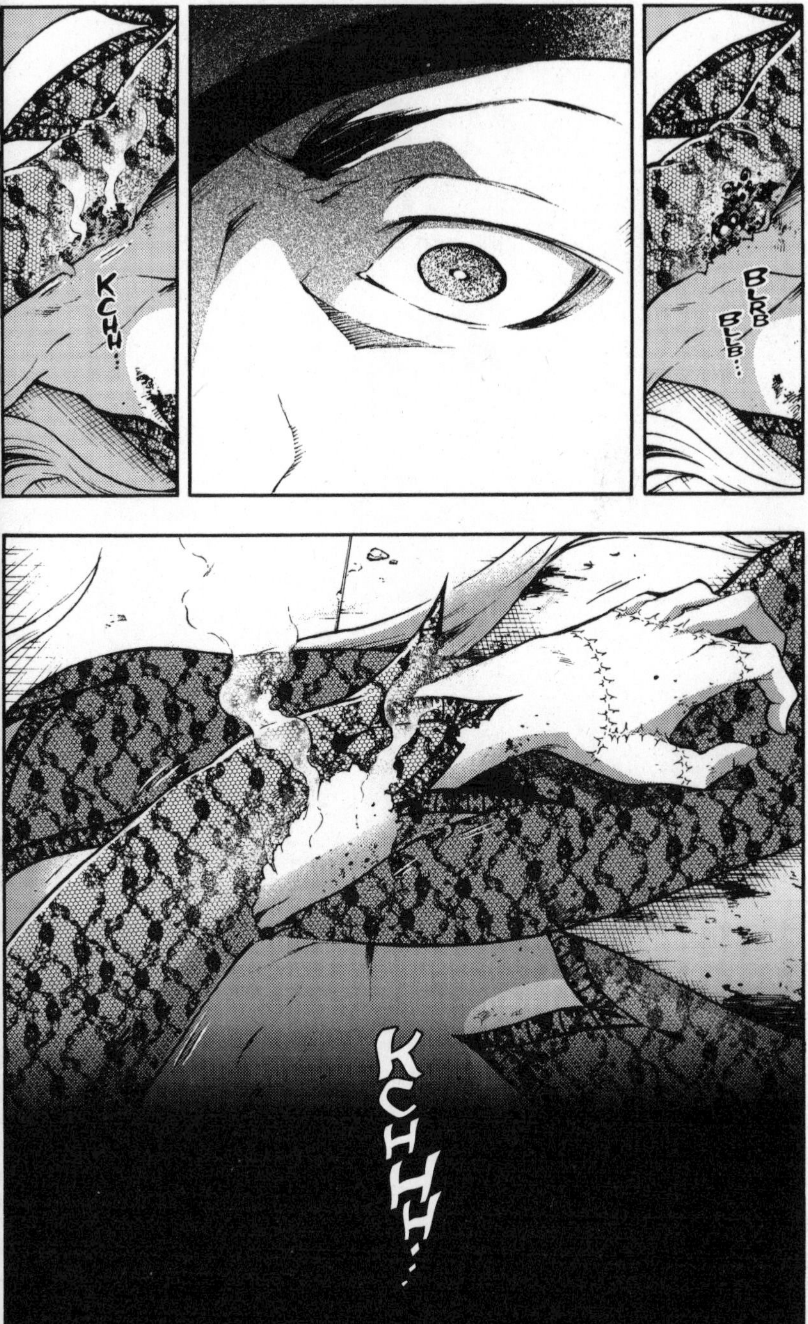
BLRB BLLB...
KCHH...
KCHHH...

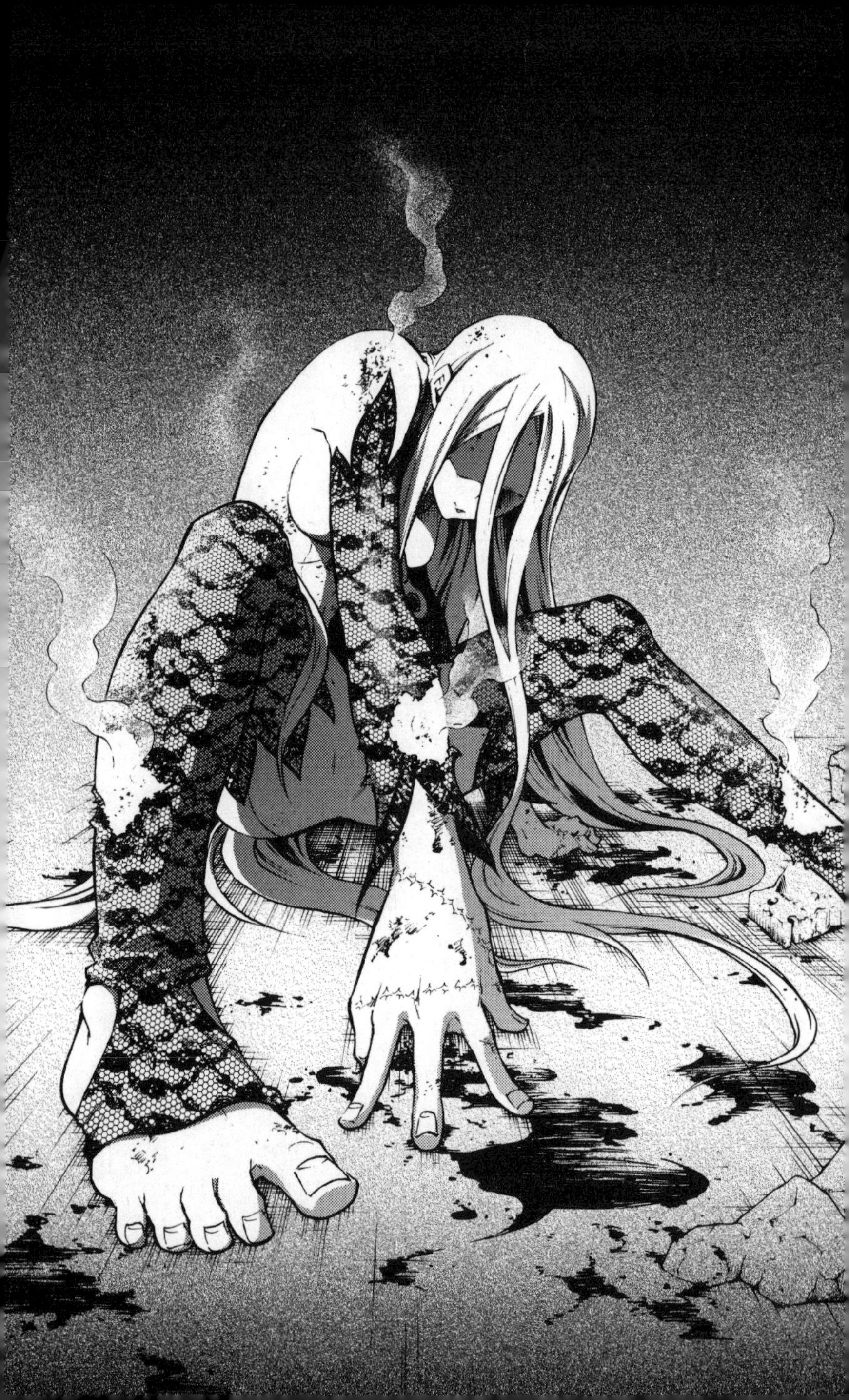

EADMA

ONDE

LAND

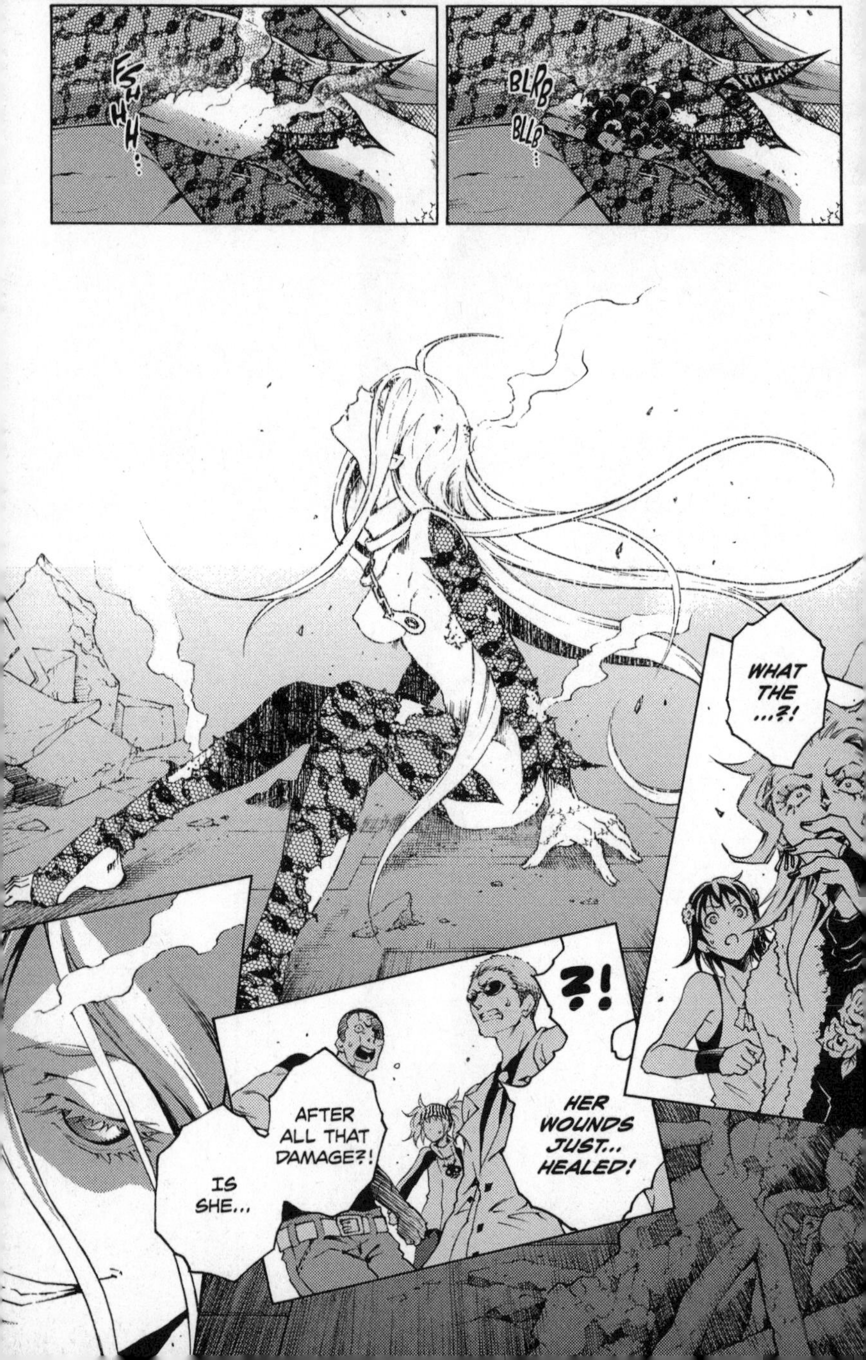
BLRB
BLLB...
FSHHH...
WHAT THE ...?!
?!
HER WOUNDS JUST... HEALED!
AFTER ALL THAT DAMAGE?!
IS SHE...

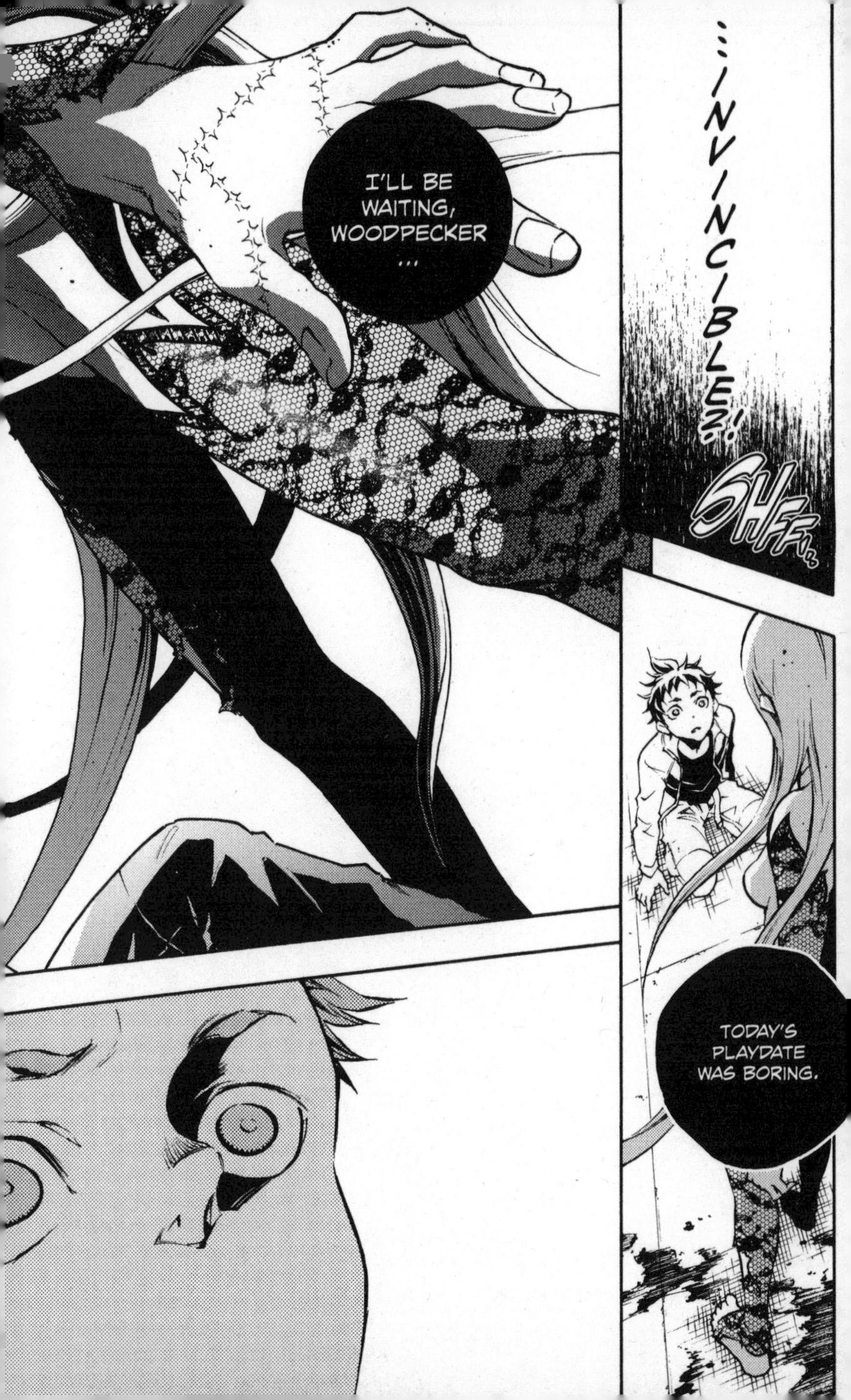
...INVINCIBLE...!
SHFF
I'LL BE WAITING, WOODPECKER...
TODAY'S PLAYDATE WAS BORING.

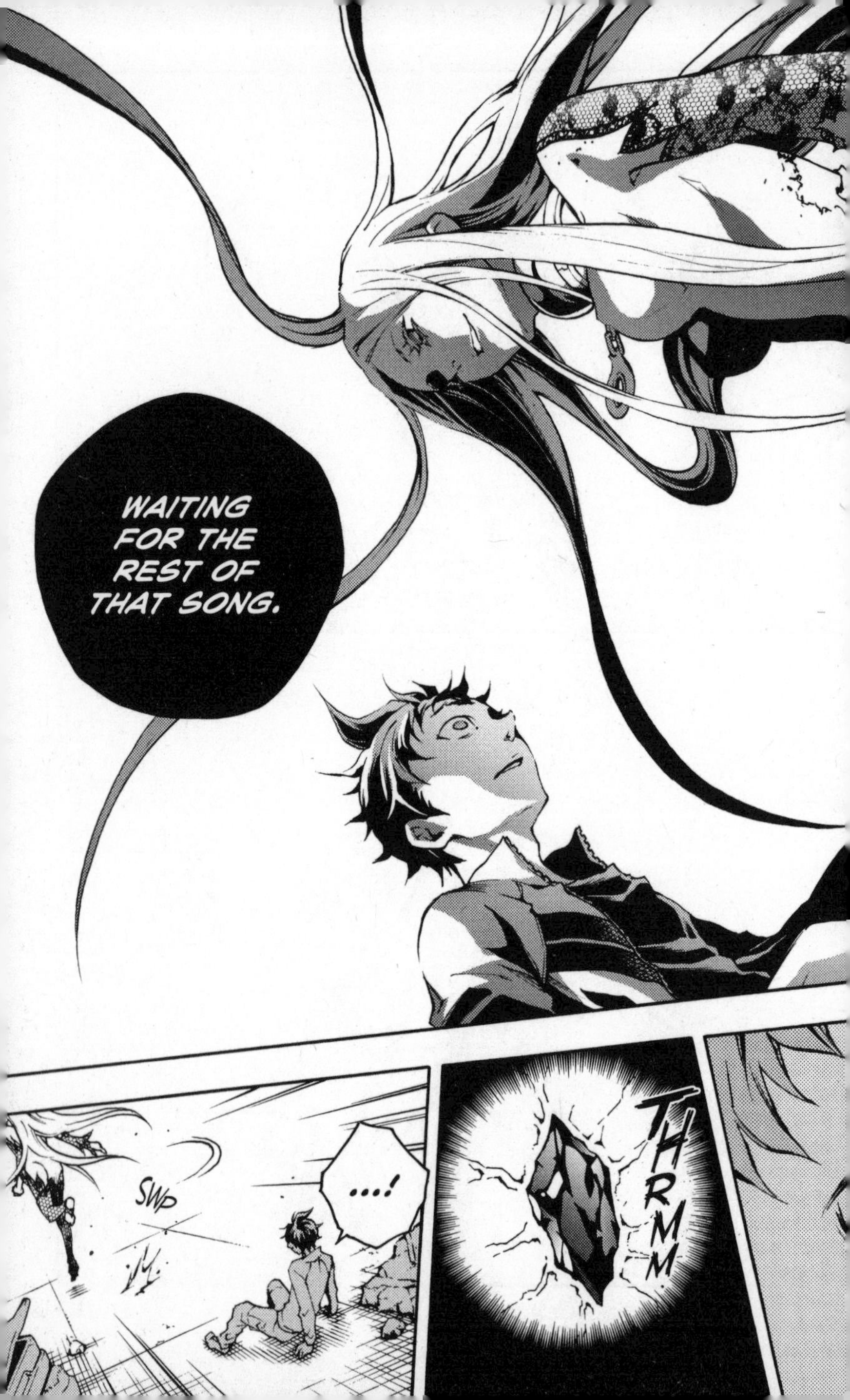
WAITING FOR THE REST OF THAT SONG.
THRMM
...!
SWP

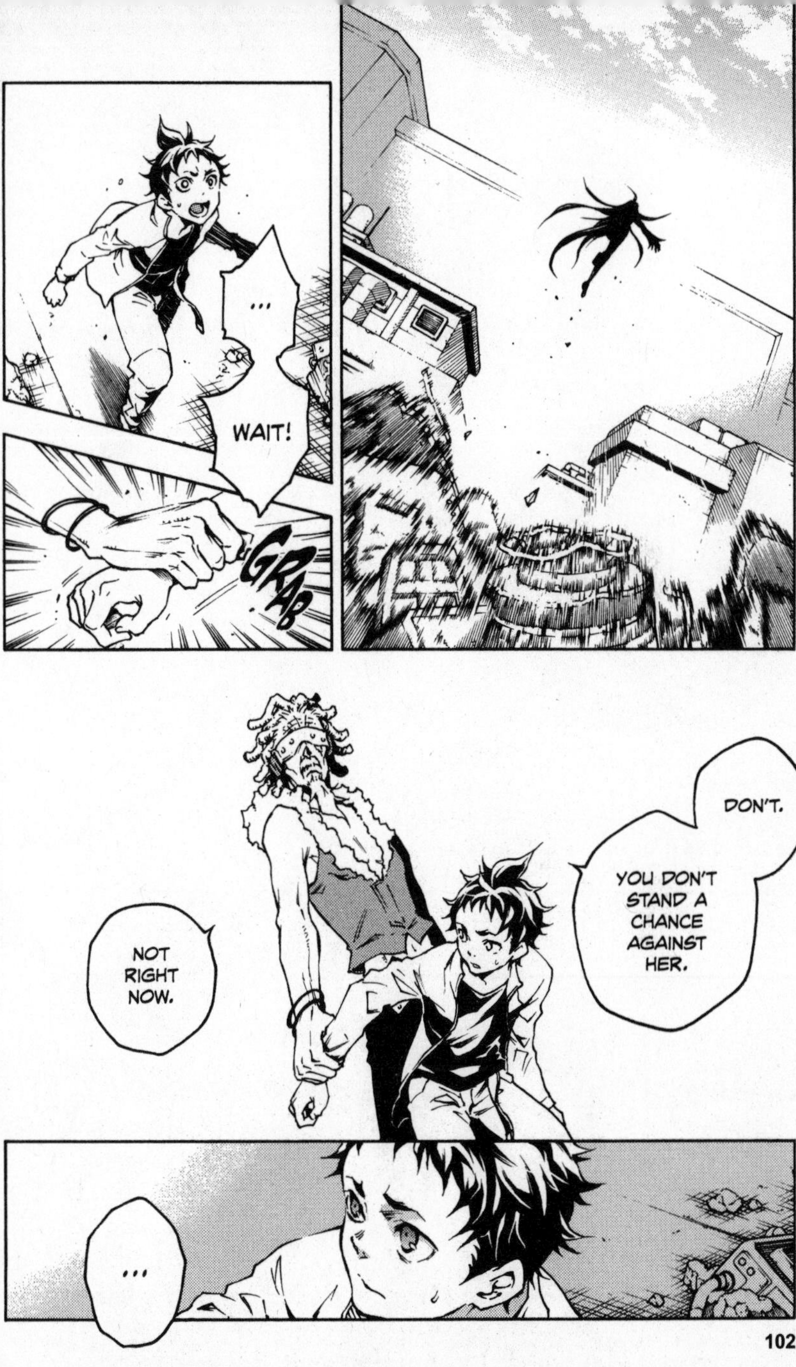
...
WAIT!
GRAB
DON'T.
YOU DON'T STAND A CHANCE AGAINST HER.
NOT RIGHT NOW.
...

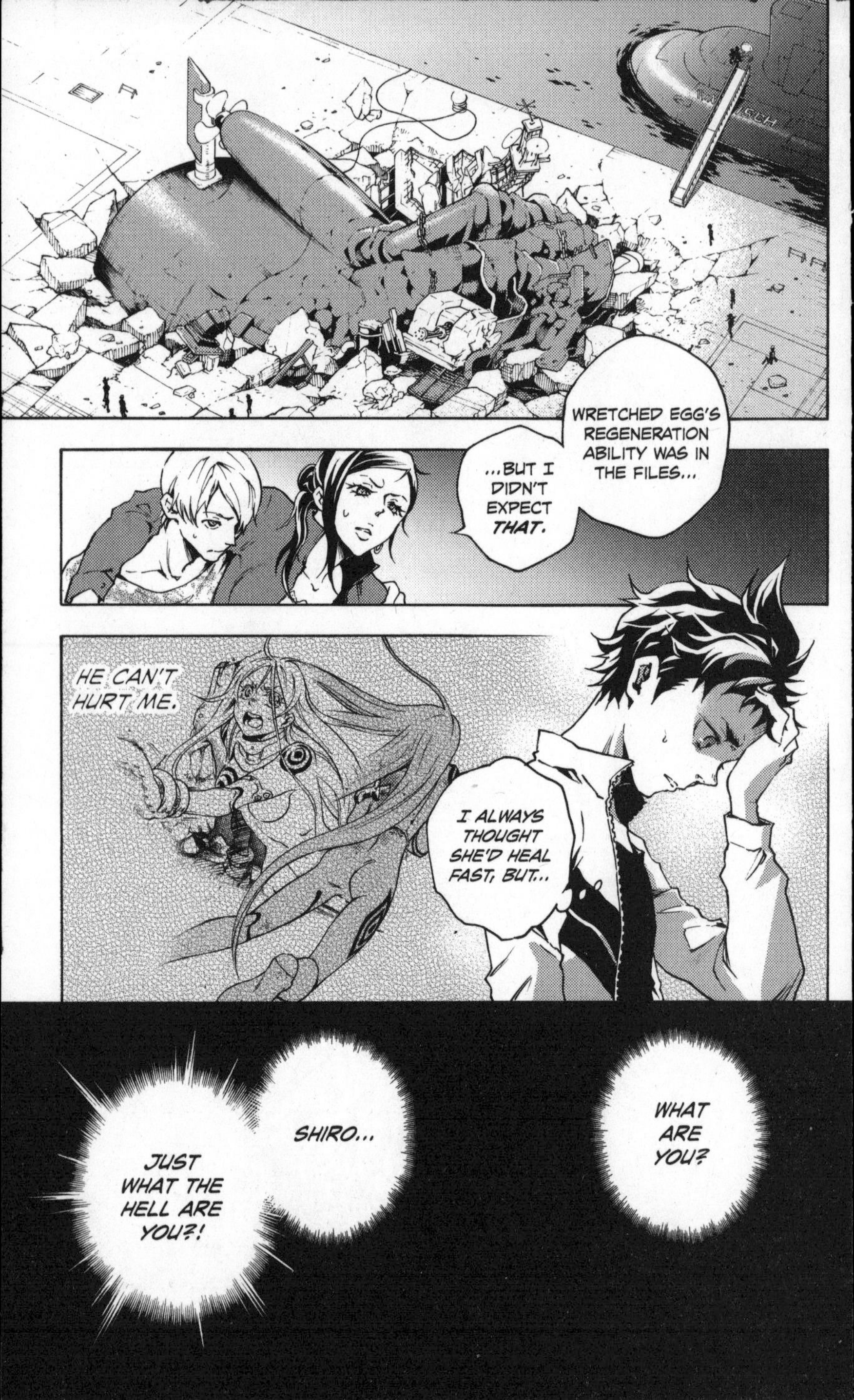
WRETCHED EGG'S REGENERATION ABILITY WAS IN THE FILES...
...BUT I DIDN'T EXPECT THAT.
I ALWAYS THOUGHT SHE'D HEAL FAST, BUT...
HE CAN'T HURT ME.
WHAT ARE YOU?
SHIRO...
JUST WHAT THE HELL ARE YOU?!

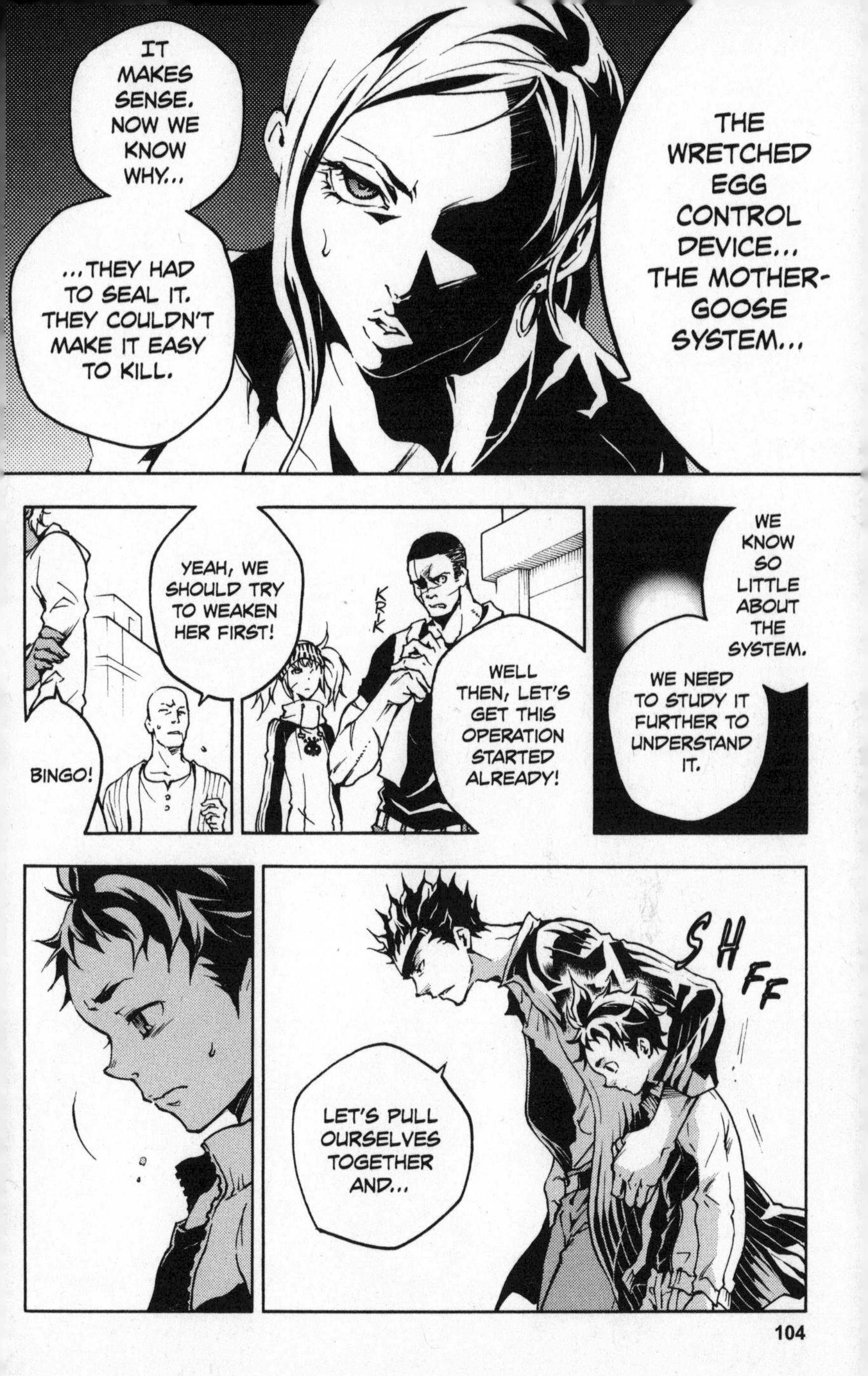
THE WRETCHED EGG CONTROL DEVICE... THE MOTHER-GOOSE SYSTEM...
IT MAKES SENSE. NOW WE KNOW WHY...
...THEY HAD TO SEAL IT. THEY COULDN'T MAKE IT EASY TO KILL.
WE KNOW SO LITTLE ABOUT THE SYSTEM.
WE NEED TO STUDY IT FURTHER TO UNDERSTAND IT.
KRIK
WELL THEN, LET'S GET THIS OPERATION STARTED ALREADY!
YEAH, WE SHOULD TRY TO WEAKEN HER FIRST!
BINGO!
SHFF
LET'S PULL OURSELVES TOGETHER AND...

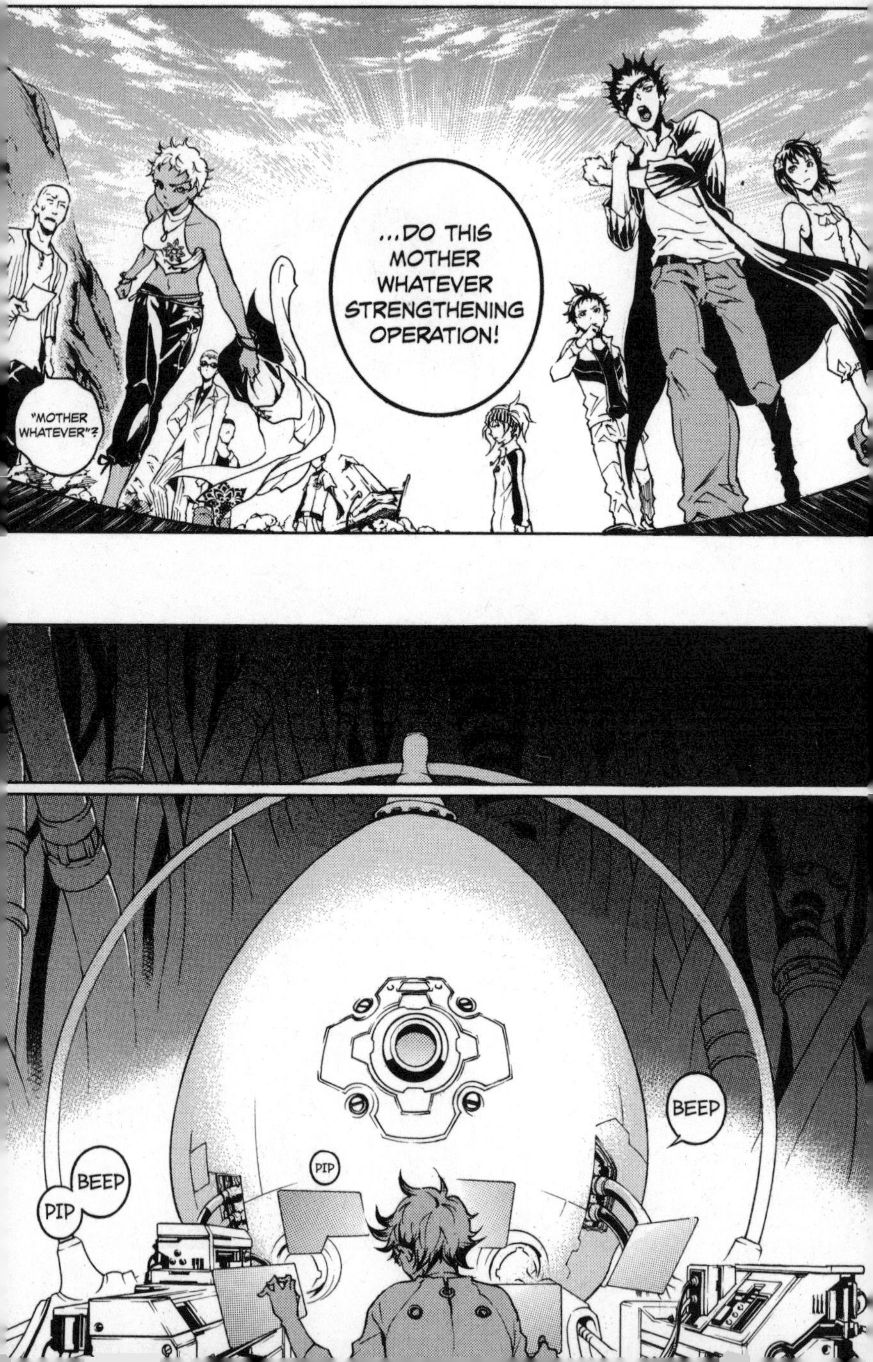
...DO THIS MOTHER WHATEVER STRENGTHENING OPERATION!
"MOTHER WHATEVER"?
BEEP
PIP
BEEP
PIP

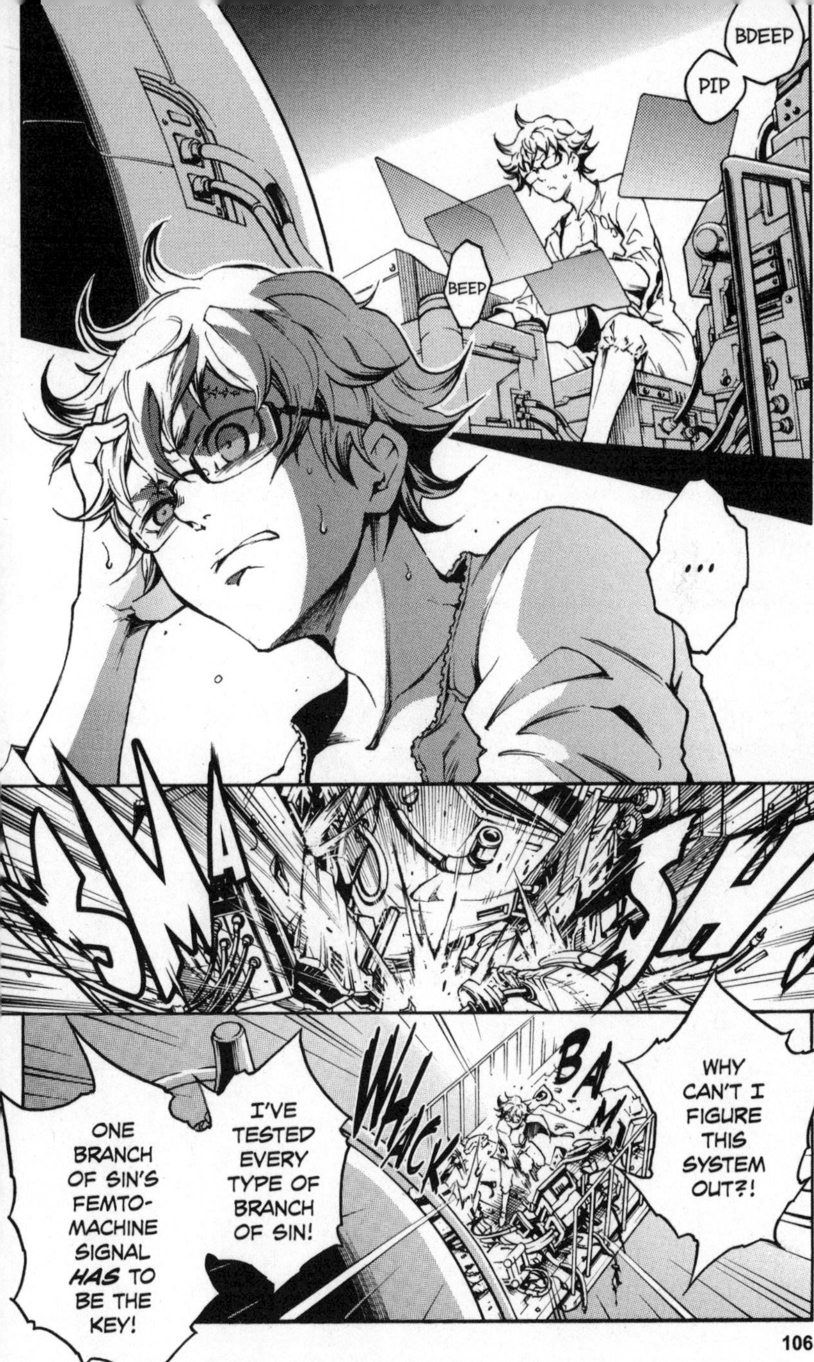
BDEEP
PIP
BEEP
...
SMASH!
WHY CAN'T I FIGURE THIS SYSTEM OUT?!
BAM
WHACK
I'VE TESTED EVERY TYPE OF BRANCH OF SIN!
ONE BRANCH OF SIN'S FEMTO-MACHINE SIGNAL ***HAS*** TO BE THE KEY!

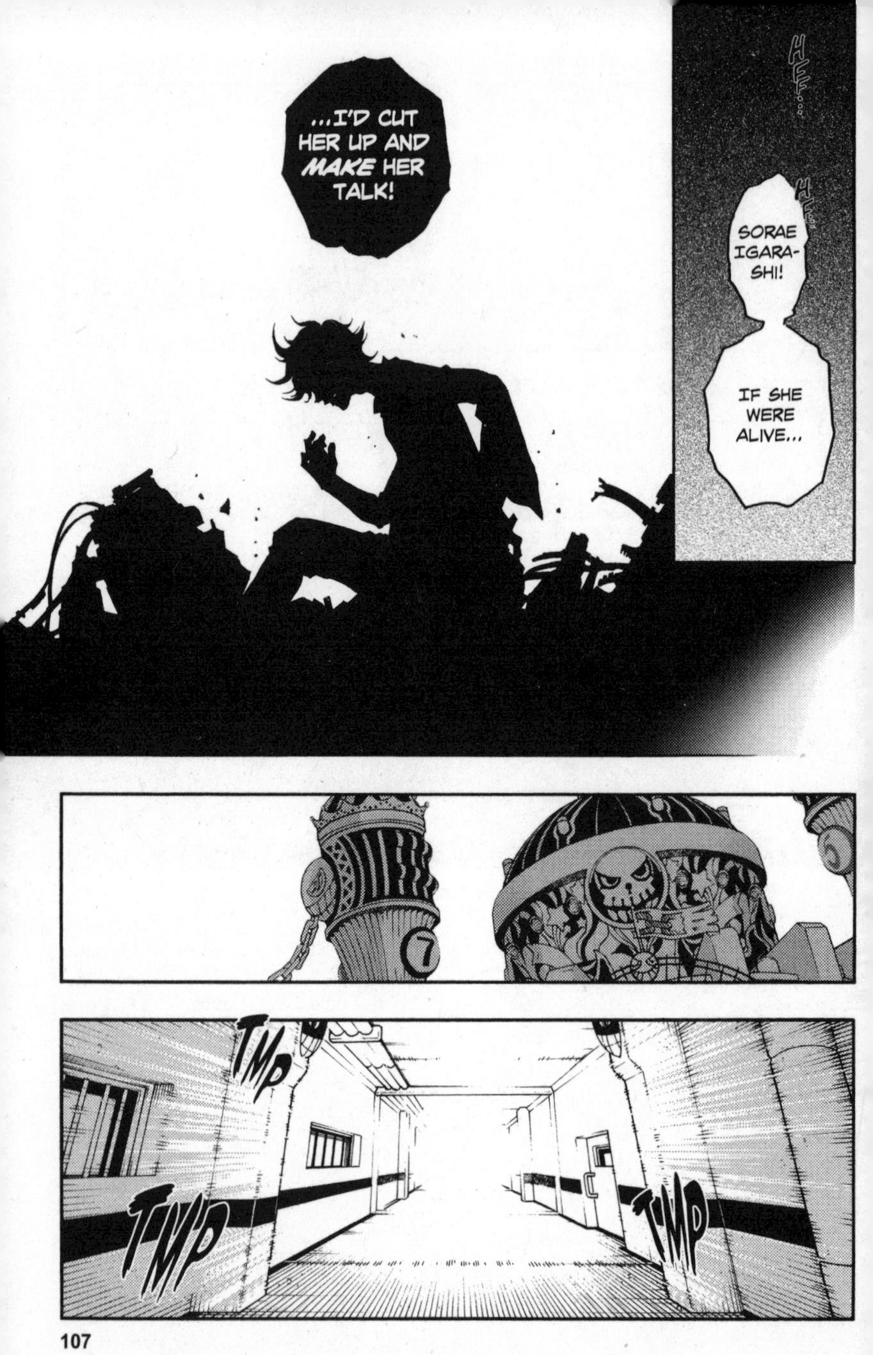
HFF...
SORAE IGARASHI!
IF SHE WERE ALIVE...
...I'D CUT HER UP AND MAKE HER TALK!
TMP
TMP
TMP

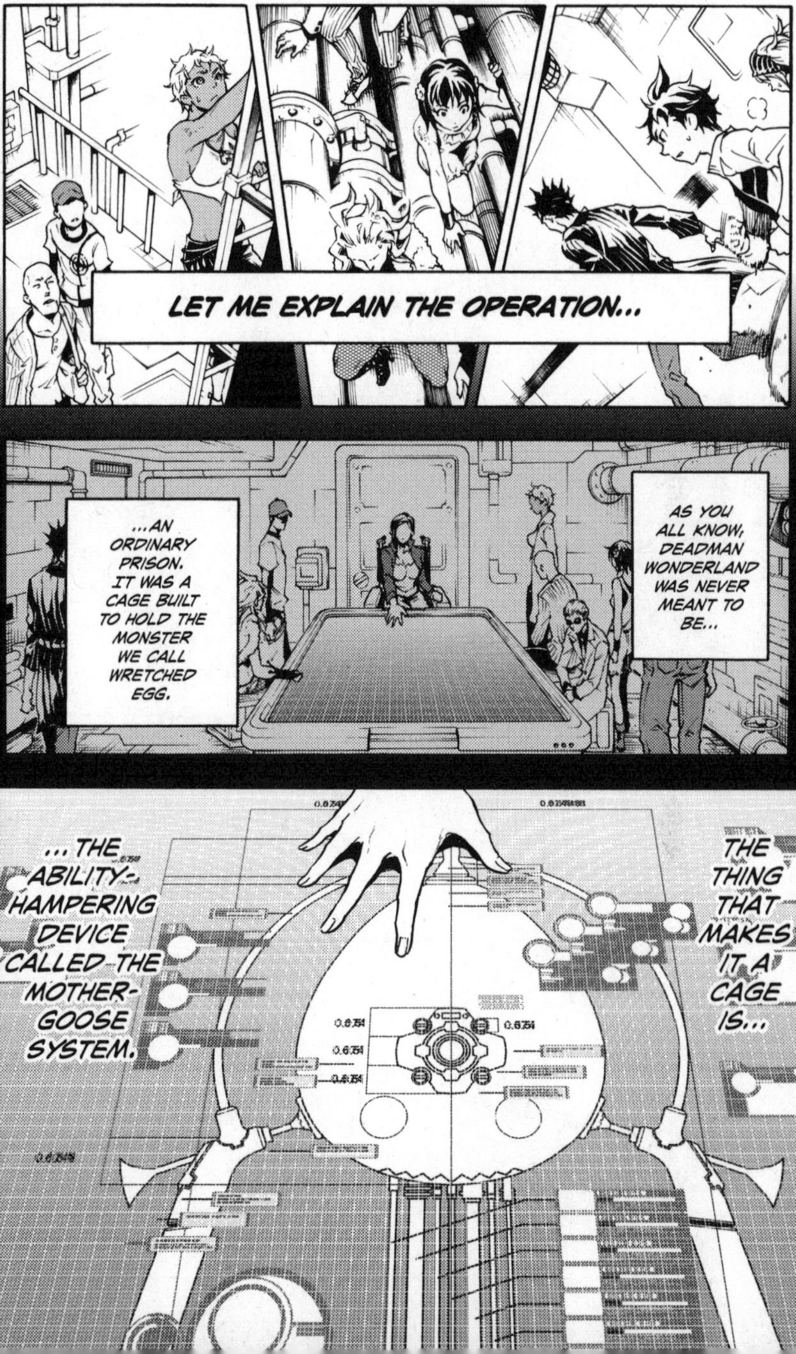
LET ME EXPLAIN THE OPERATION...
AS YOU ALL KNOW, DEADMAN WONDERLAND WAS NEVER MEANT TO BE...
...AN ORDINARY PRISON. IT WAS A CAGE BUILT TO HOLD THE MONSTER WE CALL WRETCHED EGG.
THE THING THAT MAKES IT A CAGE IS...
...THE ABILITY-HAMPERING DEVICE CALLED THE MOTHER-GOOSE SYSTEM.

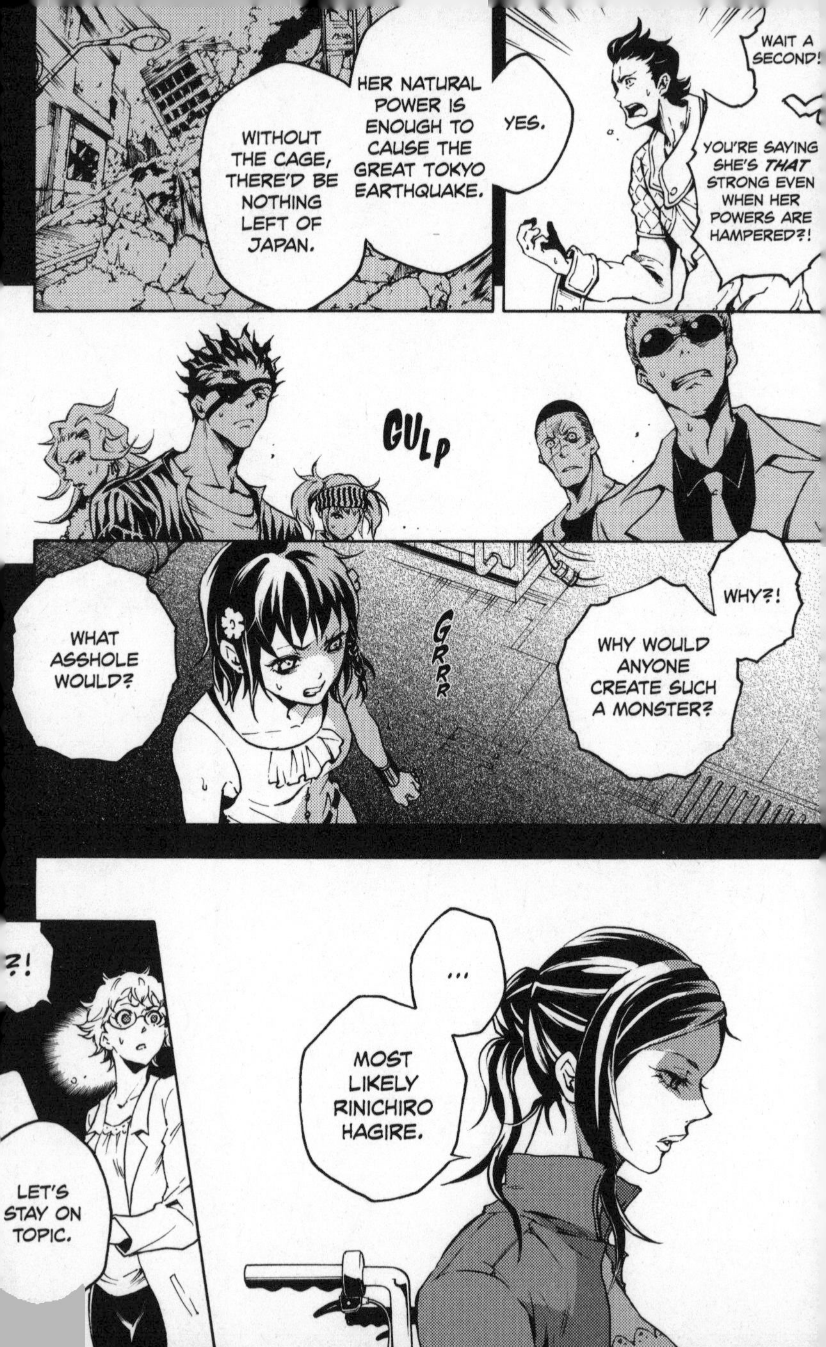
WAIT A SECOND!
YOU'RE SAYING SHE'S *THAT* STRONG EVEN WHEN HER POWERS ARE HAMPERED?!
YES.
HER NATURAL POWER IS ENOUGH TO CAUSE THE GREAT TOKYO EARTHQUAKE.
WITHOUT THE CAGE, THERE'D BE NOTHING LEFT OF JAPAN.
GULP
WHY?!
WHY WOULD ANYONE CREATE SUCH A MONSTER?
GRRR
WHAT ASSHOLE WOULD?
...
MOST LIKELY RINICHIRO HAGIRE.
?!
LET'S STAY ON TOPIC.

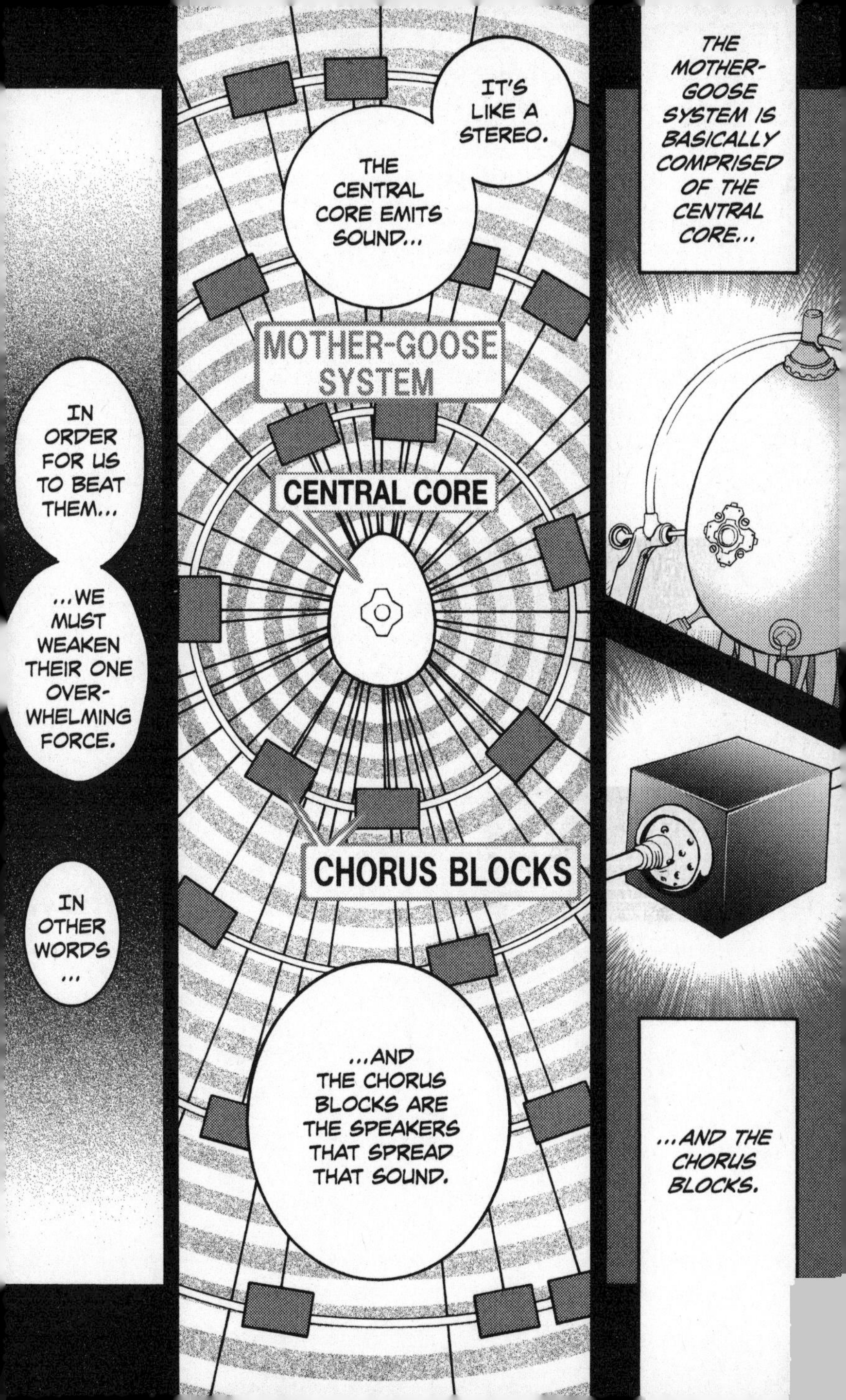
THE MOTHER-GOOSE SYSTEM IS BASICALLY COMPRISED OF THE CENTRAL CORE...
...AND THE CHORUS BLOCKS.
IT'S LIKE A STEREO.
THE CENTRAL CORE EMITS SOUND...
MOTHER-GOOSE SYSTEM
CENTRAL CORE
CHORUS BLOCKS
...AND THE CHORUS BLOCKS ARE THE SPEAKERS THAT SPREAD THAT SOUND.
IN ORDER FOR US TO BEAT THEM...
...WE MUST WEAKEN THEIR ONE OVERWHELMING FORCE.
IN OTHER WORDS...

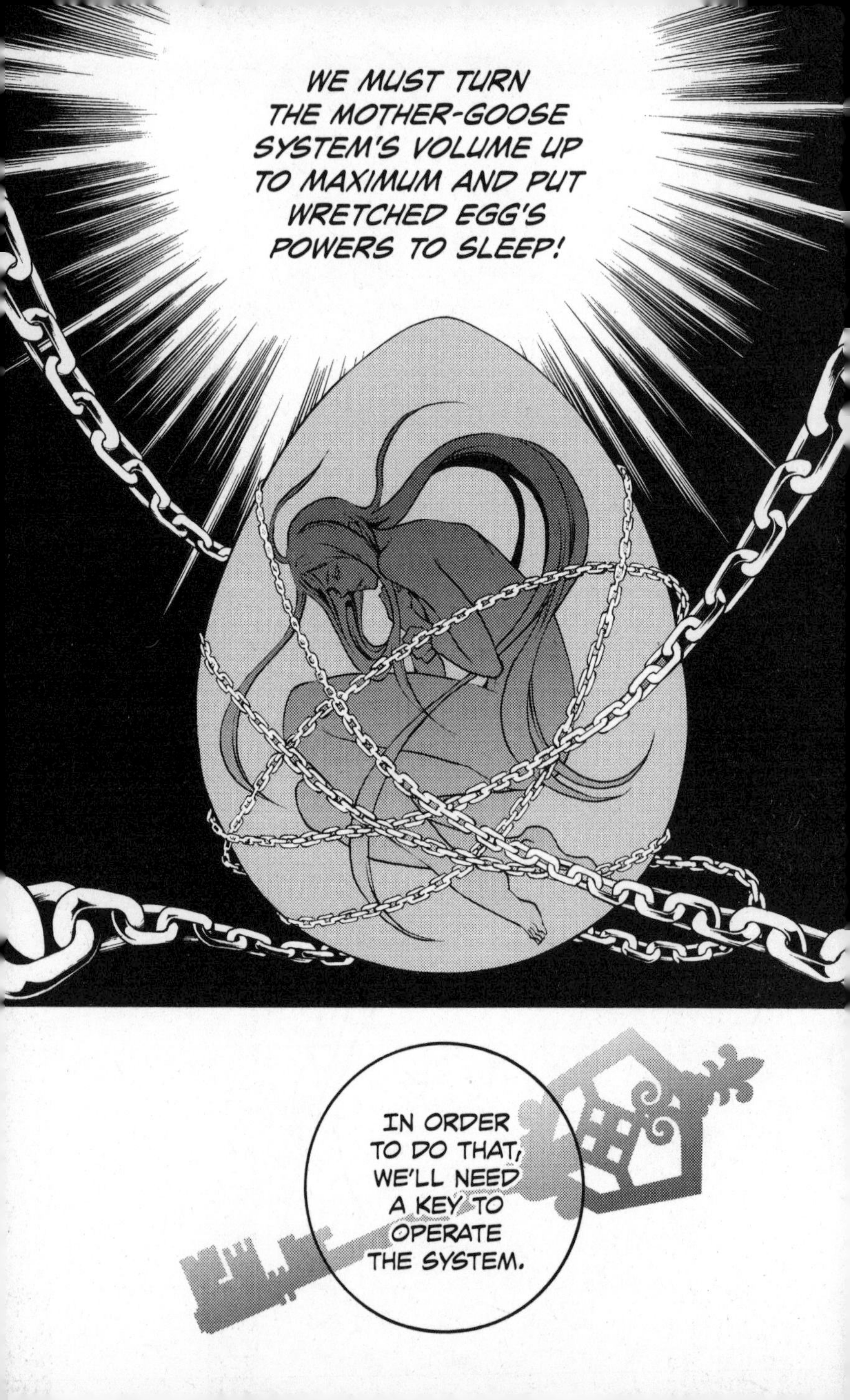
WE MUST TURN THE MOTHER-GOOSE SYSTEM'S VOLUME UP TO MAXIMUM AND PUT WRETCHED EGG'S POWERS TO SLEEP!
IN ORDER TO DO THAT, WE'LL NEED A KEY TO OPERATE THE SYSTEM.

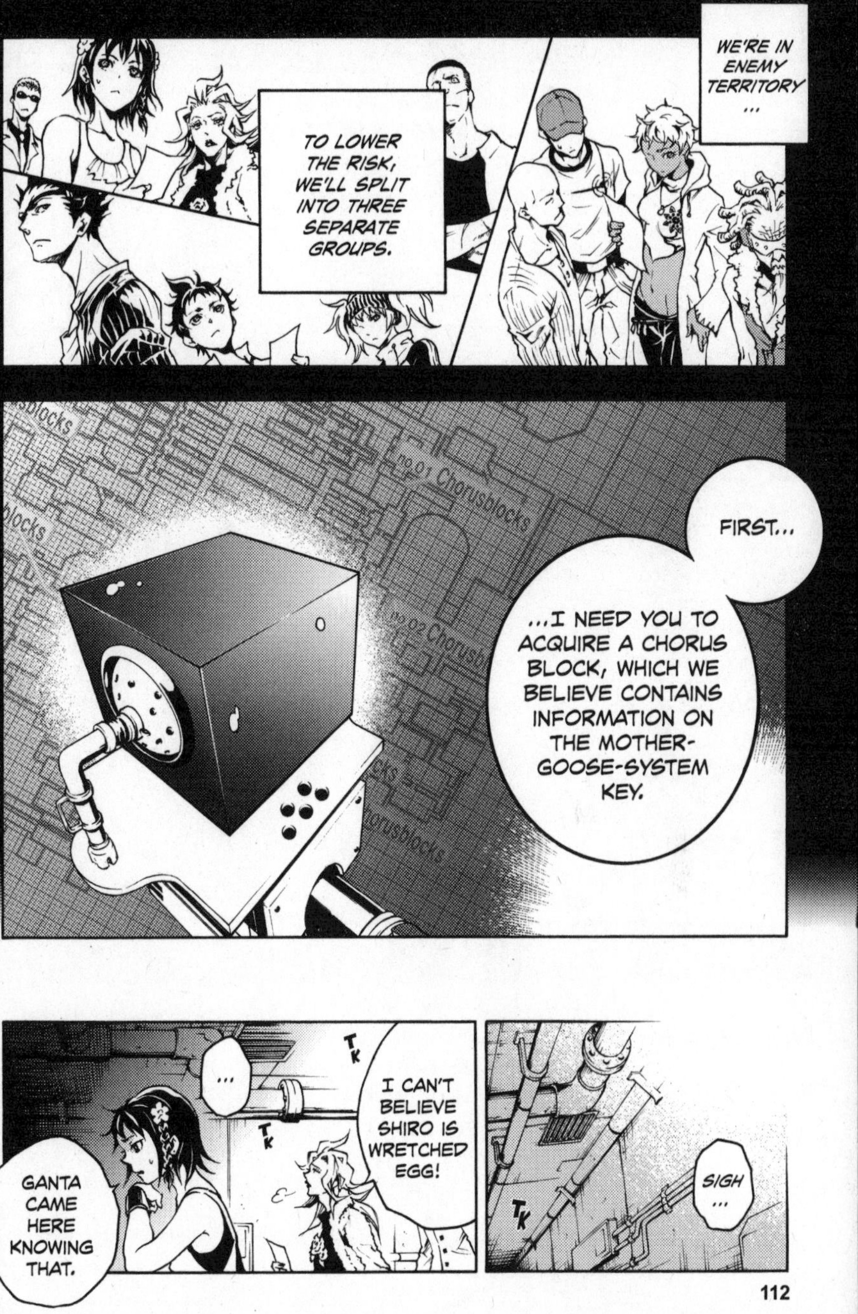
WE'RE IN ENEMY TERRITORY...
TO LOWER THE RISK, WE'LL SPLIT INTO THREE SEPARATE GROUPS.
No.01 Chorusblocks
FIRST...
...I NEED YOU TO ACQUIRE A CHORUS BLOCK, WHICH WE BELIEVE CONTAINS INFORMATION ON THE MOTHER-GOOSE-SYSTEM KEY.
TK
SIGH...
TK
TK
I CAN'T BELIEVE SHIRO IS WRETCHED EGG!
...
GANTA CAME HERE KNOWING THAT.

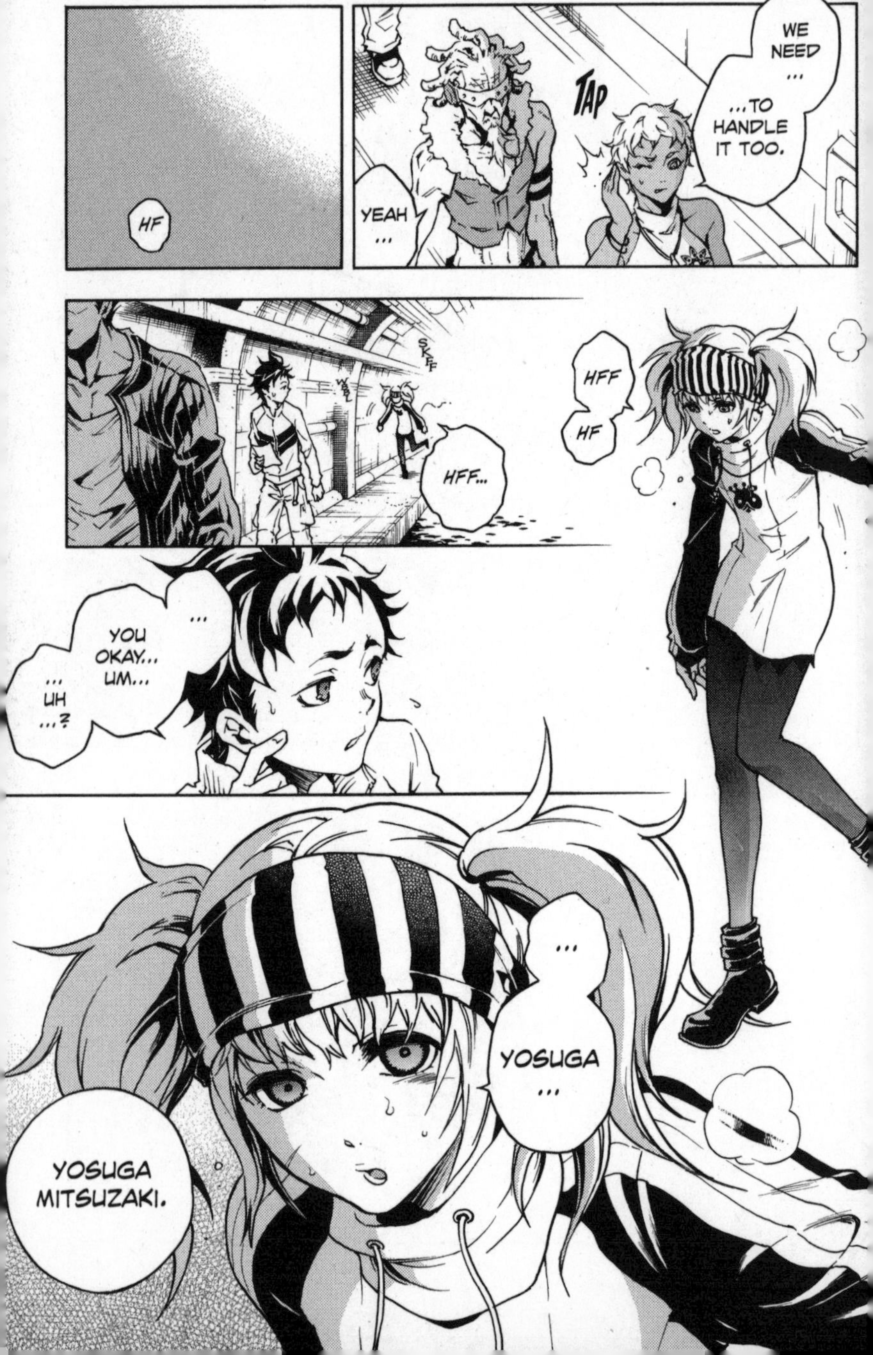
WE NEED ...
...TO HANDLE IT TOO.
TAP
YEAH ...
HF
HFF
HF
SKFF
HFF...
...
YOU OKAY... UM...
... UH ...?
...
YOSUGA ...
YOSUGA MITSUZAKI.

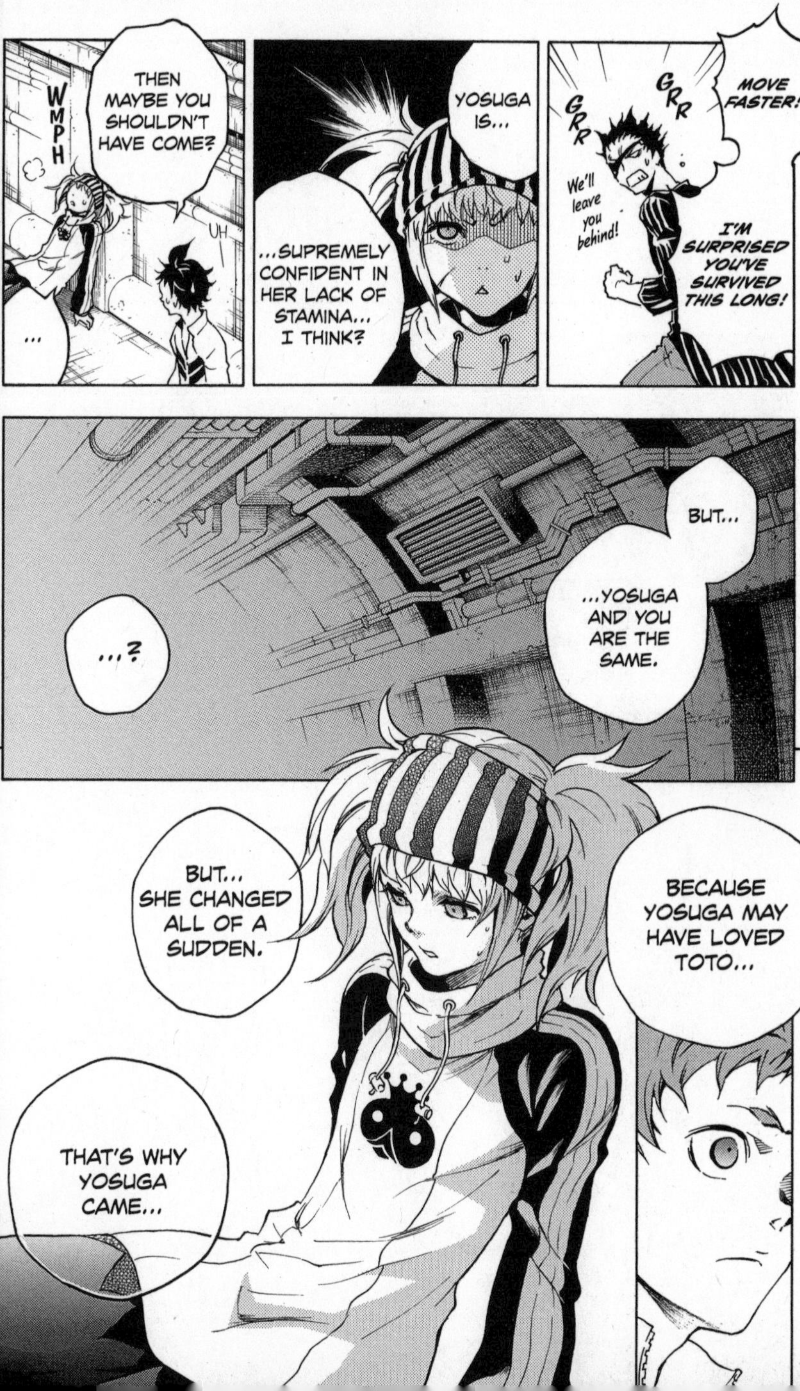
MOVE FASTER!
GRR
GRR
We'll leave you behind!
I'M SURPRISED YOU'VE SURVIVED THIS LONG!
YOSUGA IS...
...SUPREMELY CONFIDENT IN HER LACK OF STAMINA... I THINK?
THEN MAYBE YOU SHOULDN'T HAVE COME?
WMPH
UH
...
BUT...
...YOSUGA AND YOU ARE THE SAME.
...?
BECAUSE YOSUGA MAY HAVE LOVED TOTO...
BUT... SHE CHANGED ALL OF A SUDDEN.
THAT'S WHY YOSUGA CAME...

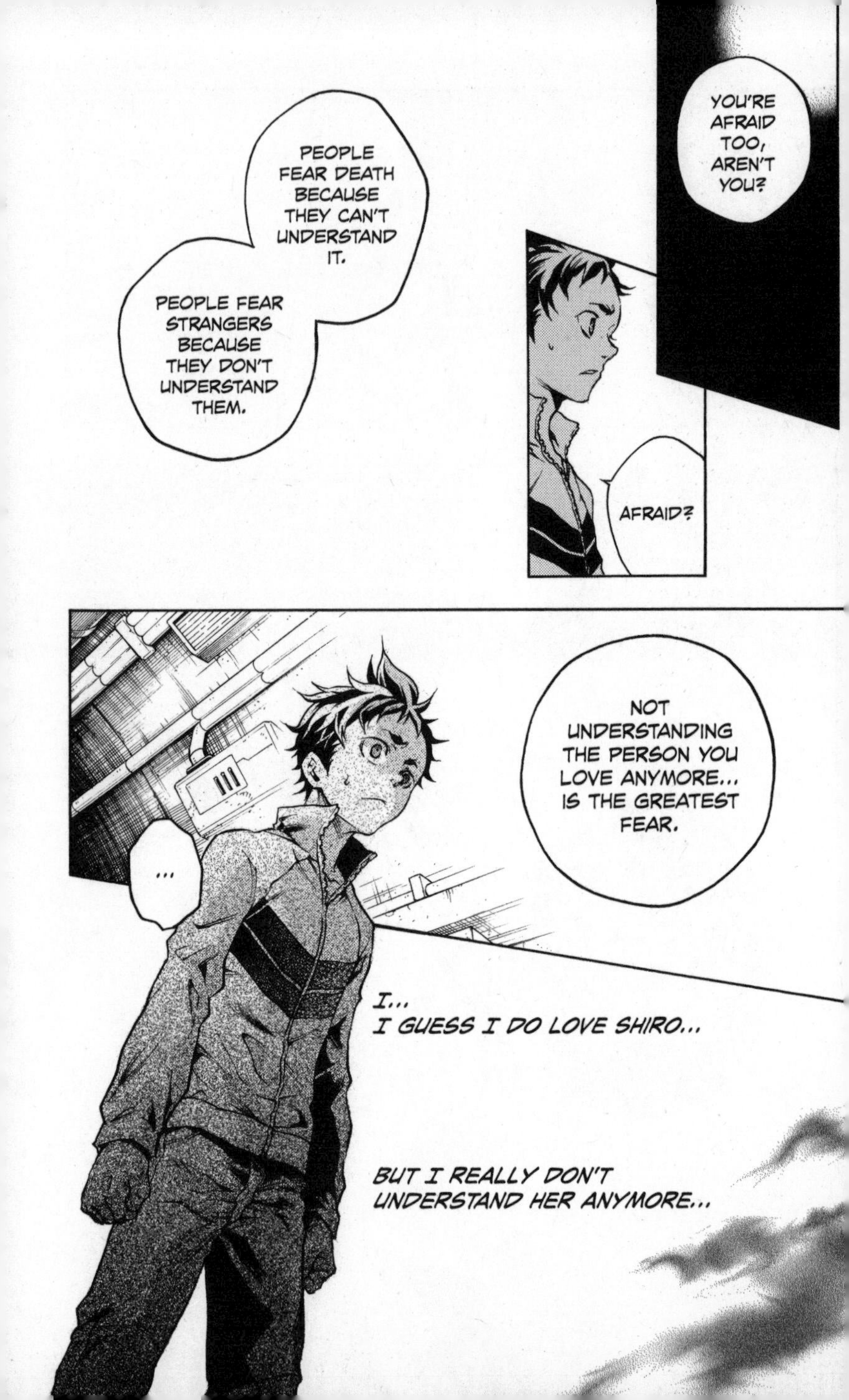
YOU'RE AFRAID TOO, AREN'T YOU?
AFRAID?
PEOPLE FEAR DEATH BECAUSE THEY CAN'T UNDERSTAND IT.
PEOPLE FEAR STRANGERS BECAUSE THEY DON'T UNDERSTAND THEM.
NOT UNDERSTANDING THE PERSON YOU LOVE ANYMORE... IS THE GREATEST FEAR.
...
I... I GUESS I DO LOVE SHIRO...
BUT I REALLY DON'T UNDERSTAND HER ANYMORE...

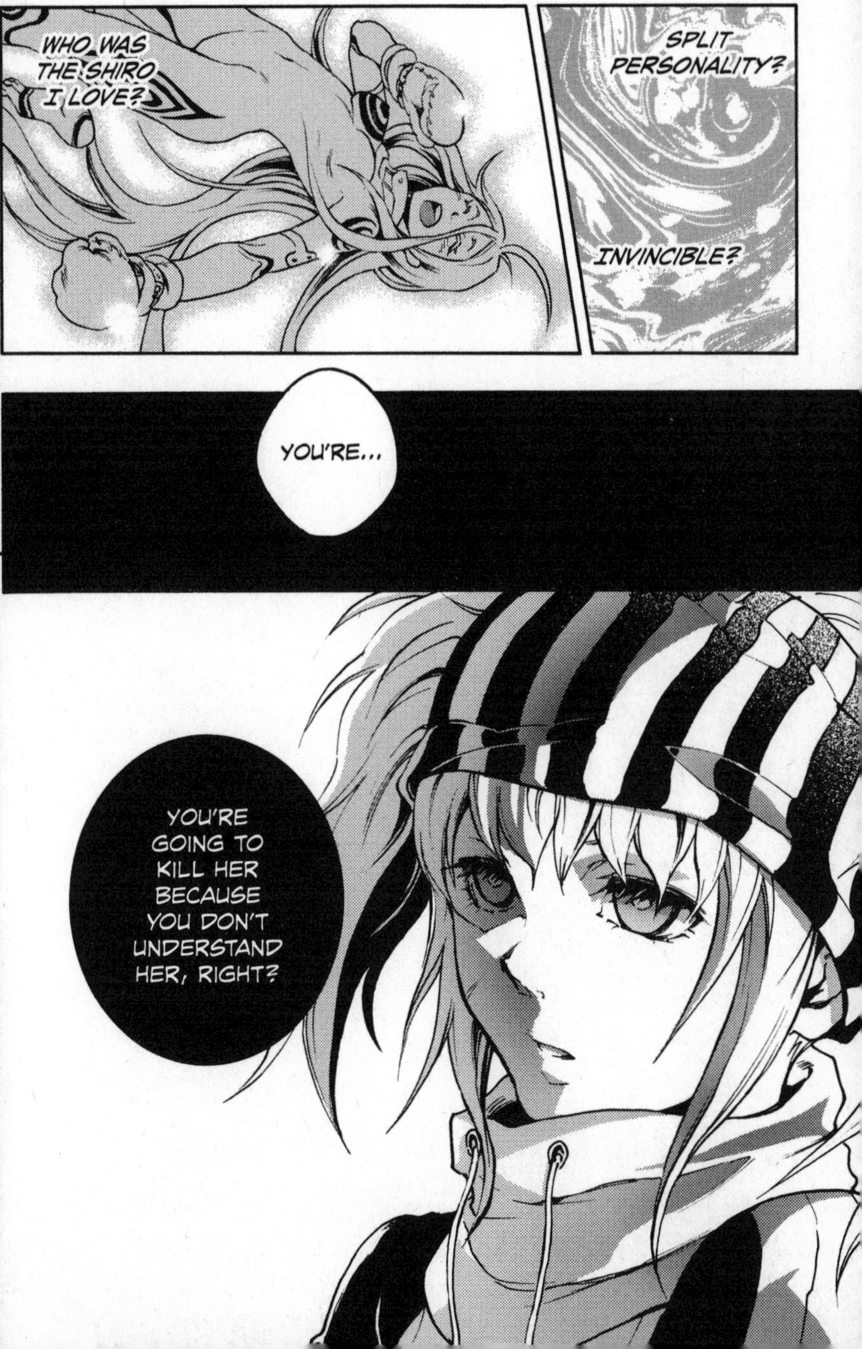
SPLIT PERSONALITY?
INVINCIBLE?
WHO WAS THE SHIRO I LOVE?
YOU'RE...
YOU'RE GOING TO KILL HER BECAUSE YOU DON'T UNDERSTAND HER, RIGHT?

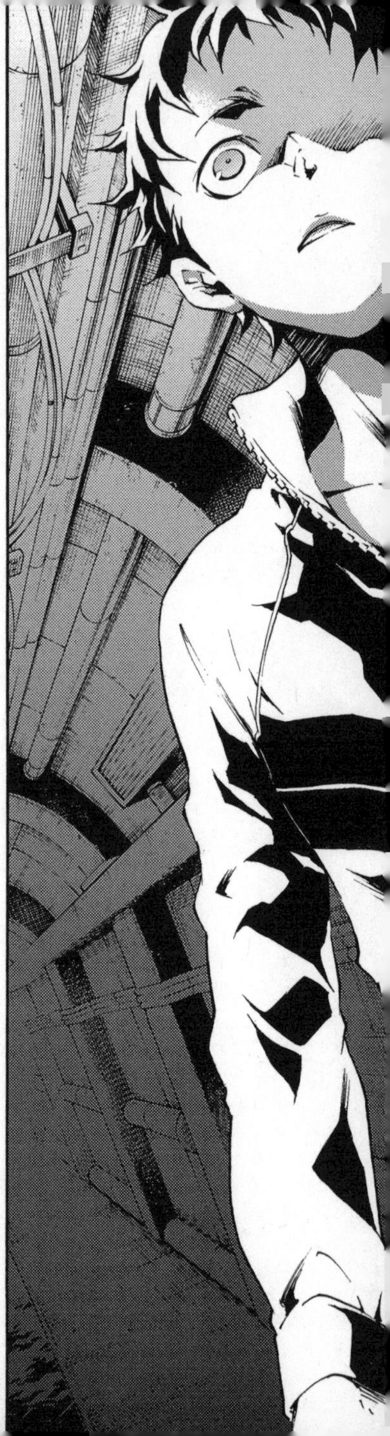

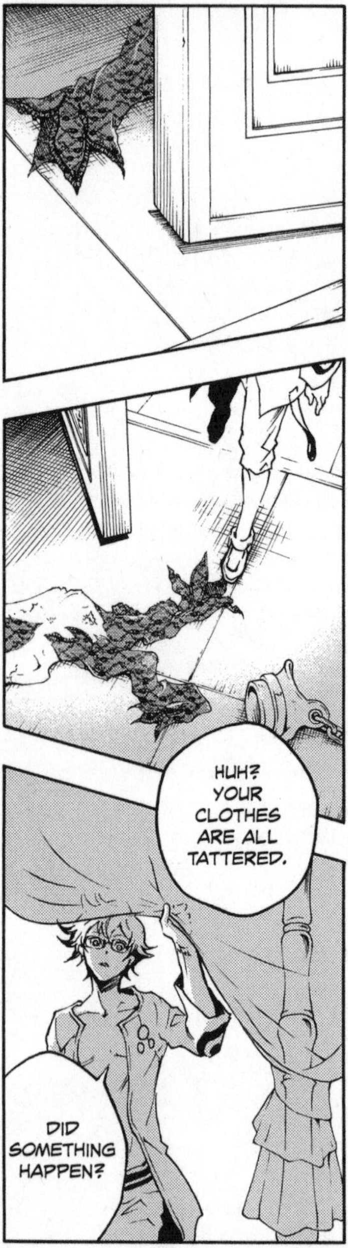
HUH? YOUR CLOTHES ARE ALL TATTERED.
DID SOMETHING HAPPEN?

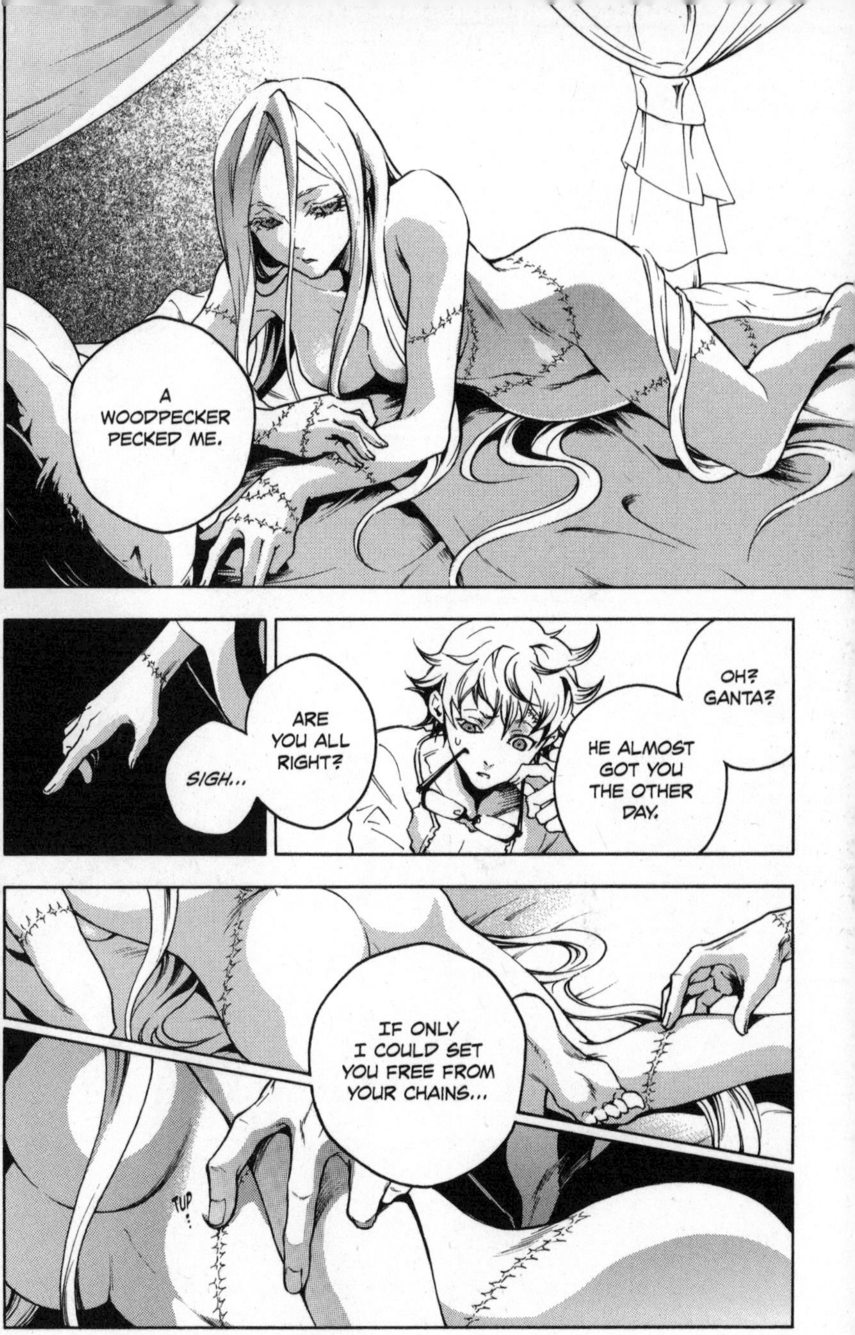
A WOODPECKER PECKED ME.
OH? GANTA?
HE ALMOST GOT YOU THE OTHER DAY.
ARE YOU ALL RIGHT?
SIGH...
IF ONLY I COULD SET YOU FREE FROM YOUR CHAINS...
TUP

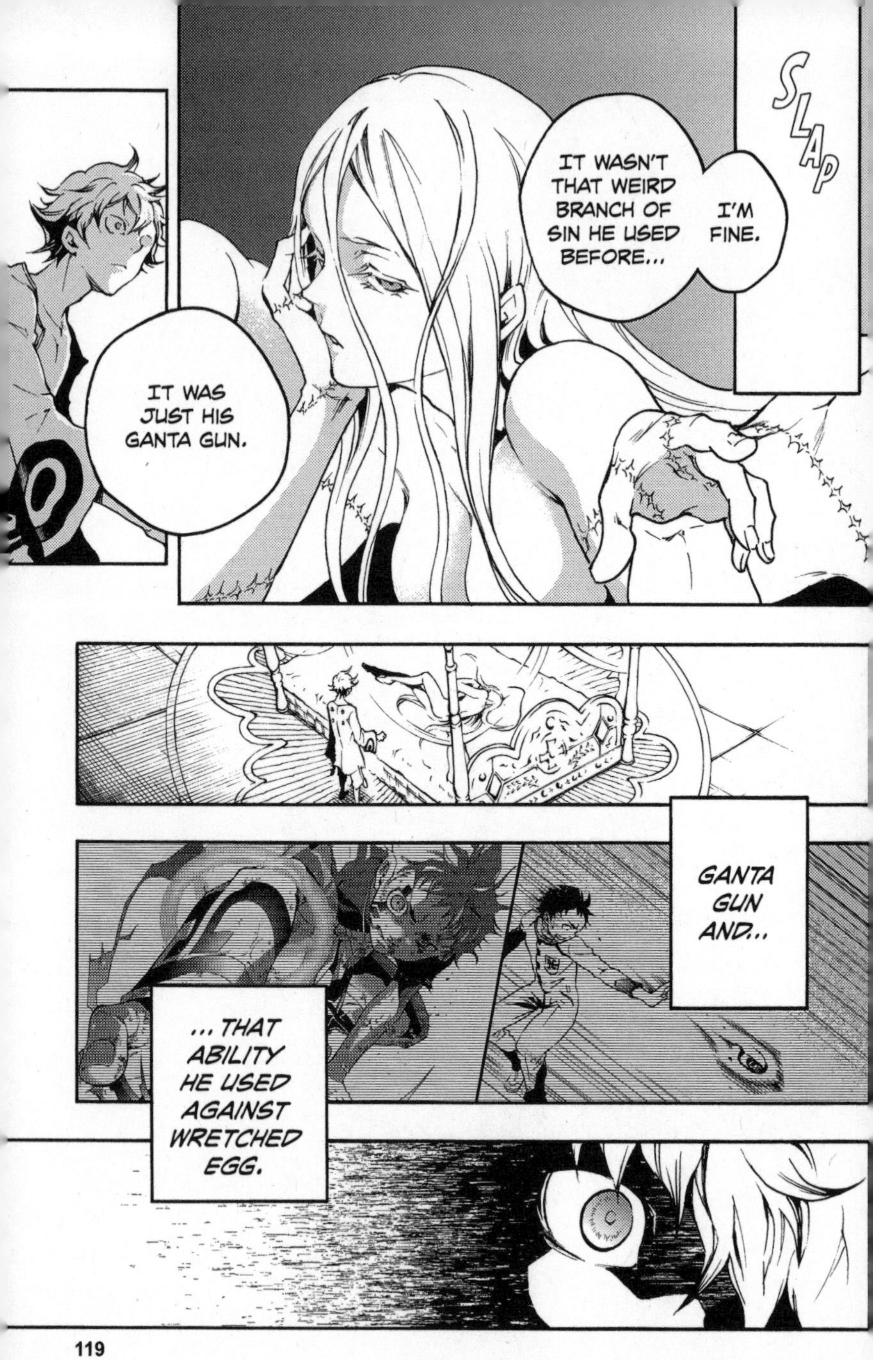
SLAP
I'M FINE.
IT WASN'T THAT WEIRD BRANCH OF SIN HE USED BEFORE...
IT WAS JUST HIS GANTA GUN.
GANTA GUN AND...
...THAT ABILITY HE USED AGAINST WRETCHED EGG.

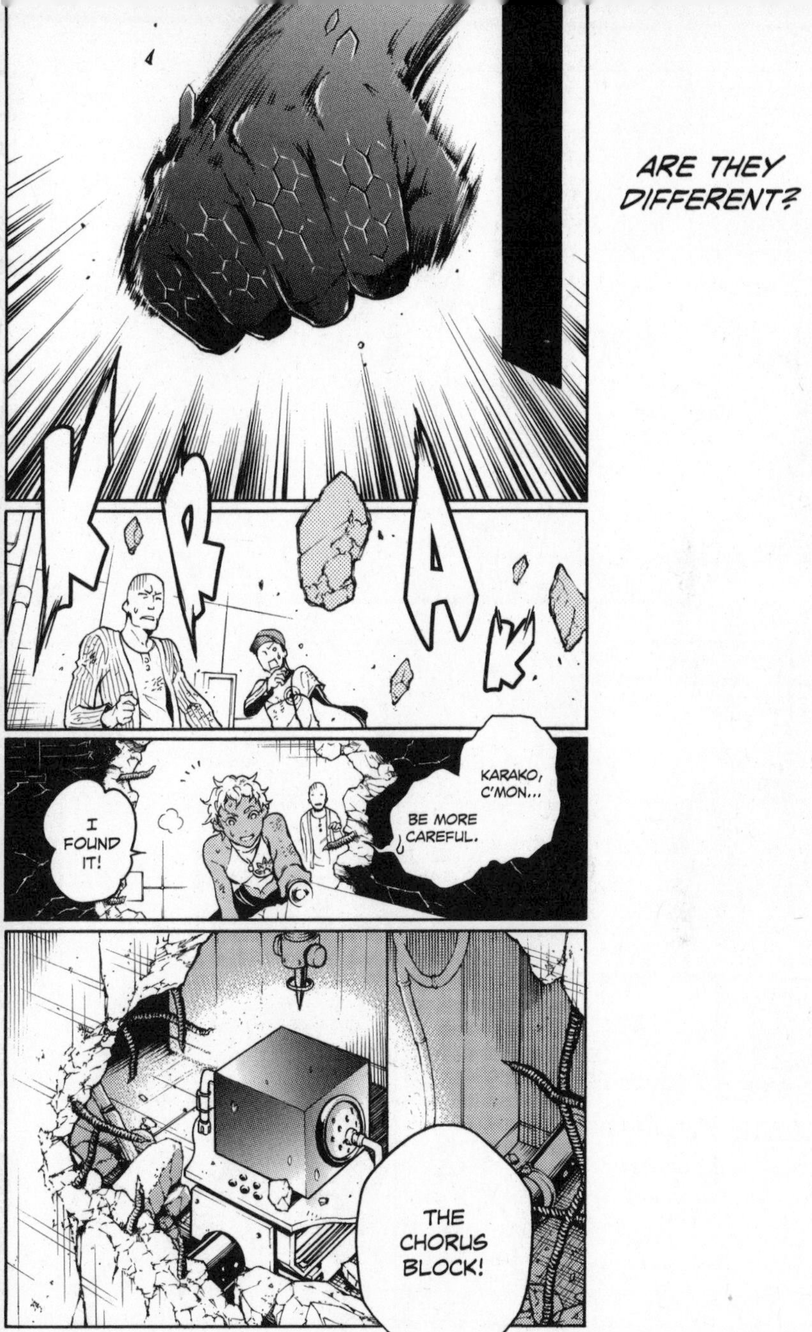
ARE THEY DIFFERENT?
KRAAK
KARAKO, C'MON... BE MORE CAREFUL.
I FOUND IT!
THE CHORUS BLOCK!

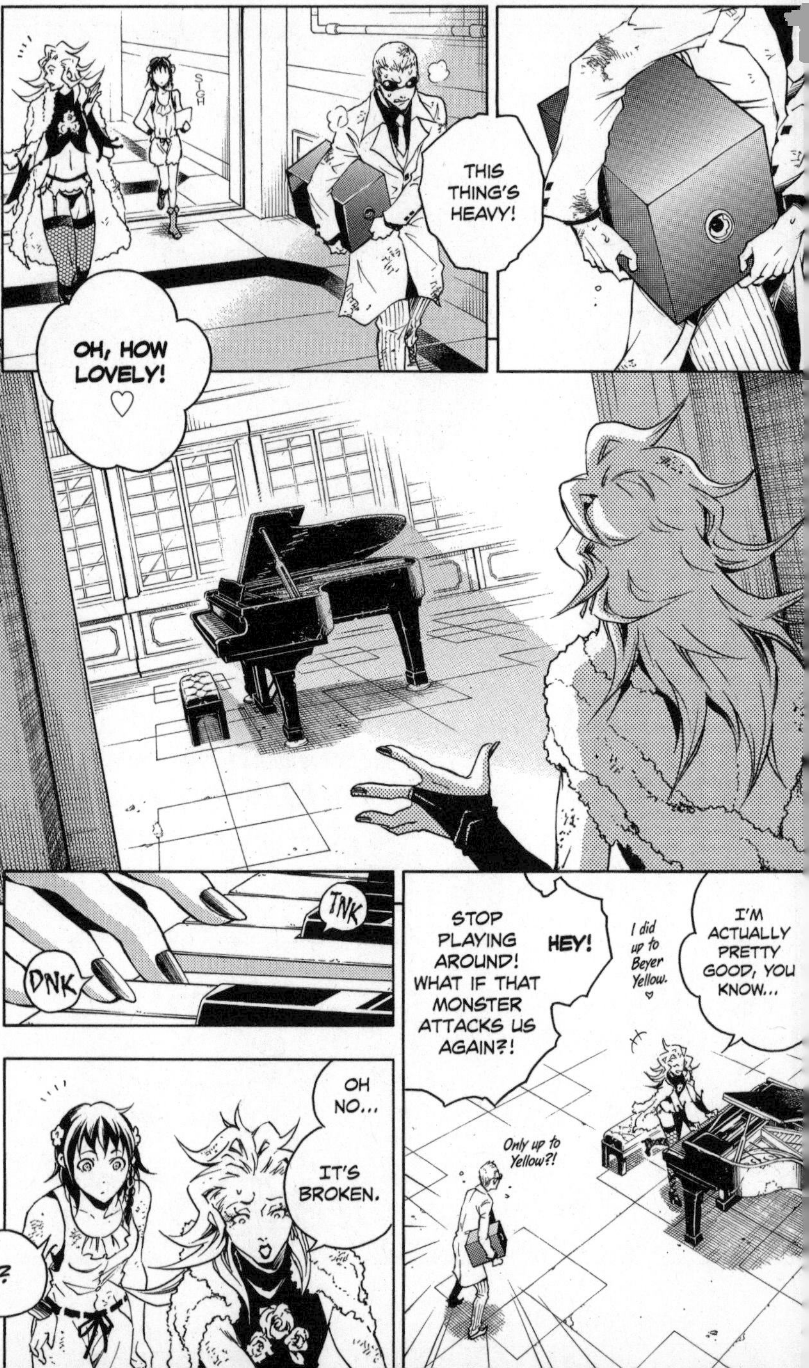
THIS THING'S HEAVY!
SIGH
OH, HOW LOVELY! ♡
I'M ACTUALLY PRETTY GOOD, YOU KNOW...
I did up to Beyer Yellow. ♡
HEY!
STOP PLAYING AROUND! WHAT IF THAT MONSTER ATTACKS US AGAIN?!
Only up to Yellow?!
TNK
DNK
OH NO...
IT'S BROKEN.
?

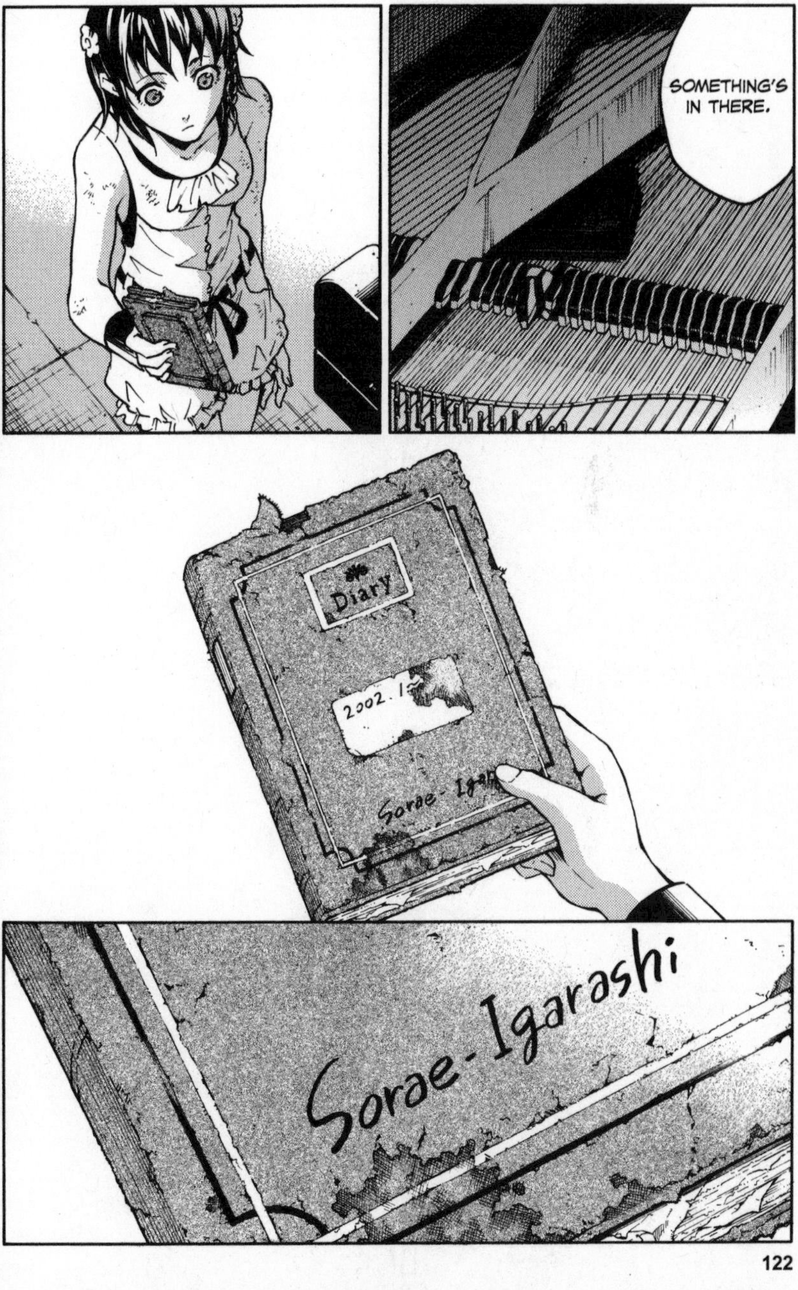
SOMETHING'S IN THERE.
Diary
2002. 1
Sorae-Igarashi

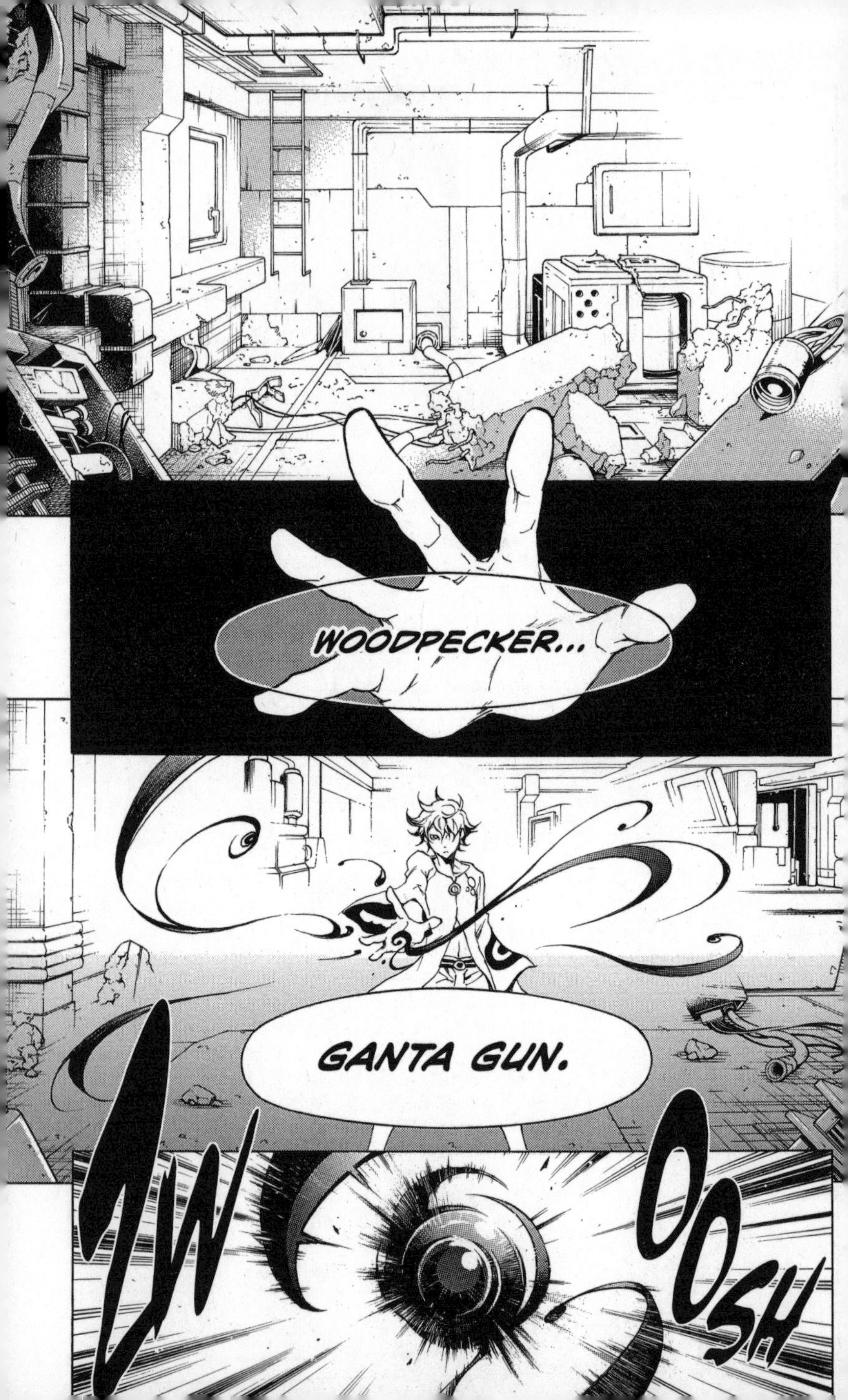
WOODPECKER...
GANTA GUN.
ZWOOSH

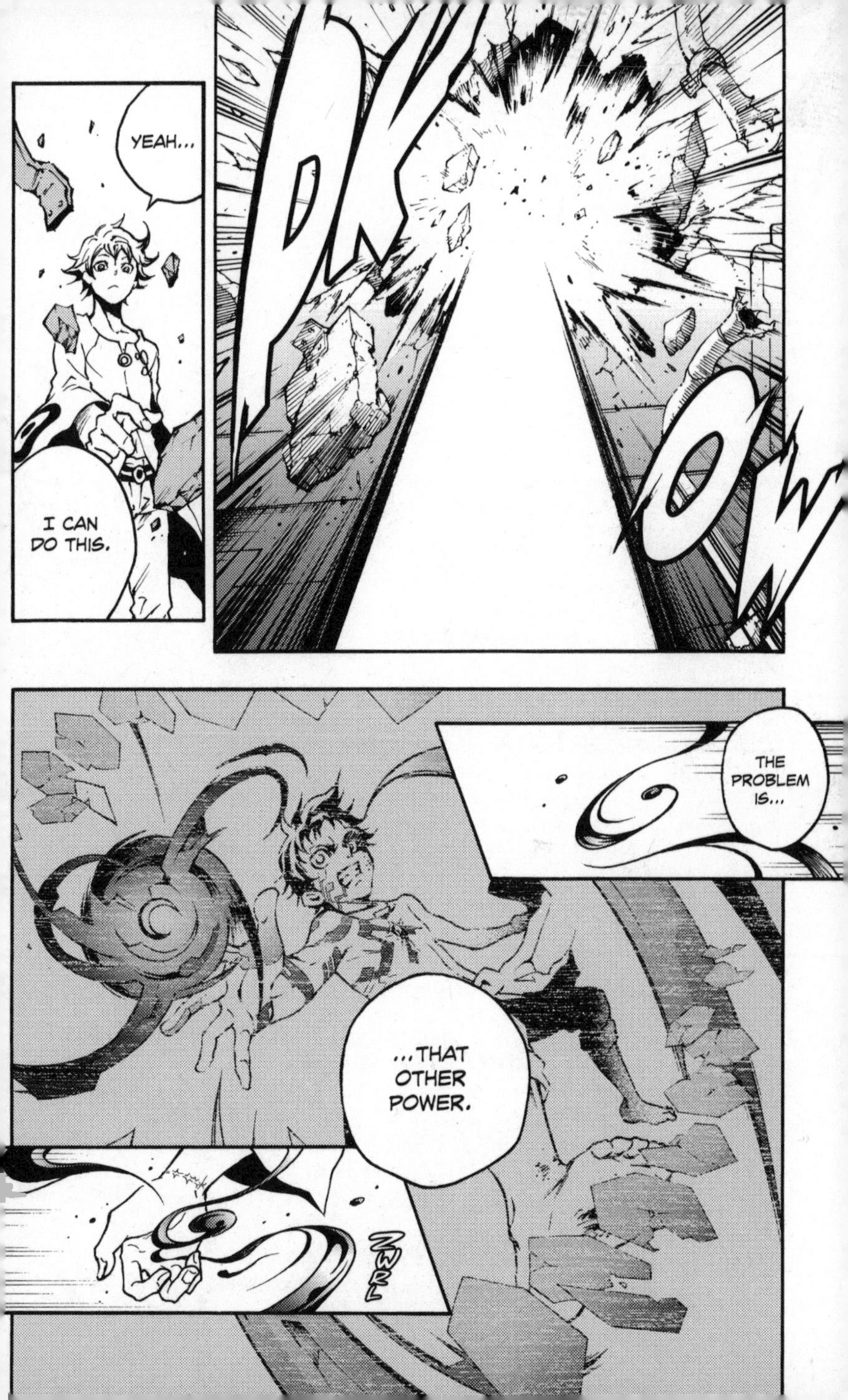
YEAH...
I CAN DO THIS.
THE PROBLEM IS...
...THAT OTHER POWER.
ZWRL

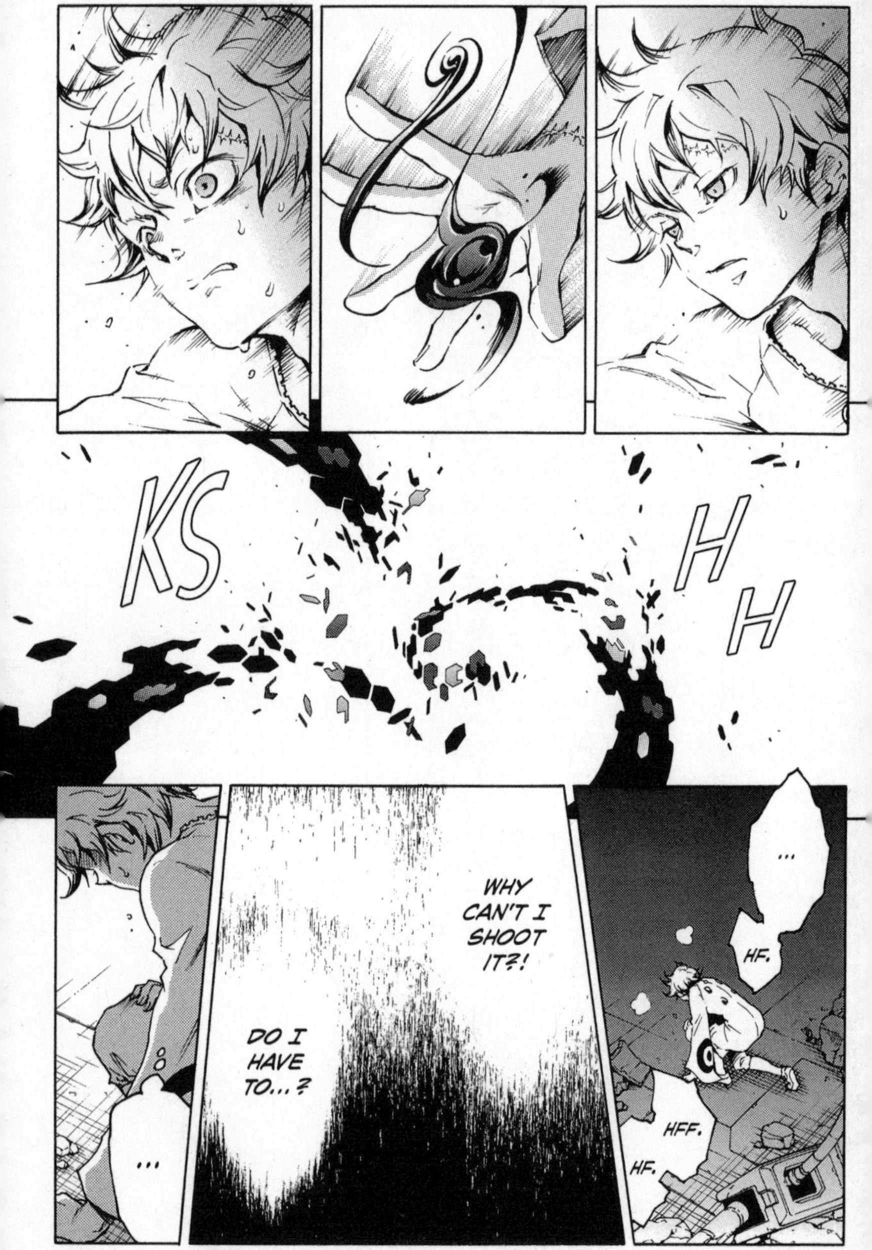
KSHH
...
HF.
HFF.
HF.
WHY CAN'T I SHOOT IT?!
DO I HAVE TO...?
...

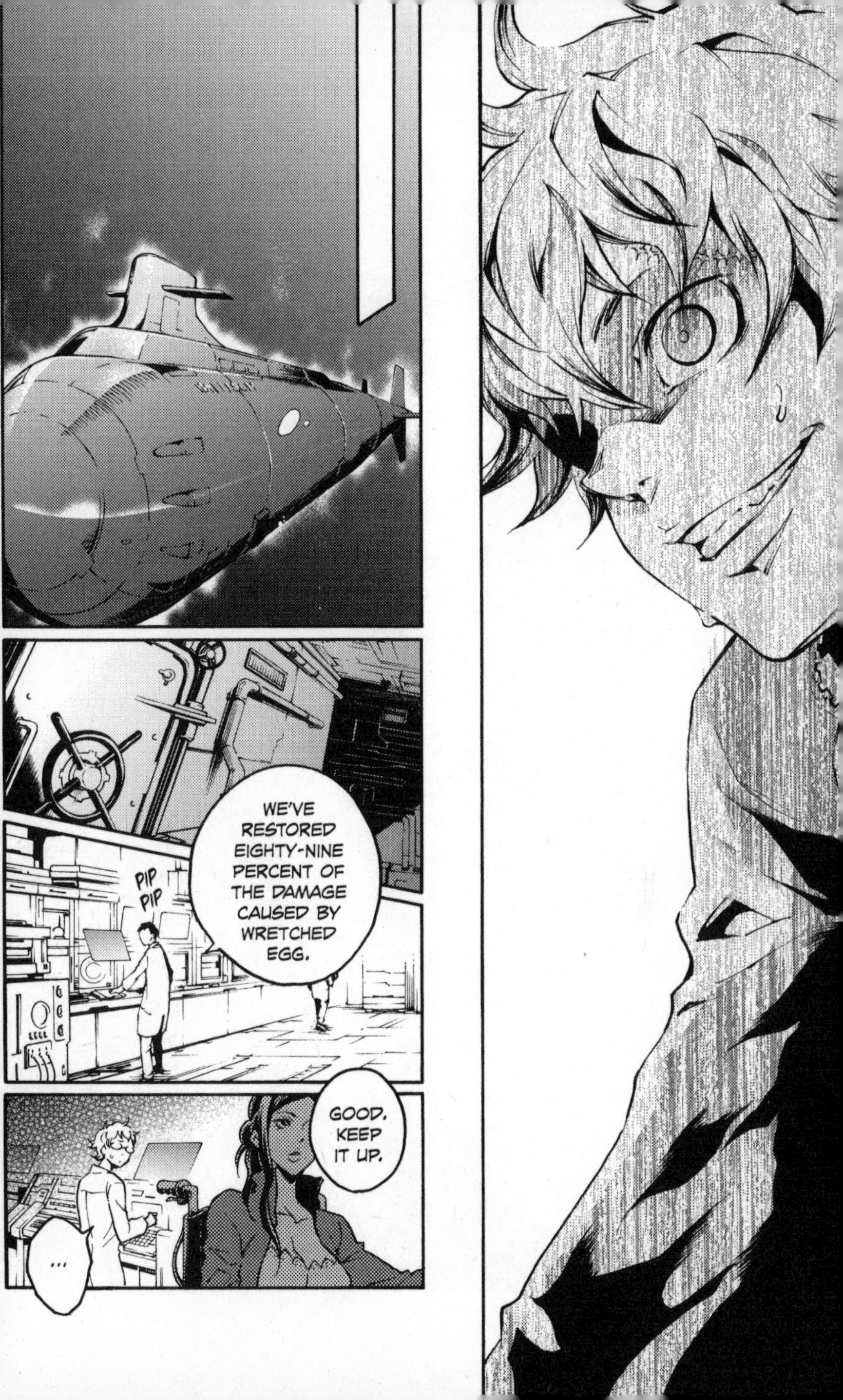
WE'VE RESTORED EIGHTY-NINE PERCENT OF THE DAMAGE CAUSED BY WRETCHED EGG.
PIP PIP
GOOD. KEEP IT UP.
...

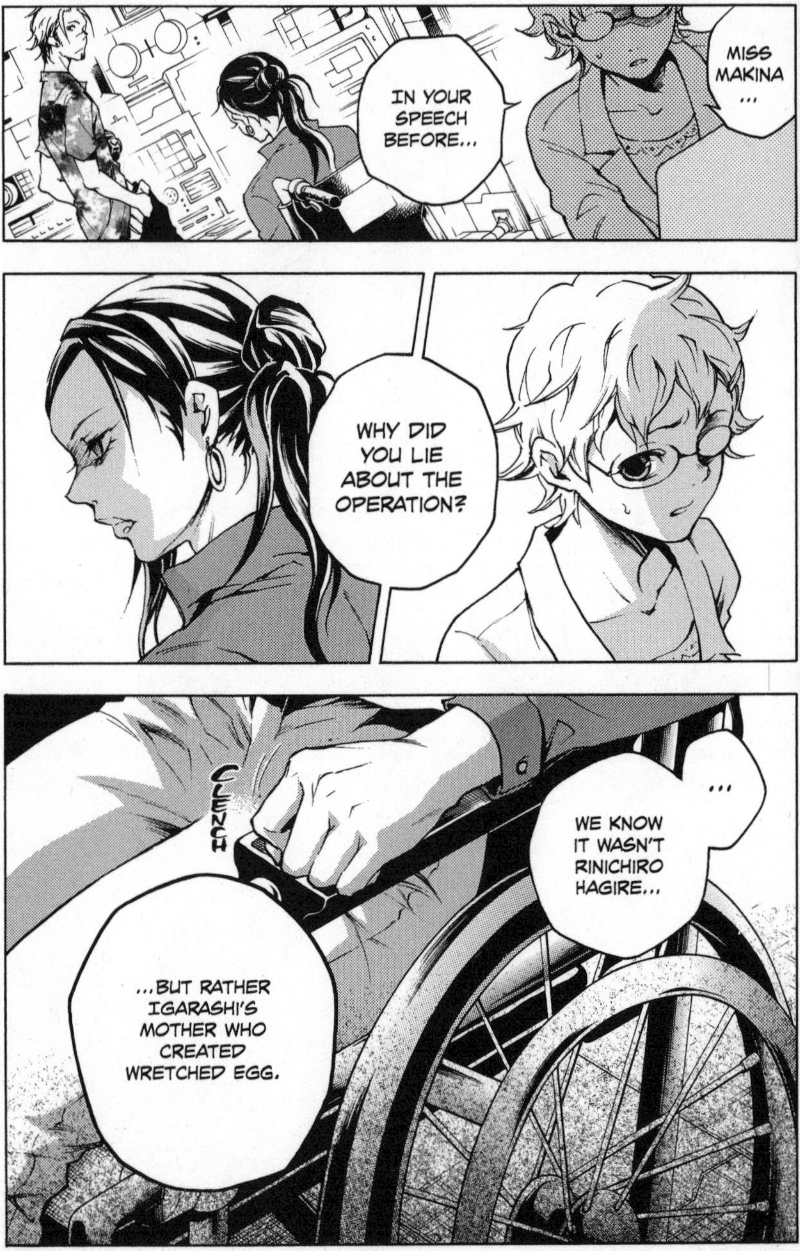
MISS MAKINA ...
IN YOUR SPEECH BEFORE...
WHY DID YOU LIE ABOUT THE OPERATION?
...
WE KNOW IT WASN'T RINICHIRO HAGIRE...
CLENCH
...BUT RATHER IGARASHI'S MOTHER WHO CREATED WRETCHED EGG.

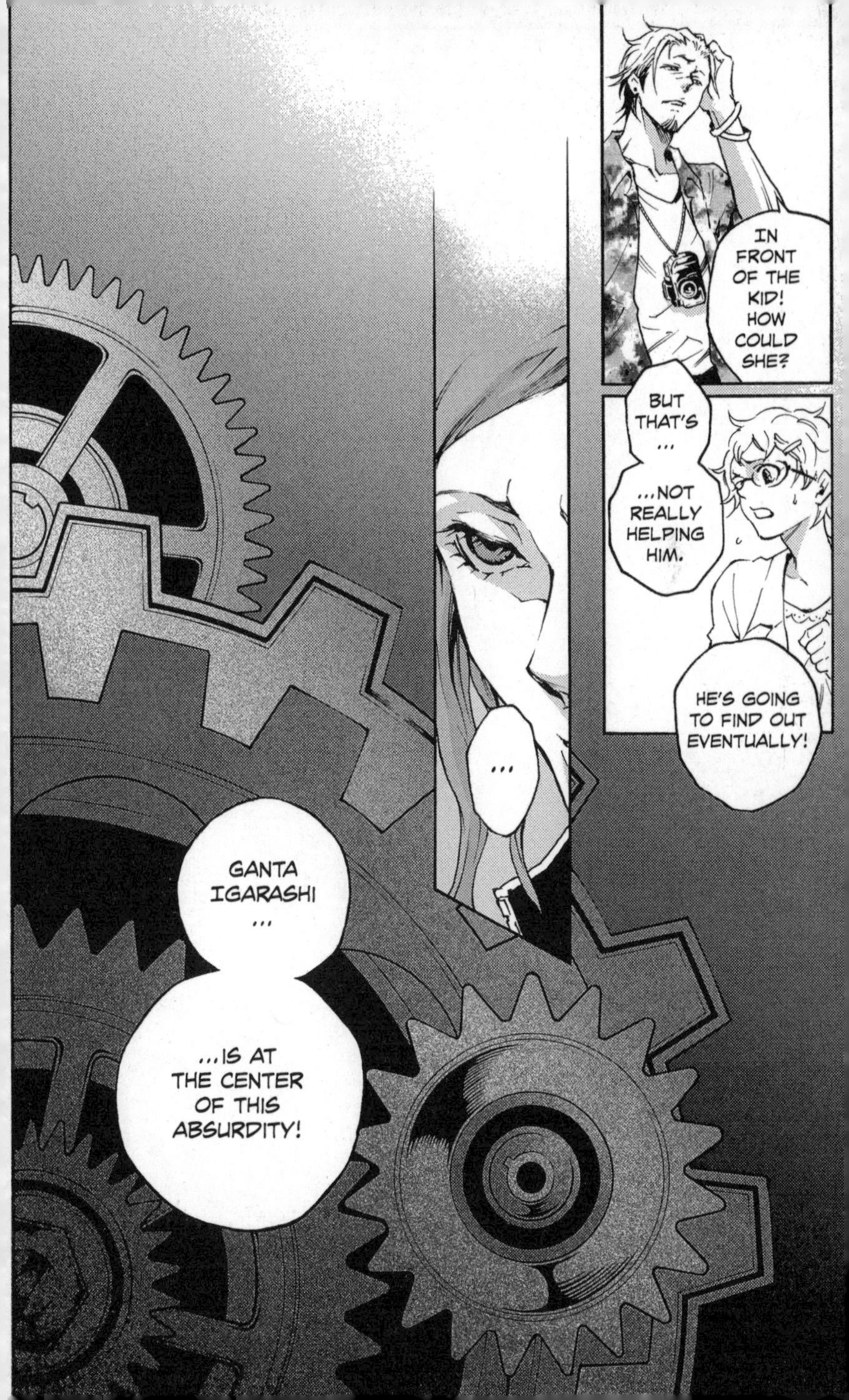
IN FRONT OF THE KID! HOW COULD SHE?
BUT THAT'S ...
...NOT REALLY HELPING HIM.
HE'S GOING TO FIND OUT EVENTUALLY!
...
GANTA IGARASHI ...
...IS AT THE CENTER OF THIS ABSURDITY!

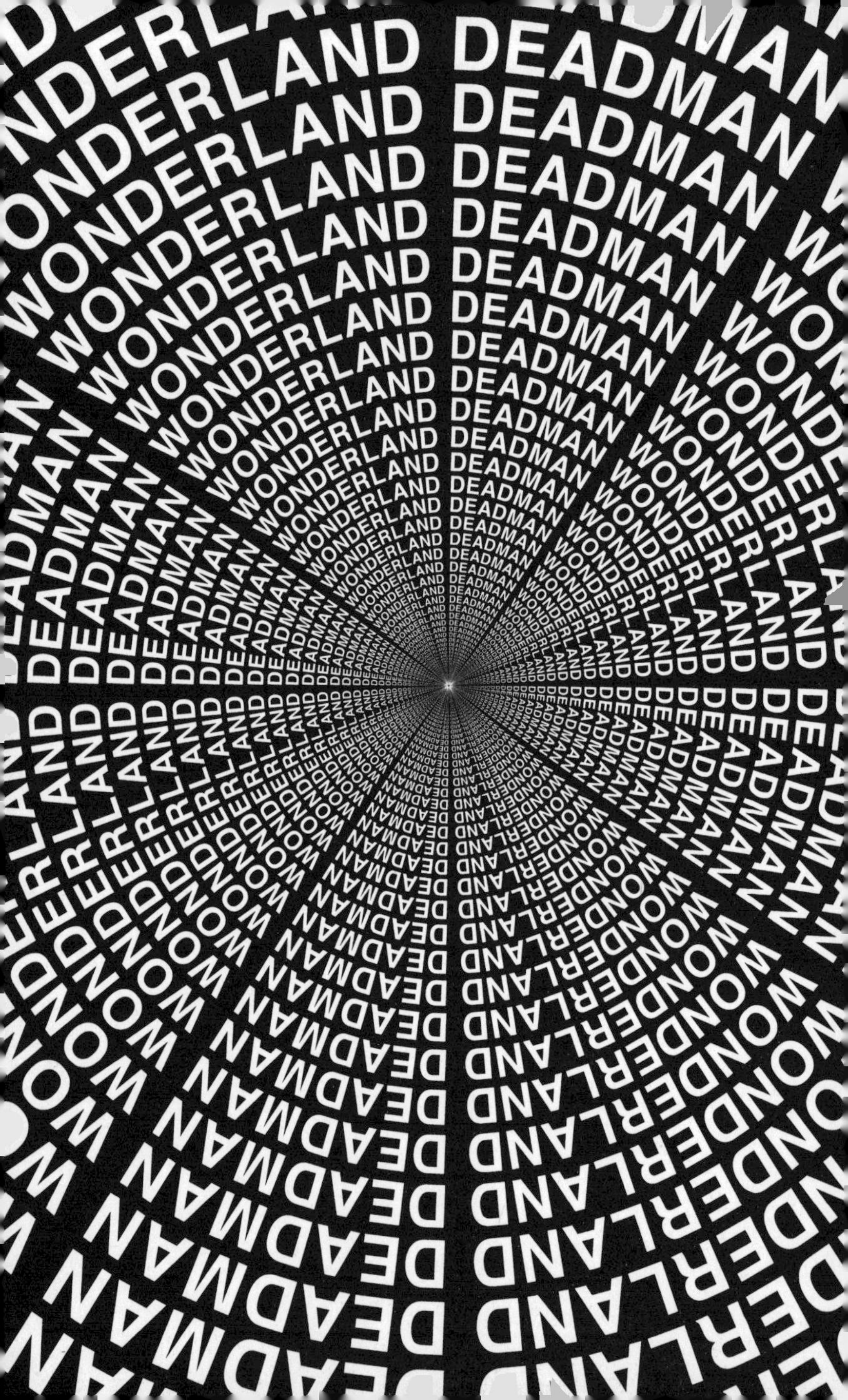
DEADMAN WONDERLAND

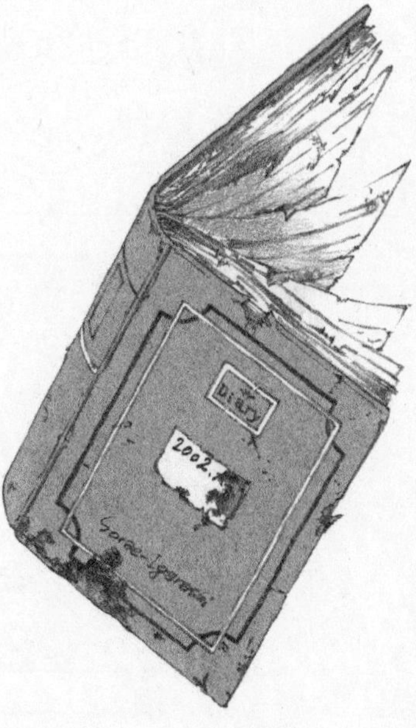
Diary
2002.

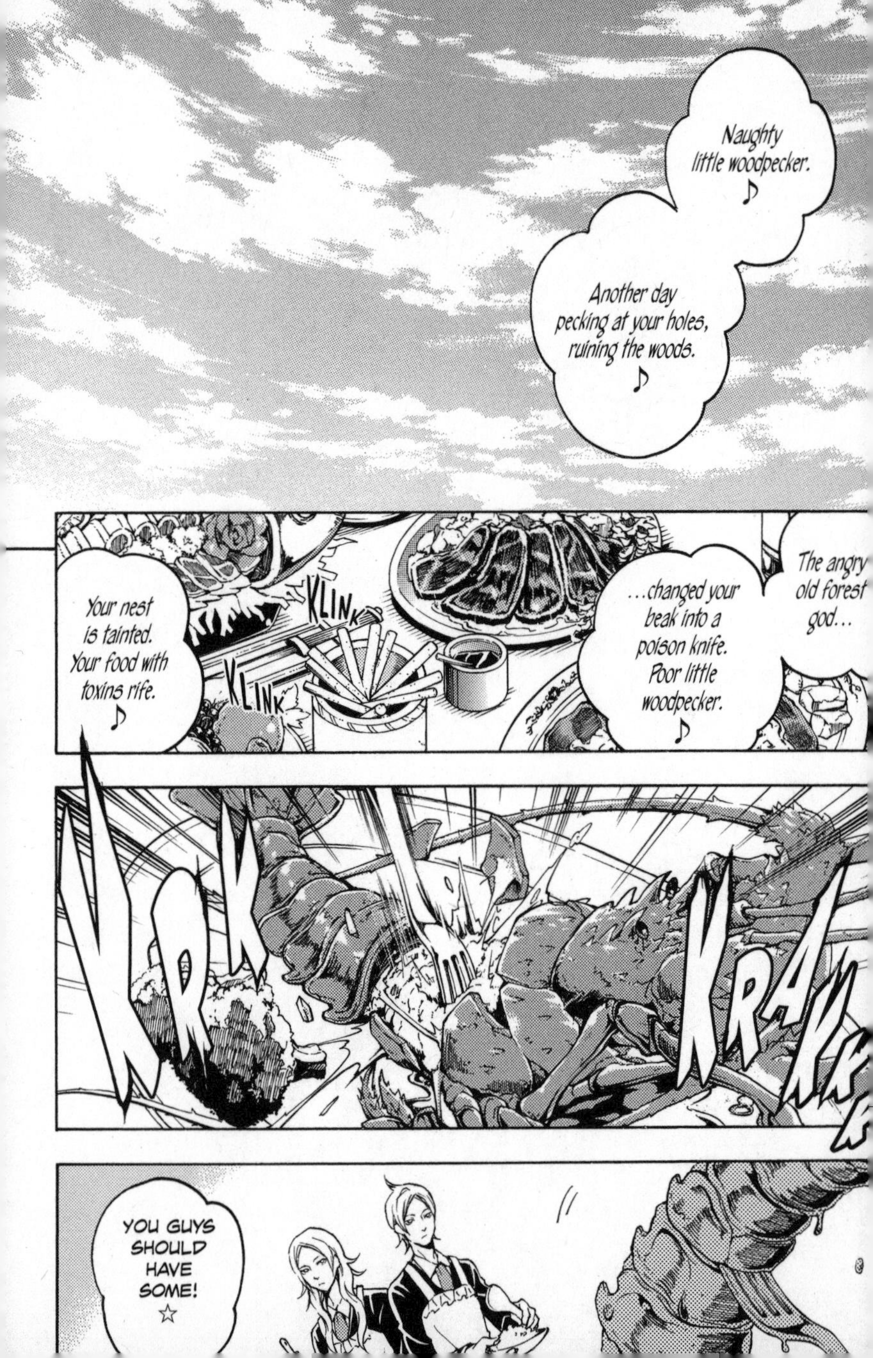
Naughty little woodpecker. ♪
Another day pecking at your holes, ruining the woods. ♪
The angry old forest god…
…changed your beak into a poison knife. Poor little woodpecker. ♪
KLINK
KLINK
Your nest is tainted. Your food with toxins rife. ♪
KRAKK
NOK
YOU GUYS SHOULD HAVE SOME! ☆

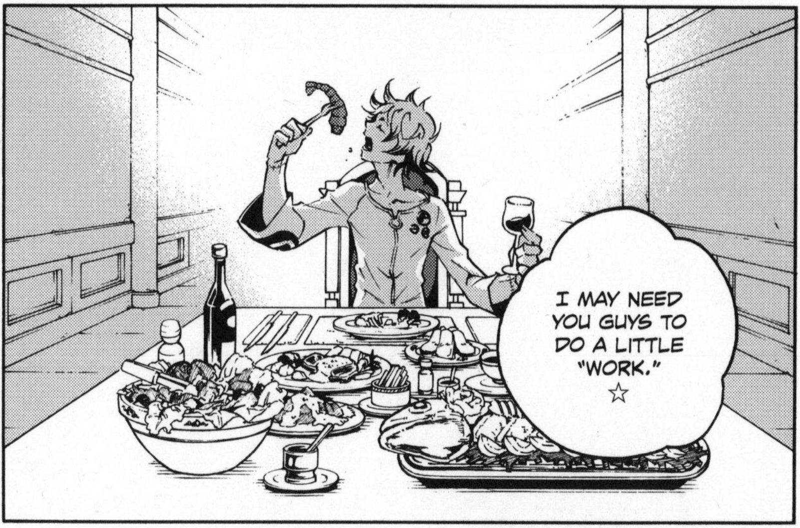
I MAY NEED YOU GUYS TO DO A LITTLE "WORK." ☆
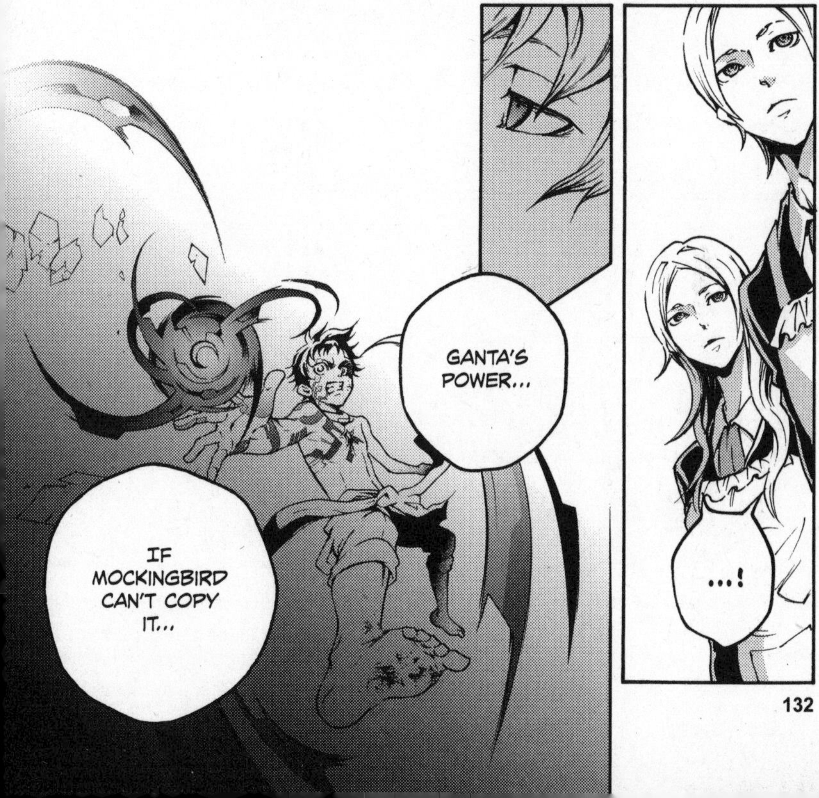
...!
GANTA'S POWER...
IF MOCKINGBIRD CAN'T COPY IT...

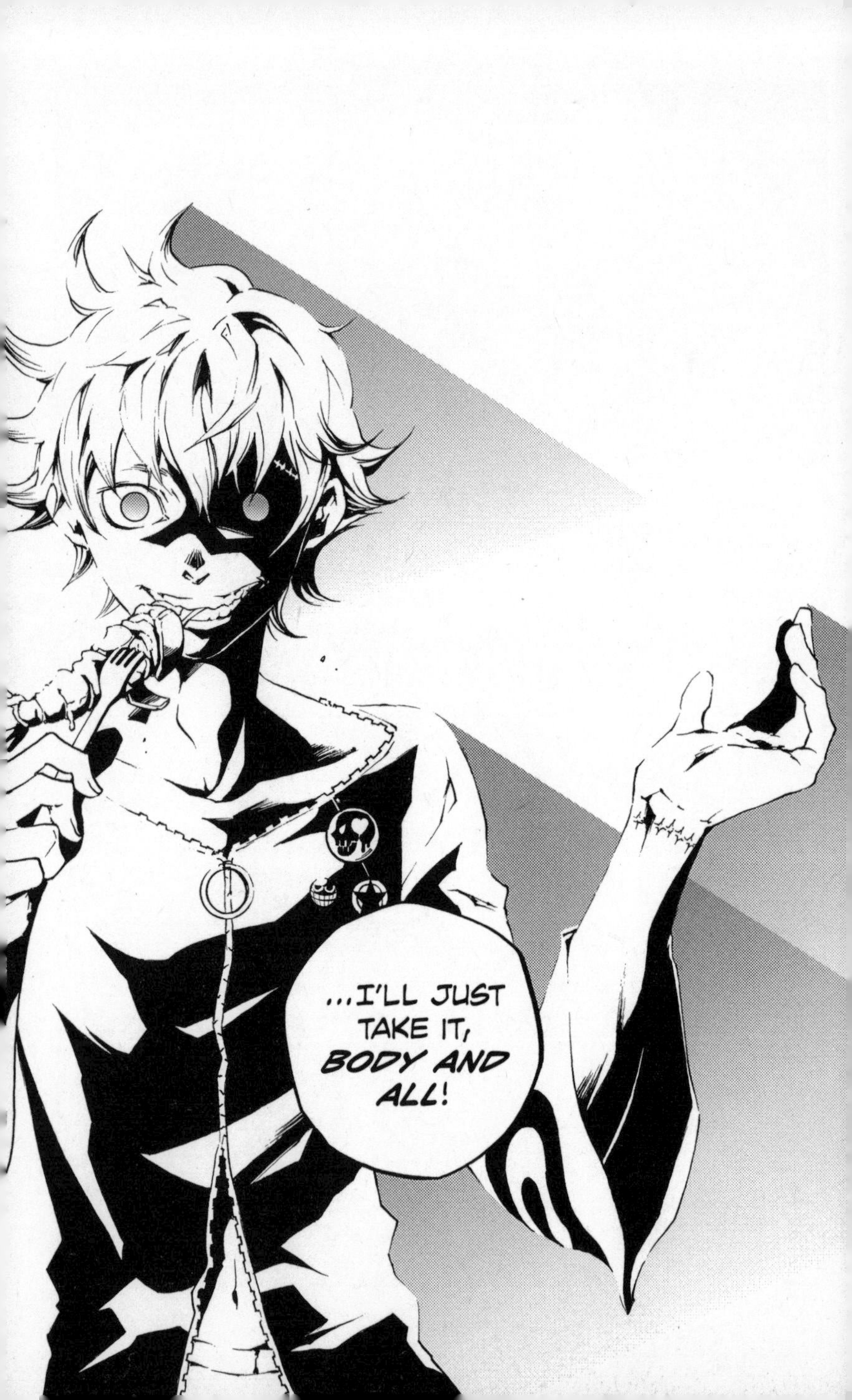
...I'LL JUST TAKE IT, BODY AND ALL!

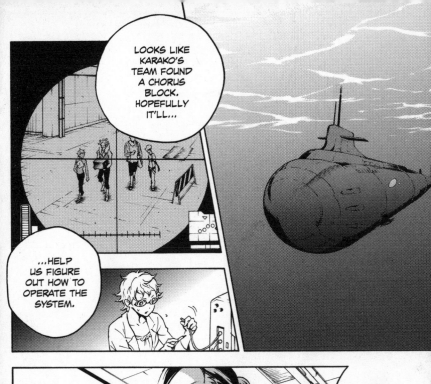

LOOKS LIKE KARAKO'S TEAM FOUND A CHORUS BLOCK. HOPEFULLY IT'LL...

...HELP US FIGURE OUT HOW TO OPERATE THE SYSTEM.

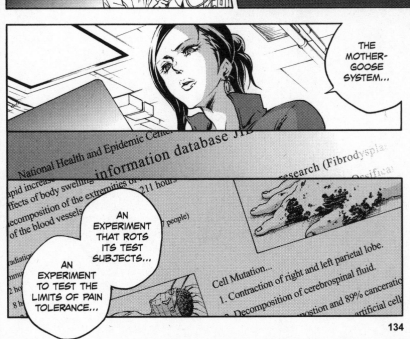

THE MOTHER-GOOSE SYSTEM...

AN EXPERIMENT THAT ROTS ITS TEST SUBJECTS...

AN EXPERIMENT TO TEST THE LIMITS OF PAIN TOLERANCE...

National Health and Epidemic Center information database

...research (Fibrodyspla...

...apid increas...
...fects of body swelling...
...composition of the extremities o...
...of the blood vessels...

...211 hours...

...l people)

Cell Mutation...

1. Contraction of right and left parietal lobe.

2. Decomposition of cerebrospinal fluid.

...ostion and 89% canceratio...

...artificial cell...

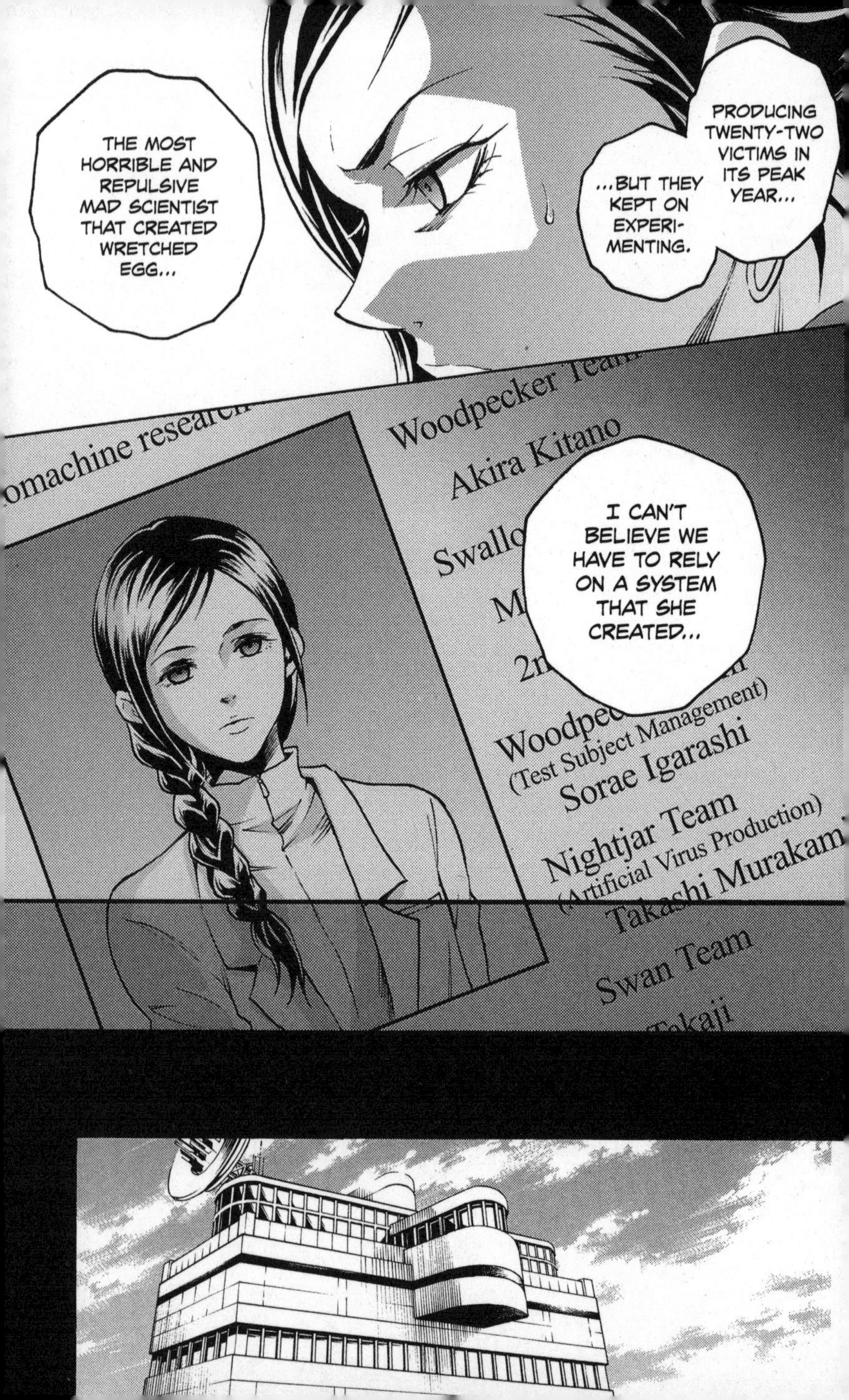
PRODUCING TWENTY-TWO VICTIMS IN ITS PEAK YEAR...
...BUT THEY KEPT ON EXPERIMENTING.
THE MOST HORRIBLE AND REPULSIVE MAD SCIENTIST THAT CREATED WRETCHED EGG...
Woodpecker
Akira Kitano
(Test Subject Management)
Sorae Igarashi
Nightjar Team
(Artificial Virus Production)
Swan Team
I CAN'T BELIEVE WE HAVE TO RELY ON A SYSTEM THAT SHE CREATED...

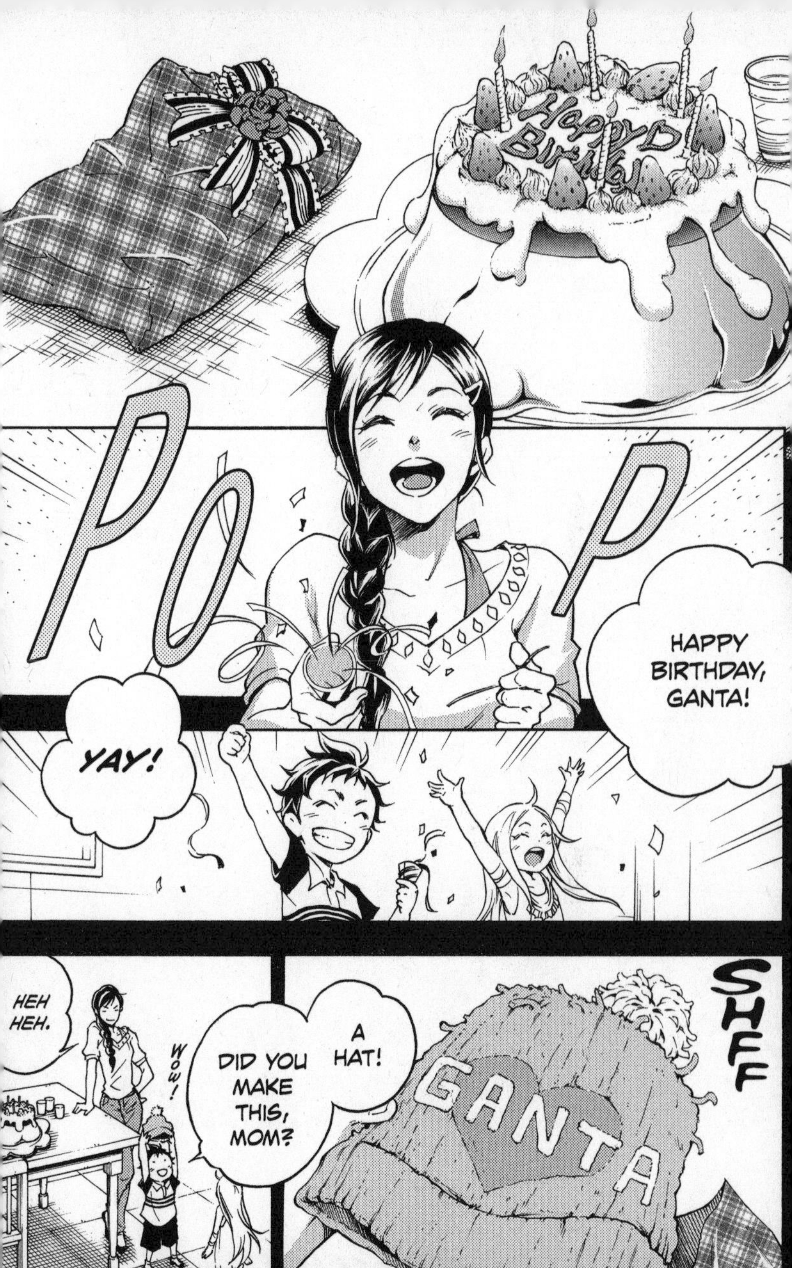
POP
HAPPY BIRTHDAY, GANTA!
YAY!
SHFF
A HAT!
GANTA
DID YOU MAKE THIS, MOM?
WOW!
HEH HEH.

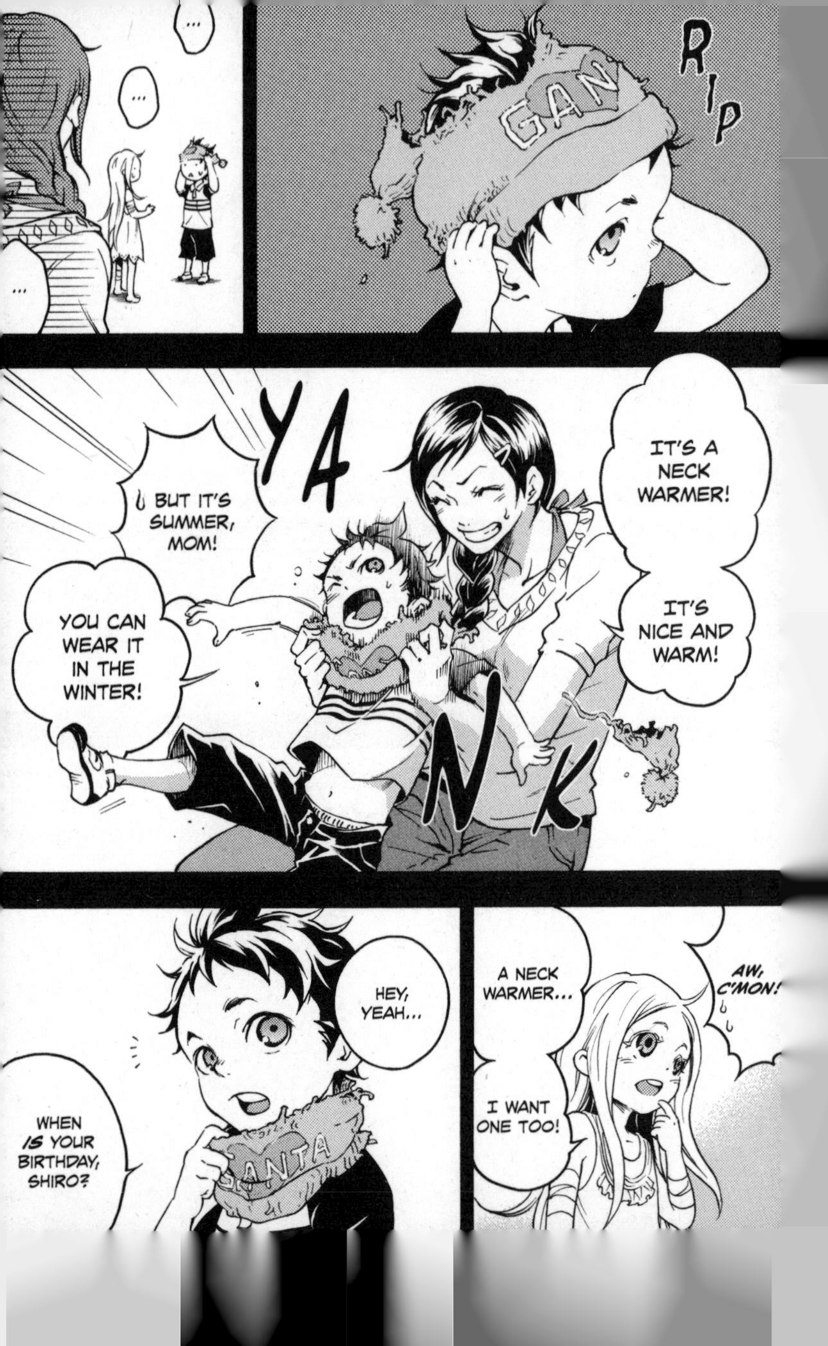
RIP
GAN
....
...
...
IT'S A NECK WARMER!
IT'S NICE AND WARM!
YANK
BUT IT'S SUMMER, MOM!
YOU CAN WEAR IT IN THE WINTER!
AW, C'MON!
A NECK WARMER...
I WANT ONE TOO!
HEY, YEAH...
WHEN *IS* YOUR BIRTHDAY, SHIRO?
SANTA

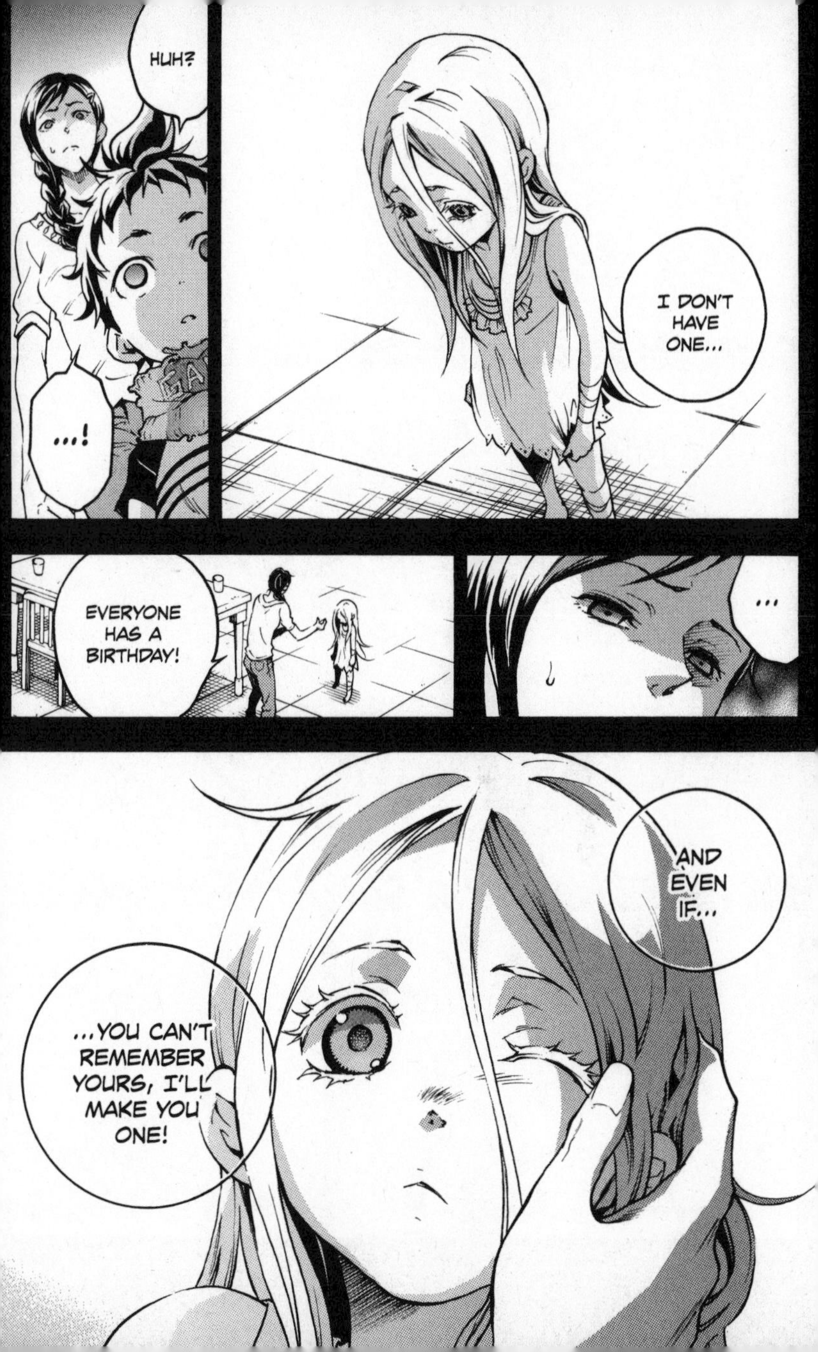
I DON'T HAVE ONE...
HUH?
...!
...
EVERYONE HAS A BIRTHDAY!
AND EVEN IF...
...YOU CAN'T REMEMBER YOURS, I'LL MAKE YOU ONE!

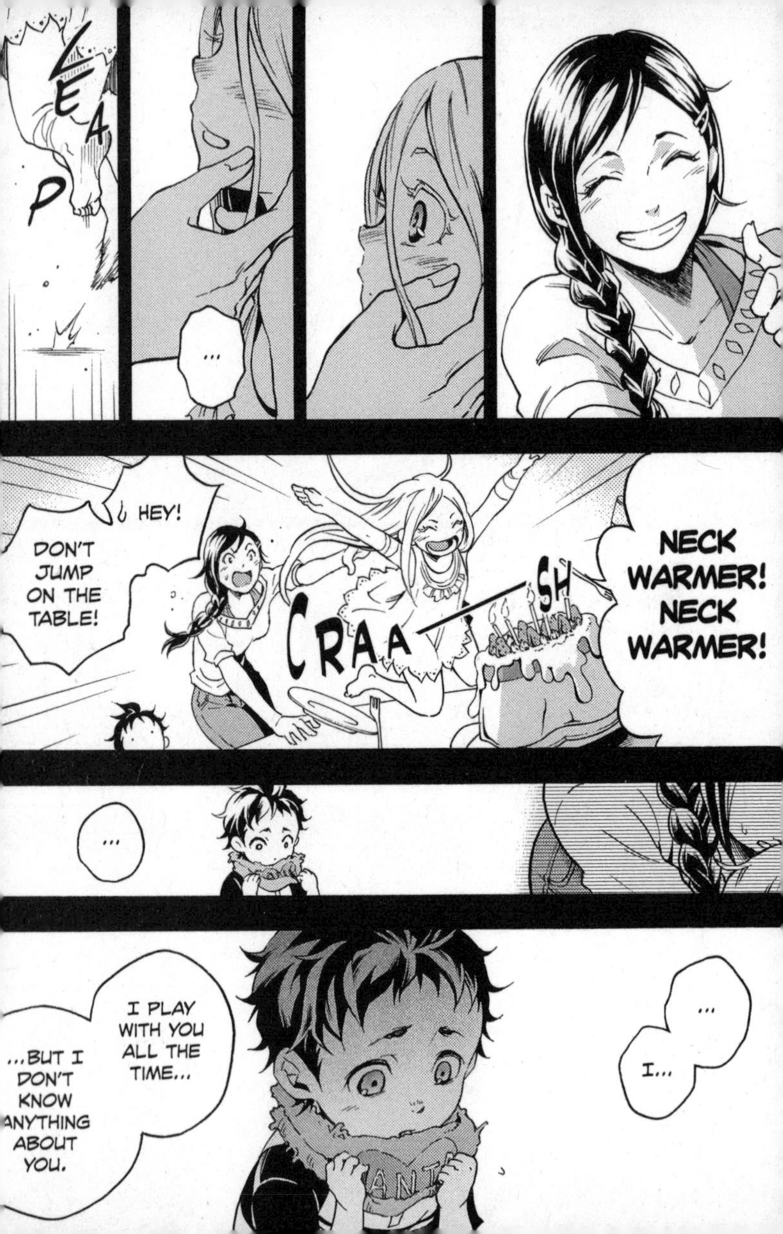
...
LEAP
NECK WARMER! NECK WARMER!
CRAASH
HEY!
DON'T JUMP ON THE TABLE!
...
...
I...
I PLAY WITH YOU ALL THE TIME...
...BUT I DON'T KNOW ANYTHING ABOUT YOU.

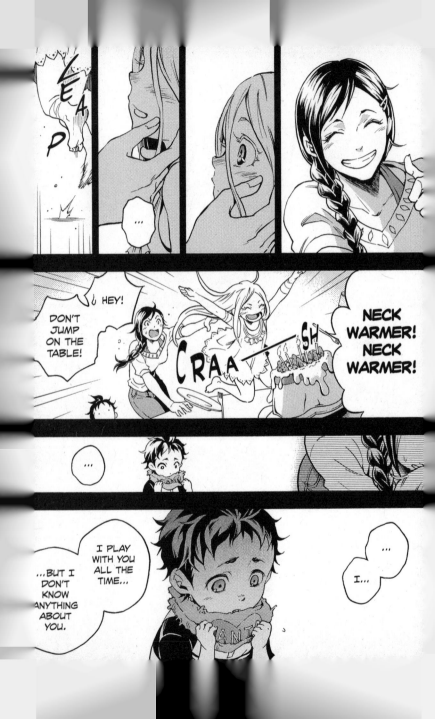

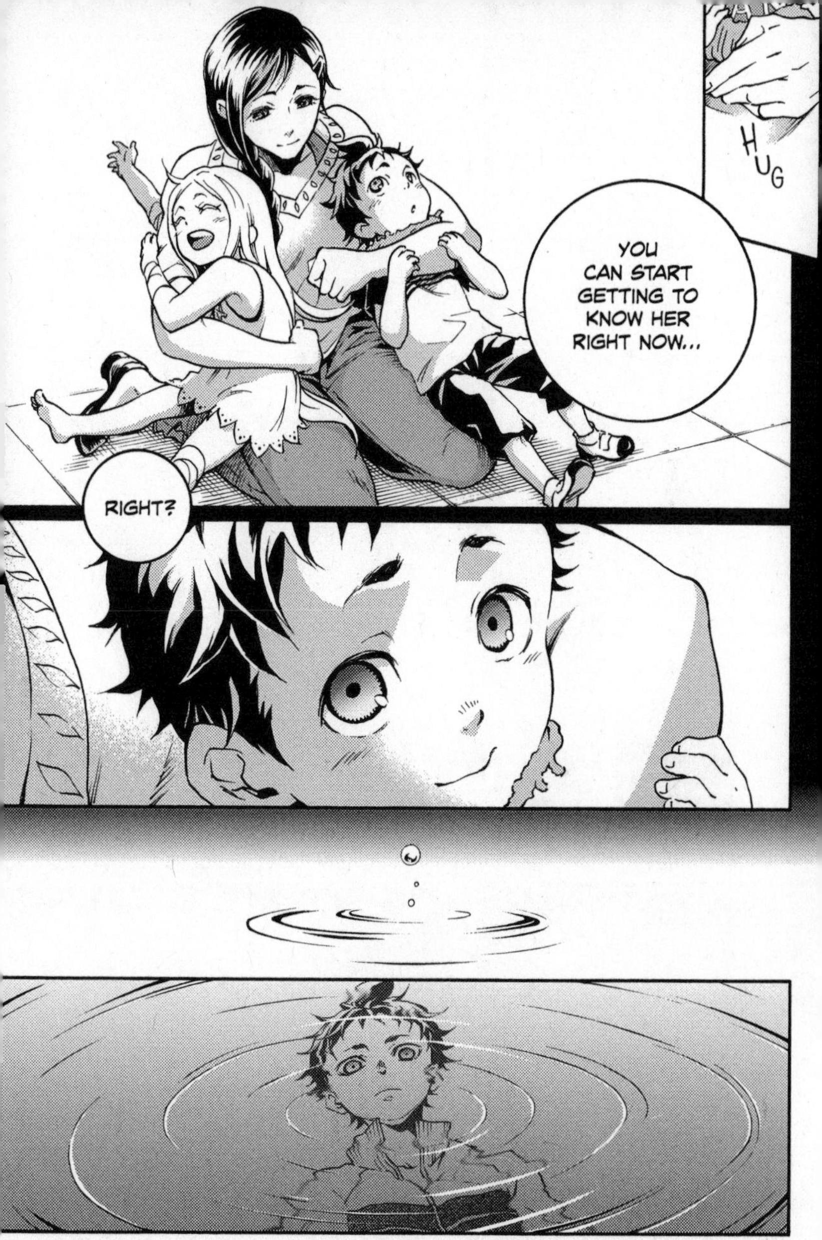
HUG
YOU CAN START GETTING TO KNOW HER RIGHT NOW...
RIGHT?

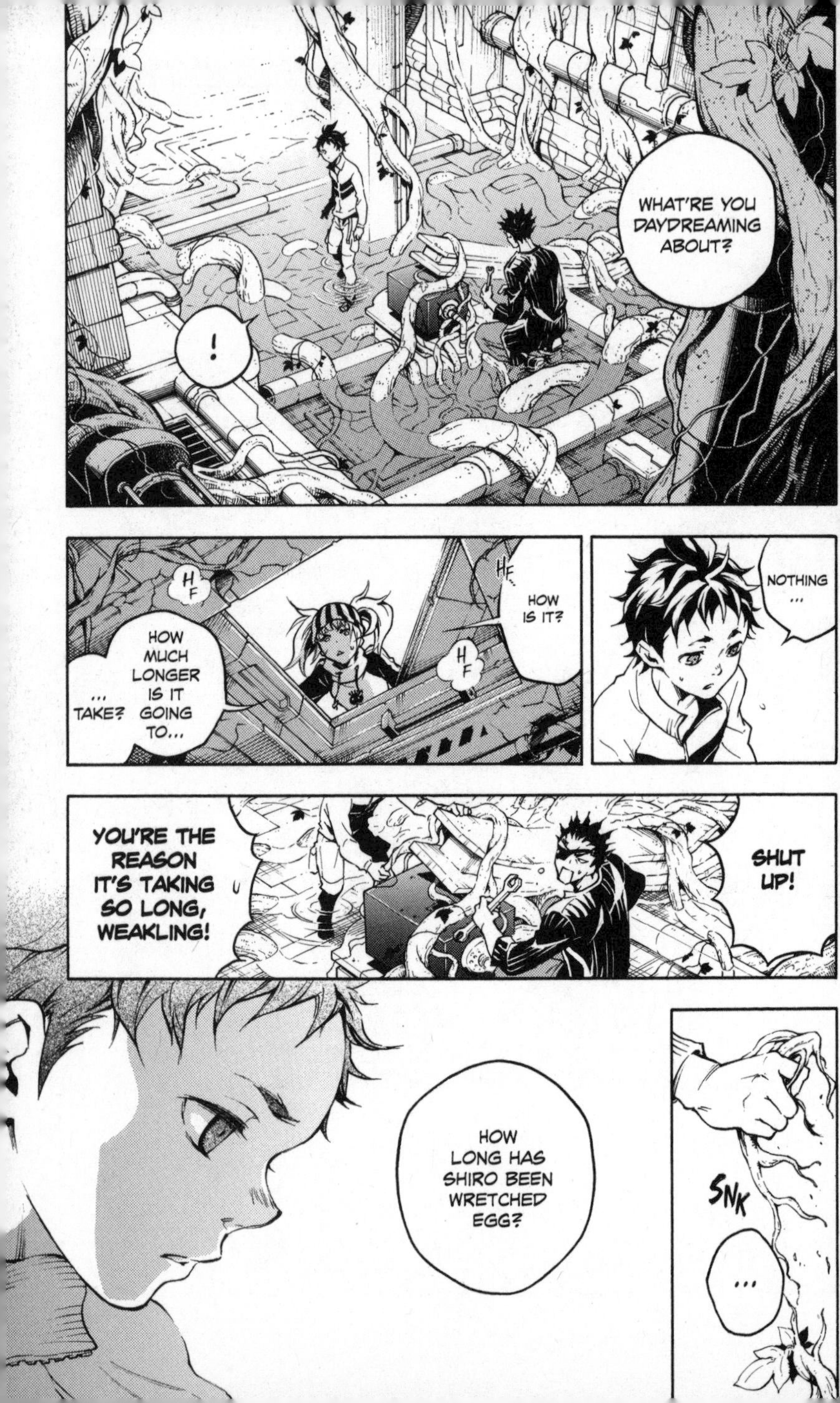
WHAT'RE YOU DAYDREAMING ABOUT?
!
NOTHING ...
HF..
HOW IS IT?
HF
HF
HOW MUCH LONGER IS IT GOING TO...
... TAKE?
SHUT UP!
YOU'RE THE REASON IT'S TAKING SO LONG, WEAKLING!
SNK
...
HOW LONG HAS SHIRO BEEN WRETCHED EGG?

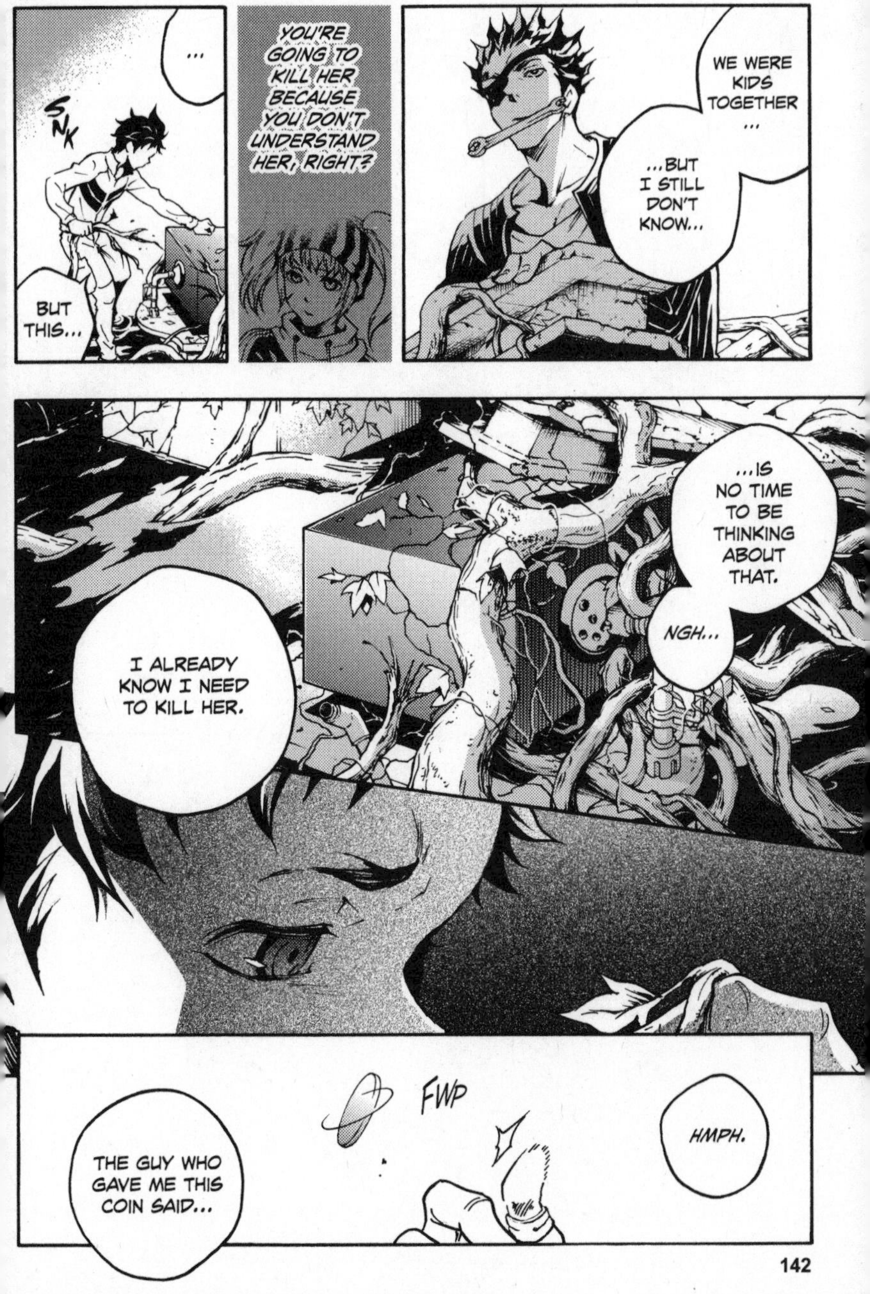
WE WERE KIDS TOGETHER ...
...BUT I STILL DON'T KNOW...
YOU'RE GOING TO KILL HER BECAUSE YOU DON'T UNDERSTAND HER, RIGHT?
...
SNK
BUT THIS...
...IS NO TIME TO BE THINKING ABOUT THAT.
NGH...
I ALREADY KNOW I NEED TO KILL HER.
HMPH.
FWP
THE GUY WHO GAVE ME THIS COIN SAID...

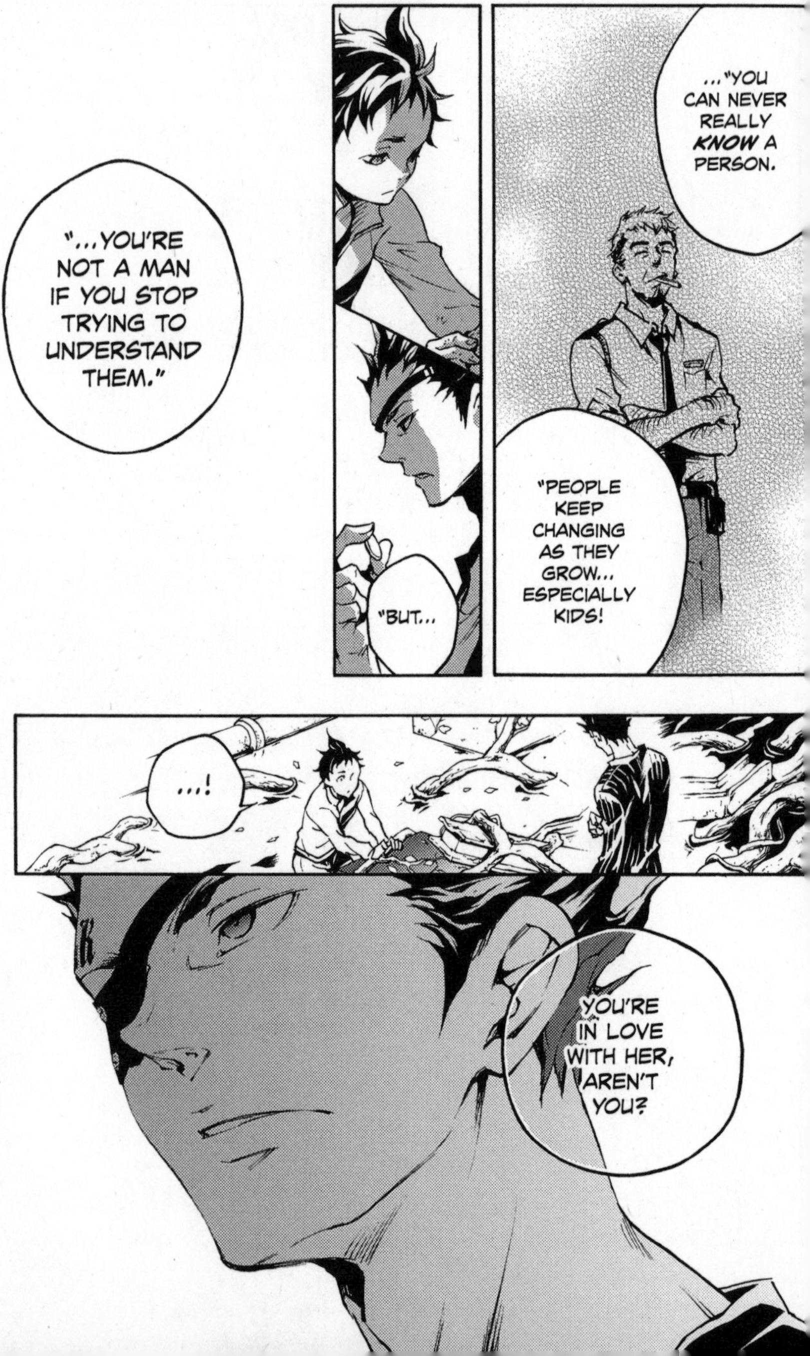
..."YOU CAN NEVER REALLY KNOW A PERSON.
"PEOPLE KEEP CHANGING AS THEY GROW... ESPECIALLY KIDS!
"BUT...
"...YOU'RE NOT A MAN IF YOU STOP TRYING TO UNDERSTAND THEM."
...!
YOU'RE IN LOVE WITH HER, AREN'T YOU?

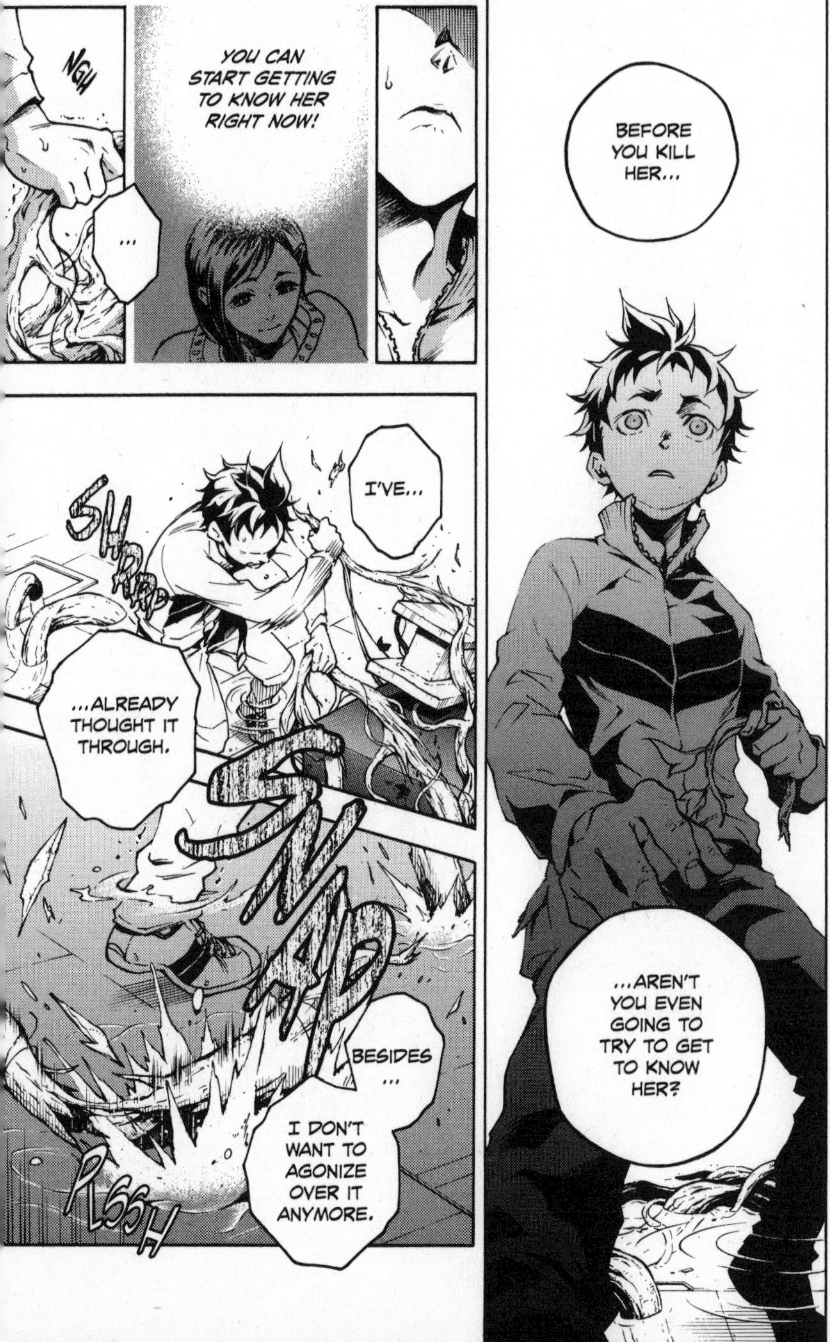
BEFORE YOU KILL HER...
...AREN'T YOU EVEN GOING TO TRY TO GET TO KNOW HER?
YOU CAN START GETTING TO KNOW HER RIGHT NOW!
NGH
...
I'VE...
SHRRRD
...ALREADY THOUGHT IT THROUGH.
SNAP
BESIDES...
I DON'T WANT TO AGONIZE OVER IT ANYMORE.
PLSSH

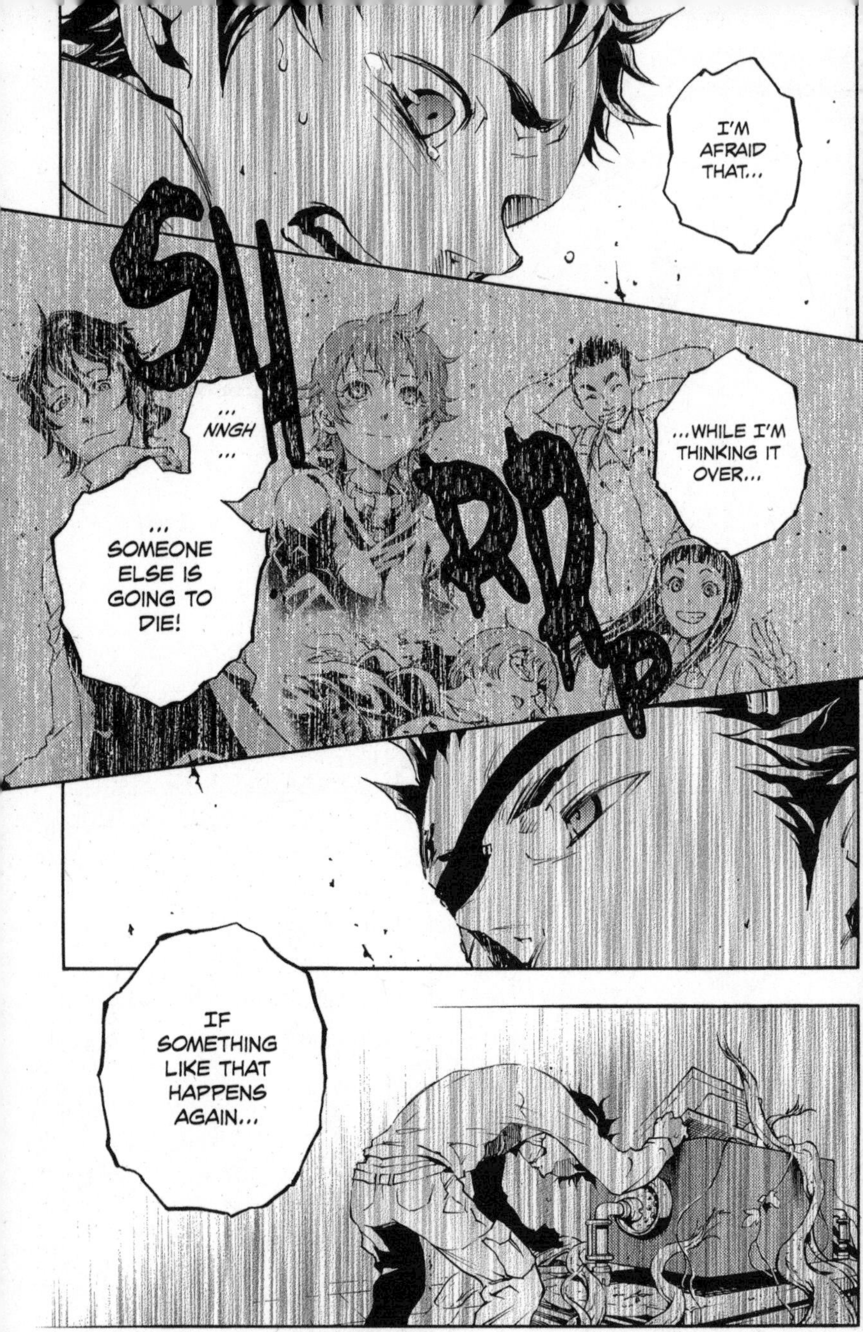
I'M AFRAID THAT...
...WHILE I'M THINKING IT OVER...
...NNGH...
...SOMEONE ELSE IS GOING TO DIE!
SHRRP
IF SOMETHING LIKE THAT HAPPENS AGAIN...

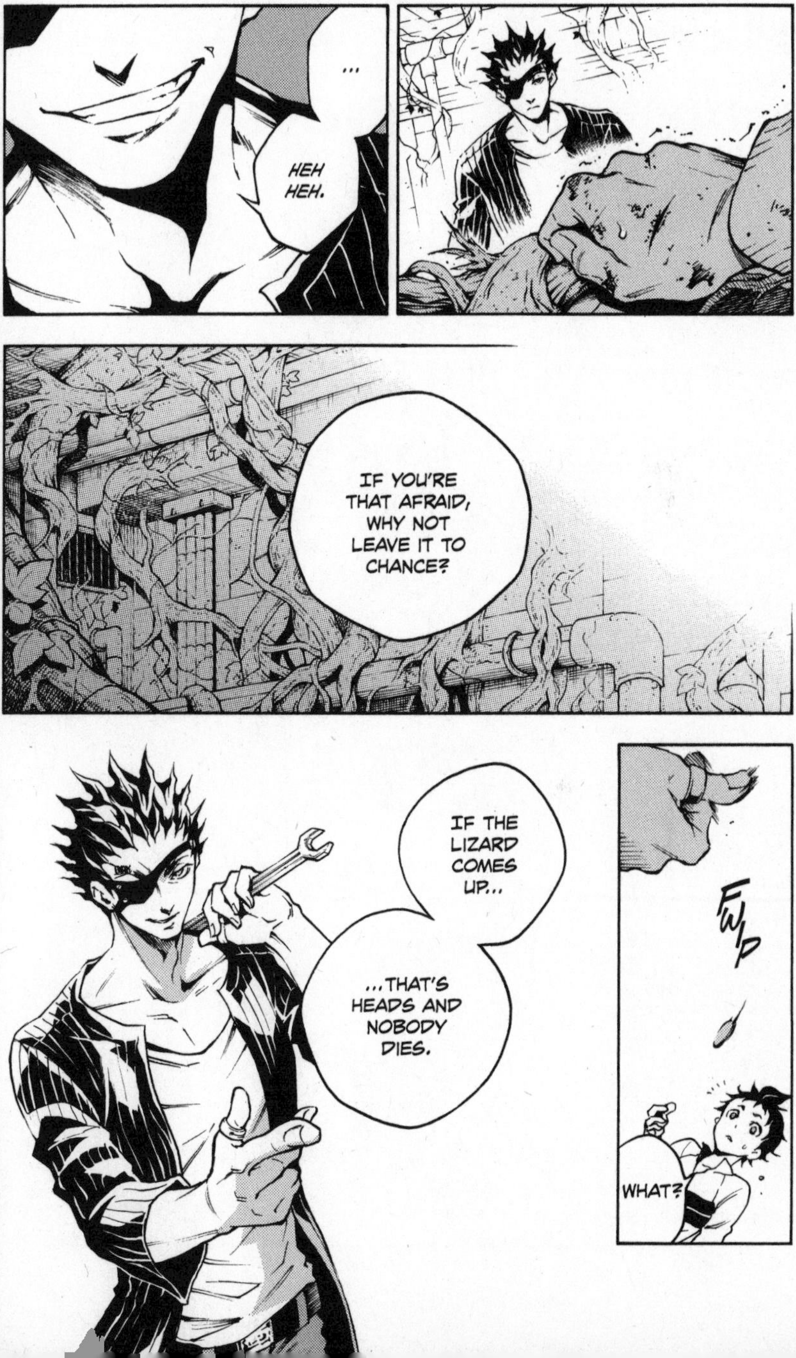
...
HEH HEH.
IF YOU'RE THAT AFRAID, WHY NOT LEAVE IT TO CHANCE?
FWIP
WHAT?
IF THE LIZARD COMES UP...
...THAT'S HEADS AND NOBODY DIES.

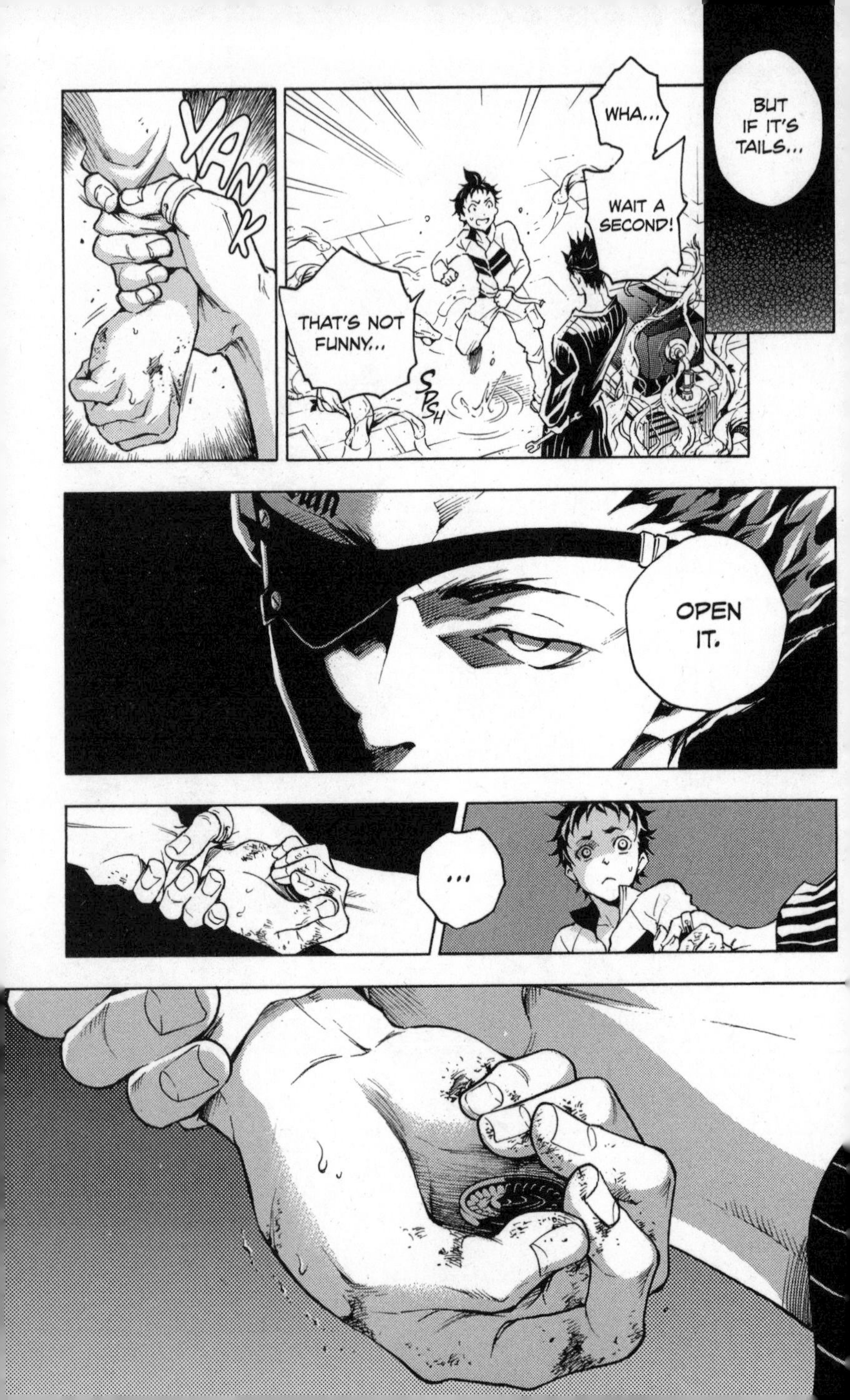
BUT IF IT'S TAILS...
WHA...
WAIT A SECOND!
THAT'S NOT FUNNY...
SPSH
YANK
OPEN IT.
...

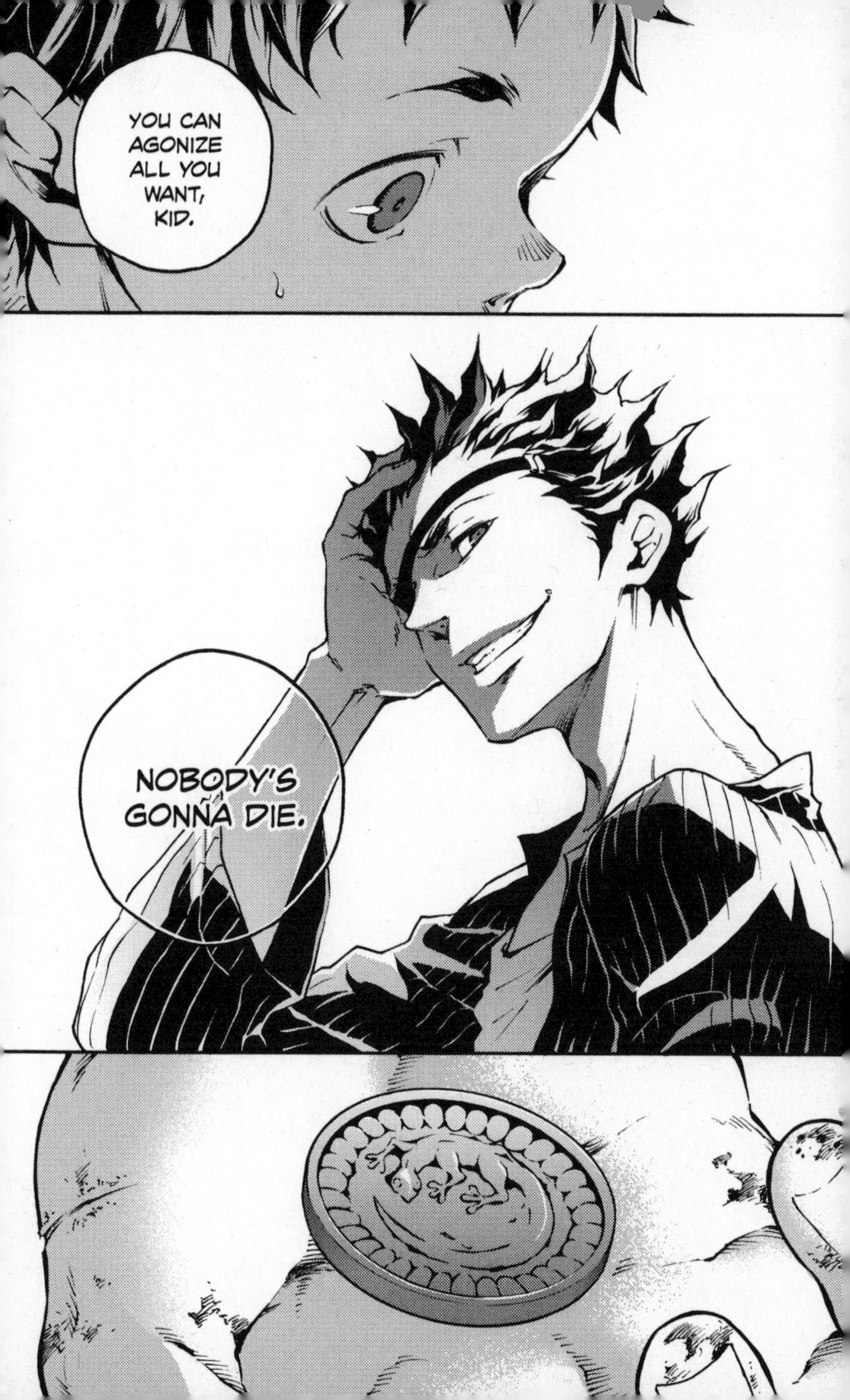
YOU CAN AGONIZE ALL YOU WANT, KID.
NOBODY'S GONNA DIE.

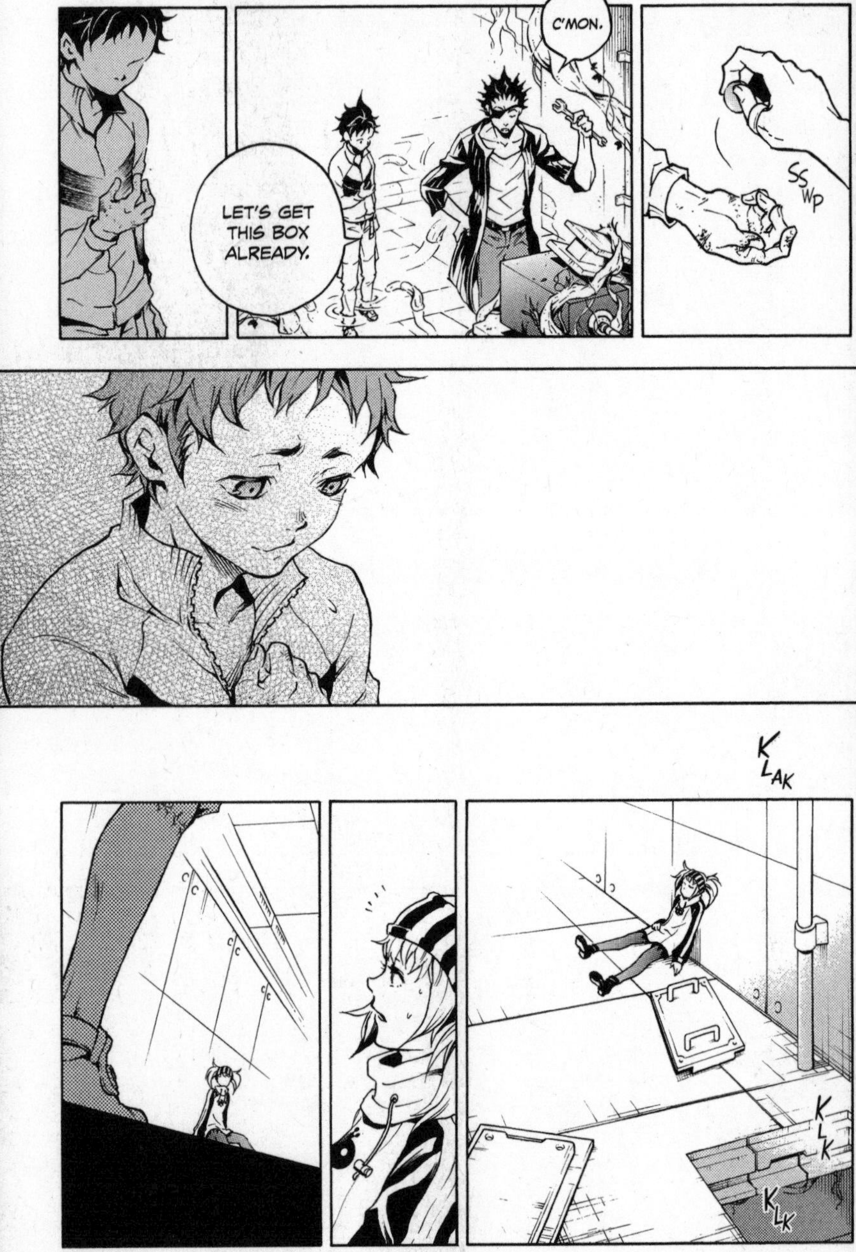
SSWP
C'MON.
LET'S GET THIS BOX ALREADY.
KLAK
KLK
KLK

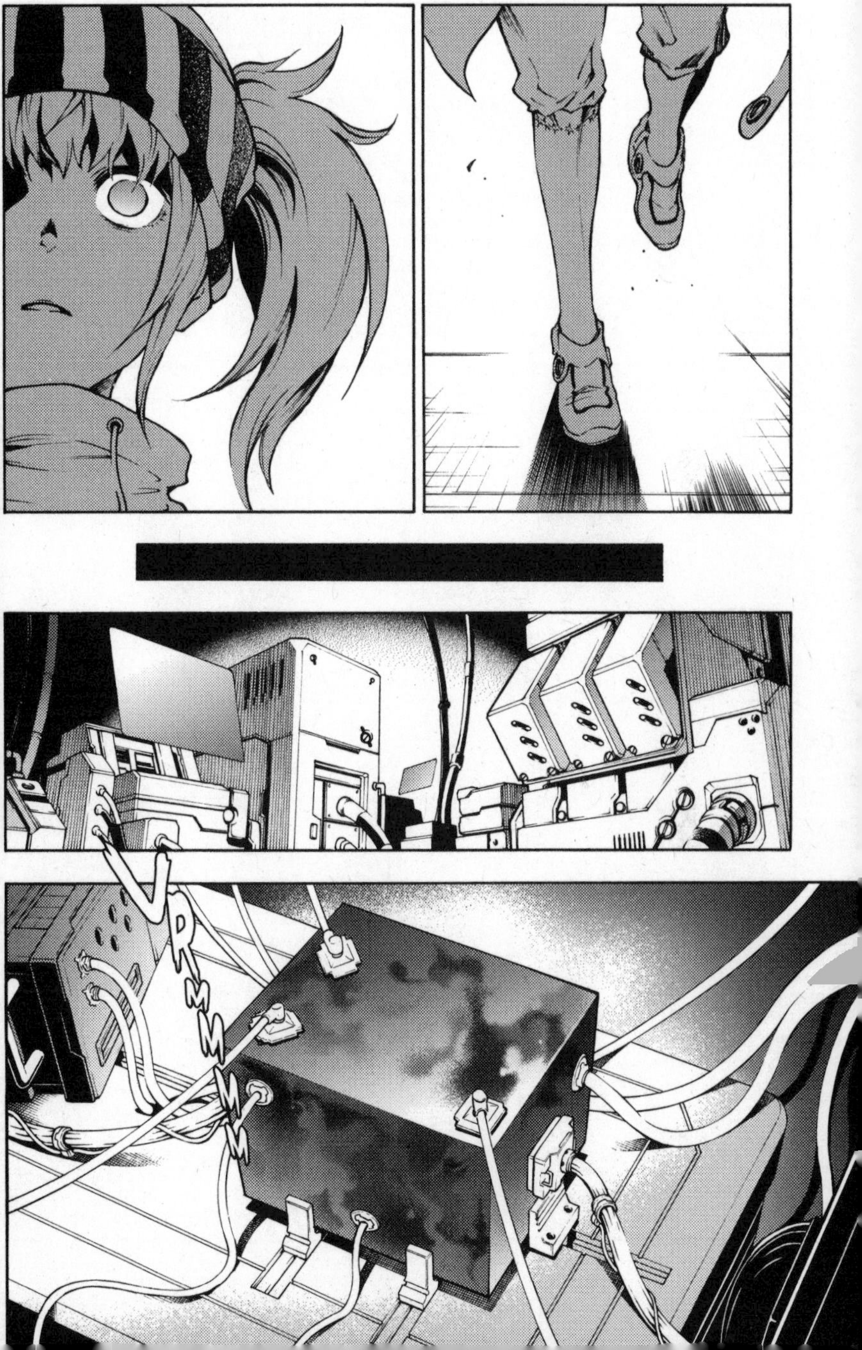
VRMMMM

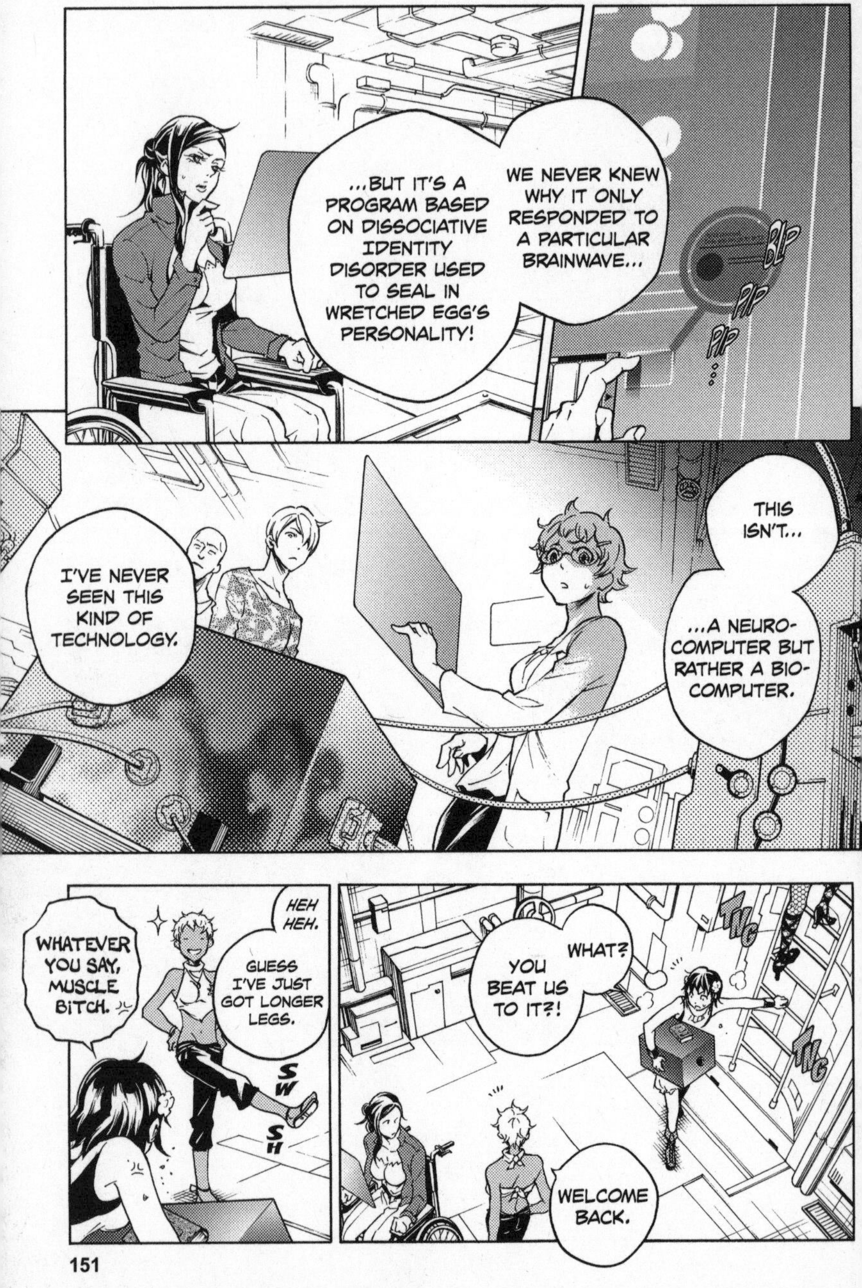
WE NEVER KNEW WHY IT ONLY RESPONDED TO A PARTICULAR BRAINWAVE...
BLIP
PIP
PIP
...BUT IT'S A PROGRAM BASED ON DISSOCIATIVE IDENTITY DISORDER USED TO SEAL IN WRETCHED EGG'S PERSONALITY!
THIS ISN'T...
...A NEURO-COMPUTER BUT RATHER A BIO-COMPUTER.
I'VE NEVER SEEN THIS KIND OF TECHNOLOGY.
TNG
TNG
WHAT?
YOU BEAT US TO IT?!
WELCOME BACK.
HEH HEH.
GUESS I'VE JUST GOT LONGER LEGS.
SWSH
WHATEVER YOU SAY, MUSCLE BITCH.

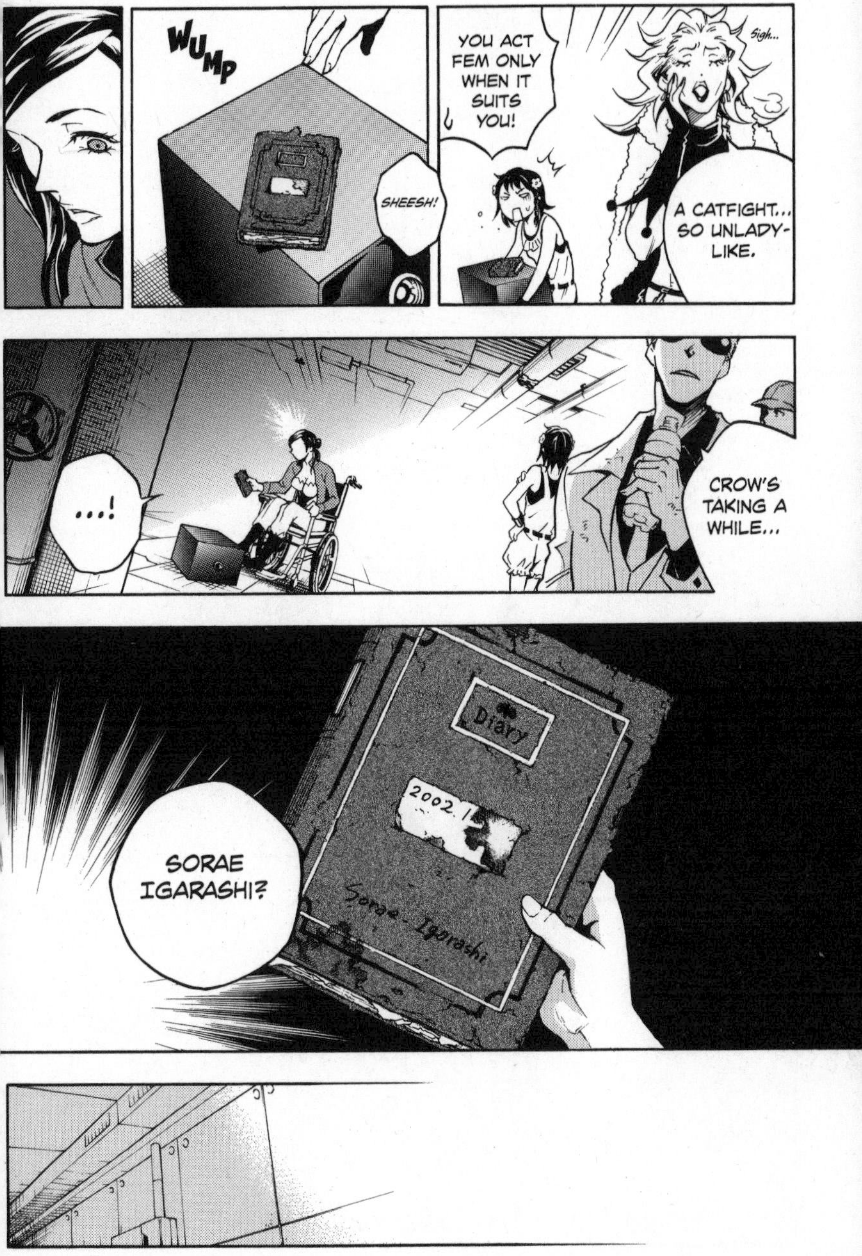
Sigh...
A CATFIGHT... SO UNLADYLIKE.
YOU ACT FEM ONLY WHEN IT SUITS YOU!
WUMP
SHEESH!
CROW'S TAKING A WHILE...
...!
Diary
2002. 1
Sorae Igarashi
SORAE IGARASHI?

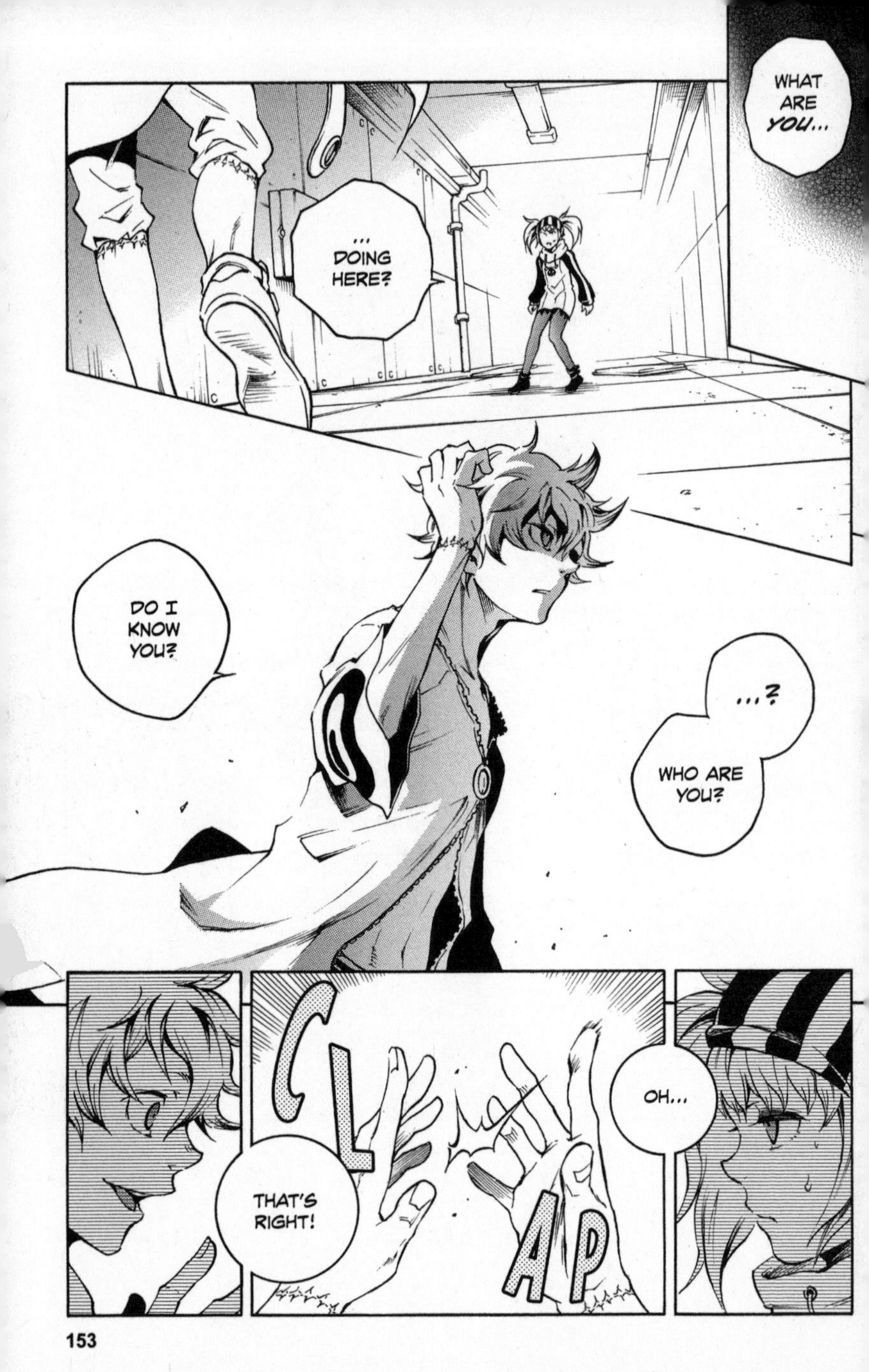
WHAT ARE YOU...
... DOING HERE?
...?
WHO ARE YOU?
DO I KNOW YOU?
OH...
CLAP
THAT'S RIGHT!

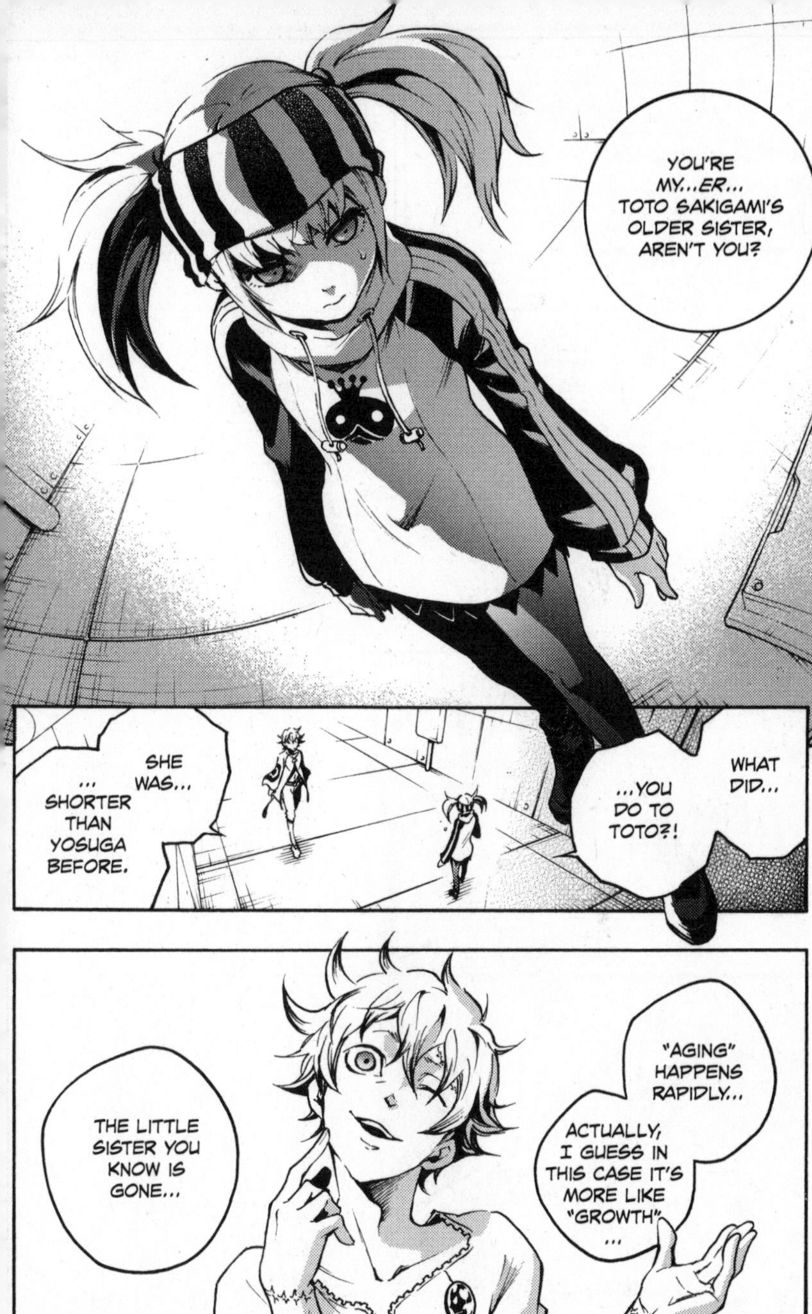
YOU'RE MY...ER... TOTO SAKIGAMI'S OLDER SISTER, AREN'T YOU?
WHAT DID...
...YOU DO TO TOTO?!
SHE WAS...
...SHORTER THAN YOSUGA BEFORE.
"AGING" HAPPENS RAPIDLY...
ACTUALLY, I GUESS IN THIS CASE IT'S MORE LIKE "GROWTH"...
THE LITTLE SISTER YOU KNOW IS GONE...

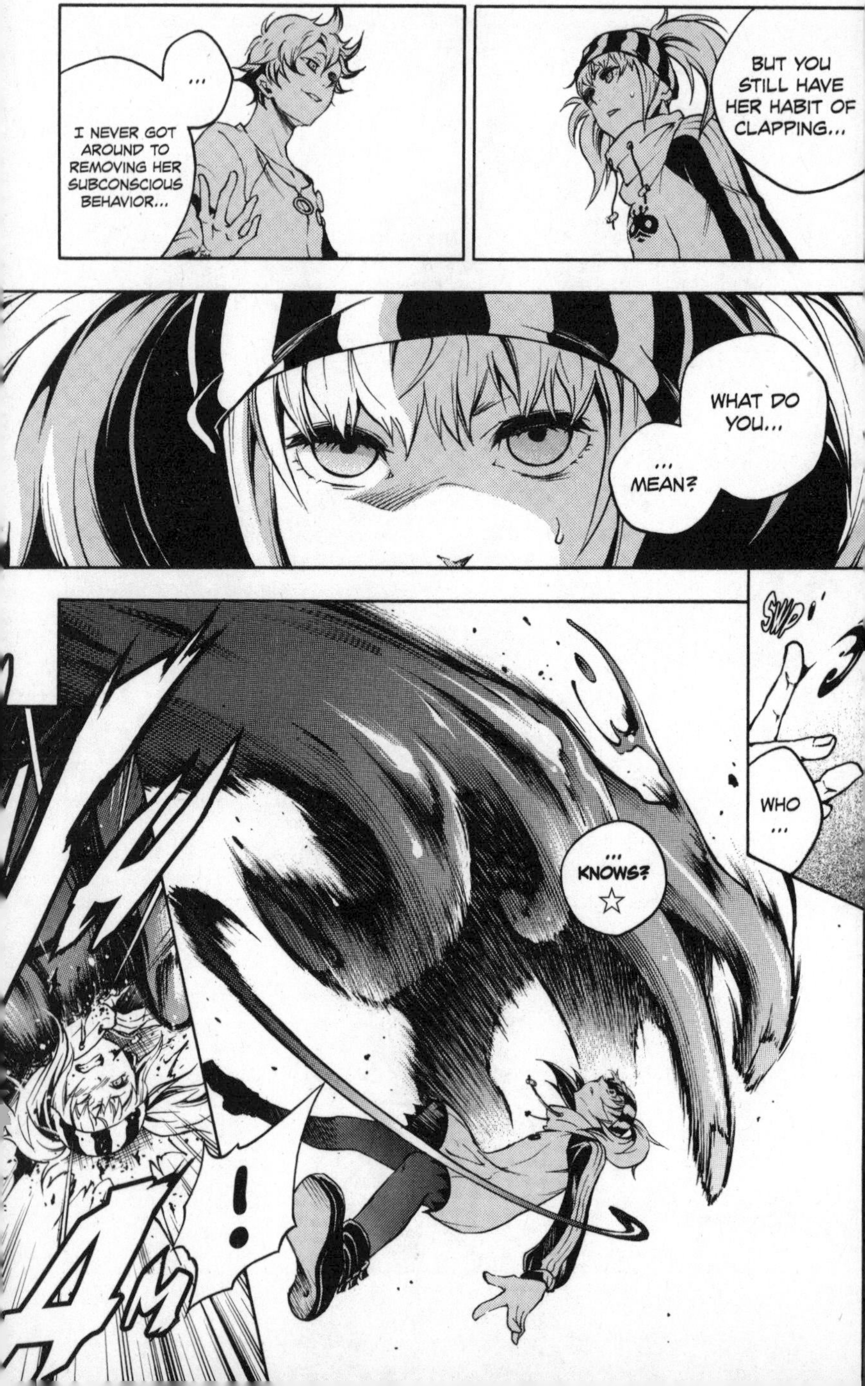
BUT YOU STILL HAVE HER HABIT OF CLAPPING...
...
I NEVER GOT AROUND TO REMOVING HER SUBCONSCIOUS BEHAVIOR...
WHAT DO YOU...
... MEAN?
SWIP
WHO ...
... KNOWS? ☆
!

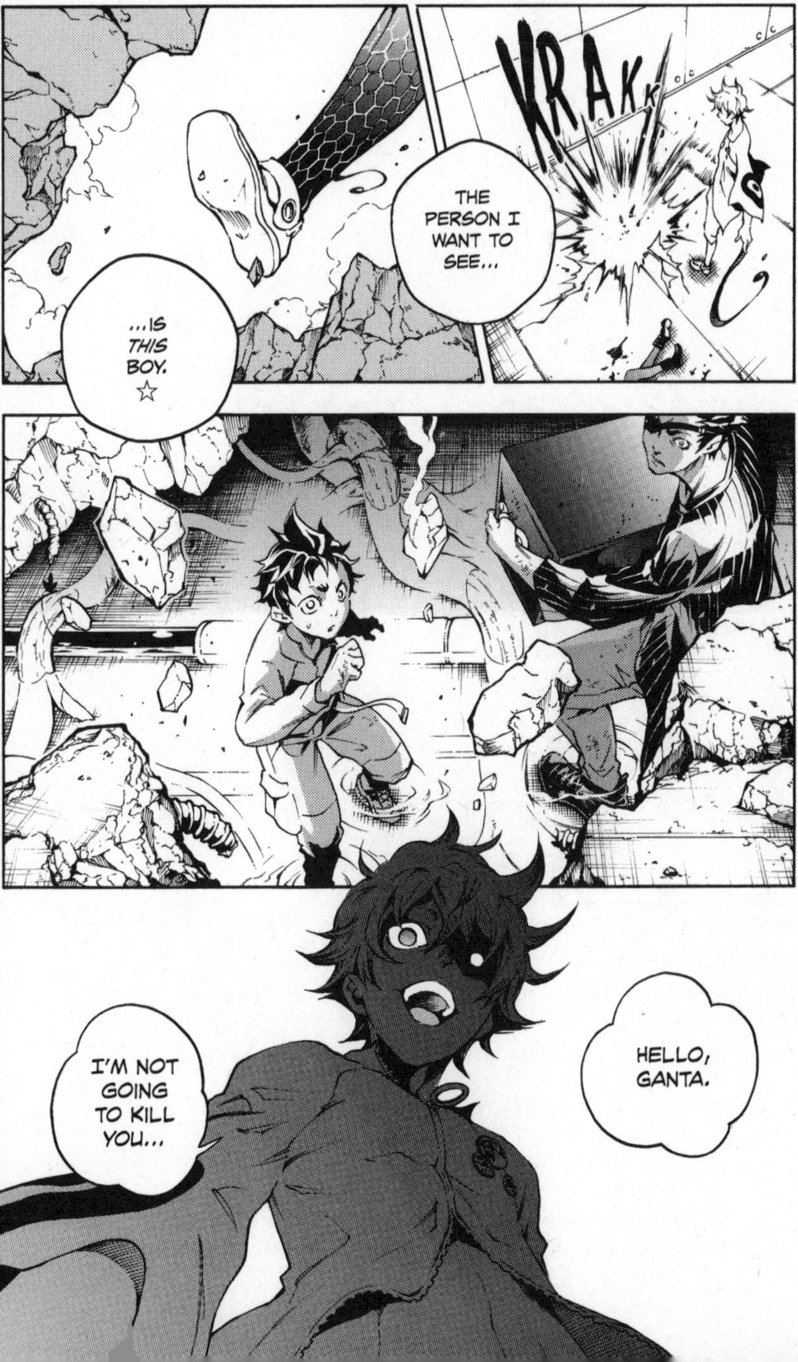
KRAKK
THE PERSON I WANT TO SEE...
...IS THIS BOY. ☆
HELLO, GANTA.
I'M NOT GOING TO KILL YOU...

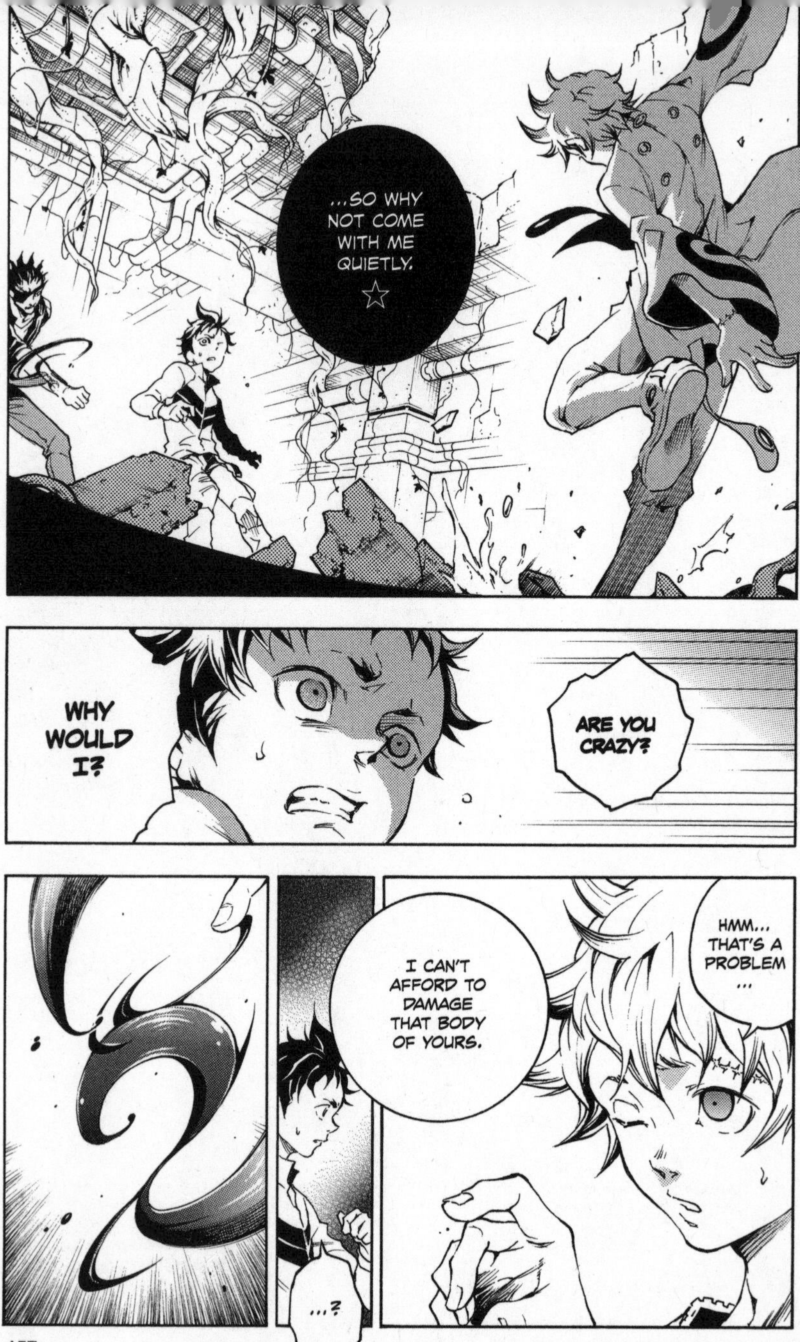
...SO WHY NOT COME WITH ME QUIETLY. ☆
ARE YOU CRAZY?
WHY WOULD I?
HMM... THAT'S A PROBLEM ...
I CAN'T AFFORD TO DAMAGE THAT BODY OF YOURS.
...?

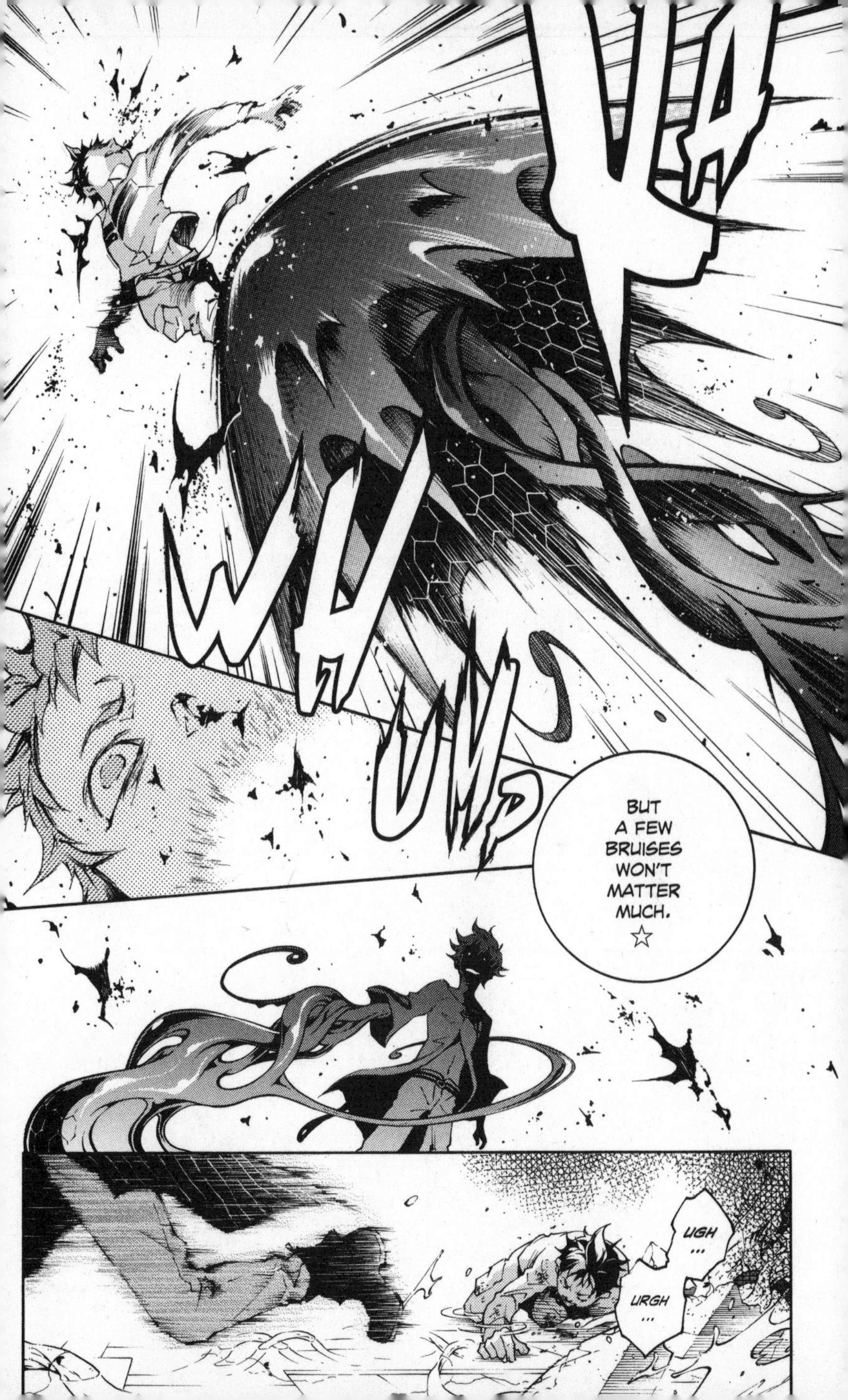
WHUMP
BUT A FEW BRUISES WON'T MATTER MUCH. ☆
UGH ...
URGH ...

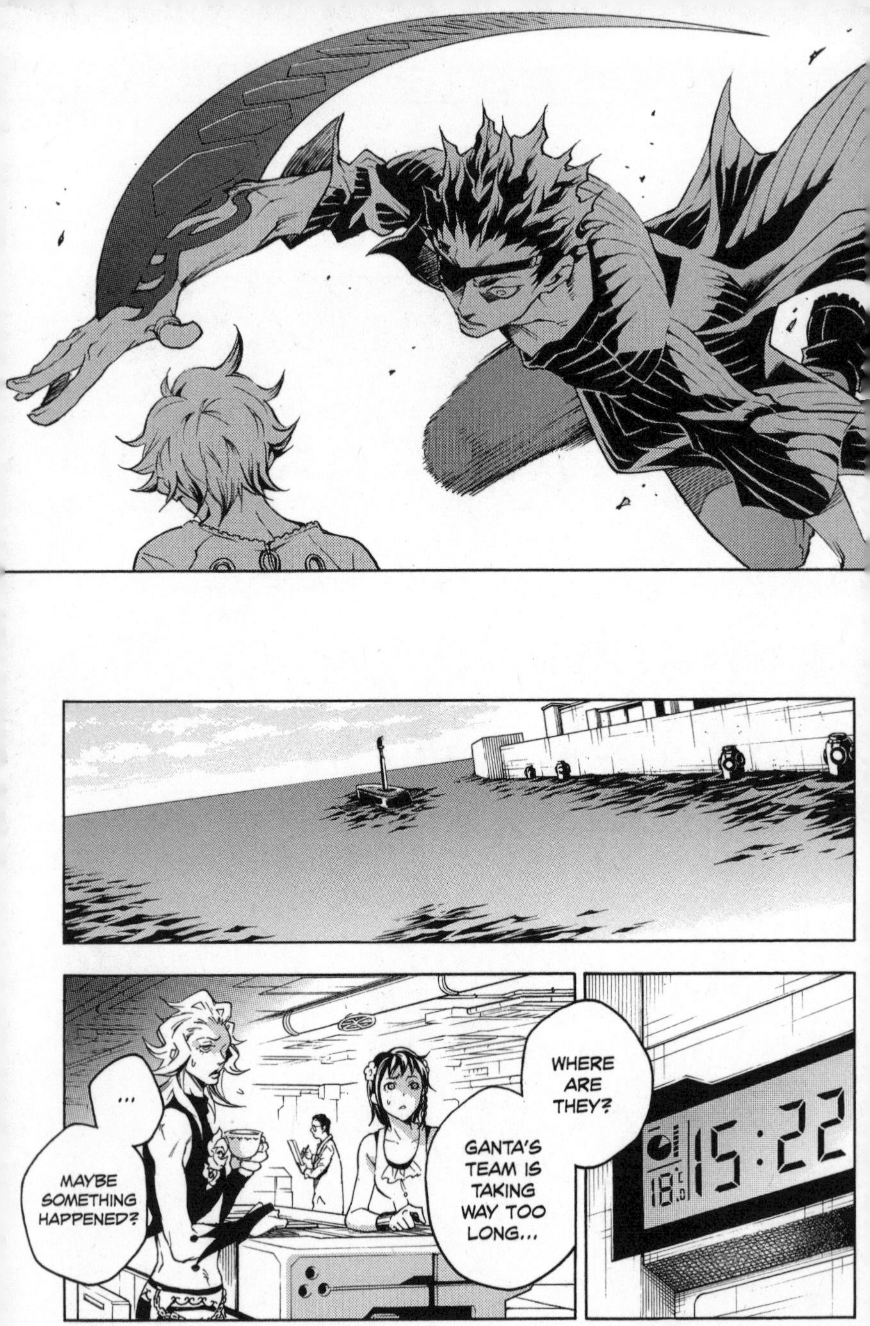
WHERE ARE THEY?
GANTA'S TEAM IS TAKING WAY TOO LONG...
...
MAYBE SOMETHING HAPPENED?

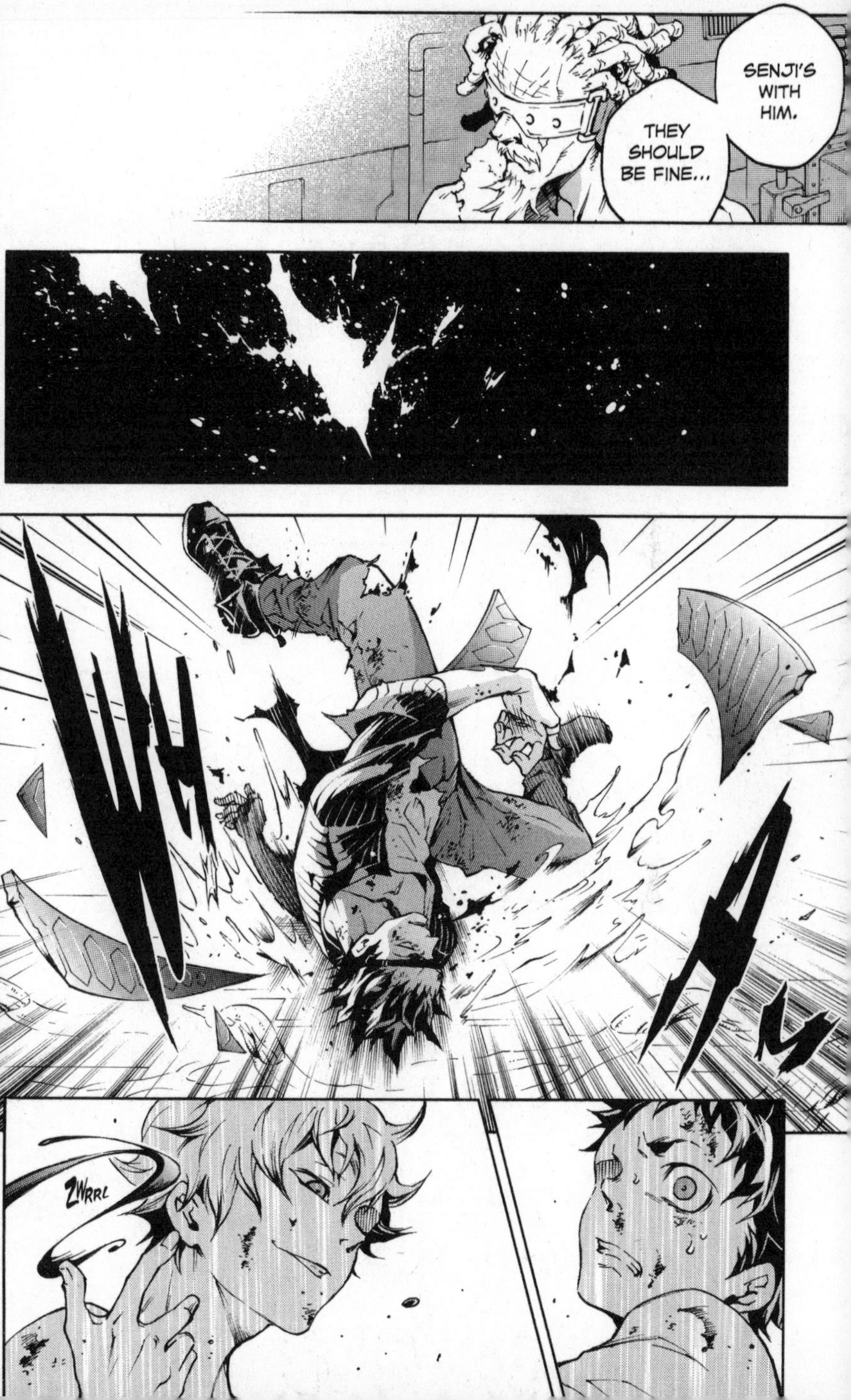
SENJI'S WITH HIM.
THEY SHOULD BE FINE...
ZWRRL

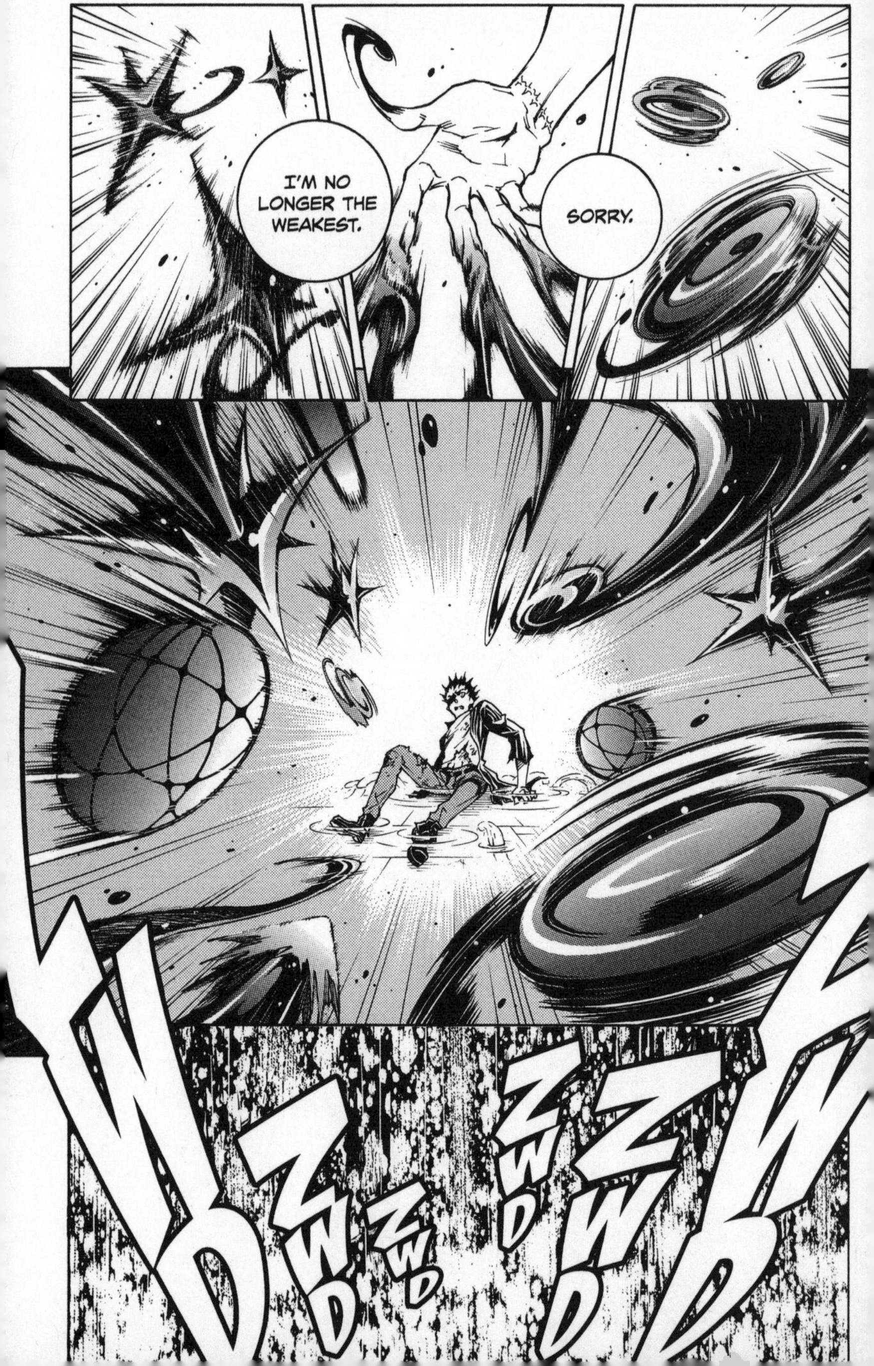
SORRY.
I'M NO LONGER THE WEAKEST.
ZWD
ZWD
ZWD
ZWD

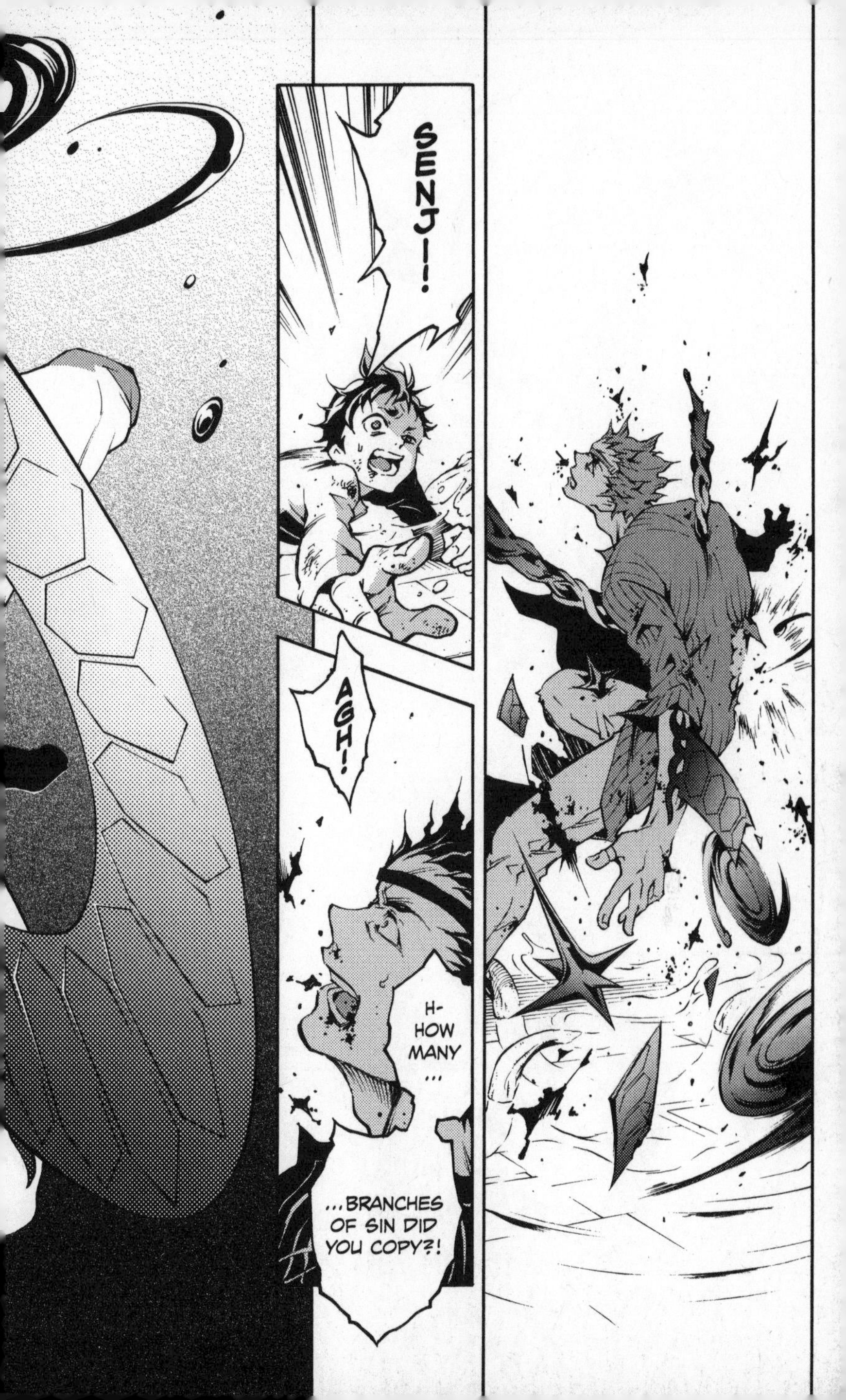
SENJI!!
AGH!
H-HOW MANY...
...BRANCHES OF SIN DID YOU COPY?!

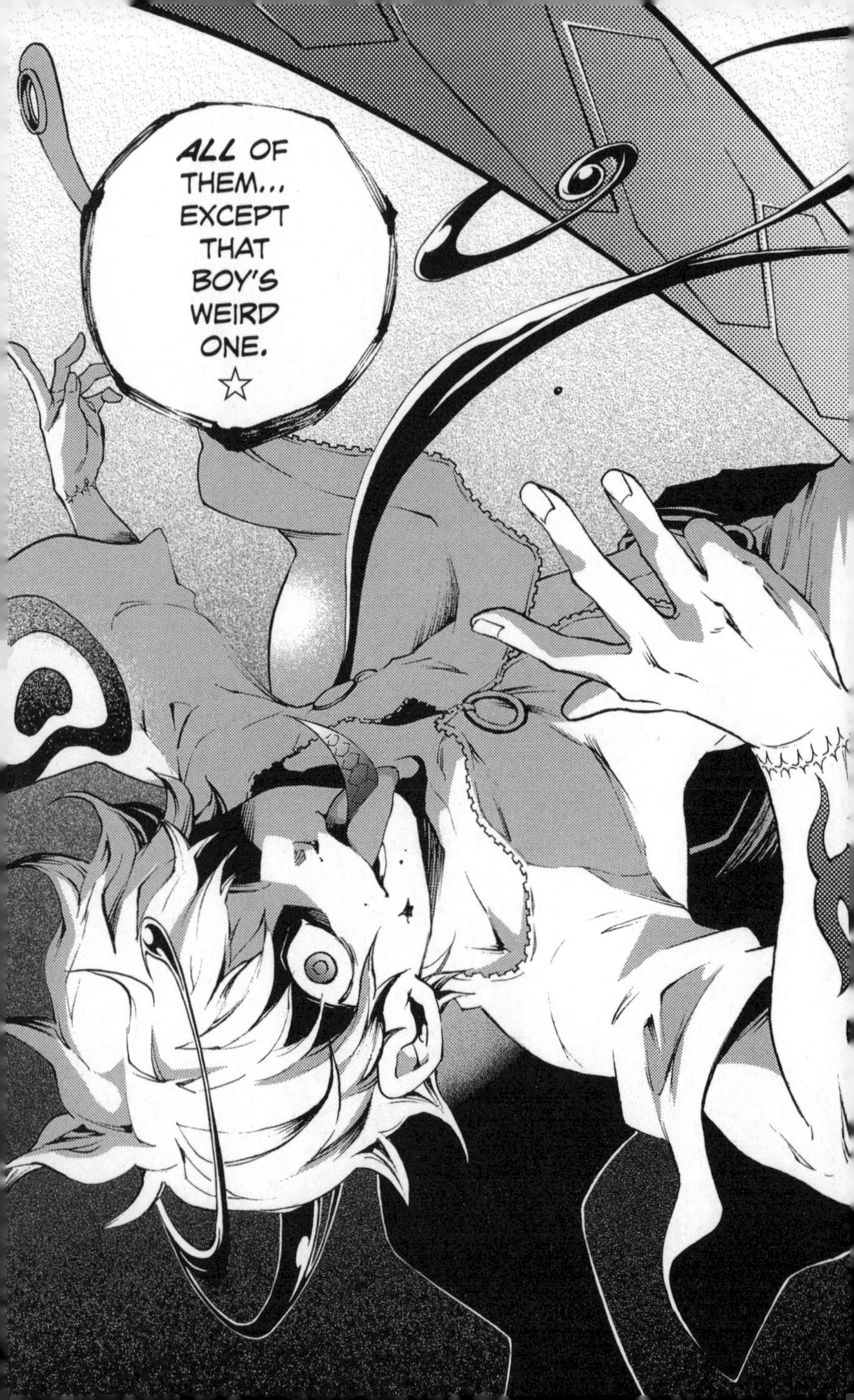
ALL OF THEM... EXCEPT THAT BOY'S WEIRD ONE. ☆

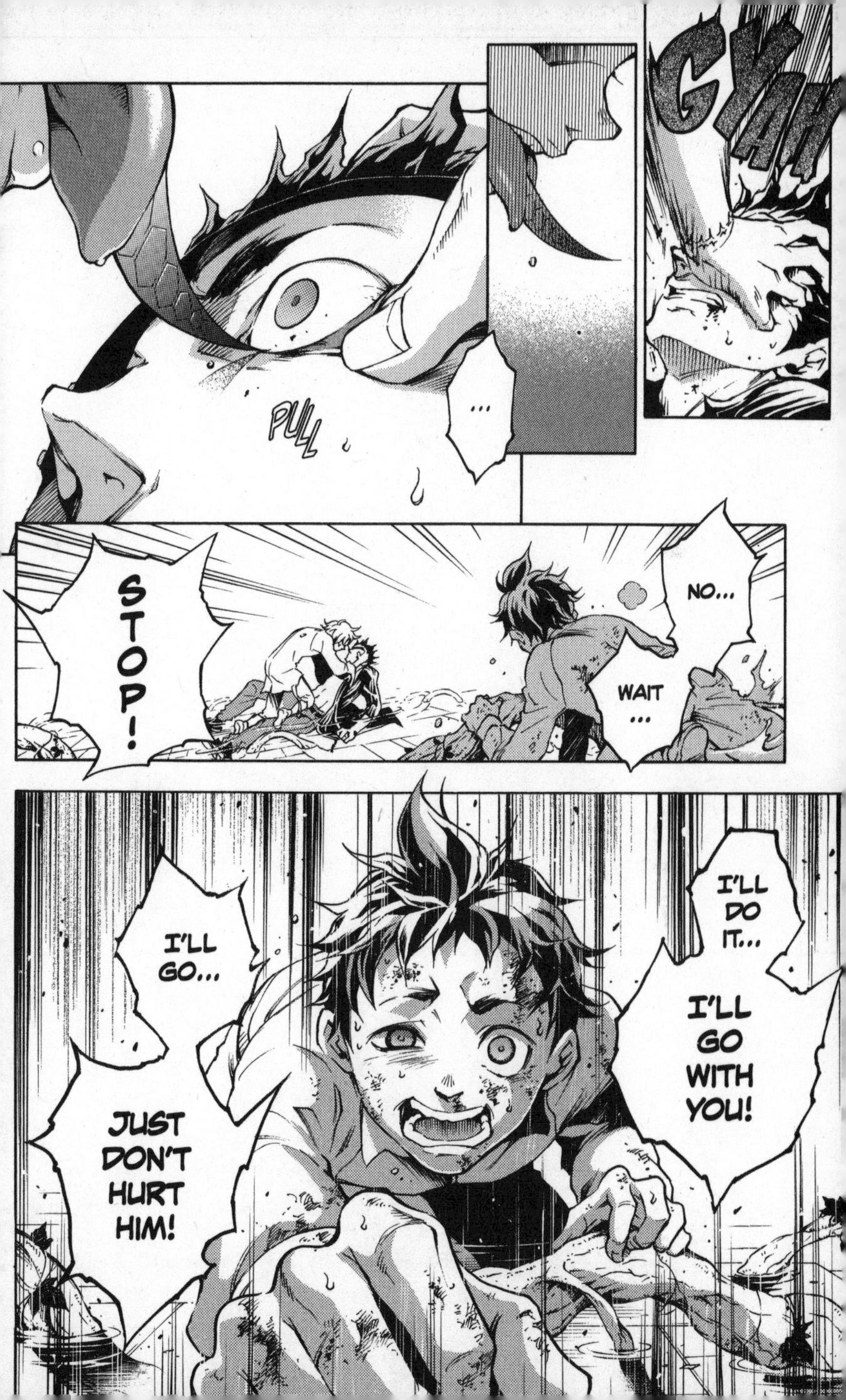
GYAH
...
PULL
NO...
WAIT...
STOP!
I'LL DO IT...
I'LL GO WITH YOU!
I'LL GO...
JUST DON'T HURT HIM!

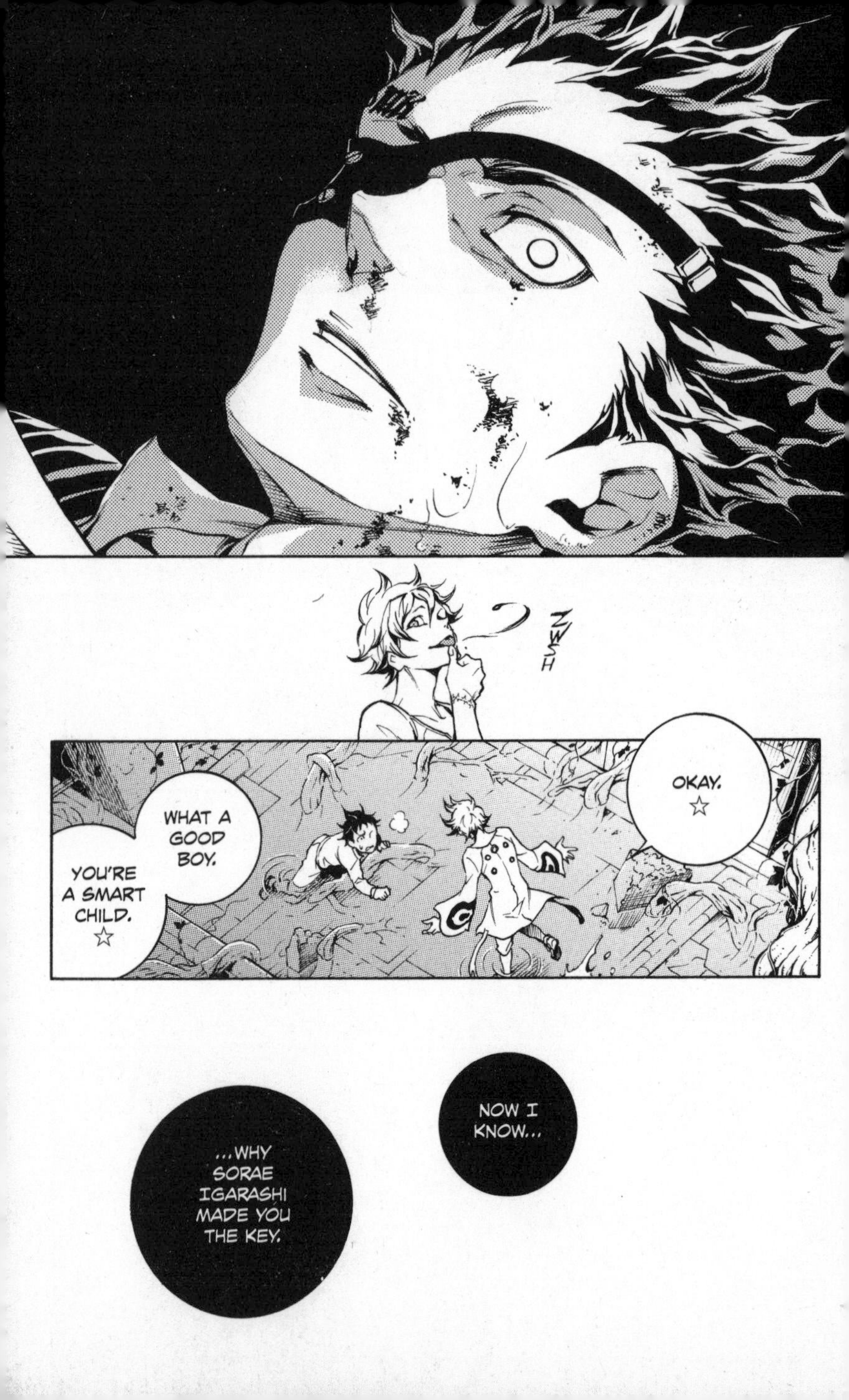
ZWSH
OKAY. ☆
WHAT A GOOD BOY.
YOU'RE A SMART CHILD. ☆
NOW I KNOW...
...WHY SORAE IGARASHI MADE YOU THE KEY.

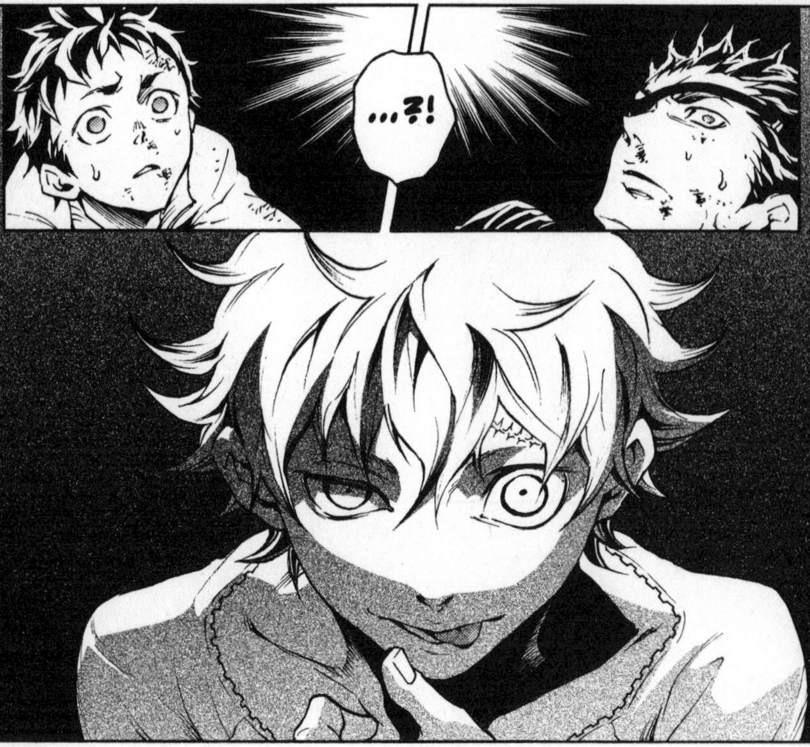
...?!

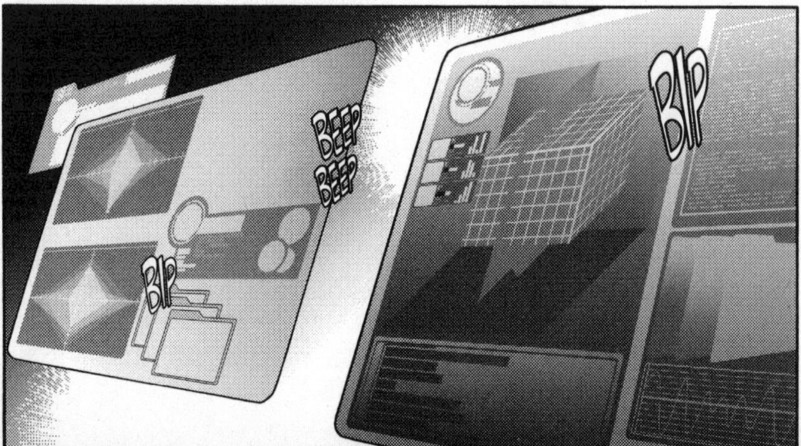
BIP
BEEP BEEP
BIP

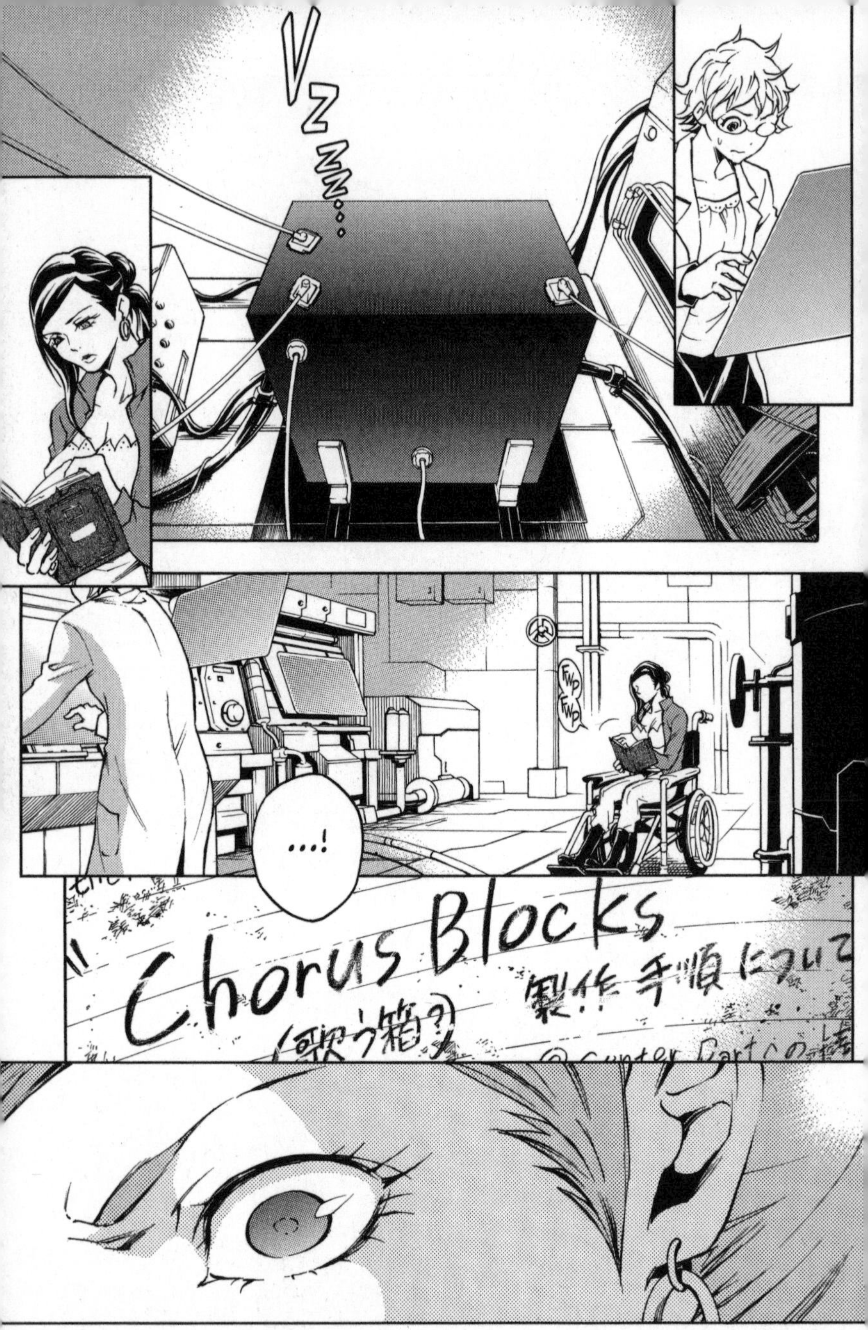
VZZZ...
FWP FWP
...!
"Chorus Blocks
(歌う箱?)
製作手順について

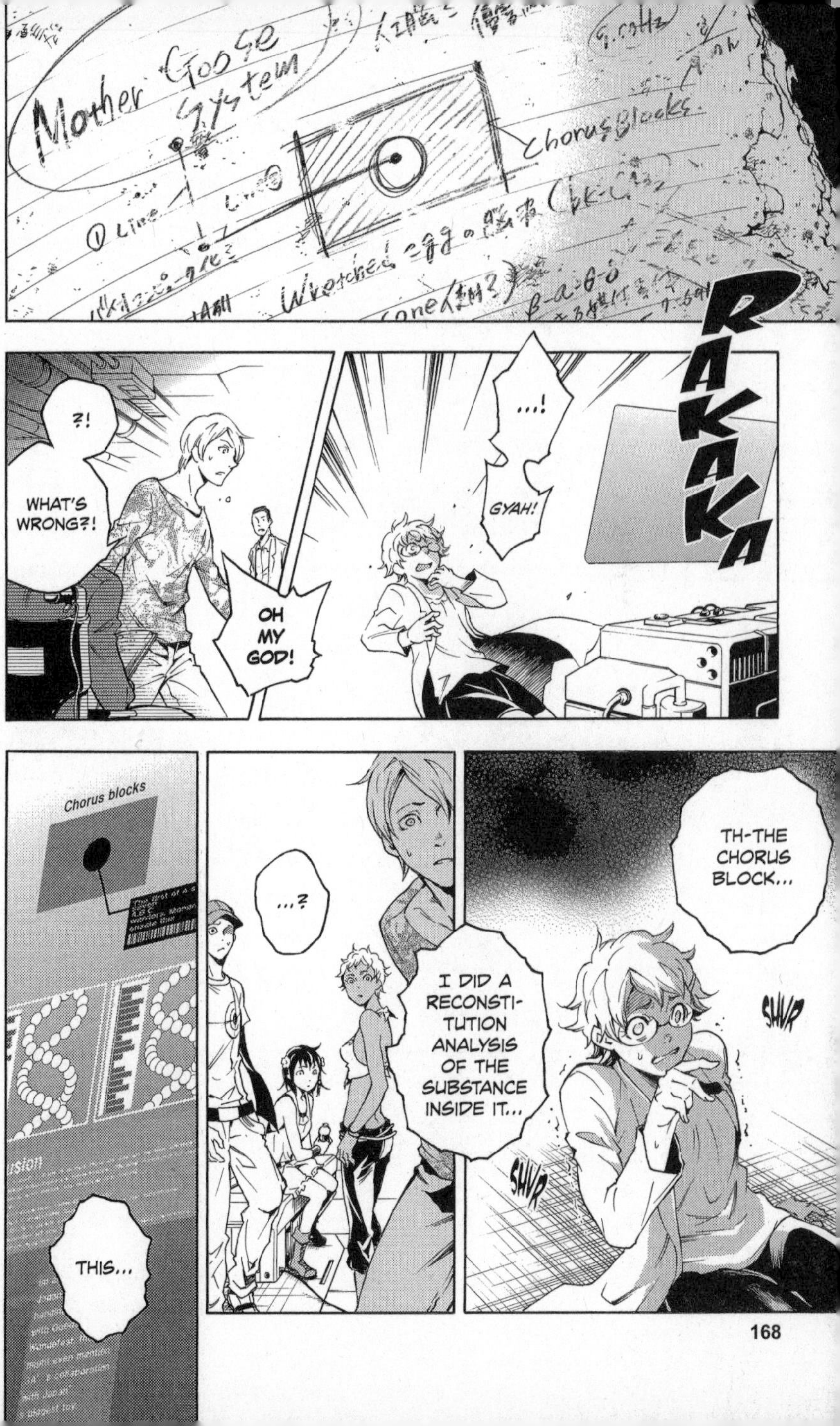
Mother Goose System
Chorus Blocks
RAKAKA
...!
GYAH!
?!
WHAT'S WRONG?!
OH MY GOD!
TH-THE CHORUS BLOCK...
SHVR
SHVR
...?
I DID A RECONSTI-TUTION ANALYSIS OF THE SUBSTANCE INSIDE IT...
Chorus blocks
THIS...

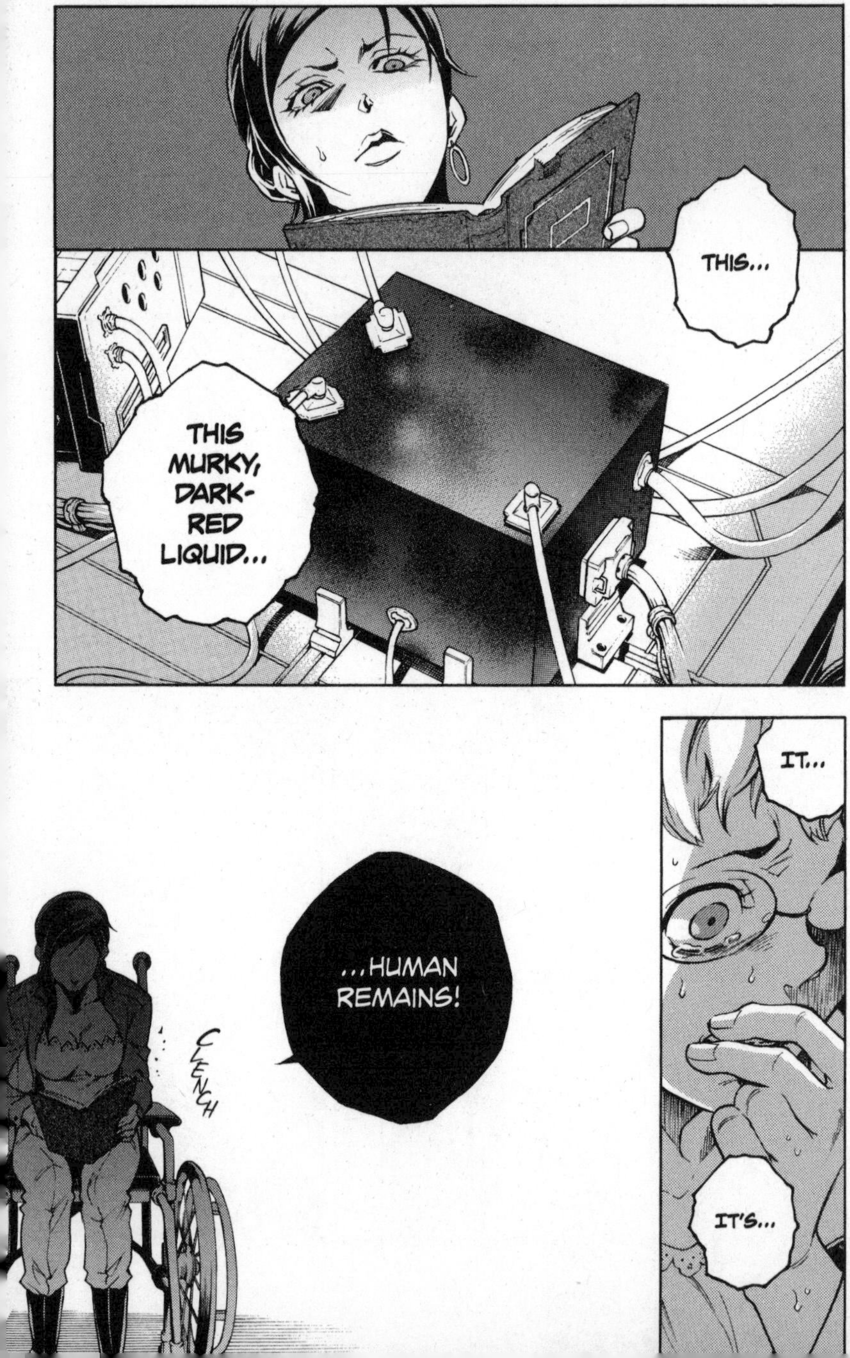
THIS...
THIS MURKY, DARK-RED LIQUID...
IT...
IT'S...
...HUMAN REMAINS!
CLENCH

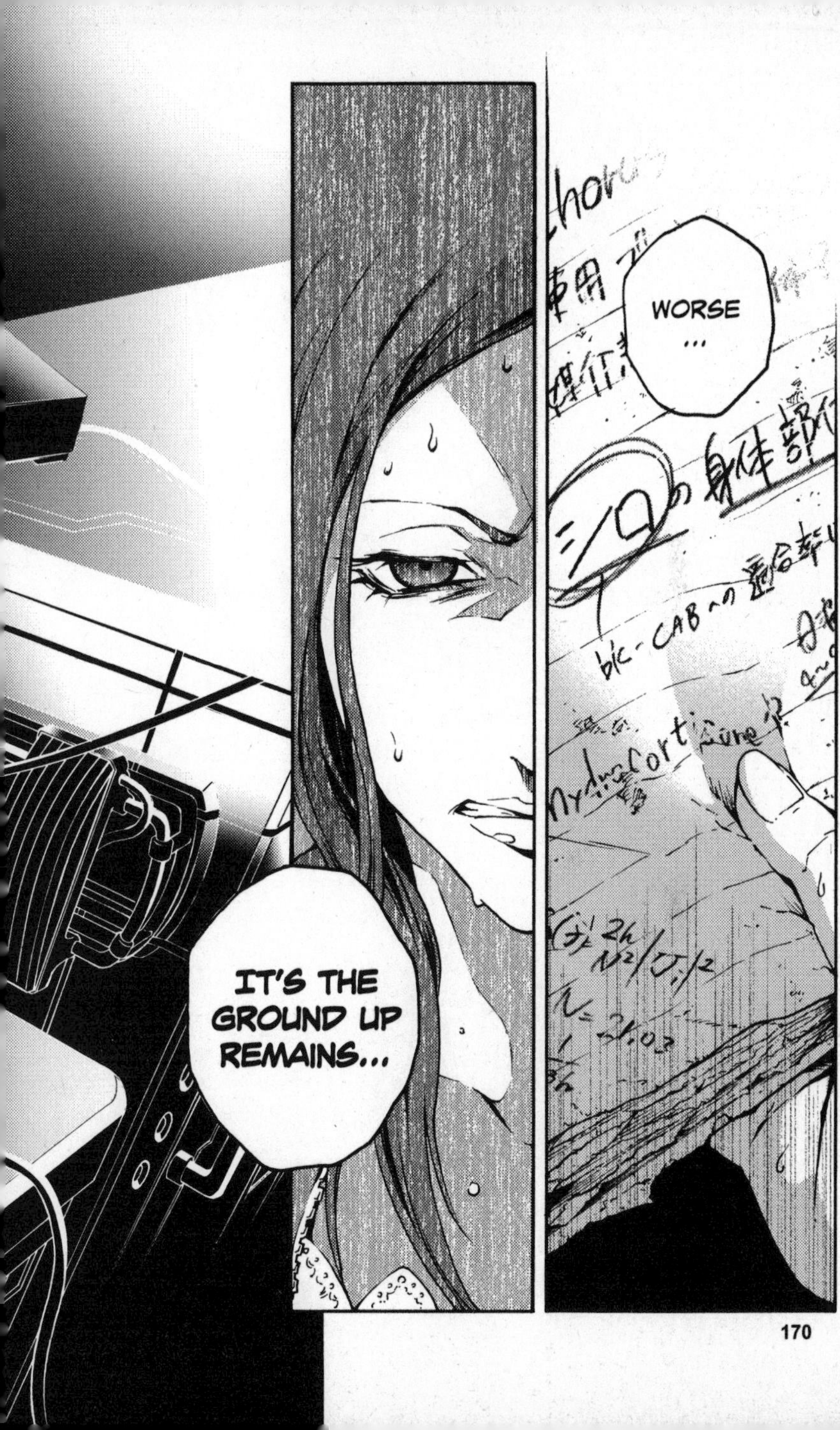
WORSE ...
IT'S THE GROUND UP REMAINS...

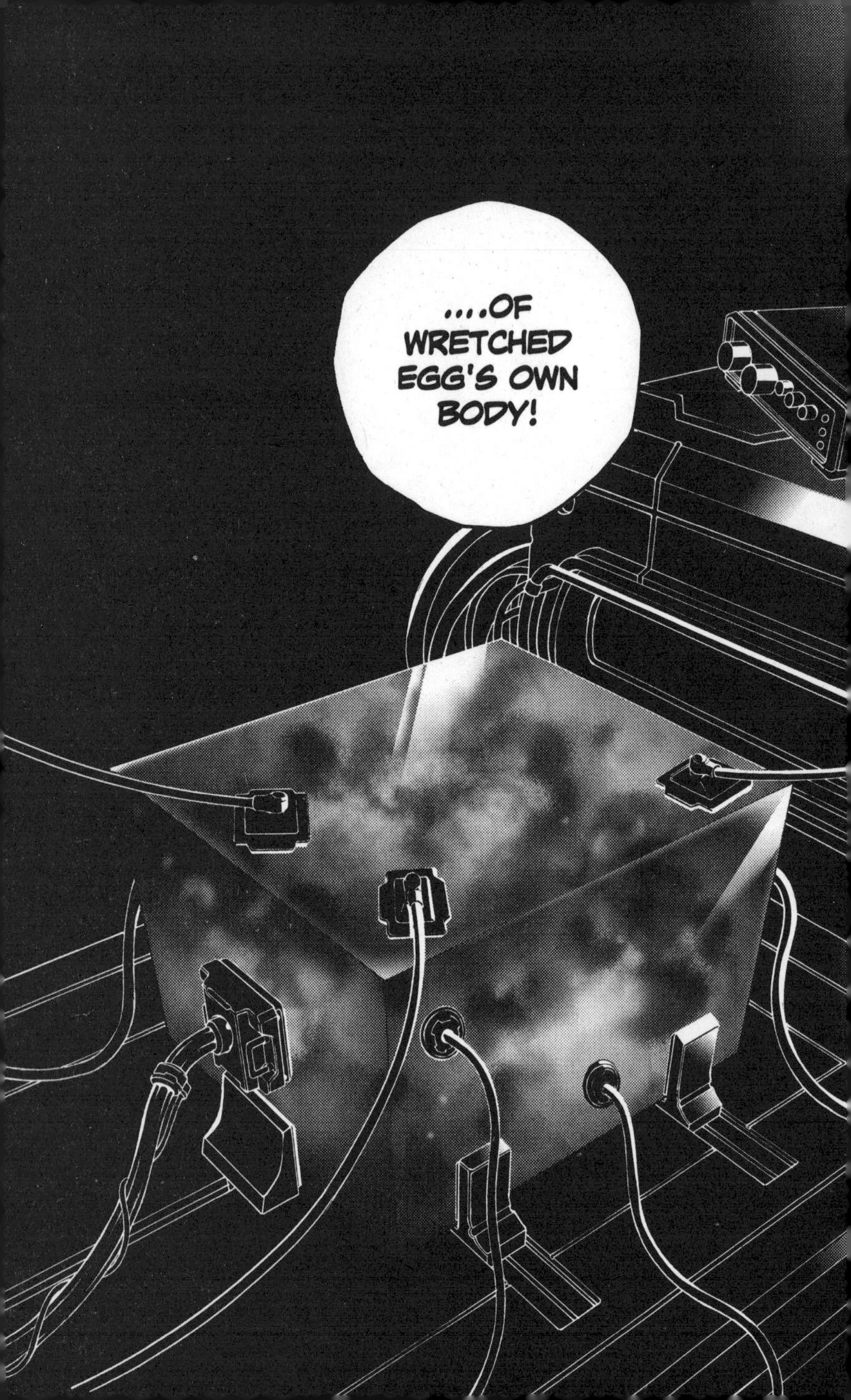
....OF WRETCHED EGG'S OWN BODY!

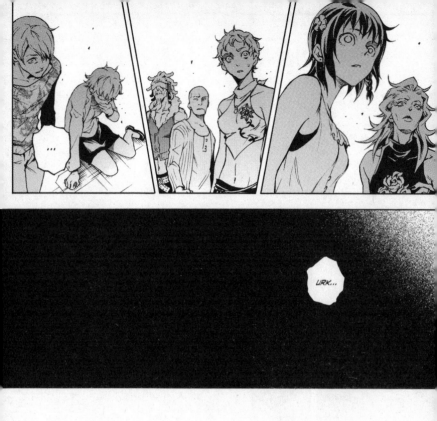

URK...

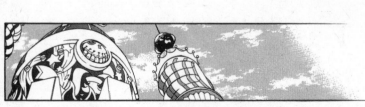

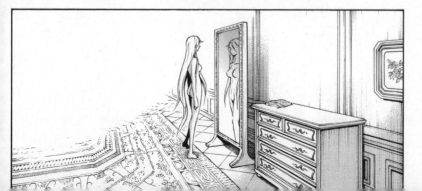

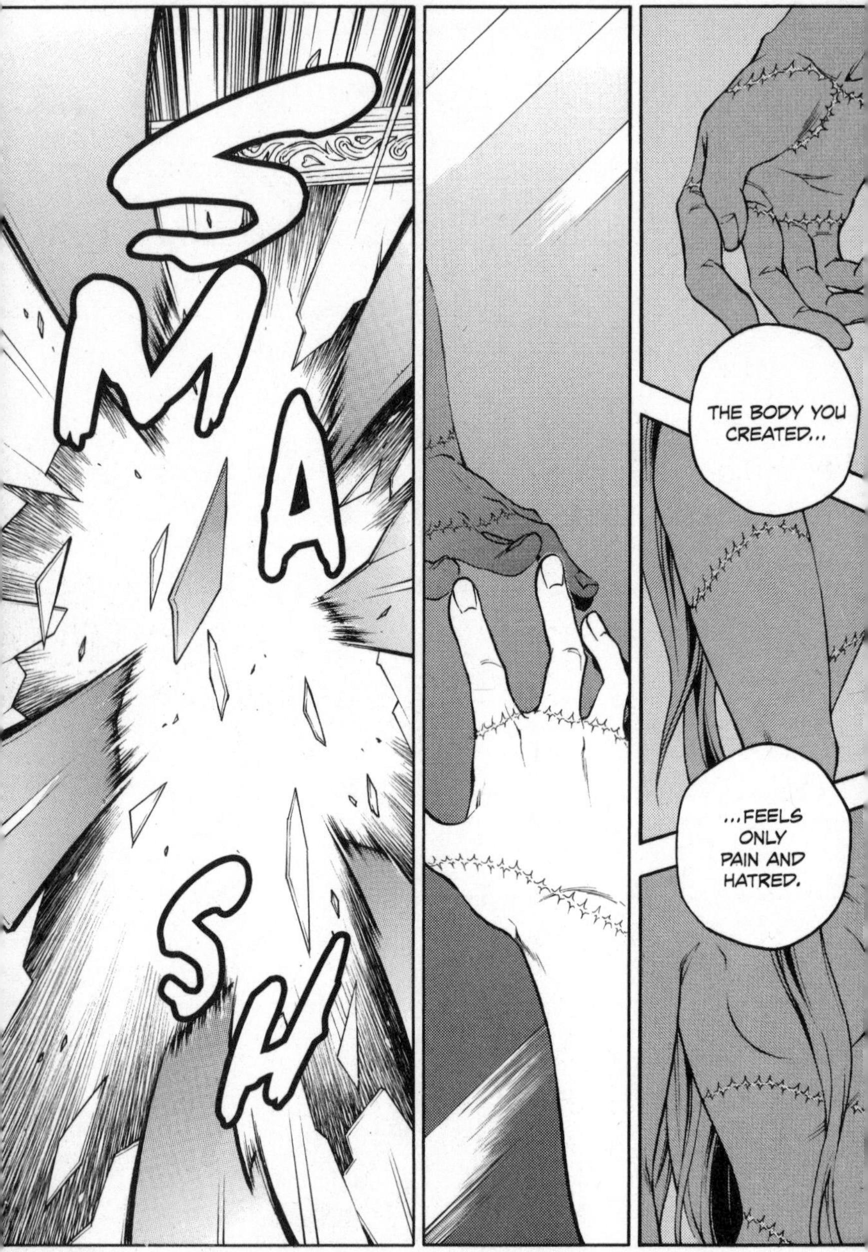
THE BODY YOU CREATED...
...FEELS ONLY PAIN AND HATRED.
SMASH

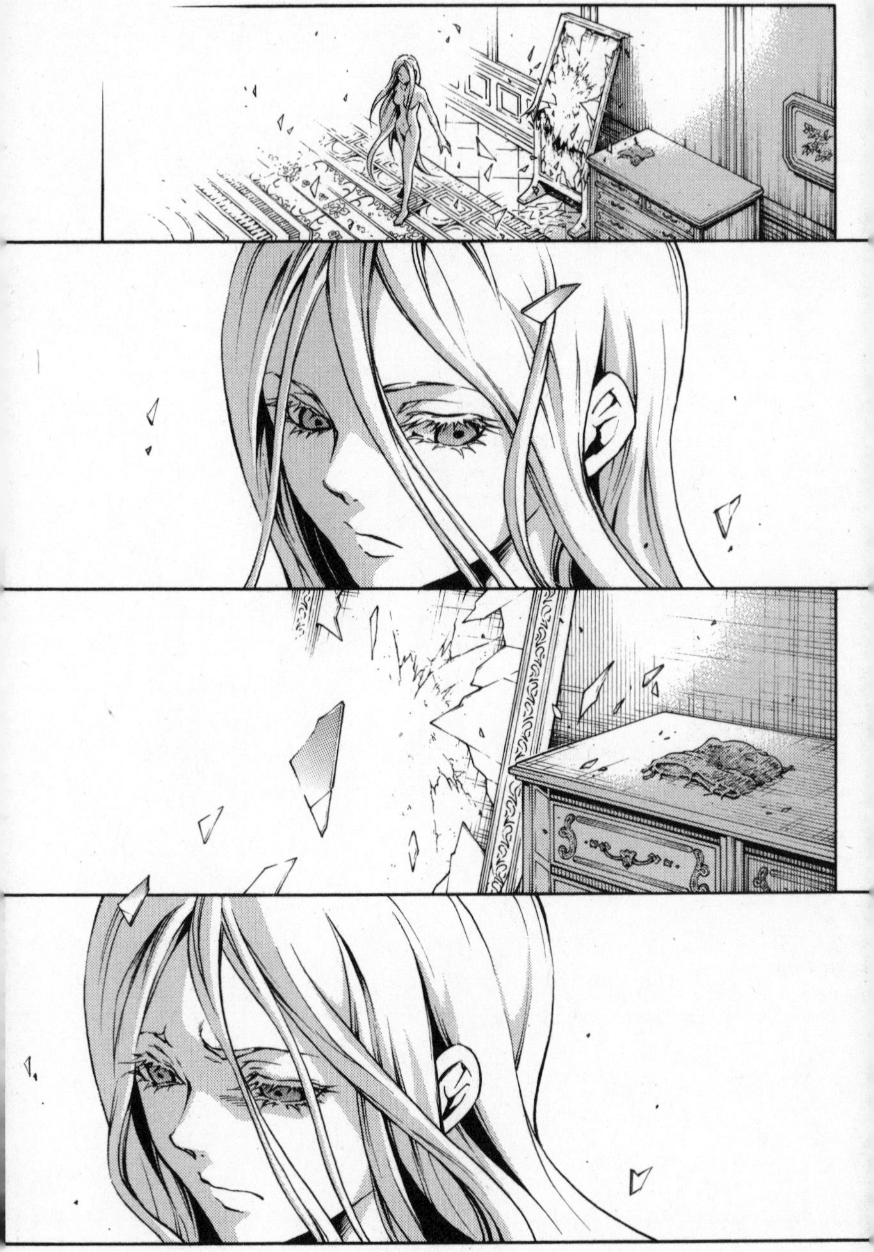

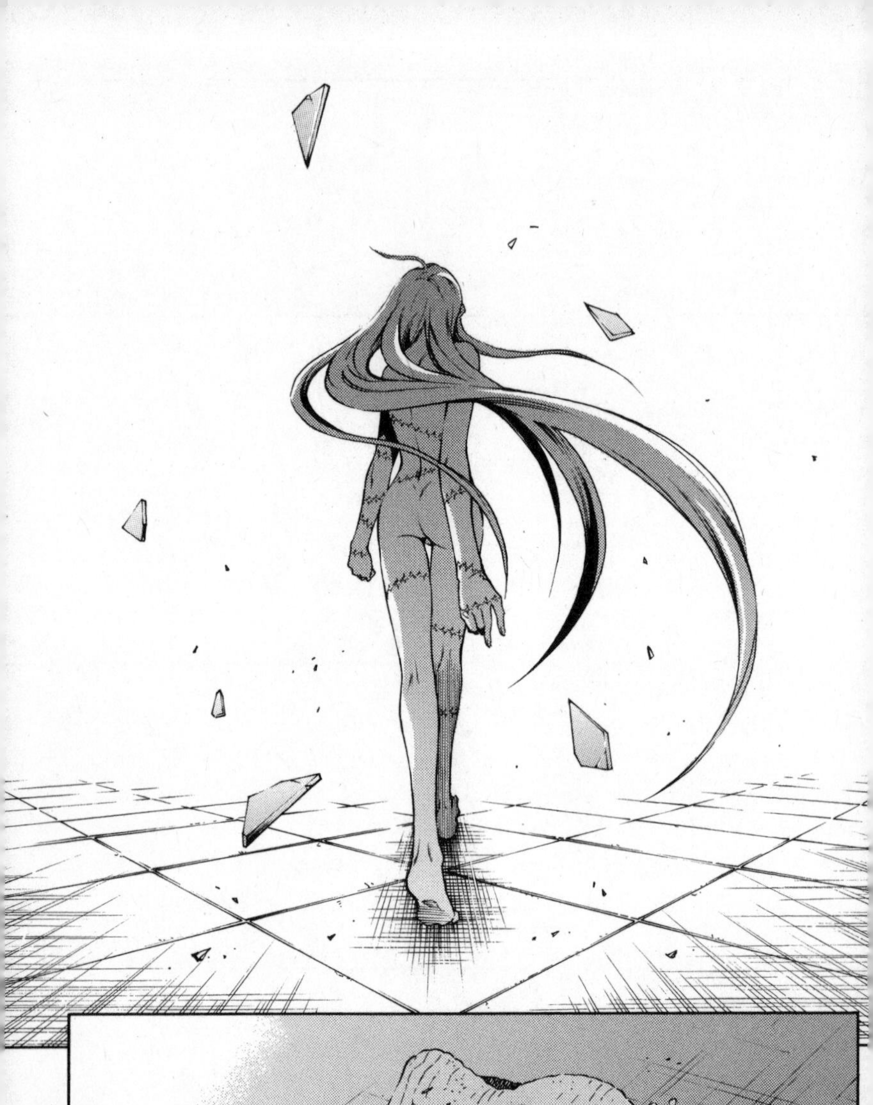

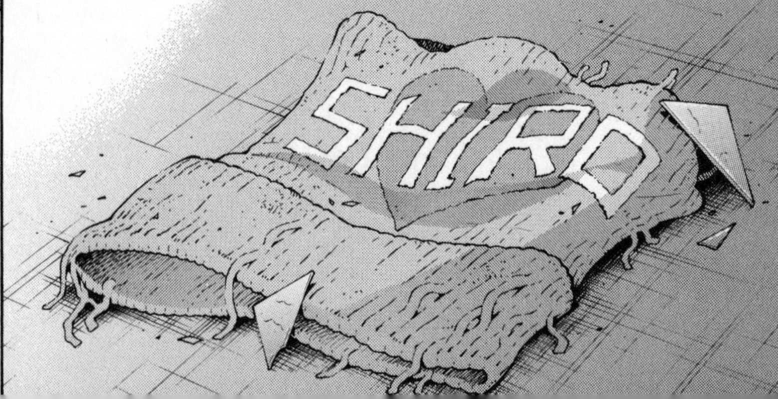
SHIRO

DEADMAN WONDERLAND 10

Jinsei Kataoka
Kazuma Kondou

STAFF

Yukitsune Amagusa

Karaiko

Shinji Sato

Taro Tsuchiya

Taku Nakamura

Toshihiro Noguchi

Wataru Ishikawa

Nao Ikegami

Official Shop

Deadman Wonderland-do

http://deadman.free.makeshop.jp

CONTINUED IN VOLUME 11

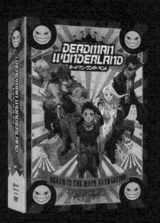

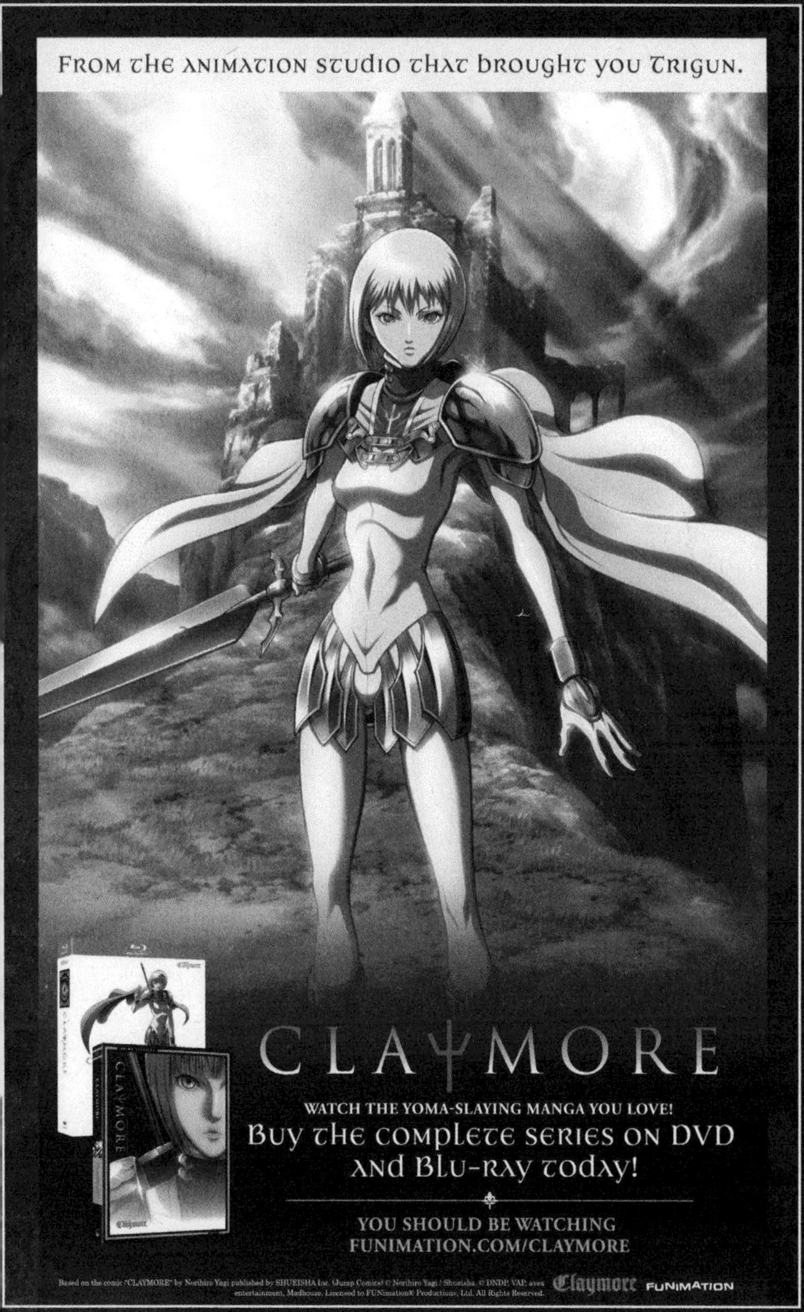

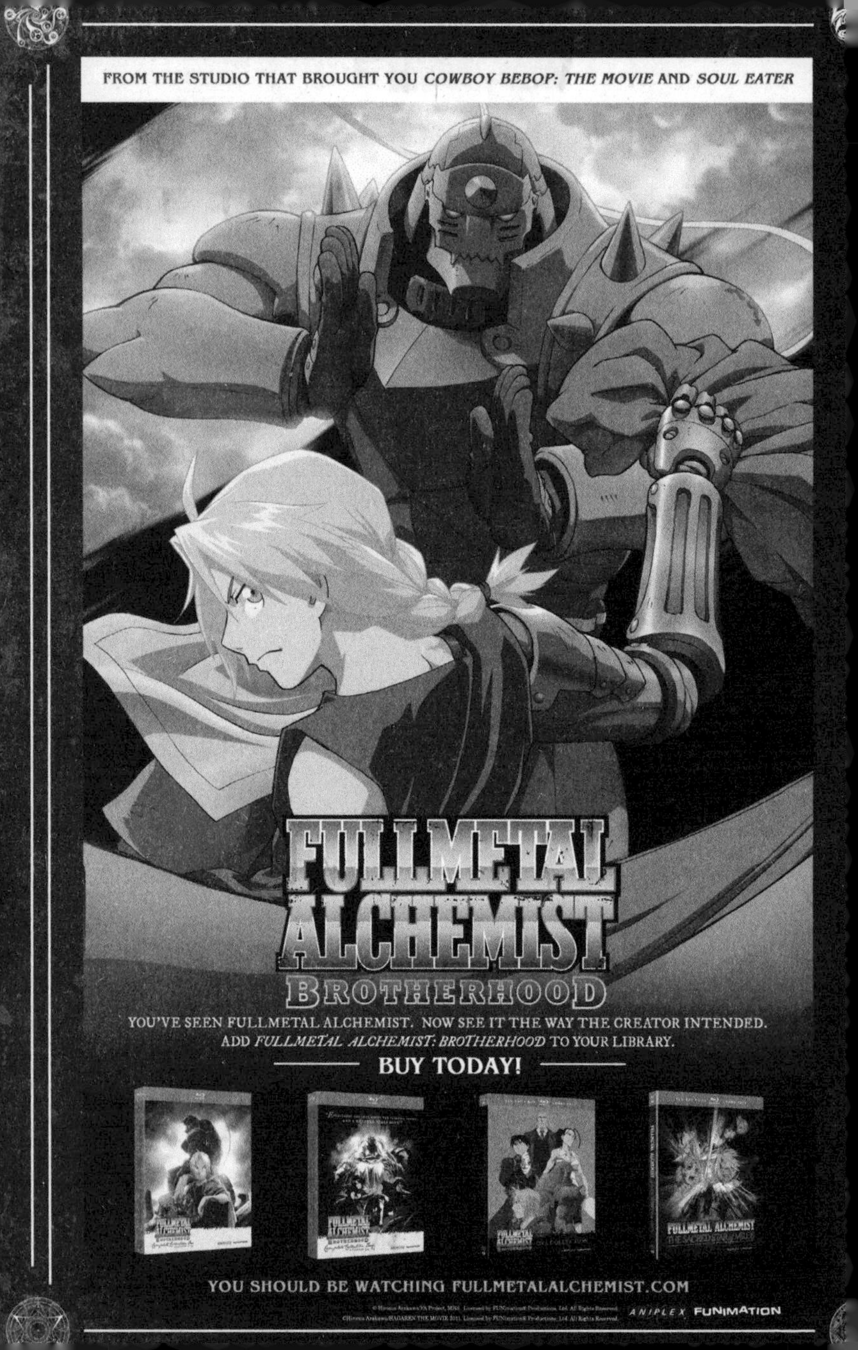

DEADMAN WON

DEADMAN WONDE
VOLUME 10
VIZ MEDIA EDITION

STORY & ART BY
JINSEI KATAOKA, KAZUMA KONDOU

DEADMAN WONDERLAND VOLUME 10

EDITED BY KADOKAWA SHOTEN
FIRST PUBLISHED IN JAPAN IN 2011 BY KADOKAWA CORPORATION, TOKYO.
ENGLISH TRANSLATION RIGHTS ARRANGED WITH KADOKAWA CORPORATION, TOKYO.

TRANSLATION/JOE YAMAZAKI
ENGLISH ADAPTATION/STAN!
TOUCH-UP ART & LETTERING/JAMES GAUBATZ
DESIGN/SAM ELZWAY
EDITOR/JENNIFER LEBLANC

PRINTED IN THE U.S.A.

PUBLISHED BY VIZ MEDIA, LLC
P.O. BOX 77010
SAN FRANCISCO, CA 94107

10 9 8 7 6 5 4 3 2
FIRST PRINTING, AUGUST 2015
SECOND PRINTING, OCTOBER 2016

viz media
www.viz.com

RATED T+ FOR OLDER TEEN

PARENTAL ADVISORY
DEADMAN WONDERLAND is rated T+ and is recommended for older teens. This volume contains scenes of supernatural horror and violence, and suggestive themes.

ratings.viz.com